Sufficient Gravity before the International Criminal Court

ELGAR INTERNATIONAL LAW

This flagship series is a forum for authored monographs that analyse current thinking and research across the spectrum of international law, rigorously examining key concepts as well as provoking debate and questions for further research.

Seeking to attract original thinking and new, challenging research, proposals are encouraged that engage with new and previously under-developed themes in the literature, or alternatively offer an innovative analysis of areas of uncertainty in the existing law.

Some books offer a strictly legal analysis of international law, whilst others weave together related fields of law, and some draw on insights from disciplines other than law, such as politics, economics or international relations. Bringing together work from both established authors and a new generation of scholars, what all books in the series have in common is that they represent a calibre of scholarship that makes significant contributions to our understanding of the field.

For a full list of Edward Elgar published titles, including the titles in this series, visit our website at www.e-elgar.com.

Sufficient Gravity before the International Criminal Court

Marco Longobardo

Reader in International Law, Westminster Law School, University of Westminster, UK

ELGAR INTERNATIONAL LAW

Edward Elgar
PUBLISHING

Cheltenham, UK • Northampton, MA, USA

Published by

Edward Elgar Publishing Limited
The Lypiatts
15 Lansdown Road
Cheltenham
Glos GL50 2JA
UK

Edward Elgar Publishing, Inc.
William Pratt House
9 Dewey Court
Northampton
Massachusetts 01060
USA

Authorised representative in the EU for GPSR queries only: Easy Access System Europe – Mustamäe tee 50, 10621 Tallinn, Estonia, gpsr.requests@easproject.com

A catalogue record for this book is available from the British Library

Library of Congress Control Number: 2026931912

This book is available electronically in the **Elgar**online Law subject collection
https://doi.org/10.4337/9781802209969

MIX
Paper | Supporting responsible forestry
FSC® C013604
FSC www.fsc.org

ISBN 978 1 80220 995 2 (cased)
ISBN 978 1 80220 996 9 (eBook)
ISBN 978 1 0494 0521 6 (ePub)

Printed and bound by CPI Group (UK) Ltd, Croydon, CR0 4YY

Ai miei genitori, Cinzia e Nicola, come sempre.
Alla memoria di Katia Petrone,
la cui risata e i cui consigli sono sempre con me.
A Lucas, che ha cambiato tutto.

Contents

Foreword

William Schabas

'Gravity' is a notion that seems to sit close to the heart of criminal law, be it domestic or international. In 'ordinary' criminal law, as practised by societies for centuries and millennia, gravity is an important factor in distinguishing between 'crimes' and 'delicts'. In the common law, 'delicts' is rendered as 'torts', but this is nothing more than a word taken from Norman French. In contemporary French, 'tort' means 'wrong'. Although all crimes are 'wrongs', not all 'wrongs' are 'crimes'. Gravity is one way this gets sorted out.

In its early iterations, dating back to the 1800s, international criminal law was concerned with punishable acts that required international cooperation for their enforcement. For example, the Convention for the Protection of Submarine Telegraph Cables, adopted in 1884, declared as a punishable offence '[t]he breaking or injury of a submarine cable, done wilfully or through culpable negligence, and resulting in the total or partial interruption or embarrassment of telegraphic communication'. It was the fact that submarine cables were mostly located outside the territory of states that mandated the international nature of the offence and not the objective seriousness of the act. There were similar treaty provisions dealing with such matters as traffic in counterfeit currency, narcotic drugs and pornography.

Only in the twentieth century do we encounter international recognition of criminal acts where 'gravity' is a significant feature in their identification. In 1915, the Triple Entente countries warned the Ottoman rulers, with whom they were at war, of their intent to punish those responsible for 'new crimes of Turkey against humanity and civilization'. Unlike the earlier suppression treaties, the problem was not one of establishing jurisdiction over acts perpetrated on territory that fell outside the territory of a sovereign state. Türkiye's genocide of the Armenians took place on its own territory. It was the gravity of the crimes, not their *locus*, that demanded their prosecution.

In 1946, at the first session of the United Nations General Assembly, a draft resolution prepared by Raphaël Lemkin and proposed by India, Cuba and Panama stated:

> Whereas the punishment of the very serious crime of genocide when committed in time of peace lies within the exclusive territorial jurisdiction of the judiciary of every State concerned, while crimes of a relatively lesser importance such as piracy, trade in women, children, drugs, obscene publications are declared as international crimes and have been made matters of international concern.

Note that genocide is described as a 'very serious crime' whereas 'piracy, trade in women, children, drugs, obscene publications' are said to be 'of a relatively lesser importance'. For no apparent reason, the paragraph didn't make it into the final version of Resolution 96(I).

Half a century later, as international criminal justice was reviving following a prolonged phase when it was rather inactive, the Appeals Chamber of the International Criminal Tribunal for the former Yugoslavia sought to distinguish what its statute labelled as 'serious violations of international humanitarian law' from those that were perhaps 'less serious'. A violation that was 'serious' should 'constitute a breach of a rule protecting important values, and the breach must involve grave consequences for the victim'. The judges said that the act of a combatant simply appropriating a loaf of bread in an occupied village would not be serious enough, although it would nevertheless violate international humanitarian law.

As Marco Longobardo explains in this study, the reference to 'gravity' in the Rome Statute can be traced to a phrase in the draft adopted by the International Law Commission in 1994. The Commission contemplated giving the proposed court the authority to refuse to consider a crime that was 'not of such gravity to justify further action by the Court'. At the time, the scope of the subject matter jurisdiction of the Court had not been clarified. It was entirely possible that the Court might retain the power to prosecute some crimes drawn from the suppression conventions that were, to borrow Lemkin's words, 'of a relatively lesser importance'. The Commission thought it might be useful to give judges the authority to decline to exercise jurisdiction in such circumstances.

When the negotiations of the Rome Statute moved from the expert level of the International Law Commission to political bodies designated by the General Assembly, momentum grew for subject-matter jurisdiction to be confined only to 'core crimes'. In a general sense, these corresponded to those that were prosecuted at Nuremberg and Tokyo. But the reference to 'gravity' remained unchanged. In a sense, the notion was entirely obsolete because the Nuremberg crimes, now somewhat repackaged as genocide, crimes against humanity, war crimes and the crime of aggression, were indubitably serious and inherently grave. The reference to 'gravity' in what became Article 17 of the Rome Statute might best be seen as a relic of early drafts, something that made some sense for a Court with very broad subject-matter jurisdiction but whose salience vanished when the core crimes focus was confirmed. In effect, the perspective had shifted during the General Assembly phase of the negotiations and at the Rome Conference itself. However, this remnant of what had become an obsolete vision remained.

The word 'gravity' appears in several provisions of the Rome Statute. For example, in the provisions on penalties, the Rome Statute declares that a term of life imprisonment is to be imposed only in cases of 'extreme gravity of the crime'. The Court has yet to impose such a sentence. Indeed, the average term with respect to convictions by the Court for core crimes is about 15 years. Although in some jurisdictions 15 years is deemed a very stiff sentence, the sentencing practice of the Court to date suggests that the prosecutor has not given that much attention to 'gravity' in the selection of cases for trial.

Gravity also figures in the definition of the crime of aggression. Only acts of aggression that by their 'character, *gravity* and scale' constitute manifest violations of the Charter of the United Nations fall within the terms of Article 8*bis*. At the Kampala Conference, the United States delegation unsuccessfully sought to narrow this even further so that unilateral military intervention in the name of humanitarian purposes would be sheltered from prosecution. Alas, the provision may never receive any judicial interpretation given the narrow jurisdictional regime imposed upon the crime of aggression.

'There is great chaos under heaven', writes Professor Longobardo, borrowing a phrase attributed to Mao Tse-tung. Indeed, the legal impact of the reference to 'sufficient gravity' in Article 17 remains elusive. In the early years of the Court, huge academic interest was focused on the issue of complementarity, which is the companion to 'sufficient gravity'. However, the Court has drifted towards an approach to Article 17 by which domestic investigations and prosecutions must 'mirror' the Prosecutor's investigation. At the practical level, this obviates any application of the criteria for admissibility listed in Article 17. If they don't pass the mirroring test, then there is no need to examine either complementarity or gravity.

As long as this narrow approach to Article 17 persists, there is unlikely to be any clarification with respect to 'sufficient gravity' in the case law of the Court. Hence, the task of elucidating the mysteries of 'gravity' falls to scholars in the discipline. Marco Longobardo's meticulously researched study, combined with his thoughtful analysis rooted in public international law principles, constitutes an immense contribution in this area.

St-Denis-le-Ferment, 25 October 2025
William Schabas OC MRIA
Professor of International Law
School of Law, Middlesex University, London

Acknowledgements

When, many years ago, I started toying with the idea of a book on the assessment of sufficient gravity before the International Criminal Court, I was plagued by a doubt: was this subject broad enough for a monograph? It is a niche topic, after all, ultimately limited to a line in the Rome Statute, Article 17(1)(d). I was also ready to quote, defensively, Antonio Cassese, who once noted, in the preface to one of his books, that 'we international lawyers should write short essays or small books consisting of brief chapters'.[1] The reader can easily judge that I spectacularly failed in the endeavour, at least when one considers my original plans for this book. It took more pages and more years than originally expected (for the latter, seven!), leading me to explore areas of international law and international criminal law that I would not have thought to examine initially.

Over these seven years, several people accompanied me on this intellectual journey, showing me more patience, solidarity, and friendship than I deserved. Although all the errors, mistakes, and absurdities in these pages are only attributable to me (or to the organs of the International Criminal Court, but that is a different story), a brief list of heartfelt acknowledgments is nonetheless warranted.

First and foremost, I would like to thank Michelle Coleman, Adil Haque, Marco Roscini, Bill Schabas, and Caleb Wheeler for the feedback they have generously provided on previous versions of this manuscript or some of its chapters. I take this opportunity to thank Bill also for the time he took to write the foreword for this book. Thanks to Marco Roscini and Federica Violi for the constant support, which kept me on track when completing this book seemed an impossible task (I prefer not to dwell on the number of embarrassing rants they had to suffer because of this book). At Westminster Law School, I would like to thank Luke Mason (now at Regent's University London) and Naomi Creutzfeldt (now at the University of Kent), who persuaded me not to abandon this project at a crucial moment when I was really determined to delete everything (though a sabbatical would have helped as well!). For many

[1] Antonio Cassese, *Self-Determination of Peoples: A Legal Reappraisal* (CUP 1995) xvi.

other reasons, all linked to friendship, support, camaraderie, and collegiality, I express my deep gratitude to Giulio Bartolini, Marcella Distefano, Federica Favuzza, Malgosia Fitzmaurice (the first person to suggest that I should write a book on this topic), Aurora Rasi, and Aldo Zammit Borda (who generously replaced me in some teaching duties when I was desperately in need of focused time to write).

Part of the research for this book was conducted during some periods that I spent as a visiting professor at the Universityies of Messina, University of Trento, and UniversitéLibre de Bruxelles. I thank Marcella Distefano, Marco Pertile, and Vaios Koutroulis for their hospitality. Additionally, I have haunted too many other libraries in search of sources for this book to name all of them. Special thanks go to Charlotte Mohr of the Library of the International Committee of the Red Cross, who provided endless assistance in locating obscure book chapters with such patience, professionalism, and grace as I have rarely seen before.

I received crucial support during the writing and production of this book as well. Ben Booth and Amber Watts at Edward Elgar have demonstrated boundless patience with my several delays in submitting the manuscript (thank you for the amazing editorial experience!). As always, I am grateful to Eden Oxley for her proofreading of my pages – my constant ally in writing in a second language.

Finally, my most special thanks go to my family, in particular my parents, Cinzia and Nicola, my brother Luca, and my partner Lucas. While I hope that they will read something that is more exciting for the wider public than this book, I would not have been able to write it without them.

This book was completed on 25 October 2025. Subsequent developments are not reflected in these pages, except when a more recent source is cited.

List of abbreviations

Abbreviation	**Definition**
AC	Appeals Chamber
AJIL	*American Journal of International Law*
AMDI	*Anuario Mexicano de Derecho Internacional*
AP	Additional Protocol I to the Geneva Conventions
App.	Application
ARSIWA	Articles on Responsibility of States for Internationally Wrongful Acts
ASP	Assembly of States Parties
AUILR	*American University International Law Review*
ARIEL	*Austrian Review of International and European Law*
CILJ	Comparative International Law Journal
CJIL	*Chinese Journal of International Law*
CJTL	*Columbia Journal of Transnational Law*
CLF	*Criminal Law Forum*
CLP	*Current Legal Problems*
CUP	Cambridge University Press
D&H	Duncker & Humblot
DUDI	*Diritti umani e diritto internazionale*
ECtHR	European Court of Human Rights
EJIL	*European Journal of International Law*
EJLS	*European Journal of Legal Studies*
FILJ	*Fordham International Law Journal*
GAOR	General Assembly Official Records
HRQ	Human Rights Quarterly
ICC	International Criminal Court

Abbreviation	**Definition**
ICJ	International Court of Justice
ICLQ	*International & Comparative Law Quarterly*
ICLR	*International Criminal Law Review*
ICmLR	*International Community Law Review*
ICTR	International Criminal Tribunal for Rwanda
ICTY	International Criminal Tribunal for the Former Yugoslavia
IER	Independent Expert Review
ILC	International Law Commission
ILJ	*International Law Journal*
ILS	*International Law Studies*
IMT	International Military Tribunal
IsLR	*Israel Law Review*
JICJ	*Journal of International Criminal Justice*
JIDS	*Journal of International Dispute Settlement*
JIL	*Journal of International Law*
JILP	*Journal of International Law and Policy*
JLP	*Journal of Law and Policy*
LGDJ	Librairie générale de droit et de jurisprudence
LJIL	*Leiden Journal of International Law*
LR	Law Review
MPEIPL	*Max Planck Encyclopedia of International Procedural Law*
MPEPIL	*Max Planck Encyclopedia of Public International Law*
MPYUNL	*Max Planck Yearbook of United Nations Law*
No.	Number
OPCV	Office of Public Counsel for Victims
OTP	Office of the Prosecutor
OUP	Oxford University Press
PTC	Pre-Trial Chamber
QIL	*Questions of International Law*
RdC	*Recueil des cours de l'Académie de droit international de La Haye*

Abbreviation	**Definition**
RDI	*Rivista di diritto internazionale*
REDI	*Revista Española de Derecho Internacional*
RGDIP	*Revue Générale de Droit International Public*
RIAA	*Reports of International Arbitral Awards*
RIDP	*Revue Internationale de Droit Pénal*
RPE	Rules of Procedure and Evidence
RQDI	*Revue Québécoise de Droit International*
RS	Rome Statute of the International Criminal Court
SCSL	Special Court for Sierra Leone
Situation in Afghanistan	Situation in the Islamic Republic of Afghanistan
Situation in Bangladesh/ Myanmar	Situation in the People's Republic of Bangladesh/ Republic of the Union of Myanmar
Situation in Burundi	Situation in the Republic of Burundi
Situation in the CAR	Situation in the Central African Republic
Situation in Côte d'Ivoire	Situation in the Republic of Côte d'Ivoire
Situation in Kenya	Situation in the Republic of Kenya
Situation in Mali	(ituation in the Republic of Mali
Situation in Palestine	Situation in the State of Palestine
Situation in Venezuela I	Situation in the Bolivarian Republic of Venezuela I
Situation in the DRC	Situation in the Democratic Republic of the Congo
Situation in the Philippines	Situation in the Republic of the Philippines
Situation on Registered Vessels	Situation on Registered Vessels of the Union of the Comoros The Hellenic Republic of Greece and the Kingdom of Cambodia
VCLT	Vienna Convention on the Law of Treaties
TC	Trial Chamber
TOAEP	Torkel Opsahl Academic EPublisher
UN	United Nations
UNGA	United Nations General Assembly
UNSC	United Nations Security Council
YIL	Yearbook of International Law
YILC	*Yearbook of the International Law Commission*

1. General introduction to the assessment of sufficient gravity

> 'Therein lies the danger. The malleability of gravity makes it easily subject to manipulation.'[1]

1. INTRODUCTION

Sufficient gravity under Article 17(1)(d) of the Rome Statute of the International Criminal Court (RS) provides a ground of inadmissibility, that is, a reason for the Court to decline to take further steps in the exercise of its jurisdiction over alleged international crimes punishable under the RS. Pursuant to this provision, 'a case is inadmissible where … it is not of sufficient gravity to justify further action by the Court'. This means that, even if a case pertains to one or more of the crimes punishable under the RS – genocide, war crimes, crimes against humanity, aggression – the International Criminal Court (ICC or Court) must decline to exercise its jurisdiction in cases that fail to meet the sufficient gravity threshold.

Notwithstanding the fact that this provision is almost three decades old, there is no agreement on how to interpret and apply the notion of sufficient gravity. Rather, visiting the website of the Office of the Prosecutor (OTP), the first document that a reader will encounter in the 'Policies and Strategies' section is entitled 'Strategic Plan 2023-2025',[2] which, at p.17, reads: '[t]he Office aims to finalize a comprehensive review and consolidation of its policy framework on *gravity*/prioritization/completion of investigations'.[3] Indeed, in 2020, the *Final Report of the Independent Expert Review (IER) of the International Criminal Court and the Rome Statute System* recommended a revision of the Court's approach to sufficient gravity, suggesting the adoption of a higher

1 Rachel López, 'The Law of Gravity' (2020) 58 CJTL 565, 570.
2 OTP, *Strategic Plan 2023–2025* (Aug 2023).
3 Ibid, para.57 (emphasis added).

threshold.[4] Although this recommendation was received with scepticism by the ICC in its response,[5] it is still part of the plan of the review of ICC policies and practices, and in 2024, the OTP has announced that it is working on a consolidated policy paper to implement the recommendations received by the IER, including those concerning sufficient gravity.[6]

Accordingly, reflecting on the content of Article 17(1)(d) and the meaning of sufficient gravity is one of the current priorities of the ICC organs.

Judicial practice before the ICC has demonstrated not only that sufficient gravity is an elusive concept, but also that it is interpreted and applied differently by different organs of the ICC (in particular, by the Chambers and the OTP). For instance, in 2006, a Pre-Trial Chamber (PTC) and the Appeals Chamber (AC) disagreed on the meaning of sufficient gravity under Article 17(1)(d) in relation to alleged crimes committed in the Democratic Republic of the Congo (DRC).[7] Moreover, in 2013, the most intense debate yet on the notion of sufficient gravity under the RS erupted in relation to the *Mavi Marmara* affair, wherein the OTP concluded that the alleged crimes committed by the Israel Defense Forces during the boarding of the vessel *Mavi Marmara* in 2010 could not be characterised as 'sufficiently grave' under Article 17(1)(d).[8] The ensuing extenuatinglitigation between the Comoros – the state of registration of the *Mavi Marmara* – and the OTP on the assessment of sufficient gravity in relation to this episode brought to light the extensive disagreement between relevant actors on the notion of sufficient gravity before the ICC.[9] The uncer-

---

4 *Independent Expert Review of the International Criminal Court and the Rome Statute System, Final Report* (30 Sep 2020) paras 648–50.

5 Overall Response of the ICC to the 'Independent Expert Review of the ICC and the RS System – Final Report', Preliminary Analysis of the Recommendations and Information on Relevant Activities Undertaken by the Court (14 Apr 2021), paras 403–5.

6 ICC, *Progress in the Assessment of the IER Recommendations Submitted Pursuant to Resolution ICC-ASP/20/Res.3*, para.11, *Matrix*, 6 Sep 2024, 28.

7 Situation in the DRC, PTC I, Decision on the Prosecutor's Application for a Warrant of Arrest, Article 58, ICC-01/04-01/06, 10 Feb 2006, paras 42–64; Situation in the DRC, AC, Judgment on the Prosecutor's appeal against the decision of PTC I entitled 'Decision on the Prosecutor's Application for Warrants of Arrest, Article 58', ICC-01/04-169-US-Exp, 13 Jul 2006.

8 Situation on Registered Vessels, OTP, Article 53(1) Report, ICC-01/13-6-AnxA, 6 Nov 2014, paras 133–48.

9 Situation on Registered Vessels, Comoros, Application for Review pursuant to Art 53(3)(a) of the Prosecutor's Decision of 6 Nov 2014 not to initiate an investigation in the Situation, ICC-01/13-3-Red, 29 Jan 2015; Situation on Registered Vessels, PTC I, Decision on the request of the Union of the Comoros to review the Prosecutor's decision not to initiate an investigation, ICC-01/13-34,

tainties resulting from these cases, coupled with the likelihood of future litigation and disagreement over what constitutes sufficient gravity, have resulted in the need for a more detailed exploration of this topic.

No one could be blamed for being puzzled by the fact that a case falling within the jurisdiction of the ICC may be considered to be insufficiently grave. The ICC has jurisdiction over some of the most serious crimes committed by human beings, those crimes that are seen as 'unimaginable atrocities that deeply shock the conscience of humanity', according to the emphatic preamble of the RS. Article 5 confirms that 'the jurisdiction of the Court shall be limited to the most serious crimes of concern to the international community as a whole', whatever the expression 'international community' means in this context.[10] Thus, *prima facie*, one could assume that every human conduct falling within the subject-matter jurisdiction of the Court meets the threshold of sufficient gravity. Who would be so insensitive as to assert that a genocide, a war crime, a crime against humanity, or an act of aggression is not sufficiently

16 Jul 2015; Situation on Registered Vessels, OTP, Notice of Prosecutor's Final Decision under Rule 108(3), ICC-01/13-57, 29 Nov 2017; Situation on Registered Vessels, Comoros, Public Redacted Version of 'Application for Judicial Review by the Government of the Union of the Comoros', ICC-01/13-58-Red, 26 Feb 2018; Situation on Registered Vessels, PTC I, Decision on the 'Application for Judicial Review by the Government of the Union of the Comoros', ICC-01/13-68, 15 Nov 2018; Situation on Registered Vessels, OTP, Request for Leave to Appeal the 'Decision on the "Application for Judicial Review by the Government of the Union of the Comoros"', ICC-01/13-69, 21 Nov 2018; Situation on Registered Vessels, AC, Judgment on the appeal of the Prosecutor against PTC I's 'Decision on the "Application for Judicial Review by the Government of the Union of the Comoros"', ICC-01/13-98, 2 Sep 2019; Situation on Registered Vessels, OTP, Notice of Prosecutor's Final Decision under rule 108(3), as revised and refiled in accordance with the PTC's request of 15 Nov 2018 and the AC's judgment of 2 Sep 2019, ICC-01/13-99, 2 Dec 2019; Situation on Registered Vessels, Comoros, Application for Judicial Review by the Government of the Comoros, ICC-01/13-100, 2 Mar 2020; Situation on Registered Vessels, PTC I, Decision on the 'Application for Judicial Review by the Government of the Comoros', ICC-01/13-111, 16 Sep 2020; Situation on Registered Vessels, Comoros, Application on behalf of the Government of the Union of the Comoros for Leave to Appeal the 'Decision on the "Application for Judicial Review by the Government of the Comoros"' of 16 Sep 2020, ICC-01/13-112, 22 Sep 2020; PTC I, Situation on Registered Vessels, Decision on the Request for Leave to Appeal the 'Decision on the "Application for Judicial Review by the Government of the Comoros"', ICC-01/13-115, 21 Dec 2020.

[10] On this notion see, generally, Christian J Tams, 'International Community' in Jean d'Aspremont and Sahib Singh (eds), *Concepts for International Law: Contributions to Disciplinary Thought* (Edward Elgar Publishing 2019) 504.

grave to deserve prosecution by the Court? Overall, the ICC exists exactly for this reason, to 'put an end to impunity for the perpetrators of these crimes and thus to contribute to the prevention of such crimes'.[11]

Nevertheless, the very existence of Article 17(1)(d) can only be justified by the idea that, in certain situations, cases resulting from crimes punishable by the RS may not be sufficiently grave to deserve prosecution within and punishment by the ICC. As discussed in this book, all the attempts to dismiss the threshold of Article 17(1)(d) as irrelevant have been rejected by the ICC organs, and correctly so: whatever the reason for Article 17(1)(d)'s adoption – and digging in the preparatory work for the RS may provide helpful insights – this provision cannot be entirely overlooked. To do so would result in a rather arbitrary abrogation of Article 17(1)(d), disguised as an act of interpretation.

The scenario is further complicated by the apposition of the adjective 'sufficient' to the word 'gravity' in Article 17(1)(d). Depending on whom you ask, a certain case may be sufficiently grave or not, creating a serious risk of rampant subjectivism.[12] If one assumes the perspective of a victim of an international crime – bearing in mind that the declared ICC victim-centred approach was saluted as one of the most relevant innovations of the RS[13] – even isolated incidents deserve prosecution. As put by the Comoros before the ICC, '[a]ny murder – and any 10 murders – are dreadfully serious to all those involved even if committed other than in an armed conflict'.[14] Let us imagine one case of rape against one civilian during an international armed conflict:[15] from the perspective of the victim, that very specific act, per se, meets the threshold of sufficient gravity. Maybe, from a different, perhaps broader perspective, that isolated act would not meet the threshold. This is particularly the case where the assessment of sufficient gravity is based on comparison between different

---

11 RS, Preamble, para.5.

12 Stuart Ford, 'The Meaning of Gravity at the International Criminal Court: A Survey of Attitudes about the Seriousness of Mass Atrocities' (2018) 24 UC Davis JILP 210, 212. For more, see below, Chapter 2, subsection 2.3.

13 See, for example, Antonio Cassese, 'The Statute of the International Criminal Court: Some Preliminary Reflections' (1999) 10 EJIL 144, 167–8. For a more recent appraisal, see Christoph Safferling and Gurgen Petrossian, *Victims Before the International Criminal Court: Definition, Participation, Reparation* (Springer 2021).

14 Situation on Registered Vessels, Comoros, Public Redacted Version with Confidential Annexes 1, 2 and 3 of Application for Review pursuant to Article 53(3)(a) of the Prosecutor's Decision of 6 Nov 2014 not to initiate an investigation in the Situation, ICC-01/13-3-Red, 29 Jan 2015, para.25.

15 Rape is considered a war crime in an international armed conflict under RS, Article 8(2)(b)(xxii).

situations, cases, and crimes: if one compares that isolated act of rape in armed conflict to the atrocities committed in the Congo Free State under Leopold II of Belgium or to the Holocaust during World War II, the former would probably not be considered sufficiently grave. Similarly problematic is trying to determine sufficient gravity based on the comparison between international crimes and domestic crimes;[16] although domestic legal systems can – and sometimes, must – prosecute international crimes, including isolated episodes, the rationale behind international criminalisation and prosecution is different from that supporting domestic criminalisation and prosecution.[17]

This line of reasoning, however, is problematic because it is not easy to rank cases involving international crimes depending on their gravity. How can one say that a case of intentional starvation of civilians[18] is necessarily graver than a case of torture?[19] More realistically, how can one compare cases involving a multitude of alleged crimes committed against a multitude of victims? Although the popular press frequently ranks atrocities,[20] for the lawyer this exercise is more difficult. To avoid this, the RS has already considered genocide, war crimes, crimes against humanity, and aggression to be sufficiently grave to fall within the subject-matter jurisdiction of the Court; therefore, why should one need to rank them to allow the Court to exercise its jurisdiction? Clearly the scenario is far more complex since Article 17(1)(d) pertains to 'cases' rather than to 'crimes' and is applied to broader situations as well – an issue that this book discusses subsequently.[21] Nevertheless, there is always the danger of an assumed shortcut between gravity as an inherent feature of international crimes, and the need to demonstrate the sufficient gravity of a case as a matter of admissibility. Overall, there is also room to wonder whether comparisons are helpful at all in determining sufficient gravity under Article 17(1)(d), or whether this provision imposes a different exercise, not based on comparison.[22]

---

[16] See, for example, Stuart Ford, 'What Investigative Resources Does the International Criminal Court Need to Succeed? A Gravity-Based Approach' (2017) 16 Washington University Global Studies LR 1, 25–45.

[17] See Chapter 3, section 3.

[18] RS, Article 8(2)(b)(xxv).

[19] Either as a war crime (RS, Article 8(2)(a)(ii) and (c)(i)) or a crime against humanity (RS, Article 7(1)(f)).

[20] For example, Samuel Osborne, '5 of the Worst Atrocities Carried Out by the British Empire', *Independent* (19 Jan 2016) https://www.independent.co.uk/news/uk/home-news/worst-atrocities-british-empire-amritsar-boer-war-concentration-camp-mau-mau-a6821756.html.

[21] See below, Chapter 3, subsection 4.2.3.

[22] See below, Chapter 5, subsection 3.3.

One could argue that all the aforementioned difficulties are speculative since, notwithstanding these conceptual problems, gravity is like US Supreme Court Justice Potter Stewart's interpretation of pornography: 'I know it when I see it.'[23] However, the frequent disagreements on sufficient gravity between different ICC organs – in particular, the OTP and the Chambers – and other relevant stakeholders such as States Parties, victims, and scholars, demonstrate that there is a need to investigate this notion in a careful way. Several delicate questions remain unanswered even after three decisions of the AC:[24] what the meaning of sufficient gravity is, how the gravity of alleged crimes can be weighted to assess whether a case is of 'sufficient' gravity, and who has the final word on the assessment of sufficient gravity. The need to explore the interpretation and application of sufficient gravity does not pertain only to the specific judicial instances mentioned above, but rather is functional to the understanding of a pivotal notion in the prosecution of international crimes before the ICC.

2. THE AIM OF THIS BOOK AND ITS CONTRIBUTION TO KNOWLEDGE

This book is built on the premise that, imperfect or baffling as it may seem at first glance, Article 17(1)(d) of the RS embodies the notion of sufficient gravity, and therefore we must find a convincing way to interpret and apply it. Accordingly, the aim of this book is to provide a better understanding of the interpretation and application of sufficient gravity as an admissibility criterion. In doing so, the analysis will focus only on the notion of sufficient

---

23 *Jacobellies v Ohio*, 378 US 184 at 197 (1964) (Stewart J concurring): 'I shall not today attempt further to define the kinds of material I understand to be embraced within that shorthand description ["hard-core pornography"], and perhaps I could never succeed in intelligibly doing so. But I know it when I see it, and the motion picture involved in this case is not that.'

24 Situation in the DRC, AC, Judgment on the Prosecutor's appeal against the decision of PTC I entitled 'Decision on the Prosecutor's Application for Warrants of Arrest, Article 58', ICC-01/04-169, 13 Jul 2006; Situation on Registered Vessels, AC, Judgment on the appeal of the Prosecutor against PTC I's 'Decision on the "Application for Judicial Review by the Government of the Union of the Comoros"', ICC-01/13-98, 2 Sep 2019; AC, Situation in the Republic of Mali, *Prosecutor v Al Hassan*, Judgment on the appeal of Mr Al Hassan against the decision of PTC I entitled 'Décision relative à l'exception d'irrecevabilité pour insuffisance de gravité de l'affaire soulevée par la défense', ICC-01/12-01/18 OA, 19 Feb 2020.

gravity under Article 17(1)(d) of the RS, and the way in which the OTP and the Chambers have interpreted and applied this provision.

Other provisions mentioning gravity – such as in relation to penalties[25] – are examined to the extent that they may contribute to a better understanding of sufficient gravity under Article 17(1)(d). The book also explores sufficient gravity under Article 53(1)(b) and (2)(b). This is not a contradiction; both paragraphs of Article 53 explicitly refer to Article 17(1)(d). This *renvoi* is the origin of significant confusion between the OTP and the Chambers, as well as among scholars, to the extent that it would be incorrect to overlook Article 53 in the analysis of sufficient gravity under Article 17(1)(d).

Providing guidance on how to interpret and apply sufficient gravity is important considering the growing role that this notion plays in prosecutorial and judicial practice, as well as considering the aforementioned plans to reform it or redefine its content. The very quick overview provided at the beginning of this chapter is enough to understand that this notion has been at the centre of ICC proceedings on several occasions, and that it is treated as a contentious issue. That there will be additional contention over the interpretation and role of sufficient gravity in the future is almost certain.

The second reason behind the decision to write this book lies in the danger of leaving the interpretation and application of 'sufficient gravity' underexplored. Sufficient gravity under Article 17(1)(d) is a ground of inadmissibility, that is, a reason for the Court to decline to exercise jurisdiction over alleged crimes falling within its jurisdiction. Article 53 of the RS allows the OTP to consider grounds of inadmissibility under Article 17(1)(d) in its decision as to whether to initiate an investigation and start the actual prosecution. Accordingly, it is important to ascertain how sufficient gravity should be assessed in order to evaluate the Chambers' and OTP's decisions not to exercise jurisdiction because of an alleged lack of sufficient gravity, despite the otherwise seriousness of the situation. For example, a better understanding of sufficient gravity will allow the reader to ascertain whether, in 2005, the OTP correctly prosecuted only alleged crimes committed by non-state actors in Uganda because those allegedly committed by state forces were not sufficiently grave;[26] whether, in 2006, it was true, as claimed by the OTP, that the alleged crimes committed in occupied Iraq by UK troops were not sufficiently

25 For example, RS, Articles 77 and 78.

26 OTP, *Statement by Chief Prosecutor Luis Moreno Ocampo* (14 Oct 2005) 3; OTP, *Statement by Luis Moreno Ocampo*, Prosecutor of the International Criminal Court, Informal Meeting of Legal Advisors of Ministries of Foreign Affairs (24 Oct 2005) 7.

grave to open an investigation;[27] whether an apparently minor attack against peacekeepers in Sudan was really sufficiently grave as claimed;[28] whether the alleged crimes committed during the *Mavi Marmara* boarding were not sufficiently grave, as claimed by the OTP and contrary to the view of a PTC and the Comoros.[29]

In all these examples, the decision whether to exercise the Court's jurisdiction rested on considerations of gravity, and one wonders whether any double standard was applied.[30] This is particularly relevant when taking into account the fact that some of these controversial gravity determinations by the OTP were taken in relation to situations where the Office was under incredible political pressure from powerful states.[31] Although there is no evidence that these pressures influenced any determination of sufficient gravity, the risk of perceived bias is a consequence of the lack of definition of sufficient gravity in the RS. In these examples, no investigation against state actors or individuals affiliated with powerful states such as Israel, the UK, and the US was opened, and the Court exercised its jurisdiction over a relatively minor incident where African Union peacekeepers were involved. As noted, the fact that 'the criteria upon which the ICC prosecutor is able to found its investigation and prosecution are not well-defined … may create the danger of subjecting such investigation and prosecution to decisions which may be easily perceived as political by the international community'.[32] However, this is not only an issue affecting the OTP; defining sufficient gravity may also prevent a similar perception of bias

---

27 OTP, *Response to Communications Received Concerning Iraq* (9 Feb 2006) 9.

28 Situation in Darfur, Sudan, *Prosecutor v Abu Garda*, PTC I, Decision on the Confirmation of Charges, ICC-02/05-02/09-243-Red, 8 Feb 2010.

29 See above, nn 8 and 9.

30 Situation on Registered Vessels, PTC I, Decision on the 'Application for Judicial Review by the Government of the Comoros', ICC-01/13-111, 16 Sep 2020, para.101. ('The Prosecutor's failure to apply the gravity requirement with consistency across cases and potential cases before the Court opens the Court up to criticism of double-standards and arbitrariness.')

31 For example, according to media reports, in 2015, the Prosecutor was seriously pressured by Israeli agents: Harry Davies, 'Revealed: Israeli Spy Chief "Threatened" ICC Prosecutor Over War Crimes Inquiry', *The Guardian* (28 May 2024), https://www.theguardian.com/world/article/2024/may/28/israeli-spy-chief-icc-prosecutor-war-crimes-inquiry; Harry Davies, 'Former ICC Chief Prosecutor Says She Faced Threats and "Thug-Style Tactics"', *The Guardian* (27 Nov 2024), https://www.theguardian.com/law/2024/nov/27/former-icc-chief-prosecutor-fatou-bensouda-threats-thug-style-tactics.

32 Geert-Jan Alexander Knoops, *Theory and Practice of International and Internationalized Criminal Proceedings* (Kluwer 2005) 114.

in relation to the Chambers. Accordingly, a clear understanding of the notion of sufficient gravity may help the ICC to present its decisions on sufficient gravity – regardless of which organ is called on to make the determination – in the best possible light, steering away from disgraceful allegations of double standards.

A third reason to write this book is to contribute to the (numerically) limited scholarship in the field. Sufficient gravity has been almost neglected in academic literature for years, with the vast majority of attention devoted to the other ground of inadmissibility: the principle of complementarity.[33] Most early works included some sparing mentions of sufficient gravity in their fine analysis of complementarity, but without any specific attention devoted to gravity as an autonomous ground,[34] even if a few exceptions can be found.[35] Still, today, international criminal law textbooks, for obvious reasons of space, do not engage extensively with sufficient gravity,[36] though a little more analysis

33 William A Schabas, *The International Criminal Court: A Commentary on the Rome Statute* (2nd edn, OUP 2016) 462.

34 See, for example, Paolo Benvenuti, 'Complementarity of the International Criminal Court to National Criminal Jurisdictions' in Flavia Lattanzi and William A Schabas (eds), *Essays on the Rome Statute of the International Criminal Court*, Vol.I (il Sirente 1999) 21, 43; John T Holmes, 'The Principle of Complementarity' in Roy S Lee (ed.), *The International Criminal Court: The Making of the Rome Statute* (Kluwer 1999) 41, 47; John T Holmes, 'Complementarity: National Courts versus the ICC' in Antonio Cassese, Paola Gaeta, and John RWD Jones (eds), *The Rome Statute of the International Criminal Court: A Commentary* (OUP 2002) 667, 673; Gabriele Della Morte, 'Potestà giurisdizionale della Corte penale internazionale: complementarità, condizioni di procedibilità, soggetti legittimati a richiedere l'esercizio dell'azione penale e *ne bis in idem*' in Gaetano Carlizzi et al (eds), *La Corte Penale Internazionale: Problemi e Prospettive* (Vivarium 2003) 1, 12; Eric David, 'La Cour Pénale Internationale' (2005) 313 RdC 325, 350; Flavia Lattanzi, 'La complementarità' in Giorgio Lattanzi and Vito Monetti (eds) *La Corte Penale Internazionale: Organi – competenza – reati – processo* (Giuffrè 2006) 179, 185–6; Young Sok Kim, *The Law of the International Criminal Court* (2nd edn, William Hein & Co 2019) 184.

35 See, for example, Paola Mori, *L'istituzionalizzazione della giurisdizione penale internazionale* (Giappichelli 2001) 236–7; Florian Razesberger, *The International Criminal Court: The Principle of Complementarity* (Peter Lang 2006) 39–40.

36 See, for example, M Cherif Bassiouni, *Introduction to International Criminal Law* (2nd edn, Brill 2013) 683; Alessandra Lanciotti, *La Corte penale internazionale e la repressione delle gravi violazioni del diritto umanitario* (Giappichelli 2013) 14; Antonio Cassese and Paola Gaeta (eds), *Cassese's International Criminal Law* (3rd edn, OUP 2013) 364; Roger O'Keefe, *International Criminal Law* (OUP 2015) 57–9; Carsten Stahn, *A Critical Introduction to International Criminal Law*

is included in works on international criminal procedure.[37] Nonetheless, since 2006 – eight years after the adoption of the RS – some works on sufficient gravity have appeared in international scholarship. These works have been a fundamental source of inspiration for researching and writing this book. They span from the growing body of academic literature that focuses on specific prosecutorial or judicial decisions on sufficient gravity (for instance in relation to the situation in the DRC,[38] the prosecutorial assessment regarding Iraq in 2006,[39] and to the *Mavi Marmara* judicial saga),[40] to the thought-provoking

---

(CUP 2019) 330, 350; Enrico Amati et al, *Introduzione al diritto penale internazionale* (4th edn, Giappichelli 2020) 39–40; Gerhard Werle and Florian Jessberger, *Principles of International Criminal Law* (4th edn, 2020 OUP) 130–31; Darryl Robinson et al, *An Introduction to International Criminal Law and Procedure* (5th edn, CUP 2024) 151–2.

[37] See, for example, Gideon Boas et al, *International Criminal Law Practitioner Library, Vol.III: International Criminal Procedure*(CUP 2011) 82–5; Christoph Safferling, *International Criminal Procedure* (OUP 2012) 222–5; William A Schabas, *An Introduction to the International Criminal Court* (6th edn, CUP 2020) 195–9; Kai Ambos, *Treatise on International Criminal Law, Vol. III: International Criminal Procedure* (2nd edn, OUP 2025) 279–92.

[38] For example, Stephen Eliot Smith, 'Inventing the Laws of Gravity: The ICC's Initial *Lubanga* Decision and Its Regressive Consequences' (2008) 8 ICLR 331; Ignaz Stegmiller, 'The Gravity Threshold under the ICC Statute: Gravity Back and Forth in *Lubanga* and *Ntaganda*' (2009) 9 ICLR 547; Mohamed M El Zeidy, 'The Gravity Threshold under the Statute of the International Criminal Court' (2008) 19 CLF 35.

[39] For example, Ray Murphy, 'Gravity Issues and the International Criminal Court' (2006) 17 CLF 281; William A Schabas, 'Prosecutorial Discretion v. Judicial Activism at the International Criminal Court' (2008) 6 JICJ 731.

[40] For example, Victor Kattan, 'The ICC and the Saga of the *Mavi Marmara*' (2015) 18 Palestine YIL 53–91; Anna Trenga, 'The Gravity Threshold of Article 17(1)(D)' (2015) 11 *Eyes on the ICC* 79; Geert-Jan Knoops and Tom Zwart, 'The *Flotilla* Case before the ICC: The Need to Do Justice While Keeping the Heaven Intact' (2015) 15 ICLR 1069; Chantal Meloni, 'The ICC Preliminary Examination of the Flotilla Situation: An Opportunity to Contextualise Gravity' (2016) 33 Zoom-in QIL 3; Ali Emrah Bozbayındır, 'The Venture of the Comoros Referral at the Preliminary Examination Stage' in Morten Bergsmo and Carsten Stahn (eds), *Quality Control in Preliminary Examination: Vol.1* (TOAPB 2018) 555; Igor Di Bernardini, '"*Mavi Marmara*": Crimini di Guerra senza responsabili? La decisione del Procuratore della Corte Penale Internazionale sull'attacco israeliano alla Freedom Flottilla per Gaza' (2020) 31 *Diritti Umani: Cronache e Battaglie* 167; Priya Urs, 'Situation on the Registered Vessels of the Union of the Comoros, the Hellenic Republic and the Kingdom of Cambodia' in *MPEPIL* (2020); Emmanouil Billis, 'The Limits of Discretion in the Investigation and Prosecution of War Crimes

monograph by Margaret deGuzman, which deals with the notion of gravity in international criminal justice (rather than before the ICC only) and advances a normative argument on the need to adopt a value-oriented approach to gravity,[41] to those illuminating books that tackle sufficient gravity from the wider perspective of studying prosecutorial discretion.[42] This book builds on the fundamental research of these great scholars to provide a comprehensive exploration of the assessment of sufficient gravity.

---

at the International Level: The *Mavi Marmara* Saga' (2022) 10 *Bergen Journal of Criminal Law and Criminal Justice* 1. This author has commented on the relevant developments in Marco Longobardo, 'Everything Is Relative, Even Gravity: Remarks on the Assessment of Gravity in ICC Preliminary Examinations, and the *Mavi Marmara* affaire' (2016) 14 JICJ 1011; 'Factors Relevant for the Assessment of Sufficient Gravity in the ICC. Proceedings and the Elements of International Crimes' (2016) 33 Zoom-In QIL 21.

[41] Margaret deGuzman, *Shocking the Conscience of Humanity: Gravity and the Legitimacy of International Criminal Law* (OUP 2020). The book draws upon a number of articles by the same author, such as 'Gravity and the Legitimacy of the International Criminal Court' (2008–2009) 32 FILJ 1400; 'How Serious Are International Crimes? The Gravity Problem in International Criminal Law' (2012–2013) 51 CJTL 18; 'The International Criminal Court's Gravity Jurisprudence at Ten' (2013) 12 *Washington University Global Studies Law* Review 475.

[42] For example, Ignaz Stegmiller, *The Pre-Investigation Stage of the ICC: Criteria for Situation Selection* (D&H 2011); Bertram Kloss, *The Exercise of Prosecutorial Discretion at the International Criminal Court: Towards a More Principled Approach* (Verlag 2017); Mohammad Hadi Zakerhossein, *Situation Selection Regime at the International Criminal Court: Law, Policy, Practice* (Intersentia 2017); Frédéric Foka Taffo, *Le pouvoir discrétionnaire du Procureur de la Cour pénale internationale* (Nomos 2018); Anni Pues, *Prosecutorial Discretion at the International Criminal Court* (Hart 2020); Farid Mohammed Rashid, *Prosecutorial Discretion in the International Criminal Court: Legitimacy and the Politics of Justice* (Routledge 2021); Jacopo Governa, *Rethinking the Prosecutor's Discretion at the International Criminal Court: Substantive Limitations and Judicial Control* (D&H 2023); Luca Poltronieri Rossetti, *To Investigate or Not to Investigate? Prosecutorial Discretion and Its Judicial Review at the International Criminal Court* (Editoriale Scientifica 2024); Priya Urs, *Gravity at the International Criminal Court: Admissibility and Prosecutorial Discretion* (OUP 2024); Cale Davis, *Prosecutorial Discretion in International Criminal Justice* (Edward Elgar Publishing 2025).

3. THE MAIN ARGUMENT, APPROACH, AND SCOPE OF THIS BOOK

This book focuses on sufficient gravity as an admissibility criterion, offering a doctrinal examination in light of primary and secondary sources of international law. Put simply, the book provides an analysis of Article 17(1)(d) of the RS, to guide ICC organs and parties before ICC proceedings in their interpretation and application of this provision, and the wider public in their understanding and evaluation of the way the ICC works. Accordingly, the book will explore how Article 17(1)(d) has been interpreted in situations and cases where it plays a role.

The central argument of the book is that sufficient gravity is a minimal threshold, and that its assessment is an act subject to the rules of legal interpretation and can be subject to legal judicial scrutiny. Accordingly, the book counters the majority view, according to which the assessment of sufficient gravity is, essentially, discretionary; it shifts the attention from prosecutorial discretion to admissibility of situations, cases, and potential cases. In doing so, the findings of this book could contribute to understanding when ICC organs have interpreted and applied sufficient gravity coherently with the RS, and whether extra-legal considerations, such as those belonging to the realm of international politics, might have played a role. The need to evaluate the assessment of sufficient gravity is particularly important since, as demonstrated by the overview above, ICC organs have determined that situations or cases did not pass the gravity threshold particularly when powerful actors (and significant pressure) were involved.

The book is structured as follows. After this introduction, Chapter 2 delineates the theoretical framework that applies to the assessment of sufficient gravity. This chapter first explores the nature of sufficient gravity from a jurisprudential point of view, then it goes on to explore which rules of treaty interpretation apply to Article 17(1)(d). Chapter 3 analyses the role of the notion of gravity in international law, international criminal law, and the RS. Usually employed to emphasise an alleged shift towards a more value-oriented approach of international law, the notion of gravity has accompanied the emergence of international criminal justice since its inception. In the RS, this notion is present in Article 17(1)(d) as an admissibility criterion – the scope of this book – and a jurisdictional component of certain crimes, as a component of the interests of justice, as a factor relevant for the determination of penalties, and as a circumstance relevant for the activity of ICC organs. Chapter 4 explores the case law of the ICC Chambers and OTP practice to ascertain which factual elements should be considered in assessing sufficient gravity under Article 17(1)(d). The chapter traces the evolution of the attitude of relevant organs, focusing on the coalescence around four factors: scale, nature, manner of commission, and impact of the crimes. Chapter 5 analyses how the word 'sufficient' should be interpreted, in relation to gravity, under Article 17(1)(d). It is argued that this provision provides a minimum threshold that should not be identified by comparison with different situations, cases, and potential cases, but rather, only through the presence of the aforementioned factors. Chapter 6 provides a granular enquiry into the available mechanisms of judicial review when it comes to the assessment of sufficient gravity performed by the OTP. The analysis focuses on the availability of these mechanisms under the RS, and in light of relevant AC decisions, and on different ways to challenge positive and negative determinations of sufficient gravity. Finally, Chapter 7 provides the conclusion.

2. The theoretical approach to the assessment of sufficient gravity

Combining jurisprudential and international law perspectives

'Law is like art in that typically it is made to be interpreted.'[1]

'Texts cannot talk – they are talked about.'[2]

1. INTRODUCTION

This chapter explores the theoretical framework that should be employed during the assessment of sufficient gravity in the Rome Statute (RS). The starting point is that the RS does not define what 'gravity' is and when it is 'sufficient' under Article 17(1)(d); rather, the concept of sufficient gravity is inherently vague and needs to be understood through its application by the International Criminal Court (ICC) organs.[3] Likewise, although Article 53 refers to sufficient gravity under Article 17(1)(d), no definition is provided. To understand how to assess sufficient gravity, then, it is necessary to investigate what the applicable theoretical framework is, considering both jurisprudence and international law.

To do so, the chapter first dispels some ideas regarding the alleged necessity for assessing sufficient gravity through non-legal instruments. The analysis is conducted from a jurisprudential perspective, exploring the nature of sufficient gravity as a combined evaluative conceptual term (section 2). Nevertheless,

[1] Joseph Raz, *Between Authority and Interpretation: On the Theory of Law and Practical Reason* (OUP 2009) 232.

[2] Ingo Venzke, *How Interpretation Makes International Law: On Semantic Change and Normative Twists* (OUP 2012) 1.

[3] On vagueness, see, for example, Roberto Guastini, *Interpretare e argomentare* (Giuffrè 2011) 52–9; Adil Ahmad Haque, 'Indeterminacy in the Law of Armed Conflict' (2019) 95 ILS 118, 126–35.

the chapter argues that the assessment of sufficient gravity is a legal issue that must be addressed through legal interpretation. The fact that sufficient gravity allows certain discretion to the organ that is tasked with the assessment does not mean that it is an inherently subjective or political notion, nor does it preclude a role for legal interpretation.

Accordingly, the chapter explores the rules on treaty interpretation that are applicable to Articles 17(1)(d) and 53 of the RS (section 3). It will be demonstrated that the rules embodied in the 1969 Vienna Convention on the Law of Treaties (VCLT) deserve specific attention because they apply to the RS as it is a treaty. Finally, the analysis focuses on the peculiar role that ICC organs, in particular the Chambers and the Office of the Prosecutor (OTP), play in interpreting the RS.

2. A JURISPRUDENTIAL EXAMINATION OF THE PERSPECTIVES FROM WHICH SUFFICIENT GRAVITY CAN BE ASSESSED

This section explores 'sufficient gravity' from a jurisprudential point of view in order to identify the appropriate legal framework that applies to the assessment of sufficient gravity. Although it is based on jurisprudential considerations, the goal of the present analysis is to make 'sufficient gravity' work in the practice of international criminal law.[4] Divergent views on the assessment of sufficient gravity are the result of different understandings of what this clause is from a jurisprudential point of view. The aim of this section is to shed some light on this issue to present a coherent argument in support of the theoretical approach adopted in this study. The combination of jurisprudential and international law sources does not aim at providing an exhaustive grand theory on this issue.

2.1 Sufficient Gravity: A Combined Evaluative Conceptual Term That Provides a Standard

From a jurisprudential point of view, 'sufficient gravity' is composed of two conceptual terms, 'sufficient' and 'gravity'. A conceptual term is a verbal representation of a concept.[5] A concept can be defined as 'the generalized idea of an empirical or normative phenomenon or state of affairs or class of such phenomena or state of affairs'.[6] Absent a legally binding definition provided by the

4 Richard Gardiner, *Treaty Interpretation* (2nd edn, OUP 2015) 9.

5 Ulf Linderfalk, 'The Functionality of Conceptual Terms in International Law and International Legal Discourse' (2013) 6 EJLS 27, 31.

6 Ibid, 49.

law-maker,[7] the utterance of conceptual terms in legal and non-legal discourse does not guide the recipient of a certain text to any final meaning, but rather, any meaning that can be given to that utterance is the consequence of the functionality of the term, that is, 'what the uttering of the term potentially does to the beliefs, attitudes or behaviour of participants at the same discourse'.[8] From this perspective, conceptual terms can help identify a meaning, but they are unable to provide for only one meaning, since this meaning depends largely on the cognitive environment of the persons that are involved.[9] Sometimes, conceptual terms are deliberate delegations of case-specific assessments from the law-maker to the recipient of the legal command,[10] but other times they are just clever negotiating solutions when there is no consensus between the drafters of a legal text in relation to the specific content of a certain norm.[11] This is particularly relevant in relation to the notion of sufficient gravity because it is based on two conceptual terms, 'sufficient' and 'gravity', which were negotiated but not defined by the states that drafted the RS.[12] According to deGuzman,

> [t]his was not a mere oversight on the part of the drafters. Rather, the decision to leave gravity ambiguous facilitated establishment of the Court by mediating between states with an expansive vision of the Court as a vehicle for human rights promotion and states that preferred to limit the Court's reach in the name of preserving sovereignty.[13]

In this, the concept of sufficient gravity is inherently evaluative, and thus, it cannot be defined once and for all through interpretation.[14] Rather, even within

---

[7] Ibid, 41.

[8] Ibid, 31.

[9] Ibid, 54–5. See also Andrea Bianchi, 'Textual Interpretation and (International) Law Reading: The Myth of (In)Determinacy and the Genealogy of Meaning' in Pieter H F Bekker, Rudolf Dolzer and Michael Waibel (eds), *Making Transnational Law Work in the Global Economy: Essays in Honour of Detlev Vagts* (CUP 2010) 34.

[10] Jeremy Waldron, 'How to Do Things with Standards' in Upendra Baxi, Christopher McCrudden and Abdul Palowala (eds), *Law's Ethical, Global and Theoretical Contexts: Essays in Honour of William Twining* (CUP 2015) 335, 336–7, 345.

[11] Linderfalk, n.5, 45.

[12] On the drafting process, see below, subsection 3.2.2.

[13] Margaret deGuzman, 'How Serious are International Crimes? The Gravity Problem in International Criminal Law' (2012–2013) 51 CJTL 18, 22.

[14] Compare Haque, n.3, 126; Waldron, n.10, 336.

the same contextual framework it is possible that reasonable actors could reach different conclusions on whether a case is sufficiently grave.[15]

This indeterminacy can be grasped by realising that, from a jurisprudential point of view, Article 17(1)(d) of the RS provides a standard, rather than a rule, when it mentions sufficient gravity. In the words of a commentator, the distinction between a rule and a standard 'is between a norm that uses relatively precise, descriptive and perhaps even operationalised predicates in its protasis and apodosis and a norm that, in its protasis and apodosis, uses evaluative [*sic*] or other vague terms whose application require thought, evaluation or judgment on the part of the norm applier'.[16] As noted, '[e]nshrined in legal rules, [standards] acquire relevance in the process of interpretation and application of the Law but, with reference to values and social usages, they mean the introduction of a different element'.[17] A famous example of the difference comes to mind in this regard: 'a speed limit is a rule; a norm that requires drivers to take reasonable care is a standard'.[18] In other words, the law-maker – in our case, the states that drafted the RS – leaves to the individuals tasked with the interpretation and application of Article 17(1)(d) the exact determination of what makes a specific situation or case of sufficient gravity.[19] The RS indicates that there is a threshold between inadmissible and admissible cases; however, the threshold is not predetermined with precision by the Statute, which incorporates a standard. Saying that a situation or a case involving ten victims has sufficient gravity would be a rule, but this is not what the RS provides for; rather, the Statute affirms that only situations and cases of sufficient gravity are admissible, thus providing a standard.

The fact that Article 17(1)(d) on sufficient gravity provides a standard rather than a rule is far from surprising since international law relies abundantly on standards and evaluative concepts in many different areas.[20] However, the nature of the standard of sufficient gravity is not an obstacle to using legal tools, in particular, legal interpretation, as a guide in its assessment.

---

15 Haque, n.3, 129

16 Waldron, n.10, 335.

17 Oriol Casanovas, *Unity and Pluralism in Public International Law* (Brill 2001) 84.

18 Waldron, n.10, 335. See also Kenneth W Abbott et al, 'The Concept of Legalization' (2000) 54 *International Organization* 401, 413.

19 Waldron, n.10, 336–7.

20 See the overview in Jean Salmon, 'Les métamorphoses de la gravité' in Marcelo G Kohen (ed.), *Promoting Justice, Human Rights and Conflict Resolution through International Law: Liber Amicorum Lucius Caflisch* (Brill 2007) 1175.

2.2 The Assessment of Sufficient Gravity as a Problem of Legal Interpretation

This subsection argues that the rules on treaty interpretation play a role in assessing sufficient gravity by narrowing the discretion left to the OTP and the Chambers in assessing it. Interpretation is often considered the core of legal analysis.[21] As affirmed, interpretation is the 'scientific knowledge of the meaning of a language, or of a tradition of customary actions',[22] even if, today, most authorities are sceptical of the 'scientific' character of interpretation.[23] According to international case law, 'par l'expression «interprétation», il faut entendre l'indication précise du «sens» et de la «portée»' of a legal text[24] and '[i]nterpretation is a legal operation designed to determine the precise meaning of a rule'.[25] Scholars concur that one of the main goals of legal interpretation[26]

---

21 See Angelo Falzea, *Introduzione alle scienze giuridiche: Parte prima: Il concetto di diritto* (4th edn, Giuffrè 1996) 234.

22 Ibid, 253.

23 On the rhetoric of 'science' and of 'art' in international law interpretation, see Ulf Linderfalk, 'Is Treaty Interpretation an Art or a Science? International Law and Rational Decision Making' (2015) 26 EJIL 169.

24 PCIJ, *Interprétation des arrêts n° 7 et 8 (usine de Chorzów), PCIJ Recueil des Arrêts*, Série A, No.13, 16 Dec 1927, 10 (only the French text is authoritative; the non-authoritative English text uses the word 'construction' rather than 'interprétation').

25 *Case concerning a boundary dispute between Argentina and Chile concerning the delimitation of the frontier line between boundary post 62 and Mount Fitzroy*, Decision of 21 Oct 1994, XXII RIAA 3, para.75.

26 See, however, Denis Alland, 'L'interprétation du droit international public' (2014) 362 *RdC* 41, 122–9 (making a distinction between interpretation to ascertain the 'sense' and interpretation to ascertain the 'signification' of a source); Jean d'Aspremont, 'The Multidimensional of Interpretation' in Andrea Bianchi, Daniel Peat and Matthew Windsor (eds), *Interpretation in International Law* (OUP 2015) 111 (separating interpretation as a content-determination operation and interpretation as a law-ascertainment operation).

is the quest for meaning or sense,[27] usually of a written text[28] in order to extrapolate from the textual provision the norm that should be applied in a specific case.[29] Today, there is significant consensus on the fact that legal interpretation cannot lead to the finding of just one true meaning, but rather, legal parameters guide the interpreter to assess a number of interpretive options that are plausible in relation to provisions that are always indeterminate to a certain extent.[30]

Hence, one may wonder whether 'sufficient gravity' under Article 17(1)(d) is a notion subject to interpretation. The answer is affirmative for multiple

---

27 See generally Francesco Carnelutti, *Teoria Generale del diritto* (Foro Italiano 1940) 376; Hans Kelsen, *Pure Theory of Law* (2nd edn, originally 1960), English trans. by Max Knight (University of California Press 1967) 348; Raz, n.1, 230; Giorgio Pino, *L'interpretazione nel diritto* (Giappichelli 2021) 7. In international law scholarship, see Georges Scelle, *Précis de droit des gens: principes et systématique, Vol.II* (Librairie du Recueil Sirey 1932–1934) 488; Hans Kelsen, *The Law of United Nations: A Critical Analysis of Its Fundamental Problems* (Stevens & Sons 1950) xiii; Mustafa Kamil Yasseen, 'L'interprétation des traités d'après la Convention de Vienne sur le droit des traité' (1976) 151 RdC 9, 9; Carlos Fernández de Casadevante Romaní, *La Interpretación de las Normas Internacionales* (Aranzadi 1996) 31–2; Jean Salmon (ed.), *Dictionnaire de droit international public* (Bruylant 2001) 603; Robert Kolb, *Interprétation at création du droit international* (Bruylant 2006) 26; Alexander Orakhelashvili, *The Interpretation of Acts and Rules in Public International Law* (OUP 2008) 285; Fuad Zarbiyev, *Le discours interprétatif en droit international contemporain: un essai critique* (Bruylant 2015) 7; Chang-fa Lo, *Treaty Interpretation under the Vienna Convention on the Law of Treaties* (Springer 2019) 3. See, however, Daniel Peat and Matthew Windsor, 'Playing the Game of Interpretation: On Meaning and Metaphor in International Law' in Andrea Bianchi, Daniel Peat and Matthew Windsor (eds), *Interpretation in International Law* (OUP 2015), 3, 9–16; Jean d'Aspremont, *After Meaning: The Sovereignty of Forms in International Law* (Edward Elgar Publishing 2021); Andrea Bianchi and Fuad Zarbiyev, *Demystifying Treaty Interpretation* (CUP 2024).

28 Falzea, n.21, 232–4; Alland, n.26, 66–96. On whether it is possible to interpret customary international law, see Panos Merkouris, Jörg Kammerhofer and Noora Arajärvi (eds), *The Theory, Practice, and Interpretation of Customary International Law* (CUP 2022); Panos Merkouris, *Interpretation of Customary International Law: Of Methods and Limits* (Brill 2024).

29 Gustavo Zagrebelsky, *Il sistema delle fonti nel diritto* (2nd edn, UTET 1991) 69; Guastini, n.3, 63–65.

30 See, with different perspectives, Kelsen, *The Law*, n.27, xv; Kelsen, *Pure Theory*, n.27, 350–352; Michele Ainis, *La legge oscura: come e perché non funziona* (Laterza 1997) 144–153; Martti Koskenniemi, *From Apology to Utopia* (CUP 2005) 527–32; Raz, n.1, 232–5; Bianchi, n.9; Fuad Zarbiyev, 'The "Cash Value" of the Rules of Treaty Interpretation' (2019) 32 LJIL 33.

reasons. Since the notion of sufficient gravity is embodied in an international treaty, it is logical to apply to it the rules on treaty interpretation that exist at the international law level. This is something that ICC Chambers do routinely in their case law, which mention the rules on treaty interpretation embodied in the VCLT as the starting point to discuss sufficient gravity.[31] Likewise, many scholars address – more or less consciously – sufficient gravity[32] and cognate inadmissibility grounds such as complementarity[33] as problems belonging to the interpretation of the RS. These circumstances are themselves valid justifications to consider sufficient gravity as an issue that falls within the realm of treaty interpretation.

More decisively, it is necessary to note that the goal of the application of the rules of treaty interpretation to sufficient gravity is not to find one and only one meaning that will clarify once and for all which situations and cases fall within the scope of sufficient gravity. Rather, legal interpretation is employed here to provide a frame[34] that limits the radius[35] of the permitted interpretations

---

31 See below, subsection 3.2.1.

32 See, for example, Ignaz Stegmiller, 'Interpretative Gravity under the Rome Statute: Identifying Common Gravity Criteria' in Carsten Stahn (ed.), *The International Criminal Court and Complementarity: From Theory to Practice* (CUP 2011) 603; Héctor Olásolo and Enrique Carnero-Rojo, 'The Application of the Principle of Complementarity to the Decision of Where to Open an Investigation: The Admissibility of "Situations"' in Carsten Stahn (ed.), The *International Criminal Court and Complementarity: From Theory to Practice* (CUP 2011) 393 393, 416–17; Kaveri Vaid, 'Discretion Operationalized Through Law: *Proprio Motu* Decision-making at the International Criminal Court' (2013) 25 Florida JIL 359, 388–402; Ghazia Popalzai and Hiba Thobani, 'The Complexities of the Gravity Threshold in the International Criminal Court: A Practical Necessity or an Insidious Pitfall?' (2017) 20 MPYUNL 150, 153; Farid Mohammed Rashid, *Prosecutorial Discretion in the International Criminal Court: Legitimacy and the Politics of Justice* (Routledge 2021) 123–76; Margaret deGuzman, *Shocking the Conscience of Humanity: Gravity and the Legitimacy of International Criminal Law* (OUP 2020) 112; Rachel López, 'The Law of Gravity' (2020) 58 CJTL 565, 621.

33 Mahnoush H Arsanjani and W Michael Reisman, 'The International Criminal Court and the Congo: From Theory to Reality' in Leila Nadya Sadat and Michael P Scharf (eds), *The Theory and Practice of International Criminal Law: Essays in Honor of M Cherif Bassiuni* (Martinus Nijhoff Publishers 2008) 325, 332–7; Muriel Ubéda-Saillard, 'Les techniques interprétatives des tribunaux pénaux internationaux' (2011) 115 RGDIP 421, 434; Aurora Rasi, 'Principio di complementarietà e interpretazione dello Statuto di Roma' (2017) 11 DUDI 5.

34 This word is borrowed from Kelsen, *Pure Theory*, n.27, 350–51.

35 See Ervin P Hexner, 'Teleological Interpretation of Basic Instruments of Public International Organizations' in Salo Engel and Rudolf A Métall (eds),

of the provision on sufficient gravity in light of legal parameters established for the interpretation of treaties. In the field of international law, it has been argued that 'critères normatifs emprisonneraient l'opération interprétative et limiteraient donc l'utilitisation de tous les moyens nécessaires pour expliquer au mieux la tâche interprétative'.[36] If legal interpretation is the hinge that joins international law and international politics,[37] then the rules on interpretation are the (quite fragile) barriers that prevent the political dimension from overcoming the legal sphere entirely.[38] The frame, in this author's opinion, is provided by the rules on treaty interpretation embodied in the VCLT, which are applicable to the RS, by those additional rules on treaty interpretation provided in the RS,[39] and by the RS itself, which is part of the relevant interpretive context as explained in the following pages.[40]

The fact that sufficient gravity is an evaluative concept and that Article 17(1)(d) provides a standard rather than a rule are not at odds with employing legal interpretation. It is true that Article 17(1)(d) does not delineate which situations, potential cases, or cases have sufficient gravity, but instead leaves this determination to the OTP and the Chambers. However, *the way in which this determination is performed*, the *ends towards which this determination is exercised*, and the *need to justify how this determination is reached*, are all governed by rules on interpretation. There is no incompatibility here between interpretation and discretion, as otherwise held by some observers:[41] treaty interpretation merely points towards the fact that interpreting sufficient grav-

---

Law, State, And International Legal Order: Essays in Honor of Hans Kelsen (The University of Tennessee Press 1964) 120, 123–4.

36 Flavia Lattanzi, 'Les techniques interprétatives des tribunaux pénaux internationaux' (2011) 115 RGDIP 435, 438, n.7.

37 Serge Sur, *L'interprétation en droit international public* (LGDJ 1974) 67 and 85.

38 López, n.32, 621. The thorny consideration that even the rules on treaty interpretation should be interpreted cannot be explored here (see Lorenzo Gradoni, 'Regole di interpretazione difficili da interpretare e frammentazione del principio di integrazione sistemica' (2010) 93 RDI 809).

39 Sonia Głogowska, 'The Complexities of Law Interpretation with Regard to the International Criminal Court' (2018) 24 Comparative LR 175, 188 ('ICC judges do not have full discretion in shaping legal norms. The content of the Statute, as a manifestation of the will of the State Parties, limits the results of creative interpretation').

40 Compare with Kelsen, *Pure Theory*, n.27, 350–51, who considers that the source or provision that is interpreted is the interpretative frame.

41 Ulf Linderfalk, 'The Exercise of Discretion in International Law – Why Constraining Criteria Have a Proper Place in the Analysis of Legal Decision-Making' (2019) 62 German YIL 407.

ity requires some discretion; legal interpretation has the additional function of guiding the way in which ICC organs exercise that discretion. At the very least, even though legal interpretation cannot identify *ex ante* which situations, potential cases, and cases pass the sufficient gravity threshold, it can be used to expose unpersuasive assessments provided by the ICC organs.

2.3 Sufficient Gravity as an Inherently Subjective Notion That Can Only Be Assessed Subjectively

Affirming that legal interpretation applies to the assessment of sufficient gravity, in abstract terms, does not necessarily mean that legal interpretation is able to clarify the notion of sufficient gravity in concrete situations. This subsection explores whether there is anything inherently subjective in the evaluative concept of sufficient gravity that makes it impossible to constrain its assessment through legal interpretation. The question of whether sufficient gravity is a subjective or an objective notion, and whether the assessment of sufficient gravity is a subjective or objective process, has significantly occupied scholars. The approach of the ICC organs to this issue is explored subsequently.[42]

Two versions of the assessment of gravity as an inherently subjective notion can be discussed. First, some scholars have considered that the assessment of sufficient gravity is inherently subjective[43] and thus, the OTP and the Chambers of the ICC have absolute discretion in concluding that a specific situation or case is sufficiently grave from their subjective perspective.[44] Certainly, in the common discourse, the determination of what is sufficiently grave can depend on individual circumstances and, as a result, it may be inherently subjective in

---

42 See below, Chapter 4, subsection 3.5.

43 Orde F Kittrie, *Lawfare: Law as a Weapon of War* (OUP 2016) 224; Stuart Ford, 'The Meaning of Gravity at the International Criminal Court: A Survey of Attitudes about the Seriousness of Mass Atrocities' (2018) 24 UC Davis JILP 209, 212 and 214; Pierre Jouette, 'La gravité en droit international pénal' (2022) 67 *McGill Law Journal* 407; Priya Urs, *Gravity at the International Criminal Court: Admissibility and Prosecutorial Discretion* (OUP 2024) 72–80.

44 Giuliano Turone, 'Powers and Duties of the Prosecutor' in Antonio Cassese, Paola Gaeta and John RWD Jones (eds), *The Rome Statute of the International Criminal Court: A Commentary* (OUP 2002) 1137, 1152; Vaid, n.32, 400; Kittrie, n.43, 224; Emanuela Piccolo Koskimies, 'Sovereignty as Responsibility at the International Criminal Court: The Frontiers of International Judicial Intervention' in Ekaterina Yahyaoui Krivenko (ed.), *Human Rights and Power in Times of Globalisation* (Brill 2018) 69; Rashid, n.32, 130–31; Richard H Steinberg, 'Politics and Justice at the International Criminal Court' (2024) 57 IsLR 308, 330. All standards are inherently subjective for Hardy Cross Dillard, 'Some Aspects of Law and Diplomacy' (1957) 91 RdC 445, 477–86.

relation to both the factors that are relevant for the notion of gravity and when those factors are sufficient.[45] However, this does not mean that the assessment of sufficient gravity in the RS cannot follow legal rules. Indeed, such a conclusion would be permissible only if one considers that the drafters of the RS abdicated their prescriptive powers in this field by entirely delegating the assessment to those individuals who, at a certain time in history and at a certain stage in the ICC procedure, must decide which case or situation is sufficiently grave.[46]

The fact that sufficient gravity is based on evaluative notions does not mean that the drafters of the RS left the assessment of sufficient gravity entirely to subjective appreciation. Rather, when a law-maker employs a standard, it provides guidance to the recipient, by using specific value-laden language in the very wording of the standard[47] – which needs to be interpreted in light of the external constraints provided by the rules on interpretation – and through the application of the rules on interpretation, to the entire source that embodies the standard.[48] Accordingly, although the assessment of which situations and cases are of sufficient gravity needs an evaluation by the OTP and the Chambers, this assessment is guided, is 'something that is supposed to represent not just their own idiosyncratic views, but a view that can stand even in their own self-application of it, in the name of the whole community'.[49] Indeed, nothing in the RS suggests that the drafters entirely delegated to the OTP or the Chambers the performance of a subjective assessment of sufficient gravity; in fact, the RS has many provisions that endeavour to limit the subjectivity of the OTP or of the Chambers on other topics.[50] Moreover, the possibility of judicial review of the assessment of sufficient gravity, when specific circumstances are met,[51] demonstrates that there is no inherently subjective character of the assessment of sufficient gravity extreme enough to remove it from legal scrutiny.

---

45 See the example above, Chapter 1, section 1.

46 See Raz, n.1, 230–31 ('Subjectivists by contrast stand at the other extreme. In holding that meaning is in the eye of the beholder they regard the receiver rather than the creator as the sole origin of meaning').

47 Casanovas, n.17, 84; Waldron, n.10, 345.

48 See below, section 3.

49 Waldron, n.10, 347, 349. See also Casanovas, n.17, 85–6; Fulvio Maria Palombino, *Fair and Equitable Treatment and the Fabric of General Principles* (Springer 2018) 22.

50 See, for example, narrow interpretation of crimes and established framework of international humanitarian law – discussed below, subsection 3.1.

51 See Chapter 6.

Second, the inherent subjectivity of the notion of sufficient gravity has led one commentator to conclude that this must be assessed by summing as many subjective perceptions as possible. This is the position championed by Stuart Ford, according to whom, 'gravity is a subjective component of crimes'.[52] Notwithstanding the reference to the components of crimes, Ford applies this subjective consideration to gravity as an admissibility criterion as well.[53] In his opinion, in the absence of a definition of sufficient gravity in the RS, and considering the inherently subjective nature of this notion, sufficient gravity should be assessed in light of 'how the population as a whole views the gravity of mass atrocities',[54] thus viewing the assessment of gravity as the result of a complex survey of subjective assessments. In line with this premise, Ford considers that sufficient gravity can only be assessed empirically and, as a result, he uses surveys to assess the attitude of the wider public[55] and legal scholars[56] to the gravity of the crimes. In this perspective, only an empirical analysis can reduce the subjectivity of gravity to a uniform standard that can be applied by the ICC.[57] However, leaving aside the fact that Ford administers these surveys only to US citizens, even though the US is not a party to the RS, nothing in the RS suggests that sufficient gravity must be assessed from this subjective perspective and in light of the broader audience of the RS. The threshold of sufficient gravity is not a norm that must be followed by the wider public in the same way as the specific prohibition not to commit a crime (for example, the ban on genocide), rather, it is a procedural norm that must be applied by specific ICC organs (mainly, the OTP and the Chambers). As such, the subjective perception of the US public (including scholars and otherwise)[58] is entirely unhelpful, since Article 17(1)(d) is not subject to self-application by all the individuals who are subject to the criminal provisions of the RS.[59] Indeed,

---

52 Ford, n.43, 212.

53 Ibid, 216.

54 Ibid, 211.

55 Ibid, passim.

56 Stuart Ford, 'Understanding Crime Gravity: Exploring the Views of International Criminal Law Experts' (2019) 27 William & Mary Bill of Rights Journal 659.

57 Ford, n.43, 212.

58 On the role of certain scholarly writings from a broader perspective, see Sandesh Sivakumaran, 'The Influence of Teachings of Publicists on the Development of International Law' (2017) 66 ICLQ 1.

59 On the role of self-application in relation to standards, see Waldron, n.10, 345 and 349.

many standards have specific addressees that reduce the relevance of the wider public's subjective perceptions.[60]

Accordingly, reducing the assessment of sufficient gravity to an inherently subjective operation is unsatisfactory because it denies any agency to the drafters of the RS who, despite the fact that they have omitted a definition of the notion, have nevertheless tasked the OTP and the Chambers with assessing it in the framework of legal proceedings. The fact that different people may have conflicting perspectives on which situations or cases meet the threshold of sufficient gravity does not mean that the drafters of the RS have left the OTP and the Chambers totally free to determine the threshold. As noted above, it is not by chance that the RS provides for mechanisms of judicial review over the OTP's assessment of sufficient gravity. The very existence of these judicial review mechanisms demonstrates that the perceived or real subjectivity of the gravity threshold is not an obstacle to the application of legal standards in its assessment. Rather, the evaluation of sufficient gravity can follow legal criteria, and the process in which sufficient gravity is assessed can be scrutinised accordingly. The legal criteria can be either provided by the primary rule demanding the assessment of sufficient gravity – in our case, the RS – or developed by the practice of relevant organs in their interpretation and application of sufficient gravity – in our case, mainly the OTP and the Chambers of the Court. Bearing in mind that there is a strict interconnection between the abstract provisions of the RS and their concrete interpretation and application by some organs, the assessment of sufficient gravity – notwithstanding the evaluative nature of this concept – is not conducted in a legal vacuum, but rather, can be scrutinised under legal principles (those governing interpretation). It is possible to consider such an assessment subjective in the sense that it is performed on a case-by-case basis by certain individuals who might reach divergent conclusions through reasonable argumentations; however, legal criteria can help to reduce the risk of extreme subjectivity that result in arbitrariness.

The idea that it is futile to try to understand the legal dimension of sufficient gravity and the legally driven processes to assess it because of its inherently subjective character should be rejected.

2.4 Sufficient Gravity as a Political – Rather Than Legal – Question

Similarly, the fact that the assessment of sufficient gravity can be influenced by political considerations does not render it extraneous to legal considerations. The subjective perception of the actors involved in the gravity assessment

[60] An example is discussed ibid, 350.

can be influenced by their appreciation of what is more grave as a matter of policy or as a matter of the perceived goals of the ICC. Indeed, authors such as Margaret deGuzman have advocated for a clear value-based and policy-oriented mandate by the Assembly of States Parties (ASP) to the Prosecutor in relation to sufficient gravity,[61] in line with the political directives imposed by the executive to prosecutors in the US.

The idea that the interpretation of certain treaties or certain provisions is mainly a political exercise is not new and has been termed 'radical legal skepticism'.[62] From this perspective: 'legal norms capable of constraining political judgment simply do not exist. Hence, whenever a certain understanding is advanced as the correct interpretation of a certain legal provision, the only question to be asked is whether the interpretation is legitimate or not.'[63] Indeed, deGuzman's analysis explicitly focuses on strengthening the legitimacy of the ICC.[64] However, her analysis, albeit provocative and well reasoned, is inapplicable to the RS as it is because it moves the responsibility for making the normative judgement on the gravity threshold from the OTP and the Chambers to the ASP. This is beyond what is provided for by the Statute. Even assuming that states agree on amending the Statute, the ASP's determination of which situations and cases cross the sufficient gravity threshold would not solve the problem of how to assess sufficient gravity. The entire operation would just strip the OTP and the Chambers of an assessment for which they are considered unsuitable – because they are perceived as organs operating mainly in a legal framework – to the ASP, from which no legal decisions are expected, only political ones. Again, how this process would help to determine sufficient gravity remains obscure to the present writer; rather, such a solution would create an almost *legibus solutus* body with the task of determining legal standards – *rectius*, making normative evaluations on the basis of legal standards – without considering itself bound by any law, except the RS itself, which is silent on this issue. The reader can assess the viability of this solution in light of what happens in relation to the action of the United Nations Security Council (UNSC), an organ that idiosyncratically, on the basis of political considerations, routinely makes political determinations on what constitutes a threat to the peace, a breach of the peace, or an act of

---

61 deGuzman, n.32, 106.

62 Ulf Linderfalk, *On the Interpretation of Treaties* (Springer 2007) 4.

63 Ibid.

64 This is evident from the very titles of some of her works: Margaret deGuzman, 'Gravity and the Legitimacy of the International Criminal Court' (2008–2009) 32 FILJ 1400, and n.32. See, also, Gus Waschefort, 'Gravity as a Requirement in International Criminal Prosecutions: Implications for South African Courts' (2014) 47 CILJ Southern Africa 38, 42–3.

aggression.[65] Scholars and judges have struggled to reconstruct this process in legal terms, and international case law was quick to conclude that the UNSC 'has functions of a political nature assigned to it' by design.[66] It is doubtful whether allowing something similar in the context of criminal proceedings would enhance the legitimacy of the ICC, despite the fact that the ASP would benefit from better representativeness than the UNSC.

Moreover, a political intervention by the ASP would never be able to determine a sufficient gravity threshold. At best, it might reduce the margins of discretion left to the OTP and the Chambers, but it is inconceivable that the ASP would be able, *ex ante*, to predict all specific cases that may arise, and make a gravity assessment applicable to them all. Remember, Article 17(1)(d) is about the sufficient gravity of situations, potential cases, and cases, rather than mere crimes. In any case, it does not seem that conceiving sufficient gravity as a political notion furthers the exploration of how it should be assessed.

Ultimately, it must be stressed that international law and international legal reasoning are fully applicable to issues that are not only legal issues, but also political ones. This is particularly the case when a judicial body is requested to intervene in the determination of a specific notion such as sufficient gravity. As stated by the International Court of Justice (ICJ) in relation to a different question, 'the circumstance that others may evaluate and interpret these facts in a subjective or political manner can be no argument for a court of law to abdicate its judicial task'.[67] The same is true in relation to the judicial function of the ICC.[68] In the field of sufficient gravity, this means that its assessment should be conducted pursuant to the RS rather than on the basis of political considerations outside the realm of international law. Overall, contemporary international

---

65 UN Charter, Article 39. On consistency in the voting behaviour of the five permanent members of the UNSC, see Tamsin Phillipa Paige, *Petulant and Contrary: Approaches by the Permanent Five Members of the UN Security Council to the Concept of 'Threat to the Peace' under Article 39 of the UN Charter* (Brill 2019).

66 *Military and Paramilitary Activities in and against Nicaragua (Nicaragua v United States of America)* (Jurisdiction and Admissibility) [1984] ICJ Reports 148, para.95. On this topic see, recently, Michael Wood and Eran Sthoeger, *The UN Security Council and International Law* (CUP 2022) 10–17.

67 *Legal Consequences of the Construction of a Wall in the Occupied Palestinian Territory* (Advisory Opinion) [2004] ICJ Reports 136, para.58.

68 Situation in Palestine, PTC I, Decision on the 'Prosecution request pursuant to article 19(3) for a ruling on the Court's territorial jurisdiction in Palestine', ICC-01/18-143, 5 Feb 2021, para.57.

law, especially in the practice of international and domestic courts, is shifting away from considering political questions as non-justiciable.[69]

Furthermore, the fact that both the OTP and the judges should perform their functions with independence[70] is a strong reminder that their actions, including those pertaining to the assessment of sufficient gravity, should not be guided primarily by political considerations but, instead governed by international law. In this case, that means that the assessment of sufficient gravity must be performed using the sources listed in Article 21 of the RS, that is, in the first place, the RS, the Elements of Crimes and its Rules of Procedure and Evidence (RPE), in the second place, applicable treaties and the principles and rules of international law, and in the third place, general principles of law derived by the Court from national laws or legal systems of the world.

Clearly, the assessment of sufficient gravity is performed by human beings, and it is impossible for the law to remove human components – including political considerations – from their actions.[71] This is particularly the case when individuals are faced with undefined notions such as that of 'sufficient gravity'. However, since the RS is silent as to whether the assessment of sufficient gravity should be undertaken from a purely political perspective, political considerations should merely be seen as part of the discourse on the legal assessment of sufficient gravity, rather than as reasons not to consider such an assessment to be governed by international law. Furthermore, although the RS does not provide for an overarching obligation to offer detailed legal reasoning in judicial decisions and prosecutorial acts, as affirmed by the Appeals Chamber (AC), 'the right to a reasoned decision is an element of the right to a fair trial'.[72] Indeed, numerous provisions of the RS demand the OTP and the Chambers provide information regarding the reasons behind their decisions, both in order to guarantee the rights of the accused and to enhance the overall transparency

---

69 See generally Daniele Amoroso, *Insindacabilità del potere estero e diritto internazionale* (Editoriale Scientifica 2012).

70 See RS, Articles 40 and 42.

71 See Kelsen, *The Law*, n.27, xiii.

72 Situation in the DRC, *Prosecutor v Lubanga*, AC, Judgment on the appeal of Mr Thomas Lubanga Dyilo against the decision of PTC I entitled First Decision on the Prosecution Requests and Amended Requests for Redactions under Rule 81, ICC-01/04-01/06-773, 13 Dec 2006, para.20. See, generally, Harvé Ascensio, 'La motivation des decisions des juridictions pénales internationales' in Hélène Ruiz Fabri and Jan-Marc Sorel (eds), *La motivation des decisions des jurisdictions internationals* (Pedone 2008) 207, 208–209; Jérémy Hall, 'CPI: Les ambiguïtés de l'obligation de motivation des charges: L'illustration par l'affaire Ongwen', Institut des Hautes Études Sur La Justice, 2016.

of ICC action.[73] In particular, Rules 105 and 106 of the RPE demand that the OTP provide 'reasons' for a decision not to open an investigation or launch prosecution for lack of sufficient gravity. These reasons are always interpreted as legal in character, rather than as pertaining to the realm of politics. There is no reason why an exception should be made in relation to the assessment of sufficient gravity.

In light of the above considerations, at this stage of the research it is possible to assume that nothing precludes a legal approach to the assessment of sufficient gravity under Article 17(1)(d). Rather, as sufficient gravity is embodied in a treaty, it is necessary to identify and apply the rules on treaty interpretation to the RS to ascertain whether they shed any light on sufficient gravity.

2.5 Sufficient Gravity as a Problem Pertaining to the Application Rather Than the Interpretation of Article 17(1)(d)

A few words are needed to finally dispel the idea that sufficient gravity is not a problem to be addressed through treaty interpretation but one that pertains to the realm of application.[74] This is not a decisive argument for denying the relevance of interpretation in relation to sufficient gravity.

Many treaties refer together to 'interpretation and application' of the law, especially in relation to the jurisdiction of an international body to settle a certain dispute.[75] Article 21(3) of the RS refers to 'the application and interpretation of law' by the ICC as if the two are separate but connected operations, a conclusion that resonates in some relevant judicial decisions.[76] On the basis of the dichotomy of interpretation versus application, most authors agree that the application of a norm is a phase distinct from the interpretation of the source that conveys that norm, and, thus, logically, interpretation precedes application.[77] As noted in the dissenting opinion of Judge Ehrlich in the *Factory of*

---

73 See, for example, RS, Articles 15, 18(1), 53(2), 58, 61, 67, 72, 74(5), 83(4). For the function of these duties, see Ascensio, ibid, 211–14; Hall, ibid, 9.

74 See Urs, n.43, 11–14.

75 Franklin Berman, 'International Treaties and British Statutes' (2005) 26(1) Statute LR 1, 10.

76 For example, Situation in the DRC, *Prosecutor v Lubanga*, AC, Judgment on the Appeal of Mr Thomas Lubanga Dyilo against the Decision on the Defence Challenge to the Jurisdiction of the Court pursuant to article 19(2)(a) of the Statute of 3 Oct 2006, ICC-01/04-01/06-772, 13 Dec 2006, para.37.

77 See HLA Hart, *The Concept of Law* (3rd edn, OUP 2012) 205. From an international law perspective, see Scelle, n.27, 488; Georg Schwarzenberger, 'Myths and Realities of Treaty Interpretation: Articles 27–29 of the Vienna Draft Convention on the Law of Treaties' (1968) 9(1) Virginia JIL 1, 7–8; Sur, n.37, 193;

Chorzow case, 'interpretation is [the process] of determining the meaning of a rule, while the other, application, is, in one sense, that of determining the consequences which the rule attaches to the occurrence of a given fact; in another sense, application is the action of bringing about the consequences which, according to a rule, should follow a fact'.[78] Similarly, the dissenting opinion of Sir Franklin Berman in the *Industria Nacional de Alimentos and Indalsa Perú v Peru* case clarified that '[w]hereas treaty interpretation can often be a detached exercise, it is virtually inevitable that treaty application will entail to some extent an assessment of the facts of the particular case and their correlation with the legal rights and obligations in play'.[79] Indeed, often, application is envisaged as the solution of a legal problem before a court, which is enacted only after the interpretation has already been performed.[80]

Suggesting that the assessment of sufficient gravity pertains to the application rather than to the interpretation of the RS, however, does not limit the role of interpretation for two reasons. First, the application of a provision can only be performed after that provision has been interpreted (and turned into a norm). Second, as mentioned above, the way in which an evaluative concept or standard is applied should be guided by legal interpretation, especially the framework of the RS, which is explicitly governed by legal rules. Accordingly, shifting the focus of the application of Article 17(1)(d) is not decisive in dispelling the role of legal interpretation.

Yasseen, n.27, 10; Kolb, n.27, 26; Gardiner, n.4, 28–29; Lo, n.27, 81–2. For a radical separation, see Anastasios Gourgourinis, 'The Distinction between Interpretation and Application of Norms in International Adjudication' (2011) 2 JIDS 31. *Contra*, see Jean Salmon, 'Le fait dans l'application du droit international' (1982) 175 RdC 257, 343. Some other authors prefer to claim that there are two forms of interpretation, one made in the abstract and pertaining to a certain provision, and the other undertaken with reference to the specific facts of the case to which the norm embodied in a provision must be applied (for example, Guastini, n.3, 15–18).

78 PCIJ, *Case concerning the Factory at Chorzów (Germany v Poland)*, Judgment of 26 Jul 1927, Series A, No.9, 2, Dissenting Opinion by M Ehrlich, 39. See also *Applicability of the Obligation to Arbitrate under Section 21 of the United Nations Headquarters Agreement of 26 June 1947* (Advisory Opinion), [1988] ICJ Reports 12, Separate Opinion of Judge Shahabuddeen, 59.

79 ICSID, *Industria Nacional de Alimentos, SA and Indalsa Perú, SA v The Republic of Peru*, ICSID Case No. ARB/03/4 - Annulment Proceeding, 5 Sep 2007, Dissenting Opinion of Sir Franklin Berman, para.15.

80 See Christian Djeffal, *Static and Evolutive Treaty Interpretation: A Functional Reconstruction* (CUP 2016) 9.

2.6 Preliminary Conclusions

This dense section has provided several answers to some preliminary questions surrounding the theoretical framework that applies to the assessment of sufficient gravity under Article 17(1)(d) of the RS. First, it has been explained that the notion of sufficient gravity is an evaluative concept, for which no definition is provided; rather, it embodies a standard through which a delegation is undertaken: the law-maker (in our case, the drafters of the RS) does not predetermine which situations, cases, and potential cases are of sufficient gravity, this assessment is left to the OTP and the Chambers.[81] However, this does not mean that the assessment of sufficient gravity is inherently subjective or political: rather, the assessment must be performed in a space governed by legal rules, and in particular by rules on the interpretation of legal instruments. In the instant case, these rules do not offer a way to reach a definitive/conclusive meaning of the expression of sufficient gravity, rather, they curb the discretion of the OTP and the Chambers in their determination of the standard of sufficient gravity.

Accordingly, it is important to assess which rules on interpretation apply to Article 17(1)(d) of the RS. These rules are the background against which the OTP and the Chambers must assess sufficient gravity.

3. RULES ON TREATY INTERPRETATION AND SUFFICIENT GRAVITY

While the preceding section has concluded that legal interpretation governs the assessment of sufficient gravity under Article 17(1)(d), this section addresses what rules on treaty interpretation actually apply to interpreting sufficient gravity in the RS. The analysis takes into consideration both specific rules embodied in the RS and those provided by the VCLT. The section demonstrates that treaty interpretation does not offer a definition of the notion of sufficient gravity – which is impossible to obtain through interpretation in light of the jurisprudential analysis above – but rather, provides guidance to the organs that are tasked with assessing sufficient gravity.

---

[81] A similar conclusion is reached, albeit through different reasoning, by Anni Pues, 'Discretion and the Gravity of Situations at the International Criminal Court' (2017) 17 ICLR 960.

3.1 The Rules on Treaty Interpretation Provided by the RS

This subsection explores whether the RS provides for any rule on treaty interpretation that should apply to sufficient gravity. According to Article 21(1) of the RS, the '[t]he Court shall apply: (a) In the first place, this Statute, Elements of Crimes and its RPE; (b) In the second place, where appropriate, applicable treaties and the principles and rules of international law, including the established principles of the international law of armed conflict'. This means that the RS takes precedence over other applicable relevant treaties such as the VCLT. Accordingly, in the field of the interpretation of sufficient gravity under Article 17(1)(d), it is necessary to explore whether the RS derogates from the rules on treaty interpretation embodied by the VCLT by providing its own rules on interpretation.

A treaty can derogate from the rules on treaty interpretation embodied in the VCLT by adopting special rules for its own interpretation. Not only is this mentioned in Article 5 of the VCLT in relation to treaties establishing international organisations,[82] it is also the consequence of a broader consideration of the rules of the VCLT as general law governing treaties that can be displaced by more specific rules embodied in a certain treaty (*lex specialis*).[83] Special rules on interpretation may be included in relation to the statutes of international organisations.[84] As mentioned, the RS in itself provides for this when it says that other treaties may be applied '[i]n the second place' while the RS is applied 'in the first place', thus giving prominence to the RS over the VCLT.[85]

---

82 'The present Convention applies to any treaty which is the constituent instrument of an international organization and to any treaty adopted within an international organization *without prejudice to any relevant rules of the organization*' (emphasis added). See generally Paolo Palchetti, 'Halfway between Fragmentation and Convergence: The Role of the Rules of the Organization in the Interpretation of Constituent Treaties' in Mads Andenas and Eirik Bjørge (eds), *A Farewell to Fragmentation: Reassertion and Convergence in International Law* (CUP 2015) 486; Jan Klabbers, *An Introduction to International Organizations Law* (4th edn, CUP 2022) 85–6.

83 Oliver Dörr, 'Articles 31–33' in Oliver Dörr and Kirsten Schmalenbach (eds), *Vienna Convention on the Law of Treaties: A Commentary* (2nd edn, Springer 2018) 559, 576.

84 Klabbers, n.82, 86.

85 Authors debate whether this creates a hierarchical relationship (see, for example, Robert Cryer, 'Royalism and the King: Article 21 of the Rome Statute and the Politics of Sources' (2009) 12 *New Criminal Law Review* 390, 393; Amit Kumar, 'Is Article 21 of the Rome Statute Aiming for Legality or Hierarchy? A Dilemma' (2020–2021) 20 *ISIL Year Book of International Humanitarian and Refugee Law* 56) or merely codifies the *lex specialis* principle in this field (see,

The RS embodies many different rules on treaty interpretation from those provided by the VCLT, even though they are scattered throughout the text. In relation to sufficient gravity pursuant to Article 17(1)(d), it must be noted that Article 17 opens with the sentence '[h]aving regard to paragraph 10 of the Preamble and [A]rticle 1'. This reference could be seen as a specific rule on treaty interpretation that applies to this provision only. It could be argued that Article 17 should be interpreted specifically in light of paragraph 10 of the Preamble and Article 1, even if it is unclear, in practice, how this specific reference would affect the interpretation beyond what is required by the need to take into account the context of the entire treaty pursuant to Article 31(2) of the VCLT. Since paragraph 10 of the Preamble refers to the principle of complementarity,[86] its contribution to the interpretation of sufficient gravity is, in any case, moot. More relevant is Article 1 of the RS, which pertains to the jurisdiction of the ICC over 'the most serious crimes of international concern' as well as to complementarity. In any case, neither of these provisions shed significant light on Article 17(1)(d).

Other clear examples of special rules on the interpretation of the RS are Articles 21(3) and 22.[87] Article 21(3) prescribes that '[t]he application and interpretation of law pursuant to this article must be consistent with internationally recognized human rights, and be without any adverse distinction founded on grounds such as gender …, age, race, colour, language, religion or belief, political or other opinion, national, ethnic or social origin, wealth, birth or other status'. The common interpretation of this provision is that it is a rule on interpretation that applies to the entirety of the RS,[88] including Article 17(1)(d). From the perspective of its nature as a rule on interpretation, this provision is akin to Article 31(3)(c) of the VCLT, according to which 'any relevant rules

efor example, J Verhoeven, 'Article 21 of the Rome Statute and the Ambiguities of Applicable Law' (2009) 33 Netherlands YIL 3, 11).

86 'Emphasizing that the [ICC] established under this Statute shall be complementary to national criminal jurisdictions.'

87 See, for example, Valérie V Suhr, *Rainbow Jurisdiction at the International Criminal Court: Protection of Sexual and Gender Minorities Under the Rome Statute* (Springer 2022) 53–128.

88 See, for example, Verhoeven, n.85, 15; Leila Nadya Sadat and Jarrod M Jolly, 'Seven Canons of ICC Treaty Interpretation: Making Sense of Article 25's Rorschach Blot' (2014) 27 LJIL 775, 759; William A Schabas, *The International Criminal Court: A Commentary on the Rome Statute* (2nd edn, OUP 2016) 530; Nathalie Clarenc Bicudo, 'Article 21' in Julian Fernandez, Xavier Pacreau and Muriel Ubéda-Saillard (eds), *Statut de Rome de la Cour Pénale Internationale: Commentaire Article par Article* (2nd edn, Pedone 2019) 957, 973.

of international law applicable in the relations between the parties' should be considered.[89]

Likewise, Article 22 embodies a rule on interpretation when it affirms that: '[t]he definition of a crime shall be strictly construed and shall not be extended by analogy. In case of ambiguity, the definition shall be interpreted in favour of the person being investigated, prosecuted or convicted.' This rule, which was clearly inspired by the canons on interpretation of criminal statutes under domestic law, has been applied by the ICC Chambers as a rule on interpretation applicable to the RS.[90] However, Article 22 has a scope limited to the definition of crimes,[91] and thus it does not affect the interpretation of Article 17(1)(d).[92]

Other provisions also have an impact on the interpretation of the RS. For instance, another rule on treaty interpretation may be seen in Article 8(2)(b) and (e), which criminalises as war crimes certain international humanitarian law violations 'within the established framework of international law'. This expression suggests a cautious and rather conservative approach in the interpretation of these crimes,[93] but does not affect the interpretation of Article 17(1)(d).

Similarly, a rule on the interpretation of crimes is provided by Article 9(1), according to which 'Elements of Crimes shall assist the Court in the interpretation and application of articles 6, 7, 8 and 8*bis*'.[94] There is thus a duplication between this provision, which contemplates the Elements of the Crimes as a rule on interpretation, and Article 21(1)(a), which mentions the Elements of the

---

89 Gerhard Hafner and Christina Binder, 'The Interpretation of Article 21 (3) ICC Statute Opinion Reviewed' (2004) 9 ARIEL 163, 169; Lattanzi, n.36, 442–3.

90 Situation in the CAR, *Prosecutor v Bemba Gombo et al*, AC, Judgment on the appeals of Mr Jean-Pierre Bemba Gombo, Mr Aimé Kilolo Musamba, Mr Jean-Jacques Mangenda Kabongo, Mr Fidèle Babala Wandu and Mr Narcisse Arido against the decision of Trial Chamber VII entitled 'Judgment pursuant to Article 74 of the Statute', ICC-01/05-01/13, 8 Mar 2018, para.11.

91 See, generally, Leena Grover, *Interpreting Crimes in the Rome Statute of the International Criminal Court* (CUP 2014); Caroline Davidson, 'How to Read International Criminal Law: Strict Construction and the Rome Statute of the International Criminal Court' (2017) 91 *St John's Law Review* 37.

92 Hafner and Binder, n.89, 169; Ubéda-Saillard, n.33, 427; Robert Kolb, 'Is There a Subject-Matter Ontology in Interpretation of International Legal Norms?' in Mads Andenas and Eirik Bjørge (eds), *A Farewell to Fragmentation: Reassertion and Convergence in International Law* (CUP 2015), 473, 481.

93 William A Schabas, *An Introduction to the International Criminal Court* (6th edn, CUP 2020) 128–9.

94 Lattanzi, n.36, 439–40.

Crimes as part of the first layer of applicable law.[95] This provision provides a self-limitation on its scope, which, again, focuses on the definition of crimes only, and is inapplicable to Article 17(1)(d).

Finally, some authors have suggested that Article 10 should be construed as a rule on the interpretation of the RS.[96] Under this provision, '[n]othing in this Part shall be interpreted as limiting or prejudicing in any way existing or developing rules of international law for purposes other than this Statute'. This provision has been interpreted as providing a rule on interpretation that 'insulate[s] at least Part Two of the Statute from any further development of international law; hence it substantially narrows the latitude for interpretation'.[97] If this view proves correct, this would be a rule potentially applicable to the assessment of sufficient gravity since Article 17(1)(d) is located in Part Two, which covers Articles 5 to 21. However, this author does not believe that this is a rule on interpretation of the RS, rather, that it pertains to the interpretation of other legal instruments that should not be prejudiced by the RS itself.[98]

Based on the preceding paragraphs, it is possible to affirm that no special rule on treaty interpretation embodied in the RS applies to the concept of sufficient gravity under Article 17(1)(d), except for the caveat that this should be interpreted consistently with international human rights law under Article 21(3). Accordingly, the special rules on treaty interpretation embodied in the RS do not displace Articles 31–33 of the VCLT in the interpretation of sufficient gravity under Article 17(1)(d).

3.2 The Application of the Rules on Treaty Interpretation in the VCLT to Article 17(1)(d)

3.2.1 The general rule under Article 31

The RS is an international law treaty with (international) criminal law content. This platitude is the basis of an existential question: should it be interpreted as an international treaty (following its form), as a criminal law statute (following

---

95 David Donat Cattin, 'Il diritto applicabile' in Giorgio Lattanzi and Vito Monetti (eds), *La Corte Penale Internazionale: Organi – competenza – reati – processo* (Giuffrè 2006) 269, 277–8.

96 Arsanjani and Reisman, n.33, 333–4; Lattanzi, n.36, 442.

97 Arsanjani and Reisman, n.33, 334.

98 Mohamed Bennouna, 'The Statute's Rules on Crimes and Existing or Developing International Law' in Antonio Cassese, Paola Gaeta and John RWD Jones (eds), *The Rome Statute of the International Criminal Court: A Commentary* (OUP 2002) 1101, 1102; Schabas, n.88, 335.

its substance), or in a hybrid way?[99] This is just one of the main areas in which the double nature of the RS, as an international law and criminal law instrument, creates apparent clashes between different kinds of *weltanschauung*.[100]

As is every treaty between states, the RS is governed by the VCLT.[101] In the absence of a more specific rule, it follows that the RS is subject to the rules on treaty interpretation mainly[102] embodied in Articles 31 to 33 of the VCLT, which correspond to customary international law.[103] Often, the ICC Chambers[104] invoke these rules to justify their interpretation of the RS.

---

99 On this conundrum regarding the statutes of other international tribunals, see William A Schabas, 'Interpreting the Statutes of the *Ad Hoc* Tribunals', in Lal Chand Vorah et al (eds), *Man's Inhumanity to Man: Essays on International Law in Honour of Antonio Cassese* (Kluwer Law International 2003) 847; Phoebe Okowa, 'Interpreting Constitutive Instruments of International Criminal Tribunals: Reflections on the Special Court for Sierra Leone' in Malgosia Fitzmaurice, Olufemi Elias and Panos Merkouris (eds), *Treaty Interpretation and the Vienna Convention on the Law of Treaties: 30 Years on* (Brill 2010) 333.

100 Antonio Cassese, 'The Statute of the International Criminal Court: Some Preliminary Reflections' (1999) 10 EJIL 144, 145.

101 VCLT, Article 5: 'The present Convention applies to any treaty which is the constituent instrument of an international organization.'

102 On whether other rules can be invoked, see generally Joseph Klingler, Yuri Parkhomenko and Constantinos Salonidis (eds), *Between the Lines of the Vienna Conventions? Canons and Principles of Interpretation in Public International Law* (Wolters Kluwer 2019).

103 Among many other works, see the authors cited above at n.27, and Sergio Neri, *Sull'interpretazione dei trattati nel diritto internazionale* (Giuffrè 1958); VD Degan, *L'interprétation des accords en droit international* (Martinus Nijhoff 1963); Myres S McDougal, Harold D Lasswell and James C Miller, *The Interpretation of International Agreements and World Public Order* (New Haven Press 1994); Jean-Marc Sorel, 'Article 31 – Convention de Vienne de 1969' in Olivier Corten and Pierre Klein (eds), *Les Conventions de Vienne sur le droit des traités: Commentaire article par article* (Bruylant 2006) 1289; Yves Le Bouthillier, 'Article 32 – Convention de Vienne de 1969', ibid, 1339; Alain Papaux, 'Article 33 – Convention de Vienne de 1969' in Olivier Corten and Pierre Klein (eds), *Les Conventions de Vienne sur le droit des traités: Commentaire article par article* (Bruylant 2006) 1373; Mark E Villiger, *Commentary on the 1969 Vienna Convention on the Law of Treaties* (Brill 2009) 413–62; Fitzmaurice, Elias and Merkouris (eds), n.99; Eirik Bjørge, *The Evolutionary Interpretation of Treaties* (OUP 2014); Gardiner, n.4; Dörr, n.83', 559; Lo, n.27.

104 See, for example, Situation in the DRC, PTC I, Decision on the Prosecutor's Application for warrants of arrest, Article 58, ICC-01/04-520-Anx2, 10 Feb 2006, para.43; Situation in the DRC, AC, Judgment on the Prosecutor's Application for Extraordinary Review of PTC I's 31 Mar 2006 Decision Denying

The main rule on treaty interpretation is provided by Article 31 of the VCLT. According to its paragraph 1, '[a] treaty shall be interpreted in good faith in accordance with the ordinary meaning to be given to the terms of the treaty in their context and in the light of its object and purpose'. Under this provision, ordinary meaning, context, and object and purpose should be assessed simultaneously, with no predominance of any particular component, as confirmed by the fact that the provision is labelled 'general rule of interpretation' (singular).[105] Often, to understand the ordinary meaning of a treaty provision, dictionaries are employed.[106] Here, in the context of the interpretation of sufficient gravity under Article 17(1)(d), this exercise is accomplished by taking into account the official English, French, and Spanish texts of the RS, while this author cannot assess the equally official Arabic, Chinese, and Russian texts[107] due to personal linguistic limitations.

In English, 'gravity' is defined as 'extreme importance or seriousness'.[108] In French, 'grave' is defined as 'qui est d'une grande importance en soi; sérieux'.[109] In Spanish, 'gravedad' is the quality of being 'grave', that is, 'grande, de mucha entidad o importancia'.[110] In legal terminology, gravity is defined as 'seriousness of harm, an offense, etc., as judged from an objective legal standpoint',[111] 'grave' is defined as 'lourd et donc de nature à influer sur le principe ou la rigueur de la sanction',[112] while 'gravedad' is defined as 'fuerza, entidad o persuasión que un determinado antecedente fáctico produce en el raciocinio del

---

Leave to Appeal, ICC-01/04-168, 13 Jul 2006, para.33; Situation in the DRC, *Prosecutor v Katanga*, TC II, Judgment pursuant to article 74 of the Statute, ICC-01/04-01/07, 7 Mar 2014, paras 43–57; Situation in Palestine, PTC I, Decision on the 'Prosecution request pursuant to article 19(3) for a ruling on the Court's territorial jurisdiction in Palestine', ICC-01/18-143, para.91.

105 Gardiner, n.4, 38 and 161–2; Dörr, n.83, 580.

106 Dörr, n.83, 581.

107 Under RS, Article 128, the texts in Arabic, Chinese, English, French, Russian, and Spanish are equally authentic.

108 Catherine Soanes (ed.), *The Oxford Compact English Dictionary* (2nd edn, OUP 2003) 484. See also *Collins Concise Dictionary* (3rd edn, Harper Collins 1995) 559 ('seriousness or importance').

109 *Lerousse Dictionnaire Français en ligne*, https://www.larousse.fr/dictionnaires/francais/grave/38010.

110 *Diccionario de la Lengua Española* (Real Academia Española 2014), https://dle.rae.es/grave?m=form.

111 Bryan A Garner (ed.), *Black's Law Dictionary* (11th edn, Thomson Reuters 2019) 845.

112 Gérard Cornu (ed.), *Vocabulaire juridique* (10th edn, PUF 2014) 496.

juez para hacerle sostener una consecuencia procesal'.[113] 'Sufficient' is defined in English as 'enough, adequate';[114] in French, 'suffisamment' is defined as 'en quantité ou d'une manière suffisante',[115] that is, 'qui est de nature à produire un certain résultat, à entraîner une certaine conséquence';[116] in Spanish, 'suficiente' is defined as 'bastante para lo que se necesita' and 'apto o idóneo'.[117] In legal terminology, 'sufficient' is described as 'adequate; of such quality, number, force, or value as it is necessary for a given purpose'.[118]

Taken all together, it looks like the ordinary meaning of the English, French, and Spanish texts of Article 17(1)(d) identifies 'sufficient gravity' as a degree of seriousness that is adequate to allow for further action in the exercise of the jurisdiction of the ICC. 'Gravity' and 'seriousness' are used as synonyms.[119] As noted in the field of human rights violations:

> the most common qualifiers for human rights violations of a certain gravity [are] serious, massive, grave, gross, flagrant, widespread, systematic, ongoing, persistent, or continuous. ... All these qualifiers are used to underline the gravity of a human rights violation. ... '[S]erious' seems to encompass the different adjectives best. It captures all shades of gravity, ... 'serious' underlines the gravity of a particular violation, irrespective of whether it is considered serious because of the specific rights violated (gross, grave, flagrant) or because of the way the violation was committed (gross, grave, systematic, massive, widespread, or persistent).[120]

However, no dictionary would be able to provide the exact content of the correct interpretation of Article 17(1)(d) because of its nature as a combined evaluative conceptual term that also provides a standard.[121]

---

[113] *Diccionario panhispánico del español jurídico*, https://dpej.rae.es/lema/gravedad.

[114] Soanes, n.108, 1150. See also *Collins Concise Dictionary*, n.108, 1345 ('enough to meet a need or purpose; adequate').

[115] *Lerousse Dictionnaire Français en ligne*, n.109 .

[116] *Lerousse Dictionnaire Français en ligne*, n.109.

[117] *Diccionario de la Lengua Española*, n.110.

[118] Garner, n.111, 1733.

[119] See, for example Norman Farrell, 'Seriousness' in Antonio Cassese (ed.), *The Oxford Companion to International Criminal Justice* (OUP 2009) 511, 512; deGuzman, n.64, 1400, n.1; Roger-Claude Liwanga, 'The Meaning of "Gross Violation" of Human Rights: A Focus on International Tribunals' Decisions over the DRC Conflicts' (2015) 44 Denver JILP 67, 70; Ford, n.43, 214. See below, subsection 3.2.3, for support for this in the rules on treaty interpretation embodied in Article 33 of the VCLT.

[120] Ilia Siatitsa, *Serious Violations of Human Rights: On the Emergence of a New Special Regime* (OUP 2022) 20–21.

[121] See above, subsection 2.1.

With reference to the object and purpose of a treaty, the Preamble of the RS can be used as a useful reference.[122] The Preamble mentions several objects and purposes, including the end of impunity and the prevention of international crimes. Scholarship has considered that the prevention of international crimes is the main object and purpose of the RS, with the end of impunity being more of an aspiration rather than an attainable goal due to the limitations of the ICC's means of enforcement.[123] More broadly, it is possible to argue that the direct object and purpose of the RS are accountability and justice, but other purposes, like truth-telling and reconciliation, should also be considered as implied purposes.[124] This conclusion applies also to the consideration that should be given to the object and purpose of the RS in assessing sufficient gravity.[125]

Article 31(2) of the VCLT clarifies that the context comprises the entirety of the treaty, including annexes and Preamble, and any other agreement concluded by the parties in connection with the treaty. This means that Article 17(1)(d) should be interpreted in light of the entire RS rather than in isolation: the RS, this way, is in itself an interpretive tool vis-à-vis the specific provision on sufficient gravity. As noted by some ICC judges, 'unless the Statute contains an indication to the contrary … a term appearing therein may be

---

[122] Mark Klamberg, *Evidence in International Criminal Trials* (Brill 2013) 23; Eric David, 'Préambule' in Julian Fernandez, Xavier Pacreau and Muriel Ubéda-Saillard (eds), *Statut de Rome del la Cour Pénale Internationale: Commentaire Article par Article* (2nd edn, Pedone 2019) 441, 444; Otto Triffterer, Morten Bergsmo and Kai Ambos, 'Preamble' in Kai Ambos (ed.), *Rome Statute of the International Criminal Court: Article-by-Article Commentary* (4th edn, Beck-Hart-Nomos 2022) 1, 4–5. On preambles and treaty interpretation, see Dörr, n.83, 585.

[123] Otto Triffterer, 'The Preventive and the Repressive Function of the International Criminal Court' in Mauro Politi and Giuseppe Nesi (eds), *The Rome Statute of the International Criminal Court: A Challenge to Impunity* (Ashgate 2001) 137, 137–8; Sadat and Jolly, n.88, 766. See, also, Situation in Kenya, *Prosecutor v Kenyatta*, TC V(b), Decision on Defence Request for Conditional Excusal from Continuous Presence at Trial, ICC-01/09-02/11-830, 18 Oct 2013, Partially Dissenting Opinion of Judge Ozaki, para.11. For a broad debate, see Patrick J Keenan, 'The Slippery Concept of "Object and Purpose" in International Criminal Law' (2023) 37 AUILR 799.

[124] See, generally, Lovisa Bådagård and Mark Klamberg, 'The Gatekeepers of the ICC: Prosecutorial Strategies for Selecting Situations and Cases at the International Criminal Court' (2017) 48 Georgetown JIL 639, 459–659; Caleb H Wheeler, *Fairness and the Goals of International Criminal Trials: Finding a Balance* (Routledge 2023).

[125] deGuzman, n.32, 98–141.

expected to have the same meaning each time it is used, in particular if it appears in the same provision'.[126] This view is particularly relevant in relation to Article 53(1)(b) and (2)(b), which refers to Article 17 (including the provision pertaining to sufficient gravity) in relation to the powers of the OTP. As discussed in the following chapter, the RS employs the notion of gravity in relation to several issues pertaining to the criminalisation, prosecution, and punishment of international crimes,[127] which should be taken into account as part of the interpretive context even though this context does not provide any definition of what constitutes sufficient gravity.

Moreover, Article 31(3) of the VCLT explains that, along with the context, it is necessary to consider also: '(a) any subsequent agreement between the parties regarding the interpretation of the treaty or the application of its provisions; (b) any subsequent practice in the application of the treaty which establishes the agreement of the parties regarding its interpretation; (c) any relevant rules of international law applicable in the relations between the parties.' The invocation of other applicable international treaties as part of the interpretation of the RS emphasises the role that international humanitarian law instruments can play in relation to the definition of certain war crimes that include references to 'gravity' and/or 'seriousness'.[128] However, no other applicable international treaty embodies an admissibility test similar to sufficient gravity as laid out in Article 17(1)(d) of the RS, making it difficult to use external sources to interpret the former provision.

3.2.2 The role of the preparatory work

The VCLT provides for supplementary means of interpretation in Article 32. Under this provision:

[r]ecourse may be had to supplementary means of interpretation, including the preparatory work of the treaty and the circumstances of its conclusion, in order to confirm the meaning resulting from the application of article 31, or to determine the meaning when the interpretation according to article 31: (a) leaves the meaning ambiguous or obscure; or (b) leads to a result which is manifestly absurd or unreasonable.

To interpret the notion of sufficient gravity, for instance, the preparatory work of the RS should be analysed to ascertain whether it can contribute to

---

[126] Situation in the DRC, *Prosecutor v Ntaganda*, AC, Public redacted version of Judgment on the appeals of Mr Bosco Ntaganda and the Prosecutor against the decision of Trial Chamber VI of 8 Jul 2019 entitled 'Judgment', ICC-01/04-02/06-2666-Anx1, 30 Mar 2021, Separate opinion of Judge Howard Morrison and Judge Piotr Hofmański on the Prosecutor's appeal, para.8.

[127] See below, Chapter 3, section 4.

[128] See below, Chapter 3, subsection 4.1.2.

clarifying this notion. However, the preparatory work is unable to clarify the notion of sufficient gravity even though it provides some useful information on why sufficient gravity was inserted in Article 17(1)(d). An examination of the preparatory work will be particularly helpful in discerning the gravity threshold, rather than the meaning of gravity, in a subsequent chapter.[129]

The document that became the RS was the product of significant drafting efforts,[130] which did not focus on the content of sufficient gravity. As it is known, the International Law Commission (ILC), after some initial efforts in the 1950s,[131] resumed its work on the drafting of a Statute for an international criminal court throughout the 1980s and 1990s, and presented, in 1994, a Draft Statute.[132] The ILC Draft Statute was conceived as a procedural mechanism coordinating the jurisdiction of the states in international criminal law matters, both in relation to core crimes and transnational crimes.[133] In this framework, the ILC Draft Statute considered that a ground for inadmissibility should be the fact that a crime 'is not of such gravity to justify further action by

[129] See belove, Chapter 5, subsection 2.2.

[130] On this topic, see generally Roy S Lee (ed.), *The International Criminal Court: The Making of the Rome Statute* (Kluwer Law 1999); James Crawford, 'The Drafting of the Rome Statute' in Philippe Sands (ed.), *From Nuremberg to The Hague: The Future of International Criminal Justice* (CUP 2003) 109; M Cherif Bassiouni and William A Schabas (eds), *The Legislative History of the International Criminal Court* (2nd edn, Brill 2016).

[131] See, for example, *Report on the Question of International Criminal Jurisdiction* by Ricardo J Alfaro, Special Rapporteur, A/CN.4/15 and Corr.1 (3 Mar 1950); *Report on the Question of International Criminal Jurisdiction* by Emil Sandström, Special Rapporteur, A/CN.4/20 (30 Mar 1950); *Draft Code of Offences Against the Peace and Security of Mankind – Report* by J Spiropoulos, Special Rapporteur, A/CN.4/25 (26 Apr 1950); *Report of the International Law Commission on its Second Session*, 5 Jun–29 Jul 1950, GAOR, Fifth session, Supplement No. 12 (A/1316); *Second Report on a Draft Code of Offences Against the Peace and Security of Mankind* by Mr J Spiropoulos, Special Rapporteur, A/CN.4/44 (12 Apr 1951); *Third Report Relating to a Draft Code of Offences Against the Peace and Security of Mankind* by J Spiropoulos, Special Report of the International Law Commission covering the work of its third session, 16 May–27 Jul 1951, A/1858, 133–7; Rapporteur, A/CN.4/85 (30 Apr 1954); *Report of the ILC Covering the Work of its Sixth Session*, 3–28 Jul 1954, GAOR, Ninth Session, Supplement No. 9 A/2693, 149–52.

[132] ILC, *Draft Statute for an ICC, Report of the ILC on the work of its forty-sixth session*, 2 May–22 Jul 1994, GAOR, Forty-ninth Session, Supplement No. 10, A/49/10, 20.

[133] See the reflections of Crawford, n.130, 137, 142–4.

the Court'.[134] So the initiative to introduce a gravity threshold came from the ILC, rather than states.[135] Special Rapporteur James Crawford thought that the ICC should: 'have power to stay a prosecution on specified grounds, a power that existed in many national jurisdictions. The grounds might include … the fact that the acts alleged were not of sufficient gravity to warrant trial at the international level.'[136] According to Crawford, discretionary use of this power should not have been left to the OTP; it was necessary to state this ground in the Statute.[137] The final commentary to the Draft Statute concludes that '[t]he grounds for holding a case to be inadmissible are, in summary, that the crime in question has been or is being duly investigated by any appropriate national authorities or is not of sufficient gravity to justify further action by the court. In deciding whether this is the case the court is directed *to have regard to the purposes of the statute as set out in the preamble*',[138] thus linking the notion of sufficient gravity to the objects and purposes of the Statute.[139]

The provision on sufficient gravity received scant attention in the subsequent rounds of negotiations, even when states decided to shift from jurisdiction over treaty-based international crimes to a jurisdiction limited to traditional core crimes.[140] In the framework of the activity of the Ad Hoc Committee on the Establishment of an ICC, 'the question of the entitlement of the accused to invoke insufficient gravity was raised',[141] but the point did not stir further debate.[142] The Chilean view in Rome that 'there was a need to explain more clearly the vague reference in paragraph 1 (d) to sufficient gravity in regard to

---

134 ILC, Draft Statute for an ICC, Article 35(c). On the ILC and sufficient gravity, see generally Susana SáCouto and Katherine Cleary, 'The Gravity Threshold of the International Criminal Court' (2008) 23 AUILR 807, 817–20.

135 The claim that sufficient gravity was introduced upon the initiative of the UK and the US (William Bourdon and Emmanuelle Duverger, *La Cour pénale internationale: Le statut de Rome* (Editions du Seuil 2000) 96) is not supported by any evidence since members of the ILC act in their personal capacity.

136 ILC, *Summary record of the 2330th meeting*, A/CN.4/SR.2330, para.9.

137 Ibid.

138 ILC, Draft Statute for an ICC, Commentary to Article 35, para.2 (emphasis added).

139 *Report of the Ad Hoc Committee on the Establishment of an ICC*, A/50/22, (1995) para.37 (in relation to complementarity).

140 On this shift, see extensively Crawford, n.130.

141 Report of the Ad Hoc Committee on the Establishment of an ICC, A/50/22, (1995) para.162.

142 deGuzman, n.64, 1424. On this topic, see below, Chapter 6, subsection 3.3.

the justification of the Court's further action'[143] did not result in any clarification.[144] Most comments by delegations pertained to the threshold of sufficient gravity, rather than to its content, a topic discussed separately subsequently.[145]

As a result, the formulation in the final text of the RS pertaining to sufficient gravity in Article 17(1)(d) remained very similar to that proposed by the ILC, with a slight change from 'such gravity' to 'sufficient gravity'. The reference to sufficient gravity survived the elimination of jurisdiction over treaty-based transnational crimes, which itself reduced the possibility of insufficiently grave cases coming before the ICC since the core crimes punishable under Article 5 of the RS are inherently grave.[146] This survival has been criticised by some observers as unnecessary in light of prosecutorial discretion.[147] However, as sufficient gravity is a feature of the RS, it must be interpreted and applied.

Overall, the preparatory work of the RS does not provide a definition of sufficient gravity, although it discusses its function and, thus, provides some guidance to the determination of the relevant threshold.[148] Accordingly, the content of sufficient gravity cannot be discerned from the preparatory work of the RS but instead must be clarified via the practice of the ICC Chambers and OTP.[149]

3.2.3 Interpretation of treaties authenticated in two or more languages

Finally, Article 33 of the VCLT governs treaties authenticated in two or more languages. This provision includes rules that are unable to shed any light on sufficient gravity, and which are briefly mentioned here only for completeness.

As mentioned above, pursuant to Article 128 of the RS, 'the Arabic, Chinese, English, French, Russian and Spanish texts [of the Statute] are equally authentic'. Article 33(3) of the VCLT affirms that '[t]he terms of the

---

143 United Nations Diplomatic Conference of Plenipotentiaries on the Establishment of an International Criminal Court, Rome, Italy 15 Jun–17 Jul 1998, A/CONF.183/C.1/SR.11, Summary Record of the 11th meeting of the Committee of the Whole, para.29.

144 deGuzman, n.64, 1424.

145 See below, Chapter 5, subsection 2.2.

146 See below, Chapter 3, subsection 4.1.

147 Schabas, n.88, 462.

148 See below, Chapter 5.

149 This is a common notation by commentators. See, for example, Florian Razesberger, *The International Criminal Court: The Principle of Complementarity* (Peter Lang 2006) 39; Karel De Meester, *The Investigation Phase in International Criminal Procedures: In Search of Common Rules* (Intersentia 2015) 256; Popalzai and Thobani, n.32, 153 and 162; Abdoul Aziz Mbaye and Sam Sasan Shoamanesh, 'Article 17' in Julian Fernandez, Xavier Pacreau and Muriel Ubéda-Saillard (eds), *Statut de Rome de la Cour Pénale Internationale: Commentaire Article par Article* (2nd edn, Pedone 2019), 867, 871.

treaty are presumed to have the same meaning in each authentic text'. The presumption is not problematic in relation to Article 17(1)(d) and sufficient gravity: *prima facie*, as demonstrated by the analysis performed in this subsection, there is no significant conflict between the words used in relation to sufficient gravity in the English version and those employed in other equally authentic texts such as the French text ('l'affaire n'est pas suffisamment grave') and the Spanish text ('gravedad suficiente').[150] Hence, there is no room to apply the rule under Article 33(4) of the VCLT, according to which 'when a comparison of the authentic texts discloses a difference of meaning which the application of articles 31 and 32 does not remove, the meaning which best reconciles the texts, having regard to the object and purpose of the treaty, shall be adopted'.

Comparing the different authentic versions of the RS is, however, helpful to demonstrate that 'seriousness' and 'gravity' are to be considered synonyms. While there is a minor discrepancy between the English text of Article 17(1)(d), referring to 'gravity', and the Preamble and Articles 1 and 5 of the RS, referring to 'serious' crimes, this discrepancy is absent in other authentic texts: the French version employs 'graves/grave' in the Preamble, Articles 1, 5, and 17(1)(b) alike, whereas the Spanish version refers to 'graves/gravedad'. Accordingly, Article 33(3) of the VCLT is a decisive authority in confirming that seriousness and gravity are synonyms in the RS.

3.3 The Constitutive Nature of the RS and Interpretive Practice of its Organs

This subsection explores whether the fact that the RS creates a new international organisation has any effect on the rules on its interpretation. The question is whether these treaties follow different rules on treaty interpretation by their nature, or whether the rules embodied in the VCLT apply differently to them.[151] The practice of ICC organs, in this context, assumes particular relevance.

---

150 See above, subsection 3.3.1.

151 On this topic, see, generally, Denys Simon, *L'interprétation judiciaire des traités d'organisations internationales: morphologie des conventions et function jurisdictionnelle* (Pedone 1981); Tetsuo Sato, *Evolving Constitutions of International Organizations: A Critical Analysis of the Interpretative Framework of the Constituent Instruments of International Organizations* (Kluwer Law International 1996).

3.3.1 Same interpretive rules but emphasis on the practice of the ICC organs

To answer the first question, it should be noted that, sometimes, authors claim that the constitutive nature of a treaty poses some challenges akin to those presented in the interpretation of domestic constitutions, so that a teleological approach should be applied.[152] Two authors, in relation to the RS, noted that 'it is appropriate, if not mandatory, to adopt a more contextual and policy-oriented hermeneutic for the interpretation' of these treaties.[153] This approach is followed by some courts created by constitutive instruments of international organisations, but practice is not uniform.[154] Rather, it is possible to appreciate a constant oscillation between 'constitutional interpretations' and 'conventional interpretations' of constitutive instruments of international organisations.[155] This oscillation is the product of the political choice of the interpreter (often a court or monitoring body) rather than the consequence of special rules on the interpretation of these treaties under international law.[156] Under the VCLT, absent any special rules on interpretation within the specific treaty at hand, departing from the rules of interpretation embodied in Articles 31–33 is hard to justify as a matter of law on the sole basis of the character of the treaty in question.[157] Indeed, the ICJ, after having recognised that treaties establishing international organisations have a special nature that should be taken into account in their interpretation,[158] in the very same decision went on to apply the rules on treaty interpretation under the VCLT with no significant departure from their usual application.[159] It should be recalled that Article 31 of the VCLT provides for a significant role for the object and purpose of a

---

[152] See, for example, Elihu Lauterpacht, 'The Development of the Law of International Organization by the Decisions of International Tribunals' (1976) 152 RdC 377.

[153] Arsanjani and Reisman, n.33, 332.

[154] For an overview, see Kolb, n.27, 186–202; Klabbers, n.82, 84–7.

[155] Kolb, n.27, 181–5. See, also, Eirik Bjørge, 'The Convergence of the Methods of Treaty Interpretation: Different Regimes, Different Methods of Interpretation?' in Mads Andenas and Eirik Bjørge (eds), *A Farewell to Fragmentation: Reassertion and Convergence in International Law* (CUP 2015) 498, 498–535.

[156] Kolb, n.27, 185–6.

[157] Klabbers, n.82, 87. See also Winfried Lang, 'Les règles d'interprétation codifiées par la Convention de Vienne sur le Droit des Traités et les divers types de traités' (1973) 24 *Österreichische Zeitschrift für öffentliches Recht* 113, 123–4; Bjørge, n.155, 535.

[158] *Legality of the Use by a State of Nuclear Weapons in Armed Conflict* (Advisory Opinion) [1966] ICJ Reports 66, para.19.

[159] Ibid.

treaty, which are mentioned as fundamental components of the general rule of interpretation. Accordingly, the purposes of an international organisation should be preserved by applying the rules on treaty interpretation embodied in the VCLT rather than looking for distinct rules on treaty interpretation that are not provided by any legal source.[160]

However, what makes the practical interpretation of constitutive instruments of international organisations – including the RS – different from other treaties is who is tasked with the interpretation, rather than the rules that need to be applied. Whereas states are the usual interpreters of treaties, when an international organisation is established, its organs are tasked with the interpretation of the constitutive instrument along with the States Parties.[161] In relation to the interpretation of the United Nations (UN) Charter, for instance, the ICJ has taken the position that each UN organ has to determine its own competence under the Charter.[162] Especially when these organs do not comprise state delegates, their actions are often led by a sense of allegiance and faithfulness to the goals of the organisation,[163] so that their interpretation of the constitutive instruments takes into particular account the object and purpose of the treaties.[164] The interpretive practice of these organs is particularly relevant since, as affirmed by the ICJ in relation to UN organs and the UN Charter, it should be taken into account when interpreting the relevant provisions of the constitutive instrument.[165]

In the same vein, the ILC has affirmed that '[p]ractice of an international organization in the application of its constituent instrument *may contribute* to

---

160 Chittharanjan F Amerasinghe, *Principles of the Institutional Law of International Organizations* (2nd edn, CUP 2005) 59–61.

161 Eric David, *Droit des organisations internationals* (Bruylant 2016) 130; Dörr, n.83, 568–70; Gardiner, n.4, 125–6; Klabbers, n.82, 87–9.

162 *Certain Expenses of the United Nations (Article 17, paragraph 2, of the Charter)* (Advisory Opinion) [1962] ICJ Reports 151, 168 ('each organ must, in the first place at least, determine its own jurisdiction').

163 Kolb, n.92, 476–7.

164 Compare with the idea mentioned above that it is the object of the interpretation, rather than the subject, to determine a teleological turn in the interpretation.

165 *Certain Expenses of the United Nations*(Advisory Opinion), [1962] ICJ Reports 151, 157; *Legality of the Use by a State of Nuclear Weapons in Armed Conflict* (Advisory Opinion), [1996] ICJ Reports 66, para.19. For concrete applications, see, for example, *Legal Consequences for States of the Continued Presence of South Africa in Namibia (South West Africa) notwithstanding Security Council Resolution 276 (1970)* (Advisory Opinion) [1971] ICJ Reports 16, para.22; *Legal Consequences of the Construction of a Wall in the Occupied Palestinian Territory (Advisory Opinion)* [2004] ICJ Reports 136, paras 27–8.

the interpretation of that instrument when applying articles 31 and 32' of the VCLT.[166] The ILC has clarified that Articles 31 and 32 of the VCLT 'permit, in particular, taking into account practice of an organization itself, including by one or more of its organs, as being relevant for the determination of the function of the international organization concerned'.[167] Moreover, Article 5 of the VCLT 'allows for the application of the rules of interpretation in articles 31 and 32 in a way that takes account of the practice of an international organization, in the interpretation of its constituent instrument, including taking into account its institutional character'.[168] The ILC clarified that although paragraph 3 of Conclusion 12 'refers to the practice of an international organization as a whole, rather than to the practice of an organ of an international organization', nevertheless '[t]he practice of an international organization in question can arise from the conduct of an organ, but can also be generated by the conduct of two or more organs',[169] that act within the competences provided for by their constitutive instruments.[170] This means that, in the framework of the RS and of the assessment of sufficient gravity, the practice of the OTP and of Chambers is particularly relevant since it is, at the same time, an act of interpretation[171] and practice relevant to future interpretation.[172]

---

166 Draft conclusions on subsequent agreements and subsequent practice in relation to the interpretation of treaties (2018), Conclusion 12(3) (emphasis added).

167 Draft conclusions on subsequent agreements and subsequent practice in relation to the interpretation of treaties (2018), Commentary to Conclusion 12(3), para.34.

168 Ibid, para.35. On the question whether the practice of the organisation can be considered as part of the 'rules of the organization' under Article 5 of the VCLT – a complex topic that cannot be explored here in detail – see, for example, Christopher Peters, 'Subsequent Practice and Established Practice of International Organizations: Two Sides of the Same Coin?' (2011) 3 Goettingen JIL 617; Kaijun Pan, 'International Organizations' Practice in the Interpretation of Their Constituent Instruments' (2025) 16 JIDS idae021.

169 Draft conclusions on subsequent agreements and subsequent practice in relation to the interpretation of treaties (2018), Commentary to Conclusion 12(3), para.36.

170 Ibid.

171 It constitutes 'operative interpretation' according to Głogowska, n.39, 185. See, also, Niels Blokker, 'Legal Facets of the Practice of International Organizations' (2024) 435 RdC 73, 217–24.

172 See generally Dörr, n.83, 576; Gardiner, n.4, 281–5; Palchetti, n.82, 494–5; Blokker, ibid, 195–204, 232. With specific reference to the ICC, see Meagan S Wong, 'The Activation of the International Criminal Court's Jurisdiction over the Crime of Aggression: International Institutional Law and Dispute Settlement Perspectives' (2020) 22 ICmLR 197, 214 and 224.

In conclusion, the constitutive nature of the RS does not allow for a different application of rules on treaty interpretation from that provided for by the VCLT. However, the practice of the ICC organs tasked with the interpretation of sufficient gravity under Article 17(1)(d) should be given proper consideration in the interpretation of this provision. Accordingly, in interpreting the notion of sufficient gravity and the way in which it should be assessed in this study, particular weight will be given to the practice of the OTP and, specifically, the Chambers.

3.3.2 The relevant practice of the ICC organs

In analysing the interplay between the OTP and the Chambers in the interpretation of sufficient gravity, this book addresses, whenever it is viable, the position of the OTP before that of the Chambers. Indeed, the first assessment of sufficient gravity is usually performed by the OTP as it must consider whether the situation, case or potential case would be admissible both upon initiating an investigation and upon starting a prosecution under Articles 15 and 53 of the RS. Accordingly, chronologically, the OTP comes first and often assesses sufficient gravity in relation to situations that will never reach the scrutiny of ICC Chambers.

The practice of the OTP in assessing sufficient gravity dates back at least as far as 2003 and has evolved over more than two decades. As noted, sometimes, the OTP has engaged directly with sufficient gravity as an admissibility ground pursuant to Article 17(1)(d), especially in relation to specific cases, whereas, at other times, it has assessed sufficient gravity to justify the selection and prioritisation of situations and cases under Articles 15 and 53 of the RS.[173] All this practice is examined together here because it sheds light on the way in which the OTP has interpreted the notion of sufficient gravity, because there is no textual differences between sufficient gravity under Article 17 and under Article 53 of the RS.

Different sources pertaining to the OTP are considered here. First, the OTP has discussed sufficient gravity before Pre-Trial Chambers (PTCs), Trial Chambers (TCs), and the AC. In these cases, the views expressed by the OTP in the relevant documents pertaining to the proceedings are analysed. However, the OTP has also expressed its view on sufficient gravity in documents that do not pertain to specific proceedings. The 2009 Regulations of the OTP (OTP Regulations) provide factors for the assessment of sufficient gravity in Article 29(2).[174] These Regulations are internal acts adopted pursuant to

[173] See above, Chapter 1, section 1. See also below, Chapter 5, section 3.

[174] OTP, Regulations of the OTP, ICC-BD/05-01-09, 23 Apr 2009.

Article 42(2) of the RS[175] and to Rule 9 of the RPE,[176] and are subject to the 'Statute, the Rules, and the Regulations of the Court and in conjunction with the Regulations of the Registry and the Staff Rules and Regulations'.[177]

Along with the OTP Regulations, the OTP has analysed the assessment of sufficient gravity in a few strategic documents and policy papers that have been adopted under Regulation 14 of the OTP Regulations, according to which: '[t]he Office shall make public its Prosecutorial Strategy and shall contribute to the Court's Strategic Plan. As appropriate, the Office shall make public policy papers that reflect the key principles and criteria of the Prosecutorial Strategy.' The adoption of these documents is commonly seen as an attempt to enhance the transparency of actions by the OTP.[178] Although judicial practice and policy papers have different aims, with the former being case specific while the latter aspires to provide a broader framework, both of these are read in conjunction here to reconstruct the position of the OTP.[179] Since formally these documents are not sources of applicable law under Article 21 of the RS, they are generally referred to as 'the practice of the OTP' in this book.[180]

However, the practice of the Chambers should hold more weight than that of the OTP since they are the ultimate arbiters of the interpretation of the Statute or, to borrow the language of the ILC, they can be seen as the 'organ[s] [that] [are] competent authoritatively to interpret the treaty'.[181] Indeed, as affirmed by the AC, 'where questions of law arise, the only authoritative interpretation of the relevant law is that espoused by the Chambers of this Court and not the Prosecutor'.[182] Among different interpretations offered by different Chambers,

---

175 Ibid, Regulation 1(1).

176 'In discharging his or her responsibility for the management and administration of the OTP, the Prosecutor shall put in place regulations to govern the operation of the Office ....'

177 Regulations of the OTP, n.174, Regulation 1(2).

178 For example, Luc Côté, 'Independence and Impartiality' in Luc Reydams, Jan Wouters, Cedric Ryngaert (eds), *International Prosecutors* (OUP 2012) 319, 355–6; Kai Ambos, *Treatise on International Criminal Law, Vol.I: Foundations and General Part* (2nd edn, OUP 2021) 42.

179 See Bådagård and Klamberg, n.124, 654.

180 On their legal value, see ibid, 684–5; Ambos, n.178, 42.

181 See Draft conclusions on subsequent agreements and subsequent practice in relation to the interpretation of treaties (2018), Commentary to Conclusion 12(4), para.40, n.582. The view that Article 21(2) does not recognise any prominence of AC decisions over Pre-Trial and Trial Chamber decisions is untenable in light of the powers of the AC to perform judicial review (see, for example, Schabas, n.88, 527).

182 Situation on Registered Vessels, AC, Judgment on the appeal of the Prosecutor against PTC I's 'Decision on the "Application for Judicial Review by

interpretations by the AC have more prominence because of its power to overturn decisions by lower chambers, even if Article 21(2) of the RS makes it clear that previous judicial decisions are not formally binding upon ICC organs.[183] The analysis of the Chambers' case law becomes particularly relevant when the relevant chamber and the OTP disagree on sufficient gravity.[184] The most famous example of such disagreement – the incident occurring in the Israeli boarding of the *Mavi Marmara* vessel flagged Comoros in 2010 – offers illuminating insights into the ways in which the OTP and the Chambers understand the assessment of sufficient gravity.[185] This disagreement is analysed here along with other relevant situations and cases.

Although this book often analyses the practice of the OTP separately from the decisions of the Chambers because of the practical activity of the ICC organs, this distinction should not be interpreted rigidly. The current understanding of sufficient gravity is the product of the interplay between the practice of the OTP and the decisions of the Chambers: the constant dialogue, tensions, agreements, and disagreements between these organs cannot be analysed in isolation, without considering how one organ's interpretation of sufficient gravity has been influenced by another's in a constant dynamic.

Finally, this book includes references to the views on sufficient gravity of other participants to the ICC proceedings, such as states, defendants, and victims. Although their practice cannot be equated to that of the OTP and the Chambers for interpretive purposes, it is helpful to reconstruct the common understanding of the gravity factors among all the participants in the ICC proceedings.

4. CONCLUSIONS

This chapter has provided the theoretical legal framework that should be applied in the assessment of sufficient gravity under Article 17(1)(d) of the RS. Rather than solving the conundrum of providing a definition for this notion, which is not provided for by the Statute itself, the analysis has provided an overview of the main theoretical issues pertaining to how sufficient gravity should be assessed.

First, jurisprudential notions have been employed to understand the challenges posed by sufficient gravity, which is a combined evaluative conceptual

---

the Government of the Union of the Comoros'", ICC-01/13 OA 2, 2 Sep 2019, para.78.

183 Schabas, n.88,, 526–528.

184 On judicial review of the assessment of sufficient gravity, see below, Chapter 6.

185 See generally authors cited above, Chapter 1, section 2, n.40.

term that also provides for a standard. This means that without a specific conceptual framework, the term of gravity is mute, and equally impossible is the assessment of when gravity is sufficient. The fact that sufficient gravity is a standard means that the drafters of the RS have tasked the organs that must apply sufficient gravity (the Chambers and the OTP mainly) with the charge of ascertaining what is sufficiently grave in relation to specific situations, potential cases, and cases. However, these jurisprudential considerations do not mean that the assessment of sufficient gravity is not governed by legal rules because it is inherently subjective or inherently political: rather, the way in which the assessment is performed is not left to the arbitrary appreciation of the ICC organs, but is guided and constrained by the rules on interpretation that are applicable to the RS.

Accordingly, the chapter has described which rules on legal interpretation apply to the assessment of sufficient gravity. The analysis has concluded that Articles 31–33 of the VCLT apply to the interpretation of Article 17(1)(d) of the RS, and that other rules on interpretation embodied specifically in the RS do not apply to sufficient gravity or, if they do, they do not alter its interpretation under the VCLT. The rules on treaty interpretation embodied in the VCLT do not contribute to the identification of a specific meaning. However, considering the work of the ILC, it is possible to emphasise that significant attention should be given to the practice of ICC organs in the interpretation of sufficient gravity. Indeed, the fact that some specific organs are tasked with the interpretation of the RS, and of sufficient gravity under Article 17(1)(d) specifically, means that their practice should be included in the framework of relevant practice for the interpretation of the RS. Accordingly, taking into account the rules on interpretation embodied in the VCLT, the next chapters will explore which factors are relevant for the assessment of sufficient gravity through an analysis of the practice of the OTP and the Chambers, as well as the relevant threshold that is embodied in Article 17(1)(d).

3. The role of gravity in the Rome Statute: Article 17(1)(d) and beyond

'The Statute has always been threaded through it the idea of gravity.'[1]

1. INTRODUCTION

This chapter offers an overview of the roles played by gravity in international criminal law and in the Rome Statute (RS), and specifically, as per the object of this book, the role of sufficient gravity under Article 17(1)(d). This wider overview may be beneficial in understanding the meaning of sufficient gravity under Article 17(1)(d), may help to situate the discussion on sufficient gravity as an admissibility criterion against the backdrop of the RS as a whole, and may contribute to a better appreciation of why sufficient gravity has such a central role in proceedings before the International Criminal Court (ICC).

This chapter is structured as follows. After a brief overview of the role of gravity in international law in general (section 2), the chapter analyses gravity as one of the main factors driving the emergence of international criminal law (section 3) and its role in the RS (section 4). In particular, this section addresses gravity as one of the main reasons why the RS criminalises certain actions (subsection 4.1), uses sufficient gravity as an admissibility criterion (subsection 4.2), includesgravity as a component of the interests of justice (subsection 4.3), mentionsgravity in the granting of interim release by states who have arrested a suspect (subsection 4.4), refers togravity in the determination of penalties (subsection 4.5), and mentionsgravity in some other instances pertaining to the functioning of the ICC (subsection 4.6).

[1] Leila Nadya Sadat, *The International Criminal Court and the Transformation of International Law: Justice for the New Millennium* (Transnational Publishers 2002) 124.

2. PRELIMINARY REMARKS ON GRAVITY IN INTERNATIONAL LAW

The notion of gravity is not a *hapax legomenon* that is embodied by the RS, but rather, it is employed in several branches of international law. Accordingly, before exploring the notion of gravity in the RS – and prior to that, the notion of gravity in international criminal law more broadly – it is necessary briefly to touch upon the role that this notion plays in other areas of international law. Although this author does not think that an overarching notion of gravity, applicable to every area of international law, exists *de lege lata*, this overview nonetheless helps to contextualise the debate surrounding gravity under the RS.

Preliminarily, it must be admitted that, in relation to gravity, in international law in general – as well as in international criminal law – there is 'great chaos under heaven and the situation is [not] excellent'.[2] The notion of gravity surfaces in legal texts along with similar notions such as 'seriousness' in an incoherent way. Scholars and practitioners of several areas of international law have struggled to disentangle (and to identify) the normative content of adjectives such as 'important', 'grave', 'substantial', 'serious', and 'significant'.[3] Although, usually, they are presumed to be synonyms, since it is clear that they are employed to convey similar ideas,[4] it is difficult to find coherence since, in different areas of international law, different legal texts such as treaties, judgments, and documents of international organisations, all embody slightly different formulations and variations on this common theme. The scenario is further complicated by the coexistence of different official languages in international legal texts: when the European Court of Human Rights discusses the differences between torture and inhuman or degrading treatment or punishment under Article 3 of the European Convention on Human Rights, in the French texts of judgments the discussion focuses on a threshold of 'gravité', whereas, sometimes, the English texts mention 'severity'.[5] All this confusion is the unavoidable consequence of the largely decentralised law-making function at the international level. Scholars must be content to accept this as simply

[2] This is a paraphrase of a sentence famously attributed to Mao Tse-tung, see https://en.wikiquote.org/wiki/Mao_Zedong.

[3] This list comes from the law on international watercourses, as mentioned by Lucius Caflisch, 'Règles générales du droit des cours d'eau internationaux' (1989) 219 RdC 9, 130. See also Ilia Siatitsa, *Serious Violations of Human Rights: On the Emergence of a New Special Regime* (OUP 2022) 20.

[4] See the discussion above, Chapter 2, subsection 3.2.3.

[5] See, for example, the European Court of Human Rights (ECtHR) in *Soering v UK*, App. No. 14038/88, 7 Jul 1989, para.100.

a feature of international law that escapes their inner desire for an orderly, Aristotelian, classification of notions and concepts.

There are various perspectives from which it is possible to assess the emergence of the notion of gravity in international law. Arguably, the notion of gravity, structurally, accompanied the evolution of international law towards what is commonly perceived as a value-centred approach. Predominantly since World War II, states have realised that international law cannot be constructed as a set of rules applicable to legal subjects irrespective of the values that are pursued and protected. To elucidate on what this means in practice, there are two examples. It became evident that the ordinary rules on the (absence of a formal) hierarchy between international sources were untenable when sources protecting fundamental values were threatened by a conflicting treaty – and thus *jus cogens* appeared in international law.[6] Similarly, the ordinary law on state responsibility appeared to be unsuitable to govern certain violations of fundamental values – and thus the International Law Commission (ILC) envisaged a regime of aggravated responsibility of states, previously under the label of 'international crimes of states'[7] and finally, in a diluted version, free from references to criminality in 2001.[8] Whether the move towards this value-

---

6 See Article 53 of the Vienna Convention on the Law of Treaties (VCLT). See generally Robert Kolb, *Théorie du ius cogens international: Essai de relecture du concept* (PUF 2001); Alexander Orakhelashvili, *Peremptory Norms in International Law* (OUP 2006); Christian Tomuschat and Jean-Marc Thouvenin (eds), *The Fundamental Rules of the International Legal Order: Jus Cogens and Obligations Erga Omnes* (Brill 2006); Daniel Costelloe, *Legal Consequences of Peremptory Norms in International Law* (CUP 2017); Ulf Linderfalk, *Understanding Jus Cogens in International Law and International Legal Discourse* (Edward Elgar Publishing 2020); Dire Tladi (ed.), *Peremptory Norms of General International Law (Jus Cogens): Disquisitions and Disputations* (Brill 2021).

7 See Article 19 of the Draft Articles on State Responsibility, in *Report of the International Law Commission on the work of its twenty-eighth session*, 3 May–23 Jul 1976, YILC, 1976-II, Part II, 75. On this notion, see, for example, Vincenzo Starace, 'La responsabilité résultant de la violation des obligations à l'égard de la communauté internationale' (1976) 153 RdC 263; Gabriella Carella, *La responsabilità dello Stato per crimini internazionali* (Jovene 1985); Joseph HH Weiler, Antonio Cassese and Marina Spinedi (eds), International Crimes of State: A Critical Analysis of the ILC's Draft Article 19 on State Responsibility (de Gruyter 1989); André de Hoogh, *Obligations Erga Omnes and International Crimes* (Brill 1996); Nina HB Jørgensen, *The Responsibility of States for International Crimes* (OUP 2000).

8 See Articles on Responsibility of States for Internationally Wrongful Acts with Commentaries, in YILC, 2001-II, Part II, 31 (ARSIWA); James Crawford,

centred approach to international law is a real change in the behaviour of states and other international subjects and actors or whether, in light of current international affairs, it is merely a discursive turn is left to the reader to appreciate.

It is not crucial for the present work to determine whether this shift is based on a perceived humanisation of international law,[9] or on an alleged verticalisation of certain values,[10] or on an apparent turn towards communitarianism[11] – or a mix of all these possible forces that affect the evolution of international law. What is relevant for this investigation is that gravity has been mentioned in these cases in order to justify the disparate treatment of certain issues. For instance, the ILC stated that 'it is not the form of a general rule of international law but the particular nature of the subject-matter with which it deals that may, in the opinion of the Commission, give it the character of *jus cogens*',[12] and the Inter-American Court of Human Rights followed through by using the notion of gravity to affirm that the prohibition on the forced disappearance of persons and the corresponding obligation to investigate and punish the perpetrators are *jus cogens*.[13] Similarly, the existence of a separate regime of state responsibility in relation to certain violations of rules protecting fundamental values is often justified on the basis of the gravity of the relevant violations: such a regime has been explained by the ILC 'on the basis of the subject-

State Responsibility: The General Part (CUP 2013) 378–94. For a recent assessment of gravity in this field, see Maurizio Arcari, 'Alla ricerca di gravità: le conseguenze delle gravi violazioni del diritto internazionale' in Paolo Benvenuti (ed.), *L'accertamento delle gravi violazioni del diritto internazionale: Dalle proposte di Gaetano Arangio-Ruiz alla prassi contemporanea* (RomaTre Press 2025) 97.

9 See, for example Theodor Meron, 'International Law in the Age of Human Rights: General Course on Public International Law' (2004) 301 RdC 278; Ruti G Teitel, *Humanity's Law* (OUP 2011); Antônio Augusto Cançado Trindade, *International Law for Humankind: Towards a New Jus Gentium* (3rd edn, Brill 2020).

10 See, for example, Paolo Picone, *Comunità internazionale e obblighi erga omnes* (3rd edn, Jovene 2013); Erika de Wet and Jure Vidmar (eds), *Hierarchy in International Law: The Place of Human Rights* (OUP 2012); Linos-Alexandre Sicilianos, 'La dimension humaine du droit international' (2024) 440 RdC 9.

11 See, for example, Bruno Simma, 'From Bilateralism to Community Interest in International Law' (1994) 250 RdC 217; Rüdiger Wolfrum, 'Solidarity and Community Interests: Driving Forces for the Interpretation and Development of International Law – General Course on Public International Law' (2021) 416 RdC 9.

12 Draft Articles on the Law of Treaties with commentaries, YILC, 1966-II, 248.

13 Inter-American Court of Human Rights, *Goiburú et al v Paraguay*, Judgment of 22 Sep 2006, para.84.

matter of the international obligation breached and, more particularly, of the *importance* which the international community attaches to obligations relating to certain matters',[14] so that 'breaches of the obligations in question are not regarded by states as falling within the category of "international crimes" unless they exhibit a certain degree of *seriousness*'.[15] Even today, with the reference to international crimes having disappeared,[16] there is an emphasis on gravity: the text of Article 40 of the Articles on Responsibility of States for Internationally Wrongful Acts (ARSIWA) states that 'this chapter applies to the international responsibility which is entailed by a *serious* breach by a state of an obligation arising under a peremptory norm of general international law'; the commentary clarifies that 'factors which may establish the seriousness of a violation would include the intent to violate the norm; the scope and number of individual violations; and the *gravity* of their consequences for the victims'.[17]

Although different perspectives on the notion of gravity in public international law are possible, very few studies have explored the use of the notion of gravity across different areas of international law. In one of them, a short but incisive essay published in 2007, Jean Salmon maps the use of the notion of gravity in international law by categorising five functions: 1) the material fact at the basis of the application of an international law rule is characterised by a certain degree of gravity; 2) an obligation to respect international law is drafted so that only a violation that reaches a certain gravity threshold is unlawful under international law; 3) an obligation to prevent or to provide compensation exists only in relation to the gravity of certain damage suffered; 4) gravity is a threshold depending on which a certain violation turns into another kind of violation; 5) gravity is a threshold that, if crossed, allows the imposition of extraordinary consequences upon states and individuals.[18] For each function of gravity, Salmon offers several examples, many of which touch upon international criminal law issues.[19] Clearly, Salmon's exercise is largely

---

14 *Report of the International Law Commission on the work of its twenty-eighth session*, 3 May–23 Jul 1976, YILC, 1976-II, Part II, 1, 97 (emphasis added).

15 Ibid, 110 (emphasis added).

16 For criticisms, see, for example, Georges Abi-Saab, 'The Uses of Article 19' (1999) 10 EJIL 339; Alain Pellet, 'Can a State Commit a Crime? Definitely, Yes!' (1999) 10 EJIL 425; Paolo Picone, 'Obblighi *erga omnes* e codificazione della responsabilità degli stati' (2005) 88 RDI 893.

17 Articles on Responsibility of States for Internationally Wrongful Acts (ARSIWA), Commentary to Article 40, 113 (emphasis added).

18 See Jean Salmon, 'Les métamorphoses de la gravité' in Marcelo G Kohen (ed.), *Promoting Justice, Human Rights and Conflict Resolution through International Law, Liber Amicorum Lucius Caflisch* (Brill 2007) 1175.

19 See, for example, ibid, 1181, 1182, 1185–8.

descriptive and there are some instances of overlap between the five groups he identifies. Nevertheless, his analysis is interesting because it grasps the fact that gravity is used in public international law to justify the application of differentiated legal regimes when some fundamental values are at stake. At the end of his overview, Salmon concludes that gravity should be measured in light of the specific rules at stake and of the values that these rules aim to protect.[20] Accordingly, there is no gravity threshold applicable to all the areas of international law, but rather, the assessment of gravity must be conducted case-by-case.[21]

This approach contrasts with that taken by Rachel López in 2020, in a thorough study that aims at unifying the legal discourse on gravity in international law, by distilling some factors that should be employed to determine gravity across international law.[22] According to López, the practice surrounding gravity that emerged in international humanitarian law, international human rights law, and international criminal law[23] demonstrates that a grave violation exists when it is universally condemned as grave, either it acutely harms a small number of people or is so widespread and systematic that the cumulative harm is severe, and it is done deliberately.[24] This study identifies three aggravating factors that should be taken into account while assessing gravity: abuse of authority, vulnerability or special status of the victims, and the duration of the violation.[25] Apparently, López's analysis is in contrast to Salmon's exploration: while the latter takes a picture of the different uses of gravity across international law without advancing an overarching definition or method to determine a gravity threshold, the former tries to identify a coherent pattern in the assessment of gravity within different disciplines of international law. The differing approach is justified by the fact that Salmon's analysis is explicitly a mapping exercise, while López looks ahead to creating a new perception of the issue.[26]

Even this brief overview on the emergence of the notion of gravity in international law is sufficient to argue that gravity is linked to the fundamental values protected by some international law rules. Although gravity is a notion that is used, with different aims, in a number of international law rules,[27] at the moment there is no consensus on how to determine its meaning; there is,

20 Ibid, 1192.

21 Ibid, 1193, with reference to the decision of the ECtHR, in *Soering v UK*, App. No. 14038/88, 7 Jul 1989, para.100.

22 Rachel López, 'The Law of Gravity' (2020) 58 CJTL 565.

23 Ibid, 583–600.

24 Ibid, 600–609.

25 Ibid, 610–15.

26 Ibid, 570.

27 Salmon, n.18, 1178–93.

however, a need to identify some unifying factors.[28] This is the background to any discussion of gravity in international criminal law, one of the areas where this notion has been playing an increasingly decisive role.

3. GRAVITY AND THE EMERGENCE OF INTERNATIONAL CRIMINAL LAW

That international criminal law is concerned with issues of a certain gravity is a platitude that nobody would seriously deny. A very cursory look at the origins and development of this branch or body of international law suffices to demonstrate it.[29]

International criminal law, *stricto sensu*, can be defined as that body of law that 'establishes individual criminal responsibility directly under international law', that 'seeks to protect fundamental values of the international legal community as a whole[,] and articulates a [*j*]*us puniendi* of that community'.[30] In pursuance of perceived value-oriented goals,[31] international criminal law ruptures the usual structure of international relations, according to which criminal activities are ordinarily left to the *jus puniendi* of each state with jurisdiction.[32] This rupture can be seen as the outcome of a historical process that experimented with different forms of international law intervention in the realm of criminal law.

For centuries, states have been the primary actors dealing with criminal law in their respective territories, reflecting the notion of territorial sovereignty. However, since criminal offences sometimes occur within more than one territory, or there are other compelling interests at stake (for example, the nationality of the victim or alleged perpetrator differs from the state exercising

---

28 López, n.22.

29 See, generally, Morten Bergsmo, Cheah Wui Ling, Song Tianying, Yi Ping (eds), Historical Origins of International Criminal Law, Vols I–IV (TOAEP 2014–2015).

30 Claus Kreß, 'International Criminal Law' in MPEPIL (2009), para.10. For more possible definitions, see Georg Schwarzenberger, 'The Problem of an International Criminal Law' (1950) 3 CLP 263–96, and, more recently, Kreß, ibid, passim.

31 M Cherif Bassiouni, Introduction to International Criminal Law (2nd edn, Brill 2013) 1. See, generally, Kirsten J Fisher, *Moral Accountability and International Criminal Law* (Routledge 2012).

32 Frédéric Mégret, 'The Creation of the International Criminal Court and State Sovereignty: The "Problem of an International Criminal Law" Re-Examined' in John Carey, William W Dunlap and R John Pritchard (eds), *International Humanitarian Law: Prospects* (Brill 2006) 47, 101.

criminal jurisdiction), international law developed certain recognised grounds for the exercise of extraterritorial criminal jurisdiction by states.[33] This, however, does not alter the fact that criminalisation, prosecution, and punishment are undertaken by states under their domestic legislation. International law only set some rules coordinating when this is permitted.

For a long time, the only way that states could pursue the prevention and punishment of certain conduct at the international level was to include obligations of domestic criminalisation in certain multilateral treaties.[34] The necessity for this may be seen as a consequence of the perceived gravity of these specific offences, which demanded – and still demands – states to criminalise, prosecute, and punish them because of an international law obligation, rather than as a mere manifestation of domestic sovereignty alone.[35] In this way, criminalisation, prosecution, and punishment is still left to domestic legal systems, but international law pressures states to criminalise, prosecute, and punish. Today, these kinds of obligations are still very common and their number is increased by the fact that, sometimes, international courts and mechanisms read obligations of domestic criminalisation into treaties that aim to protect a certain value (for instance, human rights), even in the absence of any explicit mention of using criminal law as an instrument to protect human rights.[36] However, in all these cases, international criminal law does not perform any active role; rather, states have the responsibility of criminalising, prosecuting, and punishing criminal activities pursuant to an international law obligation.[37]

Contemporary international criminal law can be seen as emerging in response to the perceived gravity of certain atrocities which were not effectively

---

33 On state jurisdiction over criminal activities, see Tullio Treves, *La giurisdizione nel diritto penale internazionale* (CEDAM 1973) 53–64; Darryl Robinson et al, *An Introduction to International Criminal Law and Procedure* (5th edn, CUP 2024) 49–68.

34 See, for example, the Slavery Convention, 25 Sep 1926, Article 6. For more historical examples, see Neil Boister, *Introduction to Transnational Criminal Law* (2nd edn, OUP 2018) 19–23; Neil Boister, Sabine Gless and Florian Jeßberger (eds), *Histories of Transnational Criminal Law* (OUP 2021).

35 On this kind of obligations, see Schwarzenberger, n.30, 266; Marco Longobardo, 'The Italian Legislature and International and EU Obligations of Domestic Criminalisation' (2021) 21 ICLR 623.

36 On this phenomenon, see Laurens Lavrysen and Natasa Mavronicola (eds), *Coercive Human Rights: Positive Duties to Mobilise the Criminal Law under the ECHR* (Hart 2020); Steven Malby, *Criminal Theory and International Human Rights Law* (Routledge 2020); Mattia Pinto, 'Historical Trends of Human Rights Gone Criminal (2020) 42 HRQ 729; Longobardo, ibid, 628–32.

37 Boister, n.34, 23.

punished by domestic legal systems.[38] In this respect, international criminal law is a legal branch of exception, which has been dormant for a long time while states criminalised, prosecuted, and punished criminal activities falling under their domestic jurisdiction. When international criminal law is at stake, its subject matter – that is, in most cases, the criminalisation, prosecution, and punishment of genocide, crimes against humanity, war crimes, and aggression – is so important for the *entire* international community, regardless of existing differences in legal cultures, that the creation of specific repressive rules to prohibit the commission of these acts becomes necessary. As a result, international criminal law deals not only with the direct criminalisation of certain conduct at the international level – either under customary international law or by virtue of specific treaties – but also provides for certain mechanisms to prosecute those crimes at the international level should the domestic legal order be unwilling or unable to do so.

International criminal law intervenes as a remedy when something particularly disruptive for the international community occurs or is likely to occur. For decades, international criminal law has arrived late and was unable to prevent atrocities. It is not by chance that the milestones in any narrative on the emergence of international criminal law are drenched in blood: the attempt to put Kaiser Wilhelm on trial for international crimes was the result of the tragedy of World War I;[39] the International Military Tribunal in Nuremberg (IMT) and the International Military Tribunal for the Far East in Tokyo (Tokyo Tribunal) were the response to the atrocities committed during World War II, in particular by Nazi and Japanese leaders;[40] the International Criminal Tribunal for the Former Yugoslavia (ICTY) and the International Criminal Tribunal for Rwanda (ICTR) – which ended a period of glaciation of international criminal law – were established by the United Nations Security Council (UNSC) to punish those very atrocities that the UNSC had been unable (or unwilling?) to prevent in pursuance of its responsibility to maintain international peace

38 See, for example, Roberto Bellelli, 'The Establishment of the System of International Criminal Justice' in Roberto Bellelli (ed.), *International Criminal Justice: Law and Practice from the Rome Statute to Its Review* (Ashgate 2010) 5, 29; Margaret M deGuzman, *Shocking the Conscience of Humanity: Gravity and the Legitimacy of International Criminal Law* (OUP 2020) 61–97. For domestic case law on this, see Ward N Ferdinandusse, *Direct Application of International Criminal Law in National Courts* (TMC Asser 2006) 177–81.

39 See William A Schabas, *The Trial of the Kaiser* (OUP 2018).

40 See, for example, Neil Boister and Robert Cryer, *The Tokyo International Military Tribunal: A Reappraisal* (OUP 2008); Guénaël Mettraux (ed.), *Perspectives on the Nuremberg Trial* (OUP 2018).

and security.[41] It is difficult not to see international criminal law as something similar to the owl of Minerva described by Hegel as the personification of philosophy: something that arrives when the night has already fallen, something that arrives too late to shape the world.[42]

Melancholic as this consideration may be, the creation of the ICC can be seen as an attempt to rectify this narrative since it places marked emphasis on the permanent character of the Court and its potential preventive effect on the commission of international crimes.[43] The very limited deterrent effect that the ICC has exercised in relation to ongoing international crimes, such as those occurring in Ukraine and Palestine at the time this book is written, may simply reaffirm that permanent 'lateness' of international criminal law. It is even possible that a failure of the ICC to meet expectations in such contexts might trigger new developments in the field of international criminal justice to wash the conscience of the international community once again.[44]

In any case, all in all, it is possible to conclude that the perceived gravity of some human action is intrinsically connected to the emergence of international

---

[41] William A Schabas, *The UN International Criminal Tribunals* (CUP 2006) 3–4.

[42] GWF Hegel, *Philosophy of Right* (originally 1821), English trans. by SW Dyde (Bell and Sons 1896) xxx (emphasis added):

> *[P]hilosophy at least always comes too late. Philosophy, as the thought of the world, does not appear until reality has completed its formative process, and made itself ready.* History thus corroborates the teaching of the conception that only in the maturity of reality does the ideal appear as counterpart to the real, apprehends the real world in its substance, and shapes it into an intellectual kingdom. When philosophy paints its grey in grey, one form of life has become old, and by means of grey it cannot be rejuvenated, but only known. *The owl of Minerva takes its flight only when the shades of night are gathering.*

[43] On this, see, for example, Fabricio Guariglia, 'Algunas reflexiones sobre el proyecto de estatuto para un Tribunal Penal Internacional Permanente' (1996) 23 *Revista Instituto Interamericano de Derechos Humanos* 57, 67; Otto Triffterer, 'The Preventive and the Repressive Function of the International Criminal Court' in Mauro Politi and Giuseppe Nesi (eds), *The Rome Statute of the International Criminal Court* (Ashgate 2001) 55; David Bosco, 'The International Criminal Court and Crime Prevention: Byproduct or Conscious Goal?' (2011) 19 Michigan State JIL 163; Song Sang-Hyun, 'Preventive Potential of the International Criminal Court' (2013) 3 Asian JIL 203.

[44] See, for example, Agreement between the Council of Europe and Ukraine on the Establishment of the Special Tribunal for the Crime of Aggression against Ukraine, 24 Jul 2025.

criminal law as it is known today.[45] In the history of international criminal law, where there has been a need to justify the rupture of the ordinary allocation of *jus puniendi* (upon the states), the notion of gravity has been invoked. Certain offences are considered too grave to be left to states' domestic jurisdiction, so states must be forced to criminalise them (through international obligations of domestic criminalisation) and, when they fail to criminalise and/or prosecute them, the institutionalised international community intervenes through repressive measures.

Accordingly, it is not a surprise that the notion of gravity accompanies the institutionalisation of international criminal justice. A few examples from the mainstream, West/Global North-centric, and increasingly challenged, narrative on the trajectory of international criminal law suffice to illustrate this point.[46] For instance, while discussing the possibility of putting the German Kaiser on trial for war crimes and crimes against peace committed during World War I, the Commission on the Responsibility of the Authors of the War and on Enforcement of Penalties created by the Preliminary Peace Conference which met at Versailles in 1919, mentioned gravity as the reason for prosecution of the Kaiser for war crimes.[47] However, in relation to crimes against peace, the Commission noted that the notion of gravity would not have justified an international trial at that time. Nonetheless, it foreshadowed a future where the gravity of these types of crime would lead to the establishment of an international tribunal.[48] After 26 years, gravity was present in the debate

---

[45] This is alluded to in the forceful defence of the distinctions between international crimes and ordinary crimes offered by Judge Kaul in Situation in Kenya, PTC II, Decision Pursuant to Article 15 of the Rome Statute on the Authorization of an Investigation into the Situation in the Republic of Kenya, ICC-01/09-19-Corr, 31 Mar 2010, dissenting opinion of Judge Hans-Peter Kaul, paras 9–10.

[46] The view that international criminal law emerged in a continuous arc from Nuremberg to the ICC is, for instance, illustrated by Philippe Sands (ed.), *From Nuremberg to The Hague: The Future of International Criminal Justice* (CUP 2003). Opponents draw attention to the fact that this narrative obliterates certain atrocities committed against non-Western individuals, such as those of the era of colonialism, while at the same time cancelling the efforts of states from the Global South to expand the scope of international criminal law as defined at Nuremberg (see, for example, Oumar Ba, 'Constructing an International Legal Order under the Shadow of Colonial Domination' (2023) 22 *Journal of Human Rights* 4; Oumar Ba, K Jo Bluen, and Owiso Owiso, 'The Geopolitics of Race, Empire, and Expertise at the ICC' in *Oxford Research Encyclopedias of International Studies Online* (2023)).

[47] 'Commission on the Responsibility of the Authors of the War and on Enforcement of Penalties, 29 Mar 1919', reprinted in (1920) 14 AJIL 95, 117.

[48] Ibid, 120.

concerning the creation of the IMT:[49] although the Charter of the IMT does not mention gravity, to justify the exercise of jurisdiction by the IMT, Robert H Jackson, the US prosecutor, affirmed: 'It is not because they yielded to the normal frailties of human beings that we accuse them. It is their *abnormal and inhuman conduct* which brings them to this bar.'[50] The very creation of genocide as a crime in the 1948 Genocide Convention refers to gravity: the request from the Delegations for Cuba, India and Panama for the inclusion of an additional item in the United Nations General Assembly (UNGA) agenda laments the fact that, at that time, 'the punishment of the very *serious* crime of genocide when committed in time of peace lies within the exclusive territorial jurisdiction of the judiciary of every state concerned, while crimes of a *relatively lesser importance* such as piracy, trade in women, children, drugs, obscene publications are declared as international crimes and have been made matters of international concern'.[51] Some years later, the ICTY concluded that 'grave violations of international humanitarian law ... were the motivating factors for the establishment of the Tribunal'.[52]

Gravity, although never specifically defined, therefore entered the realm of international criminal law, despite disagreement over its meaning, the consistency of its use by states over the years, and its axiological value.[53] As an author noted, 'the only epistemologically compelling index of whether conduct [is] sufficiently serious to merit criminalization under or pursuant to international

---

49 deGuzman, n.38, 39–40.

50 Robert H Jackson, 'Opening Address for the United States, 21 Nov 1945', reprinted in Michael R Marrus, The Nuremberg War Crimes Trial, 1945–1946: A Brief History with Documents (2nd edn, Bedford 2018) 124, 127.

51 United Nations General Assembly (UNGA), The Crime of Genocide, Request from the Delegations for Cuba, India and Panama for the Inclusion of an Additional Item in the Agenda, A/BUR/50, 2 Nov 1946 (referring to 'gravity' in the French text) (emphasis added).

52 International Criminal Tribunal for the Former Yogoslavia (ICTY), *Prosecutor v Delalic et al*, Judgment, IT-96-21-T, 16 Nov 1998, para.170.

53 See, generally, the debate in F Lenze, 'The Linguistics of Seriousness Standards Regarding Internationally Wrongful Acts of the State and Individual Crimes in the Light of the Work of the ILC and the Statute of the International Criminal Court with Special Reference to Massive or Systematic Violations of Human Rights' in Kalliopi Koufa (ed.), *The New International Criminal Law: 2001 International Law Session* (Sakkoulas 2003) 1077; Christophe Deprez, *L'applicabilité des droits humains à l'action de la Cour pénale internationale* (Bruylant 2016) 255–75; deGuzman, n.38, 81–97. For criticism of the employment of gravity in this sense, see Nikolas M Rajkovic, 'What Is a "Grave" International Crime? The Rome Statute, Durkheim and the Sociology of Ruling Outrages' (2020) 16 Loyola University Chicago International LR 65.

law [is] whether it [is] criminalized under or pursuant to international law – that is, whether it [is] defined as a crime by international law'.[54] However, and notwithstanding the nefarious double standards that accompanied the development of international criminal law and the related gravity discourse, it is undeniable that the notion of gravity coloured international criminal law from its inception.

4. THE MANY ROLES OF GRAVITY IN THE RS

This section offers an overview of the relevance of the notion of gravity in several areas of the RS. In particular, the analysis addresses gravity and the criminalisation of certain conduct in the RS, sufficient gravity as an admissibility threshold (the focus of this book), gravity as a component of the interests of justice, gravity and interim release, gravity and the determination of penalties, and gravity and the activity of the ICC organs.

4.1 Gravity and the Criminalisation of Certain Conduct

Following the observation above that gravity is perceived as one of the main reasons to criminalise certain conduct at the international level, it is no surprise that gravity in the RS is an element of some crimes. Two levels must be distinguished: gravity is both the overall reasoning for the criminalisation and punishment of certain conduct by the RS and the specific element of certain crimes described therein.

4.1.1 The overall gravity of international crimes in the RS

First, gravity shapes the contours of the ICC jurisdiction *ratione materiae* as the selection of these crimes was gravity-driven. This is in line with the role that gravity considerations have allegedly played in the affirmation of the so-called global prescriptive authority for international crimes.

As stated in the Preamble of the RS, the ICC deals with 'unimaginable atrocities that deeply shock the conscience of humanity'.[55] Indeed, 'such *grave crimes* threaten the peace, security and well-being of the world'.[56] These are 'the *most serious crimes* of concern to the international community as a whole

---

[54] Roger O'Keefe, *International Criminal Law* (OUP 2015) 58. See also the doubts of Carsten Stahn, 'Higher Gravity Threshold? A Plea for Caution' in Richard H Steinberg (ed.), *The International Criminal Court: Legal, Policy, and Political Challenges* (Brill 2025) 258, 261–2.

[55] RS, Preamble, para.2.

[56] Ibid, para.3 (emphasis added).

[and they] must not go unpunished'.[57] Rather, the 'permanent International Criminal Court' was created exactly 'with jurisdiction over the *most serious crimes* of concern to the international community as a whole'.[58]

The emphasis of the Preamble on gravity is the product of constant state attention to gravity as a driving force for international criminalisation, and permeated all the versions of the Preamble that have existed or been discussed over the years in which the RS was being drafted.[59] The 1994 Draft Statute adopted by the UN ILC already embodied a reference to gravity, stating that the Court 'is intended to exercise jurisdiction only over the most serious crimes of concern to the international community as a whole'.[60] In 1995, many states endorsed this reference: in the Ad Hoc Committee on the Establishment of an International Criminal Court created by the UNGA, several delegations expressed the idea that gravity should be used to limit the Court's jurisdiction, for a number of reasons: 'to promote broad acceptance of the court by States and thereby enhance its effectiveness; to enhance the credibility and moral authority of the court; to avoid overloading the court with cases that could be dealt with adequately by national courts; and to limit the financial burden imposed on the international community.'[61] These practical reasons were central in shaping the current RS.

Article 5 of the RS confirms the gravity-oriented terminology embodied in the Preamble by stating that: 'the jurisdiction of the Court shall be limited to the *most serious crimes* of concern to the international community as a whole. The Court has jurisdiction in accordance with this Statute with respect to the following crimes: (a) The crime of genocide; (b) Crimes against humanity; (c) War crimes; (d) The crime of aggression.'[62] Accordingly, every offence listed as genocide, crime against humanity, war crime, or aggression has sufficient gravity to be punished at the international level.[63] As noted, 'the Preamble

---

[57] Ibid, para.4 (emphasis added).

[58] Ibid, para.9 (emphasis added).

[59] On this process, see, generally, Tuiloma Neroni Slade and Roger S Clark, 'Preamble and Final Clauses' in Roy S Lee (ed.), *The International Criminal Court: The Making of the Rome Statute – Issues, Negotiations, Results* (Kluwer Law 1999) 421, 421–429; William A Schabas, *The International Criminal Court: A Commentary on the Rome Statute* (2nd edn, OUP 2016) 33–41.

[60] ILC, Draft Statute for an ICC, Commentary to Article 1, para.2, in YILC, 1994-II, Part II, 27.

[61] *Report of the Ad Hoc Committee on the Establishment of an ICC*, GAOR, Fiftieth Session Supplement No. 22 (A/50/22), 1995, para.54.

[62] RS, Article 5 (emphasis added).

[63] Andreas Zimmermann, 'Article 5: Crimes within the Jurisdiction of the Court' in Kai Ambos (ed.), *Rome Statute of the International Criminal Court:*

suggests a qualitative criterion for inclusion of crimes within the [RS]'[64] and 'there is a presumption that all crimes within the jurisdiction of the Court are serious'.[65] Absent this gravity, arguably, a specific offence would not deserve international criminalisation and punishment. In other words, the abstract configuration of each of the crimes punishable under the RS is sufficiently grave to 'shock the conscience of humanity'.

Gravity plays the same role in relation to the war crimes punished under the RS,[66] following a well-established trend in international humanitarian law and international criminal law. This is the case with the notion of 'grave breaches' in the 1949 Geneva Conventions, which introduced some obligations of domestic criminalisation for war crimes in 1949,[67] and which is today one of the four groups of war crimes punishable by the RS.[68] Similarly, the RS embodies a list of war crimes constituting 'other *serious* violations of the laws and customs applicable in international armed conflict'.[69] In relation to non-international armed conflicts, the RS embodies two lists of war crimes, one based on '*serious* violations of article 3 common to' the 1949 Geneva Conventions,[70] the other based on 'other *serious* violations of the laws and customs applicable in

---

Article-by-Article Commentary (4th edn, Beck-Hart-Nomos 2022) 107, 113.

64 Schabas, n.59, 41.

65 Ibid.

66 See, generally, Rosmerlin Estupiñan Silva, 'La gravité dans la jurisprudence de la Cour Pénale Internationale à propos des crimes de guerre' (2011) 82 RIDP 541, 546–7.

67 1949 Convention (I) for the Amelioration of the Condition of the Wounded and Sick in Armed Forces in the Field, Articles 49–50; 1949 Convention (II) for the Amelioration of the Condition of Wounded, Sick and Shipwrecked Members of Armed Forces at Sea, Articles 50–51; 1949 Convention (III) relative to the Treatment of Prisoners of War, Articles 129–130; 1949 Convention (IV) relative to the Protection of Civilian Persons in Time of War, Articles 146–147. See also 1977 Protocol Additional to the Geneva Conventions of 12 August 1949, and relating to the Protection of Victims of International Armed Conflicts, Article 85. On this topic, see, among others, Paola Gaeta, 'Grave Breaches of the Geneva Conventions' in Andrew Clapham, Paola Gaeta and Marco Sassòli (eds), *The 1949 Geneva Conventions: A Commentary* (OUP 2015) 615.

68 RS, Article 8(2)(a). This rubric has been used by other statutes of international criminal tribunals in the past, such as the ICTY (Article 2).

69 RS, Article 8(2)(b) (emphasis added).

70 RS, Article 8(2)(c) (emphasis added). Similar provisions were embodied in the statutes of other international courts and tribunals, such as the statutes of the International Criminal Tribunal for Rwanda (ICTR) (Article 4) and the Special Court for Sierra Leone (SCSL) (Article 3).

armed conflicts not of an international character'.[71] Clearly, the language of the RS mimics the terminology employed by the 1949 Geneva Conventions to justify the criminalisation of certain violations. What is relevant here is that the ICC crimes listed under these four rubrics are presumed to be sufficiently grave to deserve international criminalisation. As noted by the ICTY in relation to the grave breach regime, in the 1949 Geneva Conventions 'there is … an enumeration of offences that are regarded so serious as to constitute "grave breaches"'.[72] The four rubrics, in the RS, follow the logic of the Preamble and of Article 5.

Although gravity can be seen as the factor that dragged certain activities into the sphere of action of the ICC, the realities of international negotiations and their impact on the final text adopted in Rome must be borne in mind. While, for instance, gravity has been considered to be the driving force behind criminalising only certain violations of human rights as crimes against humanity,[73] states have been inconsistent in arguing why, on gravity considerations, specific crimes are included in the RS or excluded by its text.[74] There is, therefore, a certain confusion as to the reason for international criminalisation in some cases, with some crimes considered to be particularly grave because they threaten peace and security, whereas others are considered particularly grave because of the consequences on victims.[75]

Considerations of gravity can also be seen in reasons why certain crimes are *not* punishable by the ICC, in what has been called 'material selectivity', that is, selectivity pertaining to the subject matter of the ICC's jurisdiction.[76] Reasonable observers could, in good faith, reach different opinions on whether states have been consistent in defining the gatekeeping role of gravity in relation to the jurisdiction *ratione materiae* of the ICC. However, one must not lose sight of the fact that the negotiations that led to the adoption of the

---

71 RS, Article 8(2)(e) (emphasis added). For a similar provision, see the statutes of the ICTR (Article 4) and the SCSL (Articles 3 and 4).

72 ICTY, *Prosecutor v Tadic*, TC, Decision of the Defence Motion on Jurisdiction, IT-94-i-T, 10 Aug 1995, para.80.

73 See Lenze, n.53, 1092–104. See, for example, the discussion in ILC, *First report on the draft code of offences against the peace and security of mankind*, by D Thiam, Special Rapporteur, A/CN.4/364, 18 Mar 1983, paras 36–41.

74 See the excellent survey by Caleb H Wheeler, 'Strange Bedfellows: The Relationship between the International Criminal Court and the United States' (2024) 14 Wake Forest JLP 35, 73–5.

75 See generally deGuzman, n.38, 34–60.

76 Asad G Kiyani, 'Re-narrating Selectivity' in Margaret M deGuzman and Valerie Oosterveld (eds), *The Elgar Companion to the International Criminal Court* (Edward Elgar Publishing 2021) 307, 317–19.

RS were the result of compromises and were coloured by the prevalent forces in a certain historical moment. This also applies in relation to which actions or omissions have been considered sufficiently grave to deserve international criminalisation: if it is true that one can consider the list of crimes embodied in the RS as evidence of those actions that are considered to be sufficiently grave by the international community *as a whole* beyond specific legal traditions,[77] it is also true that groups of states have been vocal in considering other actions deserving of criminalisation at the international level due to their perceptions of gravity.

This is the case, for instance, with the longer list of international crimes included in the so-called Malabo Protocol – the treaty sponsored by the African Union to build, in the future, an International Criminal Law Section in the future African Court of Justice and Human and Peoples' Rights – which is far broader than that included in the RS.[78] It is patent from the list that the African Union has considered that, because of their perceived gravity, actions particularly heinous in African history, such as an unconstitutional change of government, piracy, mercenarism, trafficking in persons, and illicit exploitation of natural resources, deserve international criminalisation.[79] These additional crimes

> were therefore essentially justified for inclusion in the Malabo Protocol *on the basis of their nature and gravity*. They were *possessing intrinsic seriousness to the violations*, the need to protect the peace, good order and stability of African countries, and in some cases, their *serious impact on the countries and indeed the continent as a whole*. In this regard, the African Union Commission, in preparing the draft Statute, sought to draw a *gravity* of the crime based distinction between the 'serious crimes of international concern' and those 'of *serious concern to African states*'.[80]

---

77 With reference to the RS, see Héctor Olásolo, *Corte Penal Internacional: ¿Dónde Investigar? Especial Referencia a la Fiscalía en el Proceso de Activación* (Cruz Roja Española/Tirant lo Blanch 2003) 111. See, more generally, the essays in Morten Bergsmo, Emiliano J Buis and Song Tianying (eds), *Philosophical Foundations of International Criminal Law: Legally-Protected Interests* (TOAEP 2022).

78 Protocol on Amendments to the Protocol on the Statute of the African Court of Justice and Human Rights, 15 May 2014, Annex, Article 28A (not yet in force).

79 See also Ademola Abass, 'Historical and Political Background to the Malabo Protocol' in Gerhard Werle and Moritz Vormbaum (eds), *The African Criminal Court: A Commentary on the Malabo Protocol* (Springer 2017) 11, 18–19.

80 Charles C Jalloh, 'A Classification of the Crimes in the Malabo Protocol' in Charles C Jalloh, Kamari M Clarke, and Vincent O Nmehielle (eds), *The African Court of Justice and Human and Peoples' Rights in Context: Development and*

It is equally patent that former colonial powers and states still responsible for such violations directly or through multinational corporations opposed the inclusion of these crimes in the RS.[81] Accordingly, it is important to avoid the temptation to fetishise sufficient gravity as the driving force behind international criminalisation: the RS is a compromise *de minimis* covering those actions that the international community as a whole considers to be of such gravity as to deserve international criminalisation. There were undoubtedly other actions that specific states or groups of states considered equally grave that did not end up in the RS due to oppsition by other states.

4.1.2 Gravity as a specific element of certain crimes in the RS

A second role that gravity plays in relation to the criminalisation of certain activities by the RS pertains to the fact that certain crimes have a specific gravity threshold that needs to be crossed in order to be considered criminal by the RS. In these cases, the assessment of gravity is required by the RS to verify the existence of the *actus reus* of a specific crime. For these cases, the presumption of gravity in the Preamble and Article 5 is countered by the necessity of demonstrating, on a case-by-case basis, that a specific action, which in abstract corresponds to one of the crimes under ICC jurisdiction, is characterised by sufficient gravity and deserves to be criminalised by the ICC.

For instance, one of the underlying offences that may constitute genocide is 'causing *serious* bodily or mental harm to members of the group'.[82] Among crimes against humanity, the RS lists 'any other form of sexual violence of *comparable gravity*' of 'rape, sexual slavery, enforced prostitution, forced pregnancy, enforced sterilization',[83] whereas 'other inhumane acts of a similar character' are only criminalised if they 'intentionally caus[e] great suffering, or *serious* injury to body or to mental or physical health'.[84] The list of war crimes includes references to gravity as elements of the specific crimes of 'wilfully causing great suffering, or *serious* injury to body or health'[85] and 'inten-

---

Challenges (CUP 2019) 225, 247 (emphasis added) (with reference to African Union Commission, *Report of the Study on the Implications of Expanding the Mandate of the African Court of Justice and Human Rights to Try Serious Crimes of International Concern*, Oct 2010, Legal/ACJHR-PAP/5 (II), para.53).

[81] On the proposals by some African states to include a longer list of crimes in the RS, and the pressures from Western states not to include them, see Oumar Ba, 'International Justice and the Postcolonial Condition' (2017) 63 *Africa Today* 44; Ba, n.46, 6–8.

[82] RS, Article 6(b) (emphasis added).

[83] RS, Article 7(1)(g) (emphasis added).

[84] RS, Article 7(1)(k) (emphasis added).

[85] RS, Article 8(2)(a)(iii) (emphasis added).

tionally launching an attack in the knowledge that such attack will cause … widespread, long-term and *severe* damage to the natural environment which would be clearly excessive in relation to the concrete and direct overall military advantage anticipated'.[86] Finally, the definition of the crime of aggression, introduced in 2010, refers to 'planning, preparation, initiation or execution, by a person in a position effectively to exercise control over or to direct the political or military action of a State, of an act of aggression which, by its character, *gravity* and scale, constitutes a manifest violation of the Charter of the United Nations'.[87] The same definition enumerates 'the sending by or on behalf of a State of armed bands, groups, irregulars or mercenaries, which carry out acts of armed force against another State of such *gravity* as to amount to the acts listed above, or its substantial involvement therein' as an example of aggression.[88]

The legal value of these references to gravity depends on context and this is often determined by the fact that the RS incorporates international crimes that existed prior to the Rome Conference. The reference to gravity and related concepts in the definition of certain crimes makes it part of the elements of the crimes, in particular, part of the *actus reus*, that is, the 'behavioural element of a crime' which requires an action or an omission.[89] Accordingly, to demonstrate that one of these crimes within the jurisdiction of the Court has occurred, it is necessary to prove each time that all the elements of the *actus reus* exist, including the characterisation as grave. In other words, these references to gravity do not pertain to the crime *in abstracto*, but rather, to a specific human conduct *in concreto*, which must be characterised by the specific element of gravity or seriousness to be considered criminal under the RS. Unsurprisingly, the Elements of Crimes include references to gravity for most of these offences.[90] However, the Elements of Crimes are not particularly helpful in understanding gravity and related notions since, with rare exception, they merely reproduce the text of the relevant offences.

4.2 The Focus of This Book: Article 17(1)(d)

Gravity is also mentioned in the RS as a component of Article 17 of the RS, which governs issues of admissibility and refers to 'sufficient gravity'. This subsection discusses, in general terms, what this means for the exploration of

---

86 RS, Article 8(2)(b)(iv) (emphasis added).

87 RS, Article 8*bis*(1) (emphasis added).

88 RS, Article 8*bis*(2)(g) (emphasis added).

89 Iryna Marchuk, *The Fundamental Concept of Crime in International Criminal Law: A Comparative Law Analysis* (Springer 2013) 112.

90 Elements of Crimes, Articles 6(b), 7(1)(k), 8(2)(a)(iii), (b)(iv), 8*bis*.

sufficient gravity under Article 17(1)(d), taking into account the addressees of this provision and when it is relevant in the course of ICC procedures.

4.2.1 Article 17(1)(d) and the admissibility of situations, cases, and potential cases

According to Article 17(1), '[h]aving regard to paragraph 10 of the Preamble and article 1, the Court shall determine that a case is inadmissible' in four circumstances. According to Article 17(1)(a), the Court shall consider a case inadmissible where it 'is being investigated or prosecuted by a State which has jurisdiction over it, unless the State is unwilling or unable genuinely to carry out the investigation or prosecution', whereas, under Article 17(1)(b), the Court shall consider the case to be inadmissible where it 'has been investigated by a State which has jurisdiction over it and the State has decided not to prosecute the person concerned, unless the decision resulted from the unwillingness or inability of the State genuinely to prosecute'. The Court must also determine that a case is inadmissible, pursuant to Article 17(1)(c), where '[t]he person concerned has already been tried for conduct which is the subject of the complaint, and a trial by the Court is not permitted under article 20, paragraph 3'. Finally, the Court should determine that a case is inadmissible where '[t]he case is not of sufficient gravity to justify further action by the Court'.

The first two inadmissibility grounds fall within the realm of the principle of complementarity, one of the main principles characterising the work of the ICC, which governs the division of labour between the Court and domestic courts in relation to the prosecution and punishment of international crimes, favouring, in principle, domestic prosecution over international.[91] The third

[91] Within an elephantiac body of scholarship, see, at least, Flavia Lattanzi, 'Il principio di complementarietà' in Giorgio Lattanzi and Vito Monetti (eds), *La Corte Penale Internazionale: Organi – competenza – reati – processo* (Giuffrè 2006) 179; Florian Razesberger, *The International Criminal Court: The Principle of Complementarity* (Peter Lang 2006); Mohamed El Zeidy, *The Principle of Complementarity in International Criminal Law: Origin, Development and Practice* (Brill 2008); Jann K Kleffner, *Complementarity in the Rome Statute and National Criminal Jurisdictions* (OUP 2008); Jo Stigen, *The Relationship between the International Criminal Court and National Jurisdictions: The Principle of Complementarity* (Brill 2008); Sarah MH Nouwen, *Complementarity in the Line of Fire: The Catalysing Effect of the International Criminal Court in Uganda and Sudan* (CUP 2013); Ovo Catherine Imoedemhe, *The Complementarity Regime of the International Criminal Court: National Implementation in Africa* (Springer 2016); Nidal Nabil Jurdi, *The International Criminal Court and National Courts: A Contentious Relationship* (Routledge 2016); Claudia Pividori, *Il principio di complementarità della Corte penale internazionale e il processo di adattamento degli ordinamenti interni* (Editoriale Scientifica 2016); Christian M De Vos,

ground of inadmissibility pertains to the principle of *ne bis in idem*, which is also a rule protecting the accused against so-called double jeopardy.[92] Both grounds govern conflict of jurisdiction between different courts on the same cases and are usually treated together. Although sufficient gravity is seen as a specification of complementarity by some,[93] it is a distinct ground of inadmissibility that does not pertain to the division of labour between different courts.

The fact that sufficient gravity is an issue of admissibility means that Article 17(1)(d) applies only if the Court's jurisdiction is established. The rules on ICC jurisdiction can be summarised as comprising the following four relevant aspects. The Court has jurisdiction over alleged international crimes listed under Articles 5 to 8bis of the RS, that is, genocide, crimes against humanity, war crimes, and aggression (subject-matter jurisdiction); as discussed, according to many commentators, these crimes have been selected because of their perceived gravitas.[94] Only international crimes committed after the entry into force of the RS on 1 July 2002 fall within the jurisdiction of the Court (temporal jurisdiction).[95] In addition, it is also necessary to prove that the alleged crimes occurred in the territory of a State Party to the RS (territorial jurisdiction) or were allegedly committed by a national of a State Party (personal jurisdiction),[96] provided that they are above 18 years of age.[97] For these purposes, territorial jurisdiction also covers alleged crimes committed on board a vessel or aircraft if the state of registration of that vessel or aircraft is a party to the statute, as in relation to the boarding of the *Mavi Marmara*, a boat flagged Comoros.[98] Pre-Trial Chamber (PTC) I confirmed that, in cases of transbound-

---

Complementarity, Catalysts, Compliance: The International Criminal Court in Uganda, Kenya, and the Democratic Republic of Congo (CUP 2020); Patryk I Labuda, *International Criminal Tribunals and Domestic Accountability: In the Court's Shadow* (OUP 2023).

92 See generally Diane Bernard, *Juger et juger encore les crimes internationaux* (Bruylant 2014); Gaiane Nuridzhanian, *The Principle of Ne Bis in Idem in International Criminal Law: Balancing the Interests of Individuals, States, and the International Community* (Routledge 2024).

93 Lattanzi, n.91, 186.

94 See above, section 4.

95 For those states that become parties to the RS after this day, the temporal jurisdiction of the ICC applies only after the date of entry into force of the Statute for that state.

96 RS, Article 12(2)(a)–(b).

97 RS, Article 26. The ICTY considered Article 26 of the RS to provide a rule on ICC jurisdiction rather than an exemption of international criminal responsibility for individuals under 18 years of age (see ICTY, Prosecutor v Orić, TC II, IT-03-68-T, 20 Jun 2006, para.400, n.1177).

98 RS, Article 12(2)(a).

ary crimes, it is sufficient that part of an international crime occurred in the territory of a State Party to bring it within ICC jurisdiction.[99] Notwithstanding the opposition of some states, such as the US and Israel, under the RS, territorial jurisdiction and personal jurisdiction are alternative grounds rather than cumulative ones, so it is possible for the Court to have jurisdiction over nationals of non-party states if they allegedly commit international crimes within the territory of a State Party.[100] Furthermore, a state that is not a party to the RS can issue ad hoc declarations conferring jurisdiction to the Court, bringing within ICC jurisdiction alleged international crimes committed within the territory, and by nationals of, a state that is not a party to the RS, with limited retroactive effects.[101] Moreover, these ordinary rules on ICC jurisdiction can be altered by the UNSC, extending ICC territorial and personal jurisdiction beyond the limits of the RS through a referral adopted under Chapter VII of the UN Charter.[102] Finally, different rules on jurisdiction exist for the crime of aggression, thanks to the Kampala Amendments added in 2010.[103]

Only if subject-matter jurisdiction, temporal jurisdiction, and either personal or territorial jurisdiction, or both, are fulfilled, may sufficient gravity, as a matter of inadmissibility, play a role. This means that Article 17(1)(d) applies

---

[99] Situation in Bangladesh/Myanmar, PTC I, Decision on the 'Prosecution's Request for a Ruling on Jurisdiction under Article 19(3) of the Statute', ICC-RoC46(3)-01/18-37, 6 Sep 2018, paras 50–73; Situation in Bangladesh/Myanmar, PTC III, Decision Pursuant to Article 15 of the Rome Statute on the Authorisation of an Investigation into the Situation in the People's Republic of Bangladesh/Republic of the Union of Myanmar, ICC-01/19-27, 14 Nov 2019, paras 42–62. See the criticisms of Caleb H Wheeler, 'Human Rights Enforcement at the Borders: International Criminal Court Jurisdiction over the Rohingya Situation' (2019) 17 JICJ 609.

[100] See, generally, Dapo Akande, 'The Jurisdiction of the International Criminal Court over Nationals of Non-Parties: Legal Basis and Limits' (2003) 1 JICJ 618; Monique Cormier, *The Jurisdiction of the International Criminal Court Over Nationals of Non-States Parties* (CUP 2020).

[101] RS, Articles 12(2)–(3) and 11(2).

[102] RS, Article 13(b). See generally Alessandro Bufalini, *I rapporti tra la Corte penale internazionale e il Consiglio di sicurezza* (Editoriale Scientifica 2018); Alexandre Skander Galand, *UN Security Council Referrals to the International Criminal Court* (Brill 2018); Gabriel M Lentner, *The UN Security Council and the International Criminal Court: The Referral Mechanism in Theory and Practice* (Edward Elgar Publishing 2018).

[103] RS, Articles 15*bis* and 15*ter*. In a growing literature, see, for example, Claus Kreß and Stefan Barriga (eds), *The Crime of Aggression: A Commentary*, Vols 1 and 2 (CUP 2016); Carrie McDougall, *The Crime of Aggression under the Rome Statute of the International Criminal Court* (2nd edn, CUP 2021).

to cases that are already within the jurisdiction of the Court, which covers the most serious crimes under Articles 1 and 5. Yet, these cases may not reach sufficient gravity. In other words, when admissibility is at stake, although the Court has jurisdiction, there is a compelling reason not to exercise that jurisdiction further. In the context of sufficient gravity, this means that alleged international crimes, in principle sufficiently grave to be included in the RS (Articles 1 and 5, on jurisdiction), may be at the centre of cases that are not sufficiently grave under Article 17(1)(d) and therefore are inadmissible. This conclusion is confirmed by Rule 58(4) of the Rules of Procedure and Evidence (RPE), which provides that questions and challenges on jurisdiction should be heard before those on admissibility.

As noted in a different context, 'the distinction between jurisdiction and admissibility' resonates with 'analogous concepts alluding to authority to adjudicate and power to refrain from exercising adjudicative authority'.[104] Therefore, one could consider that insufficient gravity under Article 17(1)(d) is a bar to the exercise of the Court's jurisdiction.[105] Indeed, although normally sufficient gravity under Article 17(1)(d) plays a role prior to the beginning of the trial,[106] thus before ICC jurisdiction is fully exercised, a determination of admissibility can be undertaken by the Court at later moments, as demonstrated by some judgments when admissibility was exceptionally discussed and cursorily confirmed during the confirmation of charges,[107] or even in final judgments.[108] Indeed, Rule 144(1) of the RPE explicitly contemplates the possibility that the Trial Chamber could issue decisions concerning the admissibility of a case at a stage where the jurisdiction of the ICC has already been exercised.[109] Accordingly, it is more precise to say that lack of sufficient grav-

---

[104] Yuval Shany, *Questions of Jurisdiction and Admissibility before International Courts* (CUP 2015) 130.

[105] Schabas, n.59, 451.

[106] RS, Article 19(4). On this provision, see below, Chapter 6, subsection 3.3.

[107] See, for example, Situation in Darfur, Sudan, *Prosecutor v Nourain and Jamus*, PTC I, Public Redacted Version Corrigendum of the 'Decision on the Confirmation of Charges', ICC-02/05-03/09-121-Corr-Red, 7 Mar 2011, paras 27–8.

[108] See, for example, Situation in the CAR, *Prosecutor v Bemba Gombo*, TC III, Judgment pursuant to Article 74 of the Statute, ICC-01/05-01/08, 21 Mar 2016, para.4 (recalling past admissibility challenges and noting that '[t]he Chamber finds no reason to depart from these previous findings and affirms that the Bemba case is admissible').

[109] See, generally, Daniel D Ntanda Nsereko and Manuel J Ventura, 'Article 19: Challenges to the Jurisdiction of the Court or the Admissibility of a Case' in Kai Ambos (ed.), *Rome Statute* of the International Criminal Court: Article-by-Article Commentary (4th edn, Beck-Hart-Nomos 2022) 1033, 1046–7.

ity bars the Court from undertaking *further steps* in the exercise of its jurisdiction.[110] This is clear from the text of Article 17(1)(d) that refers to a case that 'is not of sufficient gravity to *justify further action* by the Court',[111] and even more explicitly in the Spanish text that considers that a case is inadmissible if there is no 'gravedad suficiente para justificar *la adopción de otras medidas por la Corte*'.[112]

Article 17(1)(d) is directed to the 'Court', which, under Article 19(1), 'may, on its own motion, determine the admissibility of a case in accordance with article 17'. While the expression 'the Court' is occasionally employed by the RS to include the Presidency, the judiciary, the Office of the Prosecutor (OTP), and the Registry,[113] the same expression is often employed in opposition to the OTP to designate only the judiciary.[114] In the context of Article 17(1), read in conjunction with Article 19(1), 'Court' means the Chambers, rather than the ICC as a whole.[115]

Accordingly, within Article 17, sufficient gravity is an admissibility threshold for cases. The Chambers of the Court must declare a case to be inadmissible if it does not have sufficient gravity, thus barring any further action in the exercise of ICC jurisdiction. The further subsection discusses how sufficient gravity centres on the activity of the OTP as well.

4.2.2 Sufficient gravity and the activity of the OTP

One of the reasons why the assessment of sufficient gravity under Article 17(1)(d) is so complex is the fact that, as already noted, Article 17 on admissibility is not the only provision within the RS relating to sufficient gravity. Rather, Article 53(1)(b) and (2)(b) of the RS, concerning the activity of the OTP, incorporate through a *renvoi* Article 17(1)(d), thus rendering the OTP one of the main organs interested in the assessment of sufficient gravity. This

---

110 For this reason, an author considers that the notion of inadmissibility pertains to decisions taken by the ICC *in limine*, whereas Article 17 pertains to legal preconditions to the exercise or the continuation of the exercise of criminal jurisdiction. See Rosario Salvatore Aitala, *Diritto internazionale penale* (Le Monnier 2021) 273.

111 Emphasis added.

112 Emphasis added.

113 See RS, Article 34.

114 Kevin Jon Heller, 'A Dissenting Opinion on the ICC and Burundi', *Opinio Juris* (29 Oct 2017), https://opiniojuris.org/2017/10/29/does-the-icc-still-have-jurisdiction-over-crimes-in-burundi/.

115 See Situation in the Philippines, *Prosecutor v Duterte*, Defence Challenge with Respect to Jurisdiction, ICC-01/21-01/25-121, 1 May 2025, paras 58 and 60. See also William A Schabas, n.59, 489.

subsection discusses the interplay between Article 17(1)(d) and Article 53, laying the groundwork for understanding the (sometimes conflicting) dynamics in play between the OTP and the Chambers in assessing sufficient gravity in subsequent chapters.

Preliminarily, it must be recalled that ICC jurisdiction is dormant until it is 'activated' or 'triggered'. Article 13 of the RS provides three triggering mechanisms, stating that the Court's jurisdiction can be activated by a referral from a State party, a referral from the UNSC, or the activity of the OTP on its own initiative (*proprio motu*). When there is a referral from a State Party or the UNSC, the OTP can immediately start an investigation; when the OTP acts *proprio motu*, it must request authorisation from a PTC under Article 15(3). The logic behind this procedural discrepancy is patent: when the jurisdiction of the ICC is triggered by the political intervention of a State Party or the UNSC through a referral, there is no need for the preliminary filter of the PTC. As said by a key negotiator at the Rome Conference and later judge of the ICC, '[t]hose who argued against granting *proprio motu* powers to the Prosecutor *feared an overzealous or politically motivated prosecutor* targeting, unfairly or in bad faith, highly sensitive political situations'.[116]

Article 53 governs two different phases of the activity of the OTP, both characterised by the need to assess sufficient gravity. Article 53(1) pertains to the activities relating to the initiation of an investigation, describing the elements that the OTP must assess before deciding to initiate an investigation. Under this provision, the OTP, in light of available information, shall 'initiate an investigation unless he or she determines that there is no reasonable basis to proceed under this Statute'. This determination is governed by three considerations: '(a) The information available to the Prosecutor provides a reasonable basis to believe that a crime within the jurisdiction of the Court has been or is being committed; (b) The case is or would be admissible under article 17; and (c) Taking into account the gravity of the crime and the interests of victims, there are nonetheless substantial reasons to believe that an investigation would not serve the interests of justice.' The reference to the evaluation of information before the OTP in this provision, along with the duty to assess jurisdiction, admissibility (including sufficient gravity), and interests of justice, suggests that, before deciding whether to initiate an investigation, the OTP is involved in the collection and analysis of information. This phase is sometimes called the 'pre-investigation phase' or, more commonly, the 'preliminary examination

---

116 Silvia Fernández de Gurmendi, 'The Role of the Prosecutor' in Mauro Politi and Giuseppe Nesi (eds), *The Rome Statute of the International Criminal Court: A Challenge to Impunity* (Ashgate 2001) 55, 56 (emphasis added).

phase', borrowing the terminology that the RS employs in Article 15(6) for such activities in cases of *proprio motu* exercise of ICC jurisdiction.[117]

For the purposes of this book, it is important to note that Article 53(1)(b) incorporates a duty for the OTP to assess admissibility under Article 17 (including sufficient gravity under Article 17(1)(d)) at the preliminary examination stage to decide whether to open an investigation. Whether this assessment is needed for every triggering mechanism for ICC jurisdiction has been debated in detail. In relation to referrals by States Parties or the UNSC, at the beginning of the Court's activity, some authors perceived as dubious the possibility that the OTP was allowed to disagree with the referring state or the UNSC.[118] However, the OTP and PTCs agreed that, even in cases of referrals, the OTP must decide whether or not to open an investigation on the basis of all the requirements listed in Article 53(1), including sufficient gravity.[119] This is confirmed by Rule 49 of the RPE, according to which '[i]n determining whether there is a reasonable basis to proceed with an investigation under article 15, paragraph 3, the Prosecutor shall consider the factors set out in article 53, paragraph 1 (a) to (c)', and Regulation 29(1) of the OTP, which states that the Office must consider 'the factors set out in article 53, paragraph 1 (a) to (c), namely issues of jurisdiction, admissibility (including gravity), as well as the

---

[117] See, generally, OTP, *Policy Paper on Preliminary Examinations* (Nov 2013). See, also, Ignaz Stegmiller, *The Pre-Investigation Stage of the ICC: Criteria for Situation Selection* (D&H 2011); David Bosco, 'Discretion and State Influence at the International Criminal Court: The Prosecutor's Preliminary Examinations' (2017) 111 AJIL 395; Carsten Stahn, 'Damned If You Do, Damned If You Don't: Challenges and Critiques of Preliminary Examinations at the ICC' (2017) 15 JICJ 413; Morten Bergsmo and Carsten Stahn (eds), *Quality Control in Preliminary Examination*, Vols 1 and 2 (TOAEP 2018); Rosemary Grey and Sara Wharton, 'The Full Picture: Preliminary Examinations at the International Criminal Court' (2019) 56 Canadian YIL 1.

[118] See, for example, the different perplexities voiced by George P Fletcher and Jens David Ohlin, 'The ICC – Two Courts in One?' (2006) 4 JICJ 428, 431; Margaret M deGuzman, 'Gravity and the Legitimacy of the International Criminal Court' (2008-2009) 32 FILJ 1400, 1413; Phani Dascalopoulou-Livada, 'The Principle of Complementarity and Security Council Referrals' in Mauro Politi and Federica Gioia (eds), *The International Criminal Court and National Jurisdictions* (Ashgate 2008) 57, 60.

[119] See, for example, OTP, *Policy Paper on Preliminary Examinations* (Nov 2013), 35; OTP, Situation in the Philippines, Prosecution's response to the Philippine Government's Appeal Brief against 'Authorisation pursuant to article 18(2) of the Statute to resume the investigation' (ICC-01/21-65 OA), ICC-01/21-68, 4 Apr 2023, para.161.

interests of justice' every time it acts 'under article 15, paragraph 3, or article 53, paragraph 1', with no distinction as to triggering mechanism.

Whether the OTP must assess sufficient gravity when acting *proprio motu* has also been a source of debate. Under Article 15(3), '[i]f the Prosecutor concludes that there is a reasonable basis to proceed with an investigation, he or she shall submit to the PTC a request for authorization of an investigation, together with any supporting material collected …'. At the beginning of the Court's activity, there was a certain consensus that Article 53(1) applies to *proprio motu* initiatives of the OTP: not only is this the plain reading of Rule 49 of the RPE quoted above, but also, PTCs have authorised investigations under Article 15(4) by applying Article 53(1) directly.[120] However, in 2020, the Appeals Chamber (AC) affirmed that, when the OTP acts on its own initiative under Article 15(3), the need to assess sufficient gravity does not originate from Article 53(1), which is inapplicable to *proprio motu* activities,[121] but from Rule 49 of the RPE.[122] On the AC's reading, Article 53(1) applies only to referrals – even if there is no textual evidence of this – because Article 15 governs, as a sort of undeclared *lex specialis*, activities *proprio motu*.[123] However, the assessment of sufficient gravity by the OTP when acting under Article 15(3) is preserved by Rule 49 of the RPE, which renders the criteria of Article 53(1)(b) applicable to *proprio motu* requests, even if Article 53(1)(b) as such does not itself apply. As discussed below, this conclusion, far from being immune to criticism, has significant implications for judicial review of sufficient gravity.[124]

---

120 Situation in Kenya, PTC II, Decision Pursuant to Article 15 of the Rome Statute on the Authorization of an Investigation into the Situation in the Republic of Kenya, ICC-01/09-19-Corr, 31 Mar 2010, paras 21–5; Situation in Côte d'Ivoire, PTC III, Corrigendum to 'Decision Pursuant to Article 15 of the Rome Statute on the Authorisation of an Investigation into the Situation in the Republic of Côte d'Ivoire', ICC-02/11-14-Corr, 15 Nov 2011, paras 16–17; Situation in Burundi, PTC III, Public redacted version of 'Decision Pursuant to Article 15 of the Rome Statute on the Authorization of an Investigation into the Situation in the Republic of Burundi', ICC-01/17-X-9-US-Exp, 25 Oct 2017, ICC-01/17-9-Red, 9 Nov 2017, para.28; Situation in Bangladesh/Myanmar, PTC III, Decision Pursuant to Article 15 of the Rome Statute on the Authorisation of an Investigation into the Situation in Bangladesh/Myanmar, ICC-01/19-27, 14 Nov 2019, para.125.

121 Situation in Afghanistan, AC, Judgment on the appeal against the decision on the authorisation of an investigation into the situation in the Islamic Republic of Afghanistan, ICC-02/17-138, 5 Mar 2020, para.33.

122 Ibid, para.35.

123 Ibid, para.33.

124 See below, Chapter 6, subsection 2.1.

Article 53(2) governs the decision whether, upon investigation, the OTP should decide to launch the prosecution of specific individuals.[125] Under this provision, the OTP, after investigation, may conclude that there is no sufficient basis for prosecution because of one of the following three grounds:

> a) There is not a sufficient legal or factual basis to seek a warrant or summons under article 58;
> b) The case is inadmissible under article 17; or
> c) A prosecution is not in the interests of justice, taking into account all the circumstances, including the gravity of the crime, the interests of victims and the age or infirmity of the alleged perpetrator, and his or her role in the alleged crime;

In these cases, 'the Prosecutor shall inform the [PTC] and the State making a referral under article 14 or the [UNSC] in a case under article 13, paragraph (b), of his or her conclusion and the reasons for the conclusion'. Article 53(2) thus concerns the investigation phase, during which the OTP must assess jurisdiction, admissibility (including sufficient gravity), and the interests of justice before deciding to request an arrest warrant or a summons to appear under Article 58.

Article 53 should be read in parallel with Article 17(1)(d) in the sense that the OTP must assess sufficient gravity prospectively, putting itself in the Chambers' shoes, to avoid investigating or prosecuting inadmissible cases. The incorporation of Article 17 (including Article 17(1)(d)) in Article 53(1) and (2) suggests that sufficient gravity is the same whether assessed by the OTP or by the Chambers. Indeed, the inclusion of a consideration of sufficient gravity under Article 17(1)(d) within the elements that must guide the OTP under Article 53(1) and (2) is easy to understand. The drafters of the RS did not want the OTP to waste time and resources in investigating and prosecuting alleged crimes only to be subsequently blocked by a Chamber declaring that the case does not reach sufficient gravity (or it is outside the jurisdiction of the Court).

4.2.3 Sufficient gravity and the distinction between situations, cases, and potential cases

Having described the role of sufficient gravity in Articles 17 and 53, in relation to the activity of the Chambers and the OTP, it is time to clarify some terminological issues related to the distinction between situations, cases, and potential cases in relation to the assessment of sufficient gravity.[126] This clarification is

---

[125] On the investigation phase, see generally Karel De Meester, *The Investigation Phase in International Criminal Procedures: In Search of Common Rules* (Intersentia 2015).

[126] On this topic see, among others, Rod Rastan, 'What Is a "Case" for the Purposes of the Rome Statute?' (2008) 19 CLF 441; Ignaz Stegmiller, n.117, 94–121;

necessary to understand the object of the assessment of sufficient gravity under Article 17(1)(d) of the RS, which is also considered by the OTP in its decision to open an investigation or to launch a prosecution (thanks to the reference to Article 17 in Article 53).

Article 17(1)(d) refers to sufficient gravity of a 'case'. There is no definition of what a case is in the RS. According to a commentator:

> a case comprises the whole of facts and charges attributed to one or several accused jointly ... A case is formed by the following elements of fact and law: a. the facts or criminal events; b. the suspect or accused; c. the charges, that is, the legal characterization of the facts; d. the mode of responsibility; and e. the standard of evidence (depending on the phase of development of the case).[127]

In PTC I's view, a case comprises 'specific incidents during which one or more crimes within the jurisdiction of the Court seem to have been committed by one or more identified suspects',[128] and 'the parameters of a "case" are those set in the document that is statutorily envisaged as defining the allegations against the person at a given stage of proceedings'.[129] The same Chamber held that a case 'entails proceedings that take place after the issuance of a warrant of arrest or a summons to appear'.[130] Since, as noted, '[t]he aim of

---

William A Schabas, 'Selecting Situations and Cases' in Carsten Stahn (ed.), *The Law and Practice of the International Criminal Court* (OUP 2015) 365, 366–8; Lovisa Bådagård and Mark Klamberg, 'The Gatekeepers of the ICC: Prosecutorial Strategies for Selecting Situations and Cases at the International Criminal Court' (2017) 48 Georgetown JIL 639, 659–61; Mohammad Hadi Zakerhossein, *Situation Selection Regime at the International Criminal Court: Law, Policy, Practice* (Intersentia 2017) 27–35; Priya Urs, *Gravity at the International Criminal Court: Admissibility and Prosecutorial Discretion* (OUP 2024) 20–22.

127 Xabier Agirre Aranburu, 'Gravity of Crimes and Responsibility of the Suspect' in Morten Bergsmo (ed.), *Criteria for Prioritizing and Selecting Core International Crimes Cases* (3rd edn, TOAEP 2024) 417, 417–18.

128 Situation in the DRC, PTC I, Public Redacted version of the Decision on the application for participation in the proceedings of VPRS 1, VPRS 2, VPRS 3, VPRS 4, VPRS 5 and VPRS 6, ICC-01/04-101-tEN-Corr, 17 Jan 2006, para.65. See also Situation in Kenya, PTC II, Decision Pursuant to Article 15 of the Rome Statute on the Authorization of an Investigation into the Situation in the Republic of Kenya, ICC-01/09-19-Corr, 31 Mar 2010, para.44.

129 Situation in Mali, *Prosecutor v Al Hassan*, PTC I, Decision on the Admissibility Challenge raised by the Defence for Insufficient Gravity of the Case, ICC-01/12-01/18-459-tENG, 27 Sep 2019, para.45.

130 Situation in the DRC, PTC I, Public Redacted version of the Decision on the application for participation in the proceedings of VPRS 1, VPRS 2, VPRS 3, VPRS 4, VPRS 5 and VPRS 6, ICC-01/04-101-tEN-Corr, 17 Jan 2006, para.65. See also Situation in Kenya, PTC II, Decision Pursuant to Article 15 of the Rome

an investigation is to identify cases',[131] cases start materialising during the investigation, and they are fully formed with the issuance of a request for an arrest warrant or summons to appear.[132] If this is correct, how is it possible that Article 53(1)(b) requires the OTP to assess the admissibility of a *case* (including regarding sufficient gravity) in order to decide whether to open an investigation if there is no case until the investigation is opened?[133]

This question cannot be answered on the basis of a literal interpretation of the RS. Likely, the incorporation of the terminology referring to a case in Article 53(1)(b) is a mistake that was overlooked in the drafting of the Statute,[134] probably for reasons of time during the negotiations at the Rome Conference.[135] To solve this issue, judicial practice makes a distinction between situations, cases and potential cases. It is important to clarify these notions to understand how sufficient gravity has been applied to them by the OTP and Chambers.

The term 'situation' appears, without definition, in the RS with reference to referrals by the UNSC and by States Parties in Articles 13 and 14 of the RS.[136] Although the RS mentions situations only in relation to state referrals and UNSC referrals, the activity of collection of information by the OTP prior to requesting authorisation to open an investigation *proprio motu* pertains to a situation as well.[137] This conclusion is confirmed by the text of Rule 49(2) of the RPE.

A situation can be defined as 'the parameters within which the Office [of the Prosecutor] conducts its investigative activities'.[138] Situations 'are generally defined in terms of temporal, territorial and in some cases personal

---

Statute on the Authorization of an Investigation into the Situation in the Republic of Kenya, ICC-01/09-19-Corr, 31 Mar 2010, para.44.

131 Bådagård and Klamberg, n.126, 675.

132 See, for example, Schabas, n.126, 367; Agirre Aranburu, n.127, 417.

133 See Carsten Stahn, 'Judicial Review of Prosecutorial Discretion: Five Years On' in Carsten Stahn and Göran Sluiter (eds), *The Emerging Practice of the International Criminal Court* (Brill 2009) 247, 268 (mentioning 'an internal contradiction in the Statute').

134 See the cautious position of Situation in Kenya, PTC II, Decision Pursuant to Article 15 of the Rome Statute on the Authorization of an Investigation into the Situation in the Republic of Kenya, ICC-01/09-19-Corr, 31 Mar 2010, paras 47–8.

135 See, for example, Stegmiller, n.117, 95.

136 Specifically, see RS, Articles 13(a), (b), and 14(1).

137 See, for example, Situation in Kenya, PTC II, Decision Pursuant to Article 15 of the Rome Statute on the Authorization of an Investigation into the Situation in the Republic of Kenya, ICC-01/09-19-Corr, 31 Mar 2010, paras 40–48. See Schabas, n.126, 367.

138 OTP, *Policy Paper on Preliminary Examinations* (Nov 2013), para.41.

parameters'.[139] On the contrary, as mentioned above, cases exist when one or more suspects have been identified for the purposes of prosecution,[140] after investigation. Accordingly, PTC I noted that there are: 'different stages of the proceedings up until trial. These stages begin with a "situation" and end with a concrete "case", where one or more suspects have been identified for the purpose of prosecution.'[141]

In practice, the OTP performs a preliminary examination of a situation to evaluate whether potential cases can be identified. This means that the OTP assesses whether, in light of the elements available, a future investigation could lead to cases that are within the jurisdiction of the Court, are admissible, and do not conflict with the interests of justice as per Article 53(1) of the RS in cases of referrals, and Rule 49 of the RPE in cases of *proprio motu* activities. If the answer is affirmative, the OTP can seek the authorisation of a PTC to start an investigation – if it is acting *proprio motu*[142] – or must proceed to the investigation if it is acting upon referral.[143] Once an investigation into a situation has been opened, the OTP must either identify potential cases for prosecution or close the investigation into the situation. Only once the prosecution starts, usually with a request for an arrest warrant or a summons to appear,[144] does a *case* finally materialise, as mentioned earlier.

PTCs have endorsed the idea that the analysis of admissibility under Article 53(1)(b), including sufficient gravity, can only focus on a situation because there is no case before an investigation, clarifying, however, that the attention should be focused on *potential cases* within a situation.[145] Accordingly, 'since it is not possible to have a concrete case involving an identified suspect for the purpose of prosecution, prior to the commencement of an investigation, *the*

---

139 Situation in the DRC, PTC I, Public Redacted version of the Decision on the application for participation in the proceedings of VPRS 1, VPRS 2, VPRS 3, VPRS 4, VPRS 5 and VPRS 6, ICC-01/04-101-tEN-Corr, 17 Jan 2006, para.65. See also OTP, *Policy Paper on Case Selection and Prioritisation* (15 Sep 2016), para.4.

140 Schabas, n.126, 367.

141 Situation in Kenya, PTC II, Decision Pursuant to Article 15 of the Rome Statute on the Authorization of an Investigation into the Situation in the Republic of Kenya, ICC-01/09-19-Corr, 31 Mar 2010, para.41.

142 See RS, Article 15(3).

143 Situation on Registered Vessels, PTC I, Decision on the request of the Union of the Comoros to review the Prosecutor's decision not to initiate an investigation, ICC-01/13-34, 16 Jul 2015, para.13.

144 RS, Article 58.

145 Situation in Kenya, PTC II, Decision Pursuant to Article 15 of the Rome Statute on the Authorization of an Investigation into the Situation in the Republic of Kenya, ICC-01/09-19-Corr, 31 Mar 2010, para.45.

admissibility assessment at this stage actually refers to the admissibility of one or more potential cases within the context of a situation'.[146] In line with this thinking, the OTP has maintained that the assessment of sufficient gravity under Article 53(1)(b) should be 'conducted bearing in mind the potential cases that would be likely to arise from an investigation of the situation'.[147] According to one author, this assessment is twofold: the assessment of sufficient gravity of the entire situation and the assessment of sufficient gravity of specific potential cases within that situation, both to be performed under Article 53(1)(b).[148] Other authors, perhaps more accurately, on the basis of some specific references in PTC decisions,[149] consider that the OTP must only perform an assessment of sufficient gravity of specific potential cases within a situation, rather than of a situation in its entirety.[150] In practice, the OTP often considers the gravity of the situation as the result of the sum of the gravity of specific potential cases.[151]

---

146 Ibid, para.48 (emphasis added). See also Situation in Georgia, PTC I, Decision on the Prosecutor's request for authorization of an investigation, ICC-01/15-12, 27 Jan 2016, para.51; Situation in Côte d'Ivoire, PTC III, Corrigendum to 'Decision Pursuant to Article 15 of the Rome Statute on the Authorisation of an Investigation into the Situation in the Republic of Côte d'Ivoire', ICC-02/11-14-Corr, 15 Nov 2011, para.202; Situation in Burundi, PTC III, Public redacted version of 'Decision Pursuant to Article 15 of the RS on the Authorization of an Investigation into the Situation in the Republic of Burundi', ICC-01/17-X-9-US-Exp, 25 Oct 2017, ICC-01/17-9-Red, 9 Nov 2017, para.184.

147 Situation on Registered Vessels, OTP, Article 53(1) Report, 6 Nov 2014, para.22.

148 Zakerhossein, n.126, 218.

149 See, for example, Situation in Georgia, PTC I, Decision on the Prosecutor's request for authorization of an investigation, ICC-01/15-12, 27 Jan 2016, para.57; Situation in Afghanistan, PTC II, Decision Pursuant to Article 15 of the Rome Statute on the Authorisation of an Investigation into the Situation in the Islamic Republic of Afghanistan, ICC-02/17-33, 12 Apr 2019, para.86; Situation on Registered Vessels, PTC I, Decision on the 'Application for Judicial Review by the Government of the Comoros', ICC-01/13-111, 16 Sep 2020, para.97.

150 See, for example, Triestino Mariniello, 'Judicial Control over Prosecutorial Discretion at the International Criminal Court' (2019) 19 ICLR 979, 986; Juan-Pablo Pérez-León-Acevedo, 'Application for Judicial Review of OTP Decision not to Open an Investigation and Authorisation of Investigation at the ICC' in André Klip and Steven Freeland (eds), *Annotated Leading Cases of International Criminal Tribunals*, Vol.LXXVI (Intersentia 2025) 339, 346.

151 See, for example, the articulation in Situation in Mali, OTP, Article 53(1) Report, 16 Jan 2013, paras 142–70.

Accordingly, this book analyses sufficient gravity under Article 17(1)(d) both in relation to cases – as per Articles 17(1)(d) and 53(2)(b) – and potential cases arising within a situation – as per Article 53(1)(b), incorporating Article 17(1)(d), interpreted as referring to potential cases because no case exists prior to investigation. The relevant benchmark is always Article 17(1)(d), as confirmed by Regulation 29(5) of the OTP Regulations, according to which: '[i]n acting under [A]rticle 53, paragraph 2, the Office shall apply *mutatis mutandis* sub-regulations 1 to 4', including sub-regulation 2 on sufficient gravity.[152]

4.2.4 A succinct overview of Chambers' judicial interventions on sufficient gravity in the RS

This subsection briefly describes when the Chambers can assess sufficient gravity during the ICC proceedings. The examination here is cursory and it is provided only to guide the reader through the relevant case law cited in the following chapters. A detailed analysis on the interplay between the assessment of the OTP and judicial review before the Chambers in matters of sufficient gravity is provided subsequently in Chapter 6.

Preliminarily, it must be noted that sufficient gravity is a more static concept than complementarity. Whether a domestic court exercises criminal jurisdiction over the same persons for the same facts can change during lengthy ICC proceedings. On the other hand, the gravity of a case is almost fixed in time since it pertains to events that have already occurred in the past. The AC elaborated on this difference between sufficient gravity and complementarity, noting that 'a Chamber determines the gravity of a case only once in the course of the proceedings because the facts underlying the assessment of gravity are unlikely to change and a party may therefore be unable to raise the same issue again in future admissibility challenges'.[153]

First, in relation to potential cases within situations, for a decade, PTCs have assessed sufficient gravity in authorising investigations under Article 15(4) of the RS upon request for an authorisation by the OTP under Article

152 OTP, Regulations of the OTP, ICC-BD/05-01-09, 23 Apr 2009, Regulation 29(5). See also Stegmiller, n.117, 340. Other authors analyse separately the practice of the Chambers and the OTP depending on whether the assessment pertains to a situation or a case: see, for example, Megumi Ochi, 'Gravity Threshold before the International Criminal Court: An Overview of the Court's Practice' (2016) 19 *International Criminal Database Brief* 1; deGuzman, n.38, 101–12.

153 Situation in Uganda, *Prosecutor v Kony et al*, AC, Judgment on the Ad Hoc Defence's Appeal on the Admissibility of the Case, ICC-02/04-01/05-408 OA3, 16 Sep 2009, para.85.

15(3).[154] Controversially, in 2020, the AC held that the RS does not allow such an assessment because, under its interpretation of Article 15(4), the PTCs can only scrutinise whether 'there is a reasonable factual basis to proceed with an investigation, in the sense of whether crimes have been committed, and whether potential case(s) arising from such investigation appear to fall within the Court's jurisdiction'.[155]

Also, in relation to potential cases within situations, Article 18 allows states to challenge the admissibility of investigations into situations. While Article 18 refers to 'admissibility' in general, its content pertains mainly to complementarity, as discussed below.[156] The only time a state has challenged sufficient gravity of a situation under Article 18(2), PTC I affirmed that sufficient gravity can be assessed under Article 18(2);[157] however, the PTC considered that the challenge at hand was about gravity as a component of ICC jurisdiction rather than admissibility, thus refusing to examine the merits of the claim.[158] This conclusion was supported by the AC.[159]

Furthermore, when the OTP acts upon a referral, the sufficient gravity of potential cases can be assessed by PTCs under Article 53(3)(a) of the RS, according to which: '[a]t the request of the State making a referral under article 14 or the Security Council under article 13, paragraph (b), the [PTC] may

[154] Situation in Kenya, PTC II, Decision Pursuant to Article 15 of the Rome Statute on the Authorization of an Investigation into the Situation in the Republic of Kenya, ICC-01/09-19-Corr, 31 Mar 2010, para.21; Situation in Côte d'Ivoire, PTC III, Corrigendum to 'Decision Pursuant to Article 15 of the Rome Statute on the Authorisation of an Investigation into the Situation in the Republic of Côte d'Ivoire', ICC-02/11-14-Corr, 15 Nov 2011, paras 16–17; Situation in Burundi, PTC III, Public redacted version of 'Decision Pursuant to Article 15 of the Rome Statute on the Authorization of an Investigation into the Situation in the Republic of Burundi', ICC-01/17-X-9-US-Exp, 25 Oct 2017, ICC-01/17-9-Red, 9 Nov 2017, para.28; Situation in Bangladesh/Myanmar, PTC III, Decision Pursuant to Article 15 of the Rome Statute on the Authorisation of an Investigation into the Situation in Bangladesh/Myanmar, ICC-01/19-27, 14 Nov 2019, para.125.

[155] Situation in Afghanistan, AC, Judgment on the appeal against the decision on the authorisation of an investigation into the situation in the Islamic Republic of Afghanistan, ICC-02/17-138, 5 Mar 2020, para.34.

[156] See below, Chapter 6, subsection 2.2.

[157] Situation in the Philippines, PTC I, Public Redacted Version of 'Authorisation pursuant to article 18(2) of the Statute to resume the investigation', ICC-01/21-56-Red, 26 Jan 2023, para.10.

[158] Ibid, para.25.

[159] Situation in the Philippines, AC, Judgment on the appeal of the Republic of the Philippines against PTC I's 'Authorisation pursuant to article 18(2) of the Statute to resume the investigation', ICC-01/21-77, 18 Jul 2023, paras 229–30.

review a decision of the Prosecutor under paragraph 1 or 2 not to proceed and may request the Prosecutor to reconsider that decision.' This provision limits the intervention of the PTCs to decisions not to open an investigation or not to launch a prosecution, as long as there is a request by the referring state or the UNSC. This provision was invoked by Comoros in relation to the *Mavi Marmara* affair when the OTP decided not to open an investigation allegedly for lack of sufficient gravity. The ensuing interventions of the PTC and AC provided the occasion for clarifying the extent of judicial review in relation to the assessment of sufficient gravity performed by the OTP.[160]

In relation to cases, in 2006, the AC, overturning a previous decision of a PTC,[161] affirmed that a decision on an application for an arrest warrant under Article 58 of the RS does not include an assessment of sufficient gravity.[162] The AC went on to analyse Article 19(1), according to which '[t]he Court may, on its own motion, determine the admissibility of a case in accordance with article 17', including sufficient gravity. According to the AC, in deciding on an application for an arrest warrant, the PTCs 'should exercise [their] discretion only when it is appropriate in the circumstances of the case, bearing in mind the interests of the suspect' and 'the rights of other participants'.[163]

As noted above, Article 19(1) confers upon the Chambers the power to determine sufficient gravity *proprio motu*. The relevant case law can be found particularly in decisions on applications for arrest warrants, as seen before, or in subsequent decisions such as on confirmation of charges or final judgments. Under Article 19(2), the accused or a person for whom a warrant of arrest or a summons to appear has been issued can bring challenges for alleged lack of sufficient gravity, too. These challenges have generated significant case law centring on incidental proceedings that all culminated in decisions rejecting the challenges brought by the accused.[164] Finally, under Article 19(3), the OTP

---

[160] See below, Chapter 6, subsection 2.3.

[161] Situation in the DRC, PTC I, Decision on the Prosecutor's Application for Warrants of Arrest, Article 58, ICC-01/04-520-Anx2, 10 Feb 2006, para.29.

[162] Situation in the DRC, AC, Judgment on the Prosecutor's appeal against the decision of PTC I entitled 'Decision on the Prosecutor's Application for Warrants of Arrest, Article 58', ICC-01/04-169, 13 Jul 2006, paras 42–5.

[163] Ibid, para.52.

[164] For example, Situation in Kenya, *Prosecutor v Muthaura et al*, PTC II, Public Redacted Version Decision on the Confirmation of Charges Pursuant to Article 61(7)(a) and (b) of the Rome Statute, ICC-01/09-02/11-382-Red, 23 Jan 2012; Situation in Côte d'Ivoire, *Prosecutor v Charles Blé Goudé*, PTC I, Decision on the Defence Challenge to the Admissibility of the Case against Charles Blé Goudé for Insufficient Gravity, ICC-02/11-02/11-185, 12 Nov 2014; Situation in Mali, *Prosecutor v Al Hassan*, PTC I, Decision on the Admissibility Challenge

may request a PTC to render a preliminary determination on admissibility. As discussed below, the Chambers have considered this provision to be applicable to both situations and cases.[165]

4.3 Gravity of the Crime as a Consideration in Assessing the Interests of Justice

Besides admissibility, gravity is mentioned again in the assessment of the interests of justice as one of the factors that should be balanced by the OTP. The notion of interests of justice is provided by Article 53 of the RS ('Initiation of an investigation') in two different formulations. Under Article 53(1)(c),

> in deciding whether to initiate an investigation, the Prosecutor shall consider whether: … [t]aking into account the *gravity* of the crime and the interests of victims, there are nonetheless substantial reasons to believe that an investigation would not serve the interests of justice.[166]

Article 53(2)(c) addresses the interests of justice at a later stage by affirming that

> If, upon investigation, the Prosecutor concludes that there is not a sufficient basis for a prosecution because: … [a] prosecution is not in the interests of justice, taking into account all the circumstances, including the *gravity* of the crime, the interests of victims and the age or infirmity of the alleged perpetrator, and his or her role in the alleged crime[,] the Prosecutor shall inform the [PTC] ... of his or her conclusion and the reasons for the conclusion.[167]

In both provisions, the concept of interests of justice constitutes a reason that the OTP may advance to justify a decision not to initiate an investigation or not to prosecute a specific person even though there are sufficient elements suggesting that a crime within ICC jurisdiction occurred and that the potential case(s) would be admissible. Accordingly, the term interests of justice refers to 'exceptional circumstances'[168] which should be assessed, taking into account 'the objects and purposes of the Statute – namely the prevention of serious crimes of concern to the international community through ending

---

raised by the Defence for Insufficient Gravity of the Case, ICC-01/12-01/18-459-tENG, 27 Sep 2019; Situation in Mali, *Prosecutor v Al Hassan*, AC, Judgment on the appeal of Mr Al Hassan against the decision of PTC I entitled 'Décision relative à l'exception d'irrecevabilité pour insuffisance de gravité de l'affaire soulevée par la défense', ICC-01/12-01/18 OA, 19 Feb 2020.

165 See below, Chapter 6, subsection 4.1.

166 Emphasis added.

167 Emphasis added.

168 OTP, *Policy Paper on the Interests of Justice* (Sep 2007), 1.

impunity'.[169] As noted by the OTP, the 'interests of justice test is a potential countervailing consideration that might produce a reason not to proceed'.[170] However, the OTP 'is not required to establish that an investigation or prosecution is in the interests of justice', because this should be presumed.[171]

From the text of Article 53, it is clear that the assessment of the interests of justice takes into account slightly different considerations depending on whether it occurs before opening an investigation or before starting a prosecution, as reflected by the different texts of Article 53(1)(c) and (2)(c).[172] For the purposes of this book, it is important to note that both provisions refer to the 'gravity of the crime' as a decisive factor – a conclusion that is shared by the AC.[173] The formulation is then different from that pertaining to gravity as an admissibility criterion, which does not refer to specific crimes, but rather, to situations, potential cases and cases.[174]

The notion of interests of justice has sparked significant academic debate, especially as an explicit manifestation of prosecutorial discretion.[175] Scholars

---

[169] Ibid. See also Situation in Afghanistan, PTC II, Decision Pursuant to Article 15 of the Rome Statute on the Authorisation of an Investigation into the Situation in the Islamic Republic of Afghanistan, ICC-02/17-33, 12 Apr 2019, para.89.

[170] OTP, *Policy Paper on the Interests of Justice* (Sep 2007), 1–2.

[171] Ibid, 2. See, also, Situation in Afghanistan, AC, Judgment on the appeal against the decision on the authorisation of an investigation into the situation in the Islamic Republic of Afghanistan, ICC-02/17-138, 5 Mar 2020, para.49.

[172] However, according to some, the list of factors in Article 53(2)(c) is not exhaustive, and the two paragraphs may match in practice. See Charles C Jalloh, 'The ICC Reform Process and the Failure to Address the African State Concerns on the Sequencing of Peace with Criminal Justice under Article 53 of the Rome Statute' (2022) 54 NYU JILP 809, 841; Catherine Maia and Ghislain Poissonnier, 'Cour pénale internationale: de la signification des «intérêts de la justice»' in Catherine Maia and Jean-Baptiste Harelimana (eds), *Réenchanter la justice internationale pénale: perspectives universelles et africaines* (Éditions du Net 2022) 61, 82–4.

[173] Situation in Afghanistan, AC, Judgment on the appeal against the decision on the authorisation of an investigation into the situation in the Islamic Republic of Afghanistan, ICC-02/17-138, 5 Mar 2020, para.49.

[174] Farid Mohammed Rashid, *Prosecutorial Discretion in the International Criminal Court: Legitimacy and the Politics of Justice* (Routledge 2021) 129. See above, subsection 4.2.1.

[175] See, for example, Talita de Souza Dias, '"Interests of Justice": Defining the Scope of Prosecutorial Discretion in Article 53(1)(c) and (2)(c) of the Rome Statute of the International Criminal Court' (2017) 30 LJIL 731; Maria Varaki, 'Revisiting the "Interests of Justice" Policy Paper' (2017) 15 JICJ 455.

are divided between those considering that the interests of justice should be interpreted narrowly and do not encompass the interests of peace[176] – a view shared by the OTP[177] – and those concluding that the interests of peace are a component of the interests of justice,[178] a notion that should be interpreted widely to favour non-retributive approaches to international justice.[179] In any case, still today, the specific content of the notion of interests of justice is not strictly defined, but rather, it is a 'mystery' that injects into the RS a wide margin of discretion for the OTP.[180] As a balance, the RS gives the PTC the power to review a decision of the OTP not to initiate an investigation or not to prosecute an individual because this would not be in the interests of justice.[181] This is the only mechanism of judicial review that is applicable to a decision of the Prosecutor *not* to initiate an investigation or *not* to prosecute an individual irrespective of whether the jurisdiction of the ICC was triggered by a state referral, by an UNSC referral, or by the OTP *proprio motu*.

Notwithstanding its potential, the concept of interests of has rarely been employed in practice. The notable exception was the 2019 decision of PTC II not to authorise an investigation into the situation in Afghanistan because of

---

176 See, for example, Errol P Mendes, *Peace and Justice at the International Criminal Court: A Court of Last Resort* (Edward Elgar Publishing 2010) 34; Diego Acosta Arcarazo, Russell Buchan and Rene Urueña, 'Beyond Justice, Beyond Peace? Colombia, the Interests of Justice, and the Limits of International Criminal Law' (2015) 26 CLF 291, 311–16; Alessandra Annoni, 'Il rapporto fra pace e giustizia nella prassi applicativa dello Statuto di Roma' in Alessandra Annoni, Serana Forlati and Pietro Franzina (eds), *Il diritto internazionale come sistema di valori: scritti in onore di Francesco Salerno* (Jovene 2021) 31, 57–8.

177 OTP, *Policy Paper on the Interests of Justice* (Sep 2007), 8; OTP, *Policy Paper on Preliminary Examinations* (Nov 2013), para.69.

178 For example, Philippa Webb, 'The ICC Prosecutor's Discretion Not to Proceed in the Interests of Justice' (2005) 50 *Criminal Law Quarterly* 305, 335–6; de Souza Dias, n.175; Varaki, n.175, 464; Jalloh, n.172; Talita de Souza Dias and Dapo Akande, 'Peace Negotiations as "Interests of Justice"' in Richard H Steinberg (ed.), *The International Criminal Court: Contemporary Challenges and Reform Proposals* (Brill 2020) 344, 350.

179 See, in particular, Claire Magnoux, '*The Sound of Silence*: le pouvoir discrétionnaire du Procureur de la Cour pénale internationale à travers l'utilisation des critères d'intérêts de la justice et de gravité lors de l'ouverture d'une enquête' (décembre 2017 - hors-série) RQDI 9.

180 See Maria Varaki, 'Introducing a Fairness-Based Theory of Prosecutorial Legitimacy before the International Criminal Court' (2016) 27 EJIL 769.

181 See RS, Article 53(3)(b). See, also, Webb, n.178, 320–21.

the interests of justice under Article 53(1)(c).[182] The Chamber concluded that 'at the very minimum, an investigation would only be in the interests of justice if prospectively it appears suitable to result in the effective investigation and subsequent prosecution of cases within a reasonable time frame'.[183] This conclusion sparked widespread outcry for reasons that cannot be scrutinised here in detail, but chiefly because the Chamber substituted its own assessment of the interests of justice for that of the Prosecutor and because the Chamber linked the interests of justice to prospective successful cases, incentivising states and individuals to oppose the exercise of ICC jurisdiction to avert the possibility of investigations and prosecutions.[184] The AC, correctly, reversed the PTC's approach, by stating that the Chamber had no power to apply the interests of justice in that decision.[185] However, and totally unnecessarily from a judicial economy perspective, the AC took the opportunity to say something on the content of the interests of justice, by affirming that the Chamber's reasoning 'was cursory, speculative and did not refer to information capable of supporting it'[186] because 'there is no indication that the [PTC] considered the gravity of the crimes and the interests of victims as articulated by the victims

---

182 Situation in Afghanistan, PTC II, Decision Pursuant to Article 15 of the Rome Statute on the Authorisation of an Investigation into the Situation in the Islamic Republic of Afghanistan, ICC-02/17-33, 12 Apr 2019.

183 Ibid, para.89. The Chamber elaborated on this:

> An investigation can hardly be said to be in the interests of justice if the relevant circumstances are such as to make such investigation not feasible and inevitably doomed to failure … [F]ocussing on those scenarios where the prospects for successful and meaningful investigations are serious and substantive is key to its ultimate success. The following factors appear to be particularly relevant: (i) the significant time elapsed between the alleged crimes and the Request; (ii) the scarce cooperation obtained by the Prosecutor throughout this time, even for the limited purposes of a preliminary examination, as such based on information rather than evidence; (iii) the likelihood that both relevant evidence and potential relevant suspects might still be available and within reach of the Prosecution's investigative efforts and activities at this stage (ibid, 89–91).

184 See, for example, Mariniello, n.150, 987–92; Luca Poltronieri Rossetti, 'The Pre-Trial Chamber's Afghanistan Decision: A Step Too Far in the Judicial Review of Prosecutorial Discretion?' (2019) 17 JICJ 585.

185 Situation in Afghanistan, AC, Judgment on the appeal against the decision on the authorisation of an investigation into the situation in the Islamic Republic of Afghanistan, ICC-02/17-138, 5 Mar 2020, para.35.

186 Ibid, 49.

themselves in conducting this assessment'.[187] No further indication of what is meant by interests of justice, or how to interpret this notion, was provided by the AC.[188]

In any case, gravity is a notion that is relevant for the assessment of the interests of justice. It should be noted as well that the assessment of the gravity of the crime to determine interests of justice is subsequent to the assessment of sufficient gravity as an admissibility criterion.[189] This means that, in principle, a situation, case, or potential case can be at the same time sufficiently grave to pass the gravity threshold for admissibility, but nevertheless, taking into account the underlying gravity of the relevant crimes, an investigation or prosecution may not be in the interests of justice. Some commentators have considered this conclusion to be absurd and that the 'gravity of the crime' should not be one of the elements to be considered in the assessment of the interests of justice.[190] However, this would go against the very text of Article 53, would obliterate the distinction between 'gravity of the crime' and gravity of situations, cases, and potential cases, and would deny the fact that the gravity of the crime must be balanced with other factors listed in Article 53 to assess the interests of justice.

For all these reasons, the assessment of the gravity of the crimes under the interests of justice should be kept separate from gravity as an admissibility criterion. This *prima facie* contradiction reinforces the idea that a situation or case should be presumed to be in the interests of justice.[191] A subsequent chapter will discuss how, in practice, sufficient gravity ended up replacing interests of justice to justify some choices of the OTP.[192]

---

187 Ibid.

188 See Joana Loyo Cabezudo, 'La llave del "interés de la justicia" en el Estatuto de Roma: su controvertido empleo en el caso de Afganistán' (2021) 73 REDI 165.

189 OTP, *Policy Paper on the Interests of Justice* (Sep 2007), 5.

190 Jan Wouters, Sten Verhoeven and Bruno Demeyere, 'The International Criminal Court's Office of the Prosecutor: Navigating between Independence and Accountability?' in José Doria, Hans-Peter Gasser and M Cherif Bassiouni (eds), *The Legal Regime of the International Criminal Court: Essays in Honour of Professor Igor Blishchenko* (Martinus Nijhoff 2009) 345, 368; Morten Bergsmo and Olympia Bekou, 'Article 53: Initiation of an Investigation' in Kai Ambos (ed.), *Rome Statute of the International Criminal Court: Article-by-Article Commentary* (4th edn, Beck-Hart-Nomos 2022), 1623, 1634.

191 OTP, *Policy Paper on the Interests of Justice* (Sep 2007), 5; Mendes, , 31.

192 See below, Chapter 5, subsection 3.3.

4.4 Gravity and the Granting of Interim Release to Individuals Arrested by National Authorities

Additionally, the gravity of the crimes is mentioned in the RS in relation to interim release. Under Article 59, when a State Party arrests an individual in pursuance of an arrest warrant or a request to surrender, the arrested person has the right to apply to the national authorities for interim release pending surrender.

Gravity of the crimes is one of the factors that national authorities should take into account in assessing whether to grant interim release. According to Article 59(4): '[i]n reaching a decision on any such application, the competent authority in the custodial State shall consider whether, given the gravity of the alleged crimes, there are urgent and exceptional circumstances to justify interim release and whether necessary safeguards exist to ensure that the custodial State can fulfil its duty to surrender the person to the Court.'[193] The relevant provisions in the RPE shed no light on the assessment of the gravity of the crimes in these procedures.[194]

Article 59(4) places the burden of assessing the gravity of the crimes for interim release upon the national authorities. Accordingly, it is possible to find some references to this issue in the scant available national case law. In 2008, the Belgian Supreme Court recognised the right of Jean-Pierre Bemba Gombo to request interim release, but it did not analyse the merits of the request in light of the gravity of the crimes.[195] In 2010, the Appeals Court of Paris analysed and rejected a request for interim release by Callixte Mbarushimana, making some cursory references to the gravity of the crimes as one of the justifications for not granting interim release, in line with the position of the French General Attorney.[196]

As such, the reference to gravity here is not particularly helpful in understanding the notion of sufficient gravity under Article 17(1)(d) of the RS. The scant national case law that is available does not illustrate the content of the

---

[193] Emphasis added.

[194] RPE, Rule 117(4) and (5).

[195] *Bemba Gombo (Jean-Pierre) v Belgium*, Cass No P 08 0896F, ILDC 1115 (BE 2008), Appeal Judgment, Court of Cassation, 18 Jun 2008, 6, reprinted in *Oxford Reports on International Law online.*

[196] The decision is reproducedin Situation in the DRC, *Prosecutor v Mbarushimana*, Rapport sur la procédure devant la Chambre de l'instruction de la Cour d'Appel de Paris, ICC-01/04-01/10-18-Anx1-Red, 21 Jan 2011, 5–7. See also the decision reproducedin Situation in the DRC, *Prosecutor v Mbarushimana*, Second Rapport sur la procédure devant la Chambre de l'instruction de la Cour d'Appel de Paris, ICC-01/04-01/10-19, 08 Nov 2010.

notion of gravity. Scholars analysing this provision similarly tend to overlook discussion of the gravity of the crimes.[197]

4.5 Gravity and the Determination of Penalties

Since gravity and sentencing in international criminal law are intrinsically linked,[198] it is no surprise that the RS employs the notion of gravity in the field of the determination of penalties. Under Article 77(1)(b), life imprisonment can only be imposed 'when justified by the extreme *gravity* of the crime and the individual circumstances of the convicted person'.[199] Similarly, Article 78(1) states that '[i]n determining the sentence, the Court shall, in accordance with the [RPE], take into account such factors as the *gravity* of the crime and the individual circumstances of the convicted person'.[200]

The provision of the RS in the field of factors guiding sentencing is complemented by the RPE. Rule 145(1)(c) provides that, besides the factors mentioned by Article 78(1) of the RS, the Court must:

> give consideration, inter alia, to the extent of the damage caused, in particular the harm caused to the victims and their families, the nature of the unlawful behaviour and the means employed to execute the crime; the degree of participation of the convicted person; the degree of intent; the circumstances of manner, time and location; and the age, education, social and economic condition of the convicted person.

This list of additional factors does not mention gravity and it is doubtful whether they can be seen as elements that are relevant to determining the gravity of the crime under Article 78(1) of the RS. In 2014, the AC did not reach a definitive conclusion, but it found merits both in the thesis that the two

---

197 For example, gravity is not discussed by Göran Sluiter, 'Human Rights Protection in the ICC Pre-Trial Phase' in Carsten Stahn and Göran Sluiter (eds), *The Emerging Practice of the International Criminal Court* (Martinus Nijhoff 2009) 459, 467–74; Schabas, n.59, 907–908; Mark Klamberg, 'Article 59' in Mark Klamberg (ed.), *Commentary on the Law of the International Criminal Court* (TOAEP 2017) 432, 433–4; Cedric Ryngaert, 'Article 59' in Kai Ambos (ed.), *Rome Statute of the International Criminal Court: Article-by-Article Commentary* (4th edn, Beck-Hart-Nomos 2022), 1732, 1742–3.

198 See, generally, Andrea Carcano, 'Sentencing and the Gravity of the Offence in International Criminal Law' (2002) 51 ICLQ 583; Jan Philipp Book, *Appeal and Sentence in International Criminal Law* (Verlag 2011); Silvia D'Ascoli, *Sentencing in International Criminal Law* (Hart 2011); Alice Riccardi, *Sentencing at the International Criminal Court: From Nuremberg to the Hague* (Eleven International 2016).

199 Emphasis added.

200 Emphasis added.

provisions refer to separate factors and in the view that Rule 145(1)(c) of the RPE should be employed to interpret Article 78(1) of the RS.[201] Subsequently, Trial Chambers (TCs) have been inconsistent, with some chambers showing reluctance in reading Rule 145(1)(c) of the RPE as a specification of the gravity requirement in Article 78(1) of the RS,[202] and others more inclined to reading both provisions as pertaining to gravity.[203]

Interpreting rules on penalties as related to the gravity of the crime is in line with what happens in some domestic criminal law systems, where the gravity of a crime is one of the guiding factors for sentencing. For instance, in the UK, the seriousness of a crime is considered one of the elements that must be considered in sentencing. The UK system provides that sentencing must be guided by legislative provisions (if any) and by sentencing guidelines adopted by the Sentencing Council for England and Wales, which identifies sentencing ranges for different categories of cases involving the commission of some offences that illustrate, in general terms, the varying degrees of seriousness with which the offence may be committed and the appropriately corresponding sentences.[204] In determining the guidelines, the Sentencing Council refers to: 'the offender's culpability in committing the offence; the harm caused, or intended to be caused or which might foreseeably have been caused, by the offence; [and] such other factors as the Council considers to be particularly relevant to the seriousness of the offence in question.'[205] The courts have a duty to assess the seriousness of each case before them and relate that case to the sentencing guidelines in order to decide which sentence should be applied.[206] Seriousness encompasses 'the offender's culpability in committing the offence, and any harm which the offence caused, was intended to cause, or might foreseeably have caused'.[207] Similarly, the Italian Criminal Code provides that judges must sentence within the limits provided by the law on the

---

201 Situation in the DRC, *Prosecutor v Lubanga*, AC, Judgment on the appeals of the Prosecutor and Mr Thomas Lubanga Dyilo against the 'Decision on Sentence pursuant to Article 76 of the Statute', ICC-01/04-01/06-3122, 1 Dec 2014, paras 61–6.

202 Situation in the CAR, *Prosecutor v Bemba Gombo*, TC III, Decision on Sentence pursuant to Article 76 of the Statute, ICC-01/05-01/08-3399, 21 Jun 2016, para.13; Situation in Mali, *Prosecutor v Al Mahdi*, TC VIII, Judgment and Sentence, ICC-01/12-01/15, 27 Sep 2016, paras 69, 75.

203 Situation in the DRC, *Prosecutor v Ntaganda*, TC VI, Sentencing Judgment, ICC-01/04-02/06, 7 Nov 2019, para.16.

204 Coroners and Justice Act 2009, Part 4, Chapter 1.

205 Ibid, s.121.

206 Sentencing Act 2020, Part 4.

207 Ibid, s.63.

basis of their discretion,[208] but the application of this discretion must be guided by the gravity of the offence and by the offensive capacity (*capacità delittuosa*) of the perpetrator.[209] The gravity of the offence is deduced in light of the nature, kind, means of commission, object, time, place and other features of the conduct, as well as of the gravity of the harm or the potential harm caused to the victim, and the intensity of *mens rea*.[210]

Both at the international and national levels, sentencing is guided by two different and intertwined considerations. On the one hand, there is the gravity *in abstracto* of each crime, which, at the domestic level, is often predetermined by the relevant statutory criminal provisions (with or without subsequent intervention of other bodies such as the Sentencing Council for England and Wales). Nothing comparable exists in the RS, where states preferred leaving to the Court the task of identifying the specific sentence for each crime.[211] The absence of consensus on the minimum and maximum penalty for each of the crimes embodied in the RS may be seen either as the result of the lack of a shared criminal policy between the drafting states,[212] or as a validation that all the crimes in the RS have the same gravity *in abstracto* and potentially deserve the most severe penalty (30 years' of imprisonment or life imprisonment).[213] From this perspective, the contrary position held by several TCs, according to which certain crimes are less grave than others, does not reflect the absence of a hierarchy in the RS.[214] However, the determination of the penalty must

---

208 Codice Penale, Article 132.

209 Ibid, Article 133.

210 Ibid.

211 Agirre Aranburu, n.127, 421. For a proposal to introduce sentencing guidelines in the ICC system, see Roger S Clark and Beti Hohler, 'Sentencing at the ICC: Is It Time for Sentencing Guidelines?' in Róisín Mulgrew and Mikkel Jarle Christens (eds), *Research Handbook on the Punishment of Atrocity Crimes* (Edward Elgar Publishing 2024) 120.

212 Alessandra Lanciotti, *La Corte penale internazionale e la repressione delle gravi violazioni del diritto umanitario* (Giappichelli 2013), 104.

213 Kai Ambos, *Treatise on International Criminal Law, Vol.II: Crimes and Sentencing* (2nd edn, OUP 2022) 326.

214 Situation in the DRC, *Prosecutor v Katanga*, TC II, Decision on Sentence pursuant to article 76 of the Statute, ICC-01/04-01/07-3484-tENG, 23 May 2014, paras 42–3; Situation in Mali, *Prosecutor Al Mahdi*, TC VIII, Judgment and Sentence, ICC-01/12-01/15, 27 Sep 2016, para.72; Situation in the DRC, *Prosecutor v Ntaganda*, TC VI, Sentencing Judgment, ICC-01/04-02/06, 7 Nov 2019, para.14. The ICTY had rejected the idea that certain crimes are more serious than others (for example, in *Prosecutor v Furundžija*, Judgment, IT-95-17/1-A, 21 Jul 2000, para.247). On this debate under the RS, see William A Schabas, 'Complementarity in Practice: Creative Solutions or a Trap for the Court?' in

also take into consideration the gravity of a specific crime *in concreto*, in light of the specific circumstances of the case before the Court.[215] This assessment requires the application of the factors listed in Articles 77 and 78 of the RS and Rule 145 of the RPE. The lack of predetermined statutory sentencing range for each crime leaves to the Court a very broad discretion in the determination of the penalties.

The relevance of these factors for the determination of sufficient gravity as an admissibility threshold under Article 17(1)(d) is explored subsequently, taking into account the practice of the relevant organs of the Court.[216]

4.6 Gravity and the Activity of the Court

The RS refers to gravity and cognate notions not only in relation to alleged crimes under ICC jurisdiction, but also in relation to the activity of the ICC's organs. Two examples suffice to illustrate this: the notion of serious misconduct or serious breach of duties as a reason for removal from office or disciplinary measures of an organ under Articles 46 and 47, and grave and manifest miscarriage of justice as a reason to claim compensation under Article 85(3).

4.6.1 Gravity and misconduct by ICC organs

The notion of seriousness is employed by the RS in relation to misconduct or breach of duties by some organs. Article 46(1)(a) provides that a 'judge, the Prosecutor, a Deputy Prosecutor, the Registrar or the Deputy Registrar shall be removed from office … in cases where that person … [i]s found to have committed serious misconduct or a serious breach of his or her duties under this Statute'. Rule 24 of the RPE defines 'serious misconduct' as conduct that '[i]f it occurs in the course of official duties, is incompatible with official functions, and causes or is likely to cause serious harm to the proper administration of justice before the Court or the proper internal functioning of the Court'.[217] If the conduct occurs outside the course of official duties, the definition encompasses cases in which the conduct 'is of a grave nature that causes or is likely to cause serious harm to the standing of the Court'.[218] Similarly, 'serious breach of duty' occurs 'where a person has been grossly negligent in the performance

---

Mauro Politi and Federica Gioia (eds), *The International Criminal Court and National Jurisdictions* (Ashgate 2008) 25, 42; O'Keefe, n.54, 160–162; Ambos, n.213, 335–42.

[215] Ambos, 337.

[216] See below, Chapter 4, subsection 3.3.

[217] RPE, Rule 24(1)(a).

[218] RPE, Rule 24(1)(b).

of his or her duties or has knowingly acted in contravention of those duties'.[219] Both definitions are accompanied by some examples.[220]

Article 47 of the RS provides that the same organ 'who has committed misconduct of a less serious nature than that set out in [Article 46(1)], shall be subject to disciplinary measures'. The RPE provides an articulated definition.[221]

Scant case law is available on these complaints since Rule 26(1) of the RPE prescribes the confidentiality of these proceedings.[222] Overall, no significant practice is available in relation to the interpretation of 'serious' and 'less serious' misconduct and breach of duty.

4.6.2 Gravity and manifest miscarriage of justice

The RS employs gravity to identify instances in which a person who has been released from detention after an acquittal can make a claim for compensation. Article 85(3) of the RS requires that some 'exceptional circumstances' exist to grant compensation in cases where 'the Court finds conclusive facts showing that there has been a grave and manifest miscarriage of justice'. The provision is complemented by Rules 173–175 of the RPE, which reproduce, in passing, the reference to gravity.

In contrast to the other instances discussed so far, Article 85(3) does not refer to the gravity of crimes. Rather, 'grave' is used as a qualifier, in conjunction with 'manifest', to limit compensation to some forms of miscarriage of justice.[223] As determined by a TC, 'a decision of acquittal, in and of itself, does not constitute a grave and manifest miscarriage of justice'.[224] Rather, a grave and manifest miscarriage of justice occurs when the miscarriage of justice is 'certain and undeniable following, for example, an erroneous decision by a trial chamber or wrongful prosecution'.[225] The Chamber went on to affirm that '[t]he miscarriage of justice must have given rise to a clear violation of the

---

219 RPE, Rule 24(2).

220 RPE, Rule 24(1)(a)(i)–(iii) and (2)(a)–(b).

221 RPE, Rule 25.

222 See Magda Karagiannakis, 'Article 46' in Kai Ambos (ed.), *Rome Statute of the International Criminal Court: Article-by-Article Commentary* (4th edn, Beck-Hart-Nomos 2022) 1547, 1551.

223 Volker Nerlich, 'Article 85' in Kai Ambos (ed.), *Rome Statute of the International Criminal Court: Article-by-Article Commentary* (4th edn, Beck-Hart-Nomos 2022) 2427, 2436.

224 Situation in the DRC, *Prosecutor v Ngudjolo*, TC II, Decision on the 'Requête en indemnisation en application des dispositions de l'article 85(1) et (3) du Statut de Rome', ICC-01/04-02/12-301-tENG, 16 Dec 2015, para.45.

225 Ibid.

applicant's fundamental rights and must have caused serious harm to the applicant' so that 'Article 85(3) of the Statute sets a high threshold in this regard and it therefore follows that not every error committed in the course of the proceedings is automatically considered a "grave and manifest" miscarriage of justice'.[226] Subsequent case law concurred with this interpretation.[227]

This rule's peculiar function does not touch upon the criminal conduct at the centre of the ICC proceedings, but rather on the proceedings themselves. This circumstance renders the reference to gravity embodied therein unsuitable to shed any light on sufficient gravity under Article 17(1)(d). Moreover, the scant case law available does not offer any significant insight on the interpretation of the word 'grave' in Article 85(3), rather, it addresses the notion of 'grave and manifest miscarriage of justice' altogether.

5. CONCLUSIONS

This chapter has laid the ground for the exploration of the assessment of sufficient gravity in this book in multiple ways. First, it has isolated the subject matter of the present book, that is, sufficient gravity as an admissibility criterion under Article 17(1)(d), from other instances in which gravity or cognate notions are relevant for international law, international criminal law, or the RS. Gravity and cognate notions are indeed commonly used in different areas of international law and have permeated international criminal law from its origins.

The chapter has explored the employment of gravity and similar notions in different areas of international law, noting a certain trend to consider the emergence of gravity as a response to an alleged value-centred approach to international law. This is particularly the case in relation to international criminal law, which the mainstream narrative describes as a response to the perceived gravity of certain actions formerly punished only as wrongful acts of the state (with individual criminal responsibility left to domestic criminal law). Indeed, gravity has a prescriptive function that has brought certain offences within the subject-matter jurisdiction of the ICC. In this sense, all the crimes punishable in the RS have, *in abstracto*, a minimum threshold of gravity that has already placed them within ICC jurisdiction, but certain specific crimes are characterised by additional gravity as part of the elements of the crimes.

Additionally, the chapter has discussed how sufficient gravity under Article 17(1)(d) fits this scenario, first describing its role under Article 17 as an

---

[226] Ibid.

[227] Situation in the CAR, *Prosecutor v Bemba Gombo*, PTC II, Decision on Mr Bemba's claim for compensation and damages, ICC-01/05-01/08-3694, 18 May 2020, para.42.

admissibility criterion, then discussing its incorporation by Article 53 in relation to the activities of the OTP. It then went on to clarify the object of the assessment of sufficient gravity, discussing the difference between situations, potential cases, and cases, and the ways in which ICC case law has interpreted the relationship between Articles 17 and 53.

Finally, the chapter has addressed other topics within the RS where the notion of gravity plays a significant role. For instance, the notion of interests of justice, which may be invoked by the OTP either in order not to open an investigation or not to proceed with a prosecution, must be construed in light of the gravity of the crimes pursuant to Article 53(1)(c) and(2)(c). Moreover, when domestic courts decide whether to grant interim release to individuals detained by States Parties, Article 59(4) requires them to consider the gravity of the crime. Finally, the gravity of the crime is also the decisive factor relating to the determination of the penalty (and the possibility of imposing life imprisonment) under Articles 77(1)(b) and 78(1).

4. Determining the factors affecting gravity through the practice of the OTP and the Chambers

> '[W]henever a new international organization is established (or later in its life), its founding fathers have choices to make about the interpretation of the law of their creation. If nothing is decided, interpretation is entirely left to practice.'[1]

1. INTRODUCTION

After having reconstructed the theoretical framework guiding the assessment of sufficient gravity and after having mapped the use of the notion of gravity in international criminal law in the previous chapters, this chapter explores the practice of the Office of the Prosecutor (OTP) and the case law of the International Criminal Court (ICC) Chambers in relation to which factors are relevant for that assessment and the way in which these factors have developed over time. The ICC organs have considered that sufficient gravity must be ascertained with reference to factors external to the elements of the crimes at hand, to keep intact the distinction between jurisdiction and admissibility. Here, the analysis is mainly divided into two temporal phases. From 2003 to 2006, the assessment of sufficient gravity was scarcely elaborated, with few references to quantitative criteria and the role of the suspect in the commission of the crimes (subsection 2.1). This phase terminated in 2006, when the views of the OTP, Pre-Trial Chamber (PTC), and Appeals Chamber (AC) clashed with respect to the elements that should be considered when assessing sufficient gravity (subsection 2.2). As a result of this disagreement, since 2006, a new approach to the assessment of sufficient gravity has emerged: the OTP and the Chambers have identified, consolidated, and developed some relevant factors for the assessment of sufficient gravity that have become the benchmark for future assessments. These factors are scale, nature, manner of commission,

1 Niels Blokker, 'Legal Facets of the Practice of International Organizations' (2024) 435 RdC 73, 221.

and impact (section 3). They are interpreted as verifiable and objective factors that do not pertain to the elements of the crimes (which are relevant for jurisdictional purposes) but are external to the elements of the crimes at hand. This chapter also demonstrates that the so-called most responsible criterion does not belong to the assessment of sufficient gravity, but rather, is an expression of prosecutorial policies in relation to the selection and prioritisation of situations and cases (section 4).

2. THE FIRST ATTEMPTS TO ASSESS SUFFICIENT GRAVITY: FROM QUANTITATIVE CONSIDERATIONS TO THREEFOLD APPROACHES (2003–2006)

2.1 The Initial Practice of the OTP

In 2014, looking back to the origin of the factors affecting gravity, the OTP argued that '[t]he position of the OTP …, which relies on multiple factors that examine the scale, nature, manner of commission, and impact of the crimes in both quantitative and qualitative terms, is apparent from its statements dating from September 2003' and from subsequent sources.[2] The accompanying footnote to the text reads: '[s]ee *Second Assembly of States Parties to the Rome Statute of the International Criminal Court Report of the Prosecutor of the ICC, Mr Luis Moreno-Ocampo*, 8 September 2003' which refers to 'the particular gravity of the crimes, both in terms of their scale and nature; their manner of commission, including summary executions, the burning of people alive, physical mutilation and the specific targeting of vulnerable groups, in particular women and children; and the effect of the crimes in causing massive displacement, exacerbated poverty, famine and disease'.[3] However, looking at that document specifically, although the OTP refers to the circumstances mentioned therein, they are never used in relation to determining sufficient gravity under Article 17(1)(d).[4]

The origin story of the OTP's understanding of the factors relevant to determining gravity starts in September 2003, but with a less sophisticated elaboration. In 2003, the OTP issued its first policy paper entitled *Paper on Some*

2 Situation in Côte d'Ivoire, *Prosecutor v Blé Goudé*, Prosecution's Response to the Defence application pursuant to Articles 19(4) and 17(1)(d) of the Rome Statute, ICC-02/11-02/11-181, 20 Oct 2014, para.31.

3 Ibid, n.47.

4 OTP, Second Assembly of States Parties (ASP) to the RS of the ICC, *Report of the Prosecutor of the ICC, Mr Luis Moreno-Ocampo* (8 Sep 2003).

Policy Issues before the Office of the Prosecutor, where, in a paragraph entitled 'Who should be prosecuted?', the OTP noted that Article 17 provides that:

> the Court (which includes the [OTP]) shall determine that a case is inadmissible where "the case is not of sufficient gravity to justify further action by the Court". The concept of gravity should not be exclusively attached to the act that constituted the crime but also to the degree of participation in its commission.[5]

This statement is interesting for at least two reasons: first, because it recognises that the OTP must take into account sufficient gravity under Article 17(1)(d) when deciding who should be prosecuted, and second, because it considers sufficient gravity as not limited to the intrinsic gravity that is a component of an ICC crime, instead leaving the door open to further considerations, particularly in relation to the participation of the accused in the commission of the crime. However, no elaboration is offered in relation to the notion of sufficient gravity.

The OTP elaborated on sufficient gravity and its assessment in relation to the situation in Uganda in 2005. Luis Moreno Ocampo, the Prosecutor at the time, justified the decision to request arrest warrants only for members of the armed group called Lord's Resistance Army (LRA) as a decision driven by considerations of gravity.[6] The OTP did not mention Article 17(1)(d), but these statements can be considered as referring to Article 53(1)(b), which incorporates a reference to the admissibility criteria under Article 17. Sufficient gravity is constructed largely as a quantitative concept. For instance, the OTP noted that '[c]rimes committed by the LRA were *much more numerous* and of *much higher gravity* than alleged crimes committed by' governmental forces.[7] Quantity was a predominant consideration particularly in relation to killings, since 'the most obvious' factor in relation to the determination of gravity: 'is the number of persons killed – as this tends to be the most reliably reported. However, [the OTP] will not necessarily limit [its] investigations to situations where killing has been the predominant crime. [It] also look[s] at number of

5 OTP, Paper on Some Policy Issues before the Office of the Prosecutor (Sep 2003), 7.

6 OTP, *Statement by the Chief Prosecutor on the Uganda Arrest Warrants* (14 Oct 2005), 2–3; OTP, *Statement of the Prosecutor at the Informal meeting of Legal Advisors of Ministries of Foreign Affairs* (24 Oct 2005), 6; OTP, *Statement of the Prosecutor at the Fourth Session of the Assembly of States Parties, 28 Nov – 3 Dec 2005* (28 Nov 2005), 1–2.

7 OTP, *Statement by the Chief Prosecutor on the Uganda Arrest Warrants* (14 Oct 2005), 2–3 (emphasis added).

victims of other crimes, especially crimes against physical integrity.'[8] Yet, at the same time, the OTP left the door open to other criteria, by admitting that '[w]e [at the OTP] are currently in the process of refining our methodologies for assessing gravity' and that '[t]he impact of the crimes is another important factor'.[9]

The year after, in early 2006, the OTP reiterated its position as mainly based on quantitative factors in relation to the possibility of opening an investigation into alleged war crimes committed in Iraq by UK nationals. The OTP announced its decision not to start an investigation in light of gravity considerations, noting that '[w]hile, in a general sense, any crime within the jurisdiction of the Court is "grave", the Statute requires an additional threshold of gravity even where the subject-matter jurisdiction is satisfied'.[10] This is a correct distinction between gravity as a jurisdictional element of the crimes and gravity as an admissibility criterion, even if the reference here is made to Article 53, regarding the powers of the OTP, rather than to Article 17(1)(d). The OTP went on to state that: '[t]he Office considers various factors in assessing gravity. A key consideration is the *number of victims* of particularly serious crimes, such as wilful killing or rape.'[11] So far, the approach to sufficient gravity was prominently quantitative and the few scholars commenting on it voiced dissatisfaction.[12] However, this quantitative approach was about to change with the beginning of an interlocution between the OTP and the Chambers.[13]

---

8 OTP, *Statement of the Prosecutor at the Informal meeting of Legal Advisors of Ministries of Foreign Affairs* (24 Oct 2005), 6.

9 Ibid.

10 OTP, *Prosecutor's Letter* (9 Feb 2006), 8.

11 Ibid, 8–9 (emphasis added).

12 See, for example, Melanie O'Brien, 'The Impact of the Iraq Communication of the Prosecutor of the International Criminal Court on War Crimes Admissibility and the Interests of Victims' (2007) 16 *University College Dublin Law Review* 109; William A Schabas, '"Complementarity in Practice": Some Uncomplimentary Thoughts' (2008) 19 CLF 5, 28–32.

13 However, even later, episodically, gravity is only assessed based on scale. See, for example, Situation in Bangladesh/Myanmar, PTC III, Decision Pursuant to Article 15 of the Rome Statute on the Authorisation of an Investigation into the Situation in Bangladesh/Myanmar, ICC-01/19-27, 14 Nov 2019, para.118.

2.2 The Initial Practice of the Chambers

2.2.1 The decision of PTC I regarding arrest warrants for Lubanga and Ntaganda

On 10 February 2006, PTC I provided the first judicial decision on sufficient gravity in the context of the issuance of arrest warrants against Lubanga and Ntaganda.[14] This decision marked a new trend in relation to the assessment of sufficient gravity and its relevant factors, although it was almost immediately overturned by the AC. Albeit short-lived, this first attempt to clarify the notion of sufficient gravity deserves attention because it contributed to the emergence of the academic debate on this topic and led to further developments in the practice of the OTP and in the decisions of the Chambers.

In analysing whether the request for arrest warrants against Lubanga and Ntaganda met the sufficient gravity test, PTC I started by noting that Article 17(1)(d) of the Rome Statute (RS) imposes an additional gravity threshold to that inherently embodied in any international crime under Article 5. According to the Chamber:

> *this gravity threshold is in addition to the drafters' careful selection of the crimes* included in articles 6 to 8 of the Statute, a selection based on gravity and directed at confining the material jurisdiction of the Court to "the most serious crimes of international concern". Hence, the fact that a case addresses one of the most serious crimes for the international community as a whole is not sufficient for it to be admissible before the Court.[15]

In this respect, the Chamber argued correctly and in line with the prosecutorial position that sufficient gravity as an admissibility test should be kept distinct from the inherent gravity of international crimes. In other words, the additional character of sufficient gravity in respect of the elements of the crimes means that the *actus reus*, *mens rea*, and modes of liability should not count for the assessment of sufficient gravity.

However, the Chamber went further in its elaboration, applying the interpretive criteria embodied in the Vienna Convention on the Law of Treaties (VCLT) to sufficient gravity.[16] After remarking that the assessment of sufficient gravity is a legal duty under the RS,[17] the Chamber, as part of the analysis of the legal context of Article 17(1)(d), identified two factors to be taken into account: the first pertains to the fact that the case must be either systematic

---

14 Situation in the DRC, PTC I, Decision on the Prosecutor's Application for Warrants of Arrest, Article 58, ICC-01/04-520-Anx2, 10 Feb 2006.

15 Ibid, para.42 (emphasis added).

16 Ibid, para.43.

17 Ibid, para.44.

(pattern of incidents) or large-scale, because: '[i]f isolated instances of criminal activity were sufficient, there would be no need to establish an additional gravity threshold beyond the gravity-driven selection of the crimes … within the material jurisdiction of the Court.'[18] The second is based on social alarm in the international community, which, in the case at hand, was 'caused by the extent of the practice of enlisting into armed groups, conscripting into armed groups and using to participate actively in hostilities children under the age of fifteen'.[19]

Without explaining how these two factors were linked to the context of the treaty provisions under interpretation, the Chamber moved on to identify a third factor relevant for the assessment of sufficient gravity on the basis of alleged teleological interpretation. According to the Chamber, a teleological interpretation of the RS should be based on the aim of putting 'an end to impunity for the perpetrators of these crimes and thus … contribute to the prevention of such crimes'.[20] To this end, the additional gravity threshold 'is a key tool provided by the drafters to maximise the Court's deterrent effect' which prevails over 'any retributory effect of the activities of the Court'.[21] This consideration allowed the Chamber to identify other factors that are relevant for the assessment of sufficient gravity.[22] In the Chamber's view, sufficient gravity was 'intended to ensure that the Court initiates cases only against the *most senior leaders* suspected of being the *most responsible* for the crimes within the jurisdiction of the Court allegedly committed in any given situation under investigation'.[23] This factor can be articulated in three sub-criteria: sufficient gravity should be assessed taking into account 1) the position of the persons against whom the arrest warrants are requested in the sense that they should focus on the most senior leaders; 2) the roles they play in the group commission of systematic or large-scale crimes; 3) the overall role played by said group in the commission of crimes within that situation (so that these persons are those suspected of being most responsible).[24] In the Chamber's opinion, 'only by concentrating on this type of individual can the deterrent effects of the activities of the Court be maximised'[25] because other senior leaders in

18 Ibid, para.47.
19 Ibid (emphasis added).
20 Ibid, para.48 (quoting para.5 of the Preamble of the RS).
21 Ibid, para.49.
22 Ibid, para.50.
23 Ibid, para.51 (emphases added).
24 Ibid, paras 52–3.
25 Ibid, para.55.

similar circumstances will then endeavour to prevent the commission of international crimes to avoid their own prosecution.[26]

After a lengthy scrutiny of precedents pertaining to the International Criminal Tribunal for the Former Yugoslavia (ICTY) and the International Criminal Tribunal for Rwanda (ICTR) aimed at justifying the prosecution of senior leaders,[27] the Chamber recalled that the 2003 Paper on Some Policy Issues before the Office of the Prosecutor agreed on the policy need to investigate and prosecute cases involving 'those who bear the greatest responsibility, such as the leaders of the State or organisation allegedly responsible for those crimes'.[28] The Chamber concluded by providing a brief recap of its view on sufficient gravity[29] – possibly in the hope that the decision would be used in the future as a jurisprudential reference on this issue.

Having done this abstract examination, the Chamber went on to apply its findings to the request for an arrest warrant at hand. According to the Chamber, the case of Lubanga met the large-scale requirement,[30] he was a senior leader of the relevant armed group,[31] and he was suspected to be the individual most responsible for the alleged crimes.[32] Consequently, the Chamber found that the case against Lubanga reached the gravity threshold of the RS.[33] However, in relation to Ntaganda, the Chamber observed that, although the large-scale and social alarms tests were met, it did not pass the test regarding being the most senior leader suspected of the commission of the crime since Ntaganda 'ranked third in the hierarchy' of the armed group[34] and did not contribute effectively to the decision-making process.[35] Since Ntaganda was not 'among the most senior leaders',[36] the Chamber concluded that the gravity test was not met.[37]

---

26 Ibid.

27 Ibid, paras 56–61.

28 Ibid, para.62 (quoting *Paper on Some Policy Issues before the Office of the Prosecutor* (Sep 2003), 7).

29 Situation in the DRC, PTC I, Decision on the Prosecutor's Application for Warrants of Arrest, Article 58, ICC-01/04-520-Anx2, 10 Feb 2006, para.64.

30 Ibid, paras 65–6.

31 Ibid, paras 67–9.

32 Ibid, para.70.

33 Ibid, para.75.

34 Ibid, para.79.

35 Ibid, paras 83 and 87.

36 Ibid, para.85.

37 Ibid, para.89.

2.2.2 Criticisms of the decision of PTC I on the arrest warrants for Lubanga and Ntaganda

PTC I's assessment of sufficient gravity in the arrest warrants decision regarding Lubanga and Ntaganda is a pivotal turning point in the discussion on gravity. On the one hand, it was the first time that a Chamber had issued a *decision* on sufficient gravity,[38] providing granular and sophisticated reasoning that, potentially, would have a lasting impact on the identification of the factors relevant for the assessment of sufficient gravity. On the other hand, the reasoning was convoluted and did not stand up to rigorous scrutiny. Unsurprisingly, the decision was quickly appealed by the OTP[39] and subsequently overturned by the AC.[40] However, the rich analysis provided by the PTC deserves attention as a testament to its effort to identify relevant factors.

The first criticism pertains to methodology. Correctly, the Chamber identified treaty interpretation as the relevant framework to be taken into account, relying on the rules embodied in the VCLT.[41] However, the Chamber did not properly explain how its threefold test was the product of the application of the criteria embodied in Article 31 of the VCLT.[42] Literal interpretation was not applied to the expression 'sufficient gravity' but only to the word 'shall' in order to conclude that the application of Article 17(1)(d) is mandatory.[43] In fact, literal interpretation was not applied to sufficient gravity at all. Moreover, the PTC did not explain how the two factors of scale and social alarm were linked to the context of Article 17(1)(d): rather, it ignored all the factors listed in Article 31(2) of the VCLT as part of the context of a treaty provision. Finally, the discussion on the object and purpose of the treaty – albeit less superficial

---

[38] Susana SáCouto and Katherine Cleary, 'The Gravity Threshold of the International Criminal Court' (2008) 23 AUILR 807, 838.

[39] Situation in the DRC, Prosecutor's Appeal against PTC I's 10 Feb 2006 'Decision on the Prosecutor's Application for Warrants of Arrest, Article 58', ICC-01/04-01/06, 14 Feb 2006; Situation in the DRC, Public Redacted Version of the Prosecutor's Document in Support of the Appeal, ICC-01/04-120-Red, 3 Mar 2006 (public redacted on 28 Jan 2011).

[40] Situation in the DRC, AC, Judgment on the Prosecutor's appeal against the decision of PTC I entitled 'Decision on the Prosecutor's Application for Warrants of Arrest, Article 58', ICC-01/04-169, 13 Jul 2006.

[41] See above, Chapter 2, subsection 3.2.

[42] Without reference to the VCLT, one author considered this 'a creative interpretation … not developed in full detail' (Carsten Stahn, 'Judicial Review of Prosecutorial Discretion: Five Years On' in Carsten Stahn and Göran Sluiter (eds), *The Emerging Practice of the International Criminal Court* (Brill 2009) 247, 274–5).

[43] Situation in the DRC, PTC I, Decision on the Prosecutor's Application for Warrants of Arrest, Article 58, ICC-01/04-520-Anx2, 10 Feb 2006, para.44.

than that of the context – lacked nuance, focusing only on one object and purpose of the RS, that is, deterrence, and linking it only to the seniority of the leaders of an armed group or army. Overall, it was unclear how the Chamber could legitimately distil distinct factors from different interpretive criteria listed in Article 31 of the VCLT: this is the general rule (singular!) on treaty interpretation, and all the criteria should be considered together when interpreting a treaty provision.[44]

Coming to the specific factors identified by the PTC, it is interesting to note that the large-scale character (quantitative element) was balanced with the qualitative element of social alarm. As discussed below, this mix between quantitative and qualitative factors has since prevailed in the practice of the OTP and in subsequent decisions of the Chamber,[45] but, at the time the PTC was articulating its decision, the assessment was limited to two factors only.[46] Social alarm is an evanescent notion that is subject to double standards. One could question whose alarm should be considered: that of States Parties to the RS? That the judges and the OTP? That highlighted by civil society (through the work of non-governmental organisations, the media, and so on)? That pertaining to the international community as a whole or the relevant local community?[47] PTC I did not offer any answers to these questions.[48] Accordingly, this factor has been criticised for being 'so ill-defined and subjective a term as to be impossible to apply with any consistency or universal acceptance'.[49] What amounts to social alarm beyond the selection of crimes provided by the drafters of the Statute may be distorted by the actions of the mass media, which 'tend to highlight certain international crimes over others … not necessarily [for] political bias, but simply because cognitive heuristics lead us all to focus our attention on the most visibly palpable of wrongs'.[50]

---

[44] See above, Chapter 2, subsection 3.2.1.

[45] See below, section 3.

[46] The need to consider more factors is noted by SáCouto and Cleary, n.38, 839–43.

[47] Ibid, 840. See also William A Schabas, 'Regions, Regionalism and International Criminal Law' (2007) 4 New Zealand YIL 3, 21.

[48] See William A Schabas, 'Prosecutorial Discretion v Judicial Activism at the International Criminal Court' (2008) 6 JICJ 731, 743.

[49] Ray Murphy, 'Gravity Issues and the International Criminal Court' (2006) 17 CLF 281, 289. See also Andreas Schüller, '"Gravity" under the Rome Statute: Procedural Filter or Instrument of Shaping Criminal Policy?' (2009) 21 *Humanitäres Völkerrecht Informationsschriften* 73, 80; Ignaz Stegmiller, *The Pre-Investigation Stage of the ICC: Criteria for Situation Selection* (D&H 2011) 349–50.

[50] Mark Osiel, 'When Law "Expresses" More than It Cares to Admit: Comments on Heller' in Carsten Stahn and Larissa Van den Herik (eds), *Future*

All in all, the ICC was not created to punish only 'spectacular' cases, which raise significant social alarm, but also 'banal' ones, which might ordinarily occur even in democratic societies.[51] Indeed, although the Preamble of the RS refers to crimes 'that deeply shock the conscience of humanity', this expression refers to the reasons behind the criminalisation of certain conduct (a problem of jurisdiction) rather than to the admissibility of cases pertaining to those crimes (as in relation to sufficient gravity).

Even those who initially supported this factor[52] ended up criticising it in unequivocally. Commenting on PTC I's 2015 decision that echoed considerations based on social alarm (by referring to 'the attention and concern that these events attracted from the parties involved, also leading to several fact-finding efforts on behalf of States and the United Nations'),[53] a commentator observed that this is 'a dangerous dicta [*sic*] – a dream come true for the ICC's critics, who have always insisted that the Court's work will be driven by politics, not law' because this paragraph 'does indeed seem to suggest that the gravity of particular crimes is a function, at least in part, of how much attention the international community pays to them'.[54] If such a factor is included in the gravity assessment, not only would it make 'a mockery of the Court's independence, [but it would] def[y] common sense: just as crimes the world obsesses over might be insufficiently grave to warrant investigation, crimes the world ignores could be more than grave enough'.[55] It is imperative to acknowledge that the assessment of sufficient gravity pertaining to alleged interna-

---

Perspectives in International Criminal Justice (TMC Asser Press 2010) 254, 257.

[51] See generally Ioannis Kalpouzos and Itamar Mann, 'Banal Crimes Against Humanity: The Detention of Asylum Seekers in Greece' (2015) 16 Melbourne JIL 1 (especially at 24–8).

[52] See Kevin Jon Heller, 'Situational Gravity under the Rome Statute' in Carten Stahn and Larissa Van den Herik (eds), *Future Perspectives in International Criminal Justice* (TMC Asser Press 2010), 227, 233–7. For some qualified support, see Melanie O'Brien, 'Prosecutorial Discretion as an Obstacle to Prosecution of United Nations Peacekeepers by the International Criminal Court: The Big Fish/Small Fish Debate and the Gravity Threshold' (2012) 10 JICJ 525, 539–40.

[53] Situation on Registered Vessels, PTC I, Decision on the request of the Union of the Comoros to review the Prosecutor's decision not to initiate an investigation, ICC-01/13-34, 16 Jul 2015, para.51.

[54] Kevin Jon Heller, 'The Most Distressing Paragraph in the Comoros Review Decision', *Opinio Juris* (19 Jul 2015), https://opiniojuris.org/2015/07/19/the-most-distressing-paragraph-in-the-comoros-review-decision/. See, also, Alexander Geert-Jan Knoops and Tom Zwart, 'The Flotilla Case before the ICC: The Need to Do Justice While Keeping the Heavens Intact' (2015) 15 ICLR 1069, 1096–7.

[55] Heller, ibid.

tional crimes must be performed 'without regard to what the international community thinks about them'.[56]

The seniority factor has also been criticised.[57] As noted, 'the [RS] does not speak of the most senior leaders; it specifically refers to the "perpetrators of the most serious crimes"', and there is the risk that PTC I's approach 'may exclude others equally culpable of heinous crimes, but who did not hold positions of authority'.[58] The celebrated aim of deterrence, employed by the PTC I to justify this factor, would thus be frustrated,[59] especially considering that senior leaders often need ordinary soldiers to commit international crimes.[60] Accordingly, the overwhelming view among observers is that the factor of seniority should not be considered a mandatory criterion under the RS; in certain cases, less senior figures should be prosecuted.[61] Indeed, the fact that PTC I quoted the *Paper on Some Policy Issues by the OTP*[62] is misleading:[63] the paper acknowledges that sometimes less senior figures can be prosecuted, since it observes that seniority is 'a general rule'.[64]

Accordingly, although PTC I should be lauded for its attempt to identify factors determining gravity through treaty interpretation and based on legal considerations, its conclusions regarding the Lubanga and Ntaganda arrest warrants are not sound. It is unsurprising that they were quickly reversed.

2.2.3 The overturn of the gravity assessment in the decision of PTC I on the arrest warrants for Lubanga and Ntaganda

The appeal by the OTP embodies many criticisms raised before or subsequently by scholars, as well as many of the solutions then adopted by the AC. To limit repetition, this subsection deals primarily with the agreement between

---

56 Ibid.

57 The less critical voice seems to be that of Schabas, n.48, 746.

58 Murphy, n.49, 293 (with references to the Preamble and to Article 5 of the RS). See also Schüller, n.49, 80.

59 Frédéric Mégret, 'La Cour pénale internationale: a-t-elle fonctionné comme prévu?' in Julian Fernandez and Olivier de Frouville (eds), *Le mutations de la justice pénale internationale?* (Pedone 2018) 81, 108.

60 Schüller, n.49, 80–81; Stahn, n.42, 275; Mégret, ibid, 108.

61 See, for example, Mohamed M El Zeidy, 'The Gravity Threshold under the Statute of the International Criminal Court' (2008) 19 CLF 35, 49; SáCouto and Cleary, n.38, 846–8.

62 Situation in the DRC, PTC I, Decision on the Prosecutor's Application for Warrants of Arrest, Article 58, ICC-01/04-520-Anx2, 10 Feb 2006, para.62.

63 El Zeidy, n.61, 50; Stahn, n.42, 275.

64 OTP, *Paper on Some Policy Issues before the Office of the Prosecutor* (Sep 2003), 7.

the OTP and the AC on why PTC I's decision was wrong in relation to sufficient gravity.

The OTP and the AC disagreed with almost every finding of PTC I in relation to the identification of the factors that should be relevant under Article 17(1)(d). In relation to the fact that the crime should be systematic or large-scale,[65] the AC rejected this finding because it confused jurisdiction and admissibility: correctly, the AC noted that, in relation to war crimes, Article 8(1) of the RS mentions large-scale commission as alternative, rather than cumulative, to the fact that the crimes are committed in pursuance of a policy.[66] In any case, the AC recalled that this requirement is not mandatory for war crimes; Article 8(1) considers that war crimes fall within the ICC's jurisdiction 'in particular' when committed on a large scale or in pursuance of a policy, rather than 'exclusively',[67] thereby leaving room for the possibility of isolated war crimes reaching sufficient gravity.[68] Finally, the AC observed that the 'systematic' commission of crimes is a jurisdictional component of Article 7 on crimes against humanity but it is not mentioned in relation to war crimes.[69] For these reasons, the AC endorsed the view of the OTP, according to which 'a legal requirement of "large-scale or systematic" within article 17 (1) (d) of the Statute would not only render inutile article 8 (1) of the Statute contrary to the principles of interpretation but would further contradict the express intent of the drafters in rejecting any such fixed requirement therein'.[70] Moreover,

---

65 Situation in the DRC, PTC I, Decision on the Prosecutor's Application for Warrants of Arrest, Article 58, ICC-01/04-520-Anx2, 10 Feb 2006, para.47.

66 Situation in the DRC, AC, Judgment on the Prosecutor's appeal against the decision of PTC I entitled 'Decision on the Prosecutor's Application for Warrants of Arrest, Article 58', ICC-01/04-169, 13 Jul 2006, para.70.

67 Ibid.

68 Confusion on the value of the *chapeau* in Article 8(1) is significant. Former Prosecutor Moreno Ocampo, discharging the value of the words 'in particular', erroneously held that '[s]uch a threshold is not an element of the crime but rather a criterion on jurisdiction' (Luis Moreno Ocampo, *War and Justice in the 21st Century: A Case Study on the International Criminal Court and its Interaction with the War on Terror* (OUP 2022) 277). Another commentator considered the chapeau as providing a special gravity threshold that should replace that in Article 17(1)(d) (Javier Dondé Matute, 'La política criminal de la Fiscalíade la Corte Penal Internacionalpara el inicio de investigaciones' (2014) 14 AMDI 31, 47).

69 Situation in the DRC, AC, Judgment on the Prosecutor's appeal against the decision of PTC I entitled 'Decision on the Prosecutor's Application for Warrants of Arrest, Article 58', ICC-01/04-169, 13 Jul 2006, para.70.

70 Ibid, para.71 (in agreement with Situation in the DRC, Public Redacted Version of the Prosecutor's Document in Support of the Appeal,

PTC I's view 'would be inconsistent with article 8 (1) of the Statute if a war crime that was not part of a plan or policy or part of a large-scale commission could not, under any circumstances, be brought before the [ICC] because of the gravity requirement'.[71]

The OTP and the AC also found that the factor of social alarm was incorrect. In the OTP's words, this 'criterion is not a relevant and reliable criterion with respect to gravity of crimes, since it depends on subjective and contingent reactions rather than the objective gravity of the crimes'.[72] The AC echoed these concerns by noting that, on the one hand, PTC I failed to explain how it had identified this factor as relevant against the silence of the RS,[73] and, on the other, that the OTP was right to consider it based on subjective and contingent reactions to crimes rather than upon their objective gravity.[74]

The OTP and the AC also agreed that the reference to most senior leaders suspected to be most responsible for the alleged crimes was unpersuasive. Although the OTP conceded that 'the extent of responsibility of the perpetrator is an appropriate factor in assessing the gravity of a case', and that this factor 'excludes cases against minor actors that clearly do not warrant an exercise of jurisdiction by the Court',[75] it disagreed with the employment of these 'more stringent standards, such as "persons most responsible", or "those bearing the greatest responsibility"' as a matter of admissibility.[76] The OTP argued that the test espoused by PTC I was even more stringent because these expressions 'are not restricted to those in high leadership positions [as in the

ICC-01/04-120-Red, 3 Mar 2006, para.46).

71 Situation in the DRC, AC, Judgment on the Prosecutor's appeal against the decision of PTC I entitled 'Decision on the Prosecutor's Application for Warrants of Arrest, Article 58', ICC-01/04-169, 13 Jul 2006, para.71 (in agreement with Situation in the DRC, Public Redacted Version of the Prosecutor's Document in Support of the Appeal, ICC-01/04-120-Red, 3 Mar 2006, para.46).

72 Situation in the DRC, Public Redacted Version of the Prosecutor's Document in Support of the Appeal, ICC-01/04-120-Red, 3 Mar 2006, para.49. See also, one decade later, in a different situation, Situation on Registered Vessels, OTP, Final decision of the Prosecution concerning the 'Article 53(1) Report', ICC-01/13-6-AnxA, dated 6 Nov 2014, as revised and refiled in accordance with the PTC's request of 15 Nov 2018 and the AC's judgment of 2 Sept 2019, ICC-01/13-99-Anx1, 2 Dec 2019, paras 49–50.

73 Situation in the DRC, AC, Judgment on the Prosecutor's appeal against the decision of PTC I entitled 'Decision on the Prosecutor's Application for Warrants of Arrest, Article 58', ICC-01/04-169, 13 Jul 2006, para.72.

74 Ibid.

75 Situation in the DRC, Public Redacted Version of the Prosecutor's Document in Support of the Appeal, ICC-01/04-120-Red, 3 Mar 2006, para.30.

76 Ibid.

Chamber's view], but also include notorious perpetrators who distinguish themselves by their extent of participation and responsibility for particularly serious or notorious crimes'.[77] Overall, the OTP disagreed with PTC I that a seniority approach would have a deterrent effect: such a restrictive view on gravity would: '[leave] the Court legally and permanently unable to address persons outside an extremely circumscribed set of perpetrators. This would undermine, not strengthen, the Court's deterrent effect.'[78] Indeed, such an approach: 'would send a disastrous signal, at the beginning of this permanent Court's operations, to other senior or mid-level leaders and perpetrators of exceptionally serious crimes that they have nothing to fear from the ICC – the ICC is legally barred from pursuing them.'[79]

The AC shared these concerns, by noting that the suggestion that: 'the deterrent effect is highest if all other categories of perpetrators cannot be brought before the Court is difficult to understand. It seems more logical to assume that the deterrent effect of the Court is highest if no category of perpetrators is per se excluded from potentially being brought before the Court.'[80] The AC went on to criticise the sub-factors assessed by PTC I in the practical ascertainment of who bears the greatest responsibility in relation to a specific crime.[81] Acutely, the AC pointed out clashes with the context of Article 17(1)(d): for instance, Article 33 of the RS clarifies that superior orders are irrelevant exactly because the drafters envisaged the possibility of prosecuting low-ranking perpetrators.[82] On these bases, the AC concluded that the assessment of sufficient gravity performed by PTC I was incorrect.[83]

It is interesting to note that the AC was not required to offer any view on sufficient gravity. In the first part of its decision, for procedural reasons that are discussed subsequently,[84] the AC considered that, when examining a request

---

77 Ibid.

78 Ibid, para.42.

79 Ibid.

80 Situation in the DRC, AC, Judgment on the Prosecutor's appeal against the decision of PTC I entitled 'Decision on the Prosecutor's Application for Warrants of Arrest, Article 58', ICC-01/04-169, 13 Jul 2006, para.73. See also ibid, para.75. For scholarly support, see, for example, Ward Ferdinandusse and Alex Whiting, 'Prosecute Little Fish at the ICC' (2021) 19 JICJ 759, 763–4.

81 Situation in the DRC, AC, Judgment on the Prosecutor's appeal against the decision of PTC I entitled 'Decision on the Prosecutor's Application for Warrants of Arrest, Article 58', ICC-01/04-169, 13 Jul 2006, paras 74–7.

82 Ibid, para.78.

83 Ibid, para.82.

84 This issue is mentioned above, Chapter 3, subsection 4.2.4, and discussed in detail below, section 3.1.

for an arrest warrant, a PTC had no power to scrutinise sufficient gravity.[85] However, the AC felt compelled to review the factors discussed by PTC I to bar them from coalescing in the early practice of the ICC.[86] Nevertheless, it limited its intervention in shaping the future developments of the factors relevant for sufficient gravity to the rejection of PTC I's test.[87] Although the OTP attempted to formulate relevant factors in the context of that appeal, the AC remained silent on which factors should be considered in the assessment of sufficient gravity. This silence, criticised by some observers as a missed opportunity,[88] permitted the OTP and Chambers to develop their own factors in subsequent cases.

3. THE FOUR MAIN GRAVITY FACTORS: SCALE, NATURE, MANNER OF COMMISSION, AND IMPACT

This section explores the convergence of the OTP and the Chambers on four well-established factors to determine gravity: scale, nature, manner of commission, and impact. Even in cases of disagreement as to the weight to be attributed to these factors, both the OTP and the Chambers still agree on the application of the same four factors to assess sufficient gravity. Accordingly, it is necessary to study how these factors emerged, consolidated, and developed since they now constitute the practice of ICC organs in the interpretation and application of Article 17(1)(d) of the RS.

---

85 Situation in the DRC, AC, Judgment on the Prosecutor's appeal against the decision of PTC I entitled 'Decision on the Prosecutor's Application for Warrants of Arrest, Article 58', ICC-01/04-169, 13 Jul 2006, paras 41–53.

86 Ibid, para.54.

87 Occasionally, and incorrectly, PTC I's view is still cited as good law. See, for example, Situation in Kenya, PTC II, *Prosecutor v Muthaura et al*, Defence Challenge to Jurisdiction, Admissibility and Prosecution's Failure to Meet the Requirements of Article 54, ICC-01/09-02/11-338, 19 Sep 2011, paras 60 and 64, and the harsh response in Situation in Kenya, *Prosecutor v Muthaura et al,* OTP, Prosecution's Response to the Defence Challenges to Jurisdiction, ICC-01/09-02/11-356, 14 Oct 2011, paras 44–5. See also the reliance by Abdoul Aziz Mbaye and Sam Sasan Shoamanesh, 'Article 17' in Julian Fernandez, Xavier Pacreau and Muriel Ubeda-Saillard (eds), *Statut de Rome de la Cour Pénale Internationale: Commentaire Article par Article* (2nd edn, Pedone 2019) 867, 871–2 (never mentioning the overturning).

88 Dov Jacobs, 'Arrest Warrants and Admissibility - Commentary' in André Klip and Göran Sluiter (eds), *Annotated Leading Cases of International Criminal Tribunals, VolXXIII: The International Criminal Court: 2005–2007* (Intersentia 2010) 113, 120; Stegmiller, n.49, 98.

This section does not deal directly with another element that is often mentioned along with the four factors as an essential component of the gravity assessment: whether the alleged perpetrator is likely the 'most responsible' for the crimes. This consideration is addressed separately below in section 4.

3.1 The Early Formulation in the OTP's Appeal against PTC I's Gravity Assessment in the Lubanga and Ntaganda Arrest Warrants

The first time the OTP articulated its view on the factors determining gravity was probably during the appeal against the Lubanga and Ntaganda arrest warrants decision by PTC I. In criticising the test laid out by PTC I, the OTP elaborated its own factors, recognising that 'the degree of *scale* and the *degree of organization* may be relevant considerations in assessing the gravity of crimes, along with other factors'.[89] Moreover, the OTP, while rejecting the social alarm test, noted that 'international reactions, including Security Council resolutions may be relevant considerations, not as a direct indicator of "social alarm", but insofar as they are evidentiary indicators that the crimes have had a significant *impact* on the community or region'.[90] Indeed, '[t]he underlying issue should remain the gravity of the crimes, with *impact being a factor for consideration* (as possibly evidenced by international reactions)'.[91]

At this point, the OTP suggested that: '[i]f the Appeals Chamber chooses to elaborate a test under Article 17 (1) (d), ... the standard should be a basic test, taking into account as factors the gravity of the crimes and the extent of responsibility of the person. ... the list of factors should be non-exhaustive, to take into account unforeseen future circumstances.'[92] The OTP went on to offer its own view on the factors that should be assessed, suggesting that 'with respect to *gravity of crimes*, relevant factors include: the *nature or severity* of the crimes; the *scale* of the crimes (including number of victims); the degree of *systematicity*, where applicable; the *impact* of the crimes; and any particularly *aggravating aspects in the manner of commission* of the crimes'.[93] The OTP added that the responsibility of the accused should also be assessed alongside the gravity of crimes, a topic that is discussed below in section 4.

---

89 Situation in the DRC, Public Redacted Version of the Prosecutor's Document in Support of the Appeal, ICC-01/04-120-Red, 3 Mar 2006, para.48 (emphases added).

90 Ibid, para.49 (emphasis added).

91 Ibid (emphasis added).

92 Ibid, para.53.

93 Ibid, para.54 (emphasis added).

All the factors subsequently endorsed – scale, nature, manner of commission, and impact – are present here in an embryonic form. This list of factors is longer than the one ultimately crystallised in judicial practice: some factors mentioned here are not be included as autonomous factors in subsequent elaborations, such as systematicity.[94] However, it is clear that the list of factors that are relevant is an open list, which can be adapted to different contexts.

3.2 The Four Factors in the OTP's Policy Papers and Regulations

After the appeal decision in the Lubanga and Ntaganda arrest warrants, both the OTP and the Chambers have consistently referred to the four factors of scale, nature, manner of commission, and impact in the assessment of sufficient gravity. The following subsections analyse how these factors have evolved in the interplay between the OTP and the Chambers, and how they are assessed as external to the *actus reus*, *mens rea*, and modes of liability (which are relevant for jurisdictional purposes). Since the consolidation of these factors is the product of the interplay between the practice and decisions of different ICC organs, it is better to describe the evolution of each of these factors through this interplay, rather than presenting the views of the OTP and the Chambers separately. In exploring this process of consolidation, it is also necessary to recall that the OTP expresses its views both in general terms, in its policy papers, and in relation to concrete situations and cases. In contrast, due to their mandate, Chambers can only assess the factors relevant to gravity in relation to specific cases brought before them, reacting to the views of the OTP and, to a lesser extent, of the defendants, victims, and states with jurisdiction over the alleged crimes.

The OTP was the driving force behind the consolidation of the four factors after they were proposed, but not accepted, in the appeal regarding the Lubanga and Ntaganda arrest warrants. In the *Report on the Activities Performed during the First Three Years (Jun 2003 – Jun 2006)*,[95] published a couple of months after the appeal decision, the OTP confirmed that '[a]lthough any crime falling within the jurisdiction of the Court is a serious matter, the [RS] (articles 53(1)(b), 53(2)(b) and 17(1)(d)) clearly foresees and requires an additional consideration of "gravity" whereby the Office must determine that a case is of sufficient gravity to justify further action by the Court'.[96] The OTP went on to determine that 'factors relevant in assessing gravity include: the scale of the crimes; the nature of the crimes; the manner of commission of the crimes; and the impact

[94] See below, subsection 3.4.3.

[95] OTP, *Report on the Activities Performed during the First Three Years (Jun 2003 – Jun 2006)* (12 Sep 2006).

[96] Ibid, 6.

of the crimes'.[97] A couple of days later, the OTP reiterated these views in the *Report on Prosecutorial Strategy*.[98] In neither document did the OTP offer any source in support of why these factors were relevant: absent any reference to treaty interpretation, the documents merely included references to a 'Draft Policy Paper on Selection Criteria' as the basis for why the factors should be considered relevant to gravity.[99] In both documents, the list of factors is not exhaustive and is introduced by the word 'include'.

The scale, nature, manner of commission, and impact of the crimes quickly became the central factors in the OTP's view on sufficient gravity. For instance, these factors were mentioned in the 2007 *Policy Paper on the Interests of Justice*, where they are presented as a higher threshold than the jurisdictional one created by the substantive rules on international crimes.[100] Similarly, the *Report on Prosecutorial Strategy (2009–2012)* lists these four factors as components of the assessment of sufficient gravity.[101]

More relevantly, in the Regulations of the OTP, which entered into force in 2009, the OTP crystallised these criteria. Article 29(2), on the initiation of an investigation or prosecution, states that: '[i]n order to assess the gravity of the crimes allegedly committed in the situation the Office shall consider various factors including their scale, nature, manner of commission, and impact.'[102] No definition of these factors is offered by the Regulations.

It is important to note the legal value of the Regulations: Article 1(1) affirms that '[t]hese Regulations have been adopted pursuant to article 42, paragraph 2 [of the RS], and rule 9 [of the RPE] and shall govern the operations of the [OTP] in relation to its management and administration'. Indeed, Article 42(2) of the RS states that '[t]he Prosecutor shall have full authority over the management and administration of the Office', while Rule 9 of the Rules of Procedure and Evidence (RPE) affirms that '[i]n discharging his or her responsibility for the management and administration of the [OTP], the Prosecutor shall put in place regulations to govern the operation of the Office'. It is clear that, by including the four gravity factors in the Regulations, the OTP meant to consolidate their position within the RS: although the Regulations 'shall be read

97 Ibid, 6.

98 OTP, *Report on Prosecutorial Strategy* (14 Sept 2006) 5.

99 OTP, *Report on the Activities Performed during the First Three Years (Jun 2003 – Jun 2006)* (12 Sept 2006), 6, n.1; OTP, *Report on Prosecutorial Strategy* (14 Sept 2006) 5, n.2.

100 OTP, *Policy Paper on the Interests of Justice* (Sept 2007) 5 (note: the word 'include' is not present, and the list of factors is presented as exhaustive).

101 OTP, *Report on Prosecutorial Strategy (2009–2012)* (1 Feb 2010), para.20.

102 OTP, Regulations of the OTP (entered into force 23 Apr 2009).

subject to the Statute, the Rules, and the Regulations of the Court'[103] – which are the primary sources that the ICC in its entirety has to apply under Article 21(1)(a) – their authority and legitimacy are anchored to the RS (which tasks the Prosecutor with the management and administration of the Office) and the RPE (which mentions the regulation as a way to manage and administer the Office).

Accordingly, the Regulations pertain to the activity of the OTP only. Formally speaking, they do not bind other ICC organs. Yet, their influence has been substantive, with various Chambers endorsing the four factors after their inclusion in the Regulations.

3.3 The Convergence of the OTP and the Chambers on the Four Factors

In relation to several situations and cases, the OTP and the Chambers have applied the four factors – or some of them – in agreement. The convergence of these different organs contributed to the consolidation of the four factors in the assessment of sufficient gravity.

On 26 November 2009, the OTP assessed sufficient gravity in its request for authorisation of an investigation pursuant to Article 15 in relation to Kenya,[104] invoking the scale of the crimes, their brutal manner of commission, and their impact on victims as a reason to consider the gravity threshold under Article 17(1)(d) of the RS to have been met.[105] In response, PTC II considered that the assessment of sufficient gravity should be performed following a quantitative and qualitative approach.[106] The Chamber went on to state that '[r]egarding the qualitative dimension, it is not the number of victims that matter but rather the existence of some aggravating or qualitative factors attached to the commission of crimes, which makes it grave'.[107] PTC II held that 'several factors concerning sentencing as reflected in rule 145(1)(c) and (2)(b)(iv) of the Rules could provide useful guidance in such an examination'.[108] In PTC II's opinion:

> [t]hese factors could be summarized as: (i) the scale of the alleged crimes (including assessment of geographical and temporal intensity); (ii) the nature of the unlawful

---

[103] Ibid, Regulation 1(1).

[104] Situation in Kenya, OTP, Request for authorisation of an investigation pursuant to Article 15, ICC-01/09-3, 26 Nov 2009.

[105] Ibid, paras 56–9.

[106] Situation in Kenya, PTC II, Decision Pursuant to Article 15 of the Rome Statute on the Authorization of an Investigation into the Situation in the Republic of Kenya, ICC-01/09-19-Corr, 31 Mar 2010, para.62.

[107] Ibid.

[108] Ibid.

behaviour or of the crimes allegedly committed; (iii) the employed means for the execution of the crimes (i.e., the manner of their commission); and (iv) the impact of the crimes and the harm caused to victims and their families.[109]

Although it appears that PTC II considered scale, nature, manner of execution, and impact as the additional or aggravating factors to be taken into account in assessing sufficient gravity, the same decision, subsequently, considered that the assessment of sufficient gravity 'is guided by factors such as the scale, nature, manner of commission, impact of crimes committed on victims *and* the existence of aggravating circumstances (i.e., qualitative dimension)',[110] thus indicating that the aggravating circumstances are additional to the four factors. However, in granting the request by the OTP, PTC II applied the four factors only.[111] In any case, the reference to 'aggravating circumstances' in general is in conflict with the fact that, earlier, PTC II mentioned only RPE, Rule 145(2)(b)(iv), which codifies only one specific aggravating circumstance ('commission of the crime with particular cruelty or where there were multiple victims'): if all the aggravating circumstances would have mattered, the Chamber should have pointed towards Rule 145(2)(b) without specifying any sub-letter.

In 2010, in relation to the situation in Darfur, Sudan, PTC I revisited the test based on the rules on penalties that had been described by PTC II, referring to Rule 145(1)(c) of the RPE. According to the Chamber, this 'rule makes reference to "the extent of damage caused, in particular, the harm caused to victims and their families, the nature of the unlawful behaviour and the means employed to execute the crime", which … can serve as useful guidelines for the evaluation of the gravity threshold required by article 17(1)(d) of the Statute'.[112] Interestingly, this passage dropped the reference to Rule 145(2)(b) on the aggravating circumstances of 'commission of the crime with particular cruelty or where there were multiple victims'.

Similarly, on 23 June 2011, the OTP mentioned sufficient gravity in its request for an authorisation of an investigation in relation to Côte d'Ivoire,[113] referring to the four factors as codified in the Regulations of the OTP.[114] In the OTP's request: 'serious crimes by their very nature such as murders, rapes,

---

109 Ibid.

110 Ibid, para.188 (emphasis added).

111 Ibid, paras 190–200 (first reviewing the submissions by the OTP, then assessing sufficient gravity on the basis of those submissions).

112 Situation in Darfur, Sudan, PTC I, Decision on the Confirmation of Charges, ICC-02/05-02/09-243-Red, 8 Feb 2010, para.32.

113 Situation in Côte d'Ivoire, OTP, Request for authorisation of an investigation pursuant to article 15, ICC-02/11-3, 23 Jun 2011.

114 Ibid, para.54.

and enforced disappearances have been committed on a large-scale, as part of a plan or in furtherance of a policy, or in the context or association with an armed conflict. Many of these crimes were committed with cruelty and on ethnic, religious or politically discriminatory grounds.'[115] In authorising an investigation, PTC III endorsed the position taken by PTC II in relation to the situation in Kenya.[116] PTC III recalled that the assessment of the gravity of the crimes requires an examination of several factors, 'including, inter alia, their scale and nature, the manner in which they were carried out, their impact on the victims, and any aggravating circumstances'.[117] No further elaboration was offered, and no reference to the rules on the determination of penalties was explicitly made.

Subsequent judicial practice demonstrated that the OTP and various ICC Chambers agreed on this convergence. For instance, in the 2014 Article 53(1) *Report on the Situation on Registered Vessels of Comoros, Greece and Cambodia*, again the OTP claimed that '[a]s stipulated in regulation 29(2) of the Regulations of the Office, the non-exhaustive factors that guide the Office's assessment include the scale, nature, manner of commission of the crimes, and their impact'.[118] In response, PTC I recalled the past judicial decisions on the four factors, which are summarised as comprising 'nature, scale, and the manner of commission of the alleged crimes, as well as their impact on victims'.[119] The coincidence of the four factors was complete, even though the OTP and PTC I disagreed on how the factors should have been applied. Likewise, when, in 2015, the OTP considered that 'scale, nature, manner of commission of the crimes, and their impact' were, on the basis of the Regulations of the OTP, the relevant non-exhaustive factors to be taken into account in assessing sufficient

115 Ibid.

116 Situation in Côte d'Ivoire, PTC III, Corrigendum to 'Decision Pursuant to Article 15 of the Rome Statute on the Authorisation of an Investigation into the Situation in the Republic of Côte d'Ivoire', ICC-02/11-14-Corr, 15 Nov 2011, para.204.

117 Ibid.

118 Situation on Registered Vessels, OTP, Article 53(1) Report, 6 Nov 2014, para.134.

119 Situation on Registered Vessels, PTC I, Decision on the Request of the Union of the Comoros to review the Prosecutor's Decision not to Initiate an Investigation, ICC-01/13-34, 16 Jul 2015, para.21. See also Situation on Registered Vessels, PTC I, Decision on the 'Application for Judicial Review by the Government of the Comoros', ICC-01/13-111, 16 Sep 2020, para.20.

gravity in relation to the situation in Georgia,[120] PTC I agreed.[121] More ambiguously, in relation to the situation in Afghanistan, upon the OTP's invocation of the four factors in relation to the assessment of sufficient gravity,[122] PTC II found that the threshold of sufficient gravity was met,[123] but it did not articulate a gravity test based on the four factors.[124]

Particularly interesting to the crystallisation of the four factors are those cases in which the defendants raised, under Article 19 of the RS, challenges to the admissibility of the case due to lack of sufficient gravity. The four factors are more or less explicitly endorsed by the defendants. For instance, the 2014 challenge brought by Blé Goudé mentioned the four factors and Rule 145(1)(c) and (2)(b)(iv) of the RPE as the guidance needed to assess sufficient gravity.[125] The OTP demonstrated its continued agreement on the four factors, albeit with no reliance on rules on penalties.[126] Ultimately, PTC I endorsed the four factors as based on Rule 145(1)(c) and (2)(b)(iv) of the RPE,[127] rejecting, however, the challenge.[128]

---

[120] Situation in Georgia, Corrected Version of 'Request for authorisation of an investigation pursuant to article 15', 16 Oct 2015, ICC-01/15-4-Corr, ICC-01/15-4-Corr2, 17 Nov 2015, para.326. See also ibid, paras 330–37.

[121] Situation in Georgia, PTC I, Decision on the Prosecutor's request for authorization of an investigation, ICC-01/15-12, 27 Jan 2016, para.51.

[122] Situation in Afghanistan, Public redacted version of 'Request for authorisation of an investigation pursuant to article 15', ICC-02/17-7-Red 20-11-2017, 20 Nov 2017, para.336.

[123] Situation in Afghanistan, Decision Pursuant to Article 15 of the Rome Statute on the Authorisation of an Investigation into the Situation in Afghanistan, ICC-02/17-33, 12 Apr 2019, paras 80 and 86.

[124] The decision, however, refers more or less explicitly to scale (ibid, paras 81–3), nature (ibid, para.82), manner of commission (ibid, paras 81–4), and impact (ibid, paras 81–4).

[125] Situation in Côte d'Ivoire, *Prosecutor v Blé Goudé*, Defence application pursuant to Articles 19(4) and 17(1)(d) of the Rome Statute, ICC-02/11-02/11-171, 27 Sep 2014, paras 23–4.

[126] Situation in Côte d'Ivoire, *Prosecutor v Blé Goudé*, Prosecution's Response to the Defence application pursuant to Articles 19(4) and 17(1)(d) of the Rome Statute, ICC-02/11-02/11-181, 20 Oct 2014, para.25.

[127] Situation in Côte d'Ivoire, *Prosecutor v Blé Goudé*, PTC I, Decision on the Defence Challenge to the Admissibility of the Case against Charles Blé Goudé for Insufficient Gravity, ICC-02/11-02/11-185, 12 Nov 2014, paras 11–12.

[128] Ibid, para.22.

Similarly, despite a lack of detailed articulation of the four factors in arguing that the case was inadmissible,[129] the 2019 challenge brought by Al-Hassan made some references to the scale of the crimes.[130] In response, PTC I took the opportunity to reaffirm the relevance of some of the factors under Rule 145(1)(c),[131] including 'the extent of the damage caused ... to the victims and their families, the nature of the unlawful behaviour and the means employed to execute the crime; the degree of participation of the convicted person; the degree of intent; the circumstances of manner, time, and location'.[132] PTC I also noted that:

> [f]or the purposes of determining whether a case is of sufficient gravity, regard has also been had to the existence of any of the aggravating circumstances listed in rule 145(2)(b) of the Rules, inter alia, the "[c]ommission of the crime where the victim is particularly defenceless", the "[c]ommission of the crime with particular cruelty or where there were multiple victims" and the "[c]ommission of the crime for any motive involving discrimination".[133]

In reviewing this decision in 2020, the AC endorsed the four factors and their derivation from the rules on penalties by noting that:

> some factors listed in rule 145(1)(c) and 145(2)(b) of the Rules in relation to sentencing could provide relevant guidance to the assessment of gravity pursuant to article 17(1)(d), including the extent of the damage caused, the nature of the unlawful behaviour, the means employed to execute the crime, the degree of participation of the accused person, the degree of intent, the circumstances of manner, time and location, the existence of particularly defenceless victims, the commission of crimes with particular cruelty or where there are multiple victims, and the commission of crimes for any motive involving discrimination.[134]

The AC went on to state that

---

129 Situation in Mali, *Prosecutor v Al Hassan*, OTP, Public redacted version of 'Submissions for the confirmation of charges', CC-01/12-01/18-394-Red, 9 Jul 2019, paras 256–86.

130 Al Hassan, however, claimed that the charges against him did not reach the necessary scale: ibid, paras 263–5.

131 Situation in Mali, *Prosecutor v Al Hassan*, PTC I, Decision on the Admissibility Challenge raised by the Defence for Insufficient Gravity of the Case, ICC-01/12-01/18-459-tENG, 27 Sep 2019, para.48.

132 Ibid.

133 Ibid.

134 Situation in Mali, *Prosecutor v Al Hassan*, AC, Judgment on the appeal of Mr Al Hassan against the decision of PTC I entitled 'Décision relative à l'exception d'irrecevabilité pour insuffisance de gravité de l'affaire soulevée par la défense', ICC-01/12-01/18 OA, 19 Feb 2020, para.89.

> [a]lthough gravity under article 78(1) of the Statute and rule 145(1)(c) and 145(2)(b) of the Rules is assessed at a different stage of the proceedings (after a conviction has been entered), the [AC] considers that some of the factors pertinent to determining the appropriate sentence of a convicted person can serve as useful guidelines for the evaluation of the gravity requirement in article 17(1)(d) of the Statute as well. *This ensures a consistent understanding of gravity throughout the Statute.* The [AC] has recently confirmed that this assessment may include consideration of, inter alia, the extent of the damage caused, the nature of the unlawful behaviour, the circumstances of time and the degree of participation of the convicted person.[135]

This is the final word on the convergence of the four factors, which, in the Chambers' view, is the consequence of the application of certain rules on penalties.

Overall, from these examples, it is possible to conclude that, since 2006, the Chambers of the ICC, including the AC, have converged on the application of the four factors of scale, nature, manner of commission, and impact in the assessment of sufficient gravity under Article 17(1)(d). In doing so, the Chambers have echoed the OTP's position that these factors should be understood as the product of both quantitative and qualitative considerations, and that the list is not meant to be exhaustive. The distinctive contribution of the Chambers is that the factors determining gravity should be anchored to the rules on the determination of penalties as provided by Article 78(1) of the RS and Rule 145(1)(c) and (2)(b) of the RPE. In the *Al Hassan* case, the AC correctly noted that such an interpretation 'ensures a consistent understanding of gravity throughout the Statute'.[136]

The application of these four factors has become established case law within the ICC system.[137] Scholars usually consider the list of relevant factors favourably.[138] The following subsection explores the way in which each of the factors has evolved.

---

135 Ibid, para.93 (emphasis added).

136 Ibid. Approval is voiced by Kai Ambos, *Treatise on International Criminal Law: Vol.III: International Criminal Procedure* (2nd edn, OUP 2025) 286.

137 Aziz Mbaye and Sasan Shoamanesh, n.87, 873; Harmen van der Wilt, 'Selectivity in International Criminal Law: Asymmetrical Enforcement as a Problem for Theories of Punishment' in Florian Jessberger and Julia Geneuss (eds), *Why Punish Perpetrators of Mass Atrocities? Purposes of Punishment in International Criminal Law* (CUP 2020) 305, 312.

138 See the survey conducted (although among US international scholars) by Stuart Ford, 'Understanding Crime Gravity: Exploring the Views of International Criminal Law Experts' (2019) 27 *William & Mary Bill of Rights Journal* 659.

3.4 The Evolution of the Four Factors

This subsection traces the evolution of the four factors in the practice of the OTP and the Chambers. All the factors – scale, nature, manner of commission, and impact – are the product of assessing quantitative and qualitative considerations together.

3.4.1 Scale

As already noted, the factor of scale is the first factor that the OTP has invoked in its practice that predates the litigation on sufficient gravity in relation to the Lubanga and Ntaganda arrest warrants.[139] In its policy papers and judicial practice, the OTP has clarified that scale includes: 'the number of direct and indirect victims, the extent of damage caused by the crimes, in particular bodily or psychological harm caused to the victims and their families, or their geographical or temporal spread (high intensity of the crimes over a brief period or low intensity of crimes over an extended period).'[140] While references to numbers of victims and extent of damage points towards the quantitative character of this factor, geographical and temporal spread, with comparisons between intensity and timeframe of the crime, inject qualitative concerns into the assessment of scale.

In practice, the quantitative aspect is preponderant in the OTP's assessment of scale in specific instances. For instance, the OTP assessed scale in relation to the *Mavi Marmara* boarding in light of the overall passengers onboard, the casualties among them, and the number of the injured.[141] In relation to Afghanistan, the OTP considered as relevant both the fact that a multitude of international crimes appeared to have been committed and the fact that a multitude of direct and indirect victims could be identified,[142] noting that 'crimes are alleged to have occurred in every province throughout the territory of Afghanistan, with increasing frequency each year as the insurgency

---

[139] See above, section 2.1.

[140] OTP, *Policy Paper on Preliminary Examinations* (Nov 2013), para.62; OTP, *Policy Paper on Case Selection and Prioritisation* (15 Sept 2016), para.38; OTP, *Policy on Addressing Environmental Damage through the Rome Statute* (Dec 2025), para.20. See also Situation in Côte d'Ivoire, *Prosecutor v Blé Goudé*, Prosecution's Response to the Defence application pursuant to Articles 19(4) and 17(1)(d) of the Rome Statute, ICC-02/11-02/11-181, 20 Oct 2014, para.32.

[141] OTP, Situation on Registered Vessels, Article 53(1) Report, 6 Nov 2014, para.138.

[142] OTP, Situation in Afghanistan, PTC III, Public redacted version of 'Request for authorisation of an investigation pursuant to article 15', ICC-02/17-7-Conf-Exp, 20 Nov 2017, paras 339–40.

gained in strength'.[143] In 2023, in relation to the Philippines, the OTP cursorily noted that sufficient gravity was fulfilled because 'at least more than 5,000 and possibly as many as 30,000 civilians (including children) have been killed by police or by "unidentified" perpetrators apparently acting in coordination with police' and because 'the available information indicates that torture, other inhumane acts, and other crimes were also committed in connection with the "war on drugs" campaign'.[144] All in all, '[w]hile quantitative criteria alone (such as the number of victims) may not be dispositive of the gravity of a given case, it may be a significant factor in [a specific] instance'.[145]

Similarly, Chambers have approached scale mainly through a quantitative lens. In disagreeing that the scale of crimes allegedly committed in the *Mavi Marmara* incident did not reach the gravity threshold, PTC I noted that scale included the 10 victims and 50–5 cases of injuries, amounting to 'possibly hundreds of instances of outrages upon personal dignity, or torture or inhuman treatment'.[146] In 2016, PTC I observed that sufficient gravity was met in relation to scale because of: '51-113 killings, the destruction of over 5,000 dwellings and the forced displacement of 13,400 – 18,500 persons constituting, in the estimation of the Prosecutor, a 75 % decrease in the ethnically Georgian population in South Ossetia.'[147] In 2019, PTC I considered that the assessment of scale should have considered the fact that the charges 'amount[ed] to 13 counts of crimes against humanity and war crimes allegedly committed against the civilian population in Timbuktu and its region over a period of around 10 months'.[148] In this regard, the AC reflected on the role of scale in

---

[143] Ibid, para.340.

[144] OTP, Situation in the Philippines, Prosecution's response to the Philippine Government's Appeal Brief against 'Authorisation pursuant to article 18(2) of the Statute to resume the investigation' (ICC-01/21-65 OA), ICC-01/21-68, 4 Apr 2023, para.163.

[145] Situation in Afghanistan, Public redacted version of 'Prosecution's application under article 58 for a warrant of arrest against Abdul Hakim HAQQANI', ICC-02/17-225-Red, 23 Jan 2025, para.167; Situation in Afghanistan, Public redacted version of 'Prosecution's application under article 58 for a warrant of arrest against Haibatullah AKHUNDZADA', ICC-02/17-224-Red, 23 Jan 2025, para.166.

[146] Situation on Registered Vessels, PTC I, Decision on the Request of the Union of the Comoros to Review the Prosecutor's Decision Not to Initiate an Investigation, ICC-01/13-34, 16 Jul 2015, para.26.

[147] Situation in Georgia, PTC I, Decision on the Prosecutor's request for authorization of an investigation, ICC-01/15-12, 27 Jan 2016, para.54.

[148] Situation in Mali, *Prosecutor v Al Hassan*, PTC I, Decision on the Admissibility Challenge raised by the Defence for Insufficient Gravity of the Case, ICC-01/12-01/18-459-tENG, 27 Sep 2019, para.57.

light of participating victims, stating that it is not mere maths on the number of victims that matters,[149] but rather:

> the number of victims is a relevant consideration in the assessment of the gravity requirement under article 17(1)(d) of the Statute, pertaining to the quantitative gravity assessment. … [W]hile relevant, quantitative criteria are not per se determinative of the gravity of a given case … in determining the number of victims, the number of participating victims may provide some indication of the scope of victimhood within the context of a case.[150]

The conclusion of the AC is that '[t]he relevance of the number of participating victims to a gravity assessment pursuant to article 17(1)(d) must be assessed on a case-by-case basis',[151] as a component of the factor of scale that needs to be weighed against other factors.[152]

The inclusion of scale as a factor in the assessment of sufficient gravity is easy to explain. A case with significant scale implies that harm and damage occurred to a large number of victims. Since the RS places victims at the centre of the entire international criminal justice project, as emphasised in the Preamble and in the rules on victims' participation and reparations, a vast number of victims makes a case sufficiently grave.[153]

3.4.2 Nature

The nature of the crimes is a factor that has sparked some significant judicial debate due to its inherent elusiveness. The evolution of the way in which this factor has been construed and applied by the OTP shows that nature is interrelated to the other factor of the manner of commission, with significant overlap and confusion.[154] In the 2013 *Policy Paper on Preliminary Examinations*, the 2014 *Policy Paper on Sexual and Gender-Based Crimes*, and the 2016 *Policy*

---

149 Situation in Mali, *Prosecutor v Al Hassan*, AC, Judgment on the appeal of Mr Al Hassan against the decision of PTC I entitled 'Décision relative à l'exception d'irrecevabilité pour insuffisance de gravité de l'affaire soulevée par la défense', ICC-01/12-01/18 OA, 19 Feb 2020, para.121

150 Ibid, para.97.

151 Ibid.

152 Ibid, paras 101–102.

153 Mohammad Hadi Zakerhossein, *Situation Selection Regime at the International Criminal Court: Law, Policy, Practice* (Intersentia 2017) 221–2.

154 Indeed, in a different context, the International Law Commission (ILC) discussed the meaning of the 'nature of the crime' under the RS, by noting that '[s]eriousness can be deduced either by the nature of the act in question (cruelty, monstrousness, barbarity, etc.)' (ILC, *Report of the International Law Commission on the Work of Its Thirty-ninth Session* (4 May–17 Jul 1987), A/42/10 (1987), para.66, Article 1(2)).

Paper on Case Selection and Prioritisation, the OTP argued that: '[t]he nature of the crimes refers to the specific elements of each offence such as killings, rapes and other crimes involving sexual or gender violence and crimes committed against children, persecution, or the imposition of conditions of life on a group calculated to bring about its destruction.'[155] This position was nuanced in a 2025 *Policy on Cyber-Enabled Crimes under the Rome Statute* that refers to 'factual nature' rather than 'nature'.[156] However, in 2025, a totally different definition was provided in the *Policy on Addressing Environmental Damage through the Rome Statute*, according to which, the assessment of the nature of the relevant crimes focuses on 'whether the environmental crimes were committed against or affected particularly marginalised victims or in vulnerable situations, including but not limited to women, children, the elderly, the disabled, Indigenous People, people of African descent, and peasants'.[157] This subsection argues that a correct interpretation of the factor of nature should be based on whether the crimes are committed for discriminatory purposes or against victims in particularly vulnerable conditions, contrary to most of the available documents of the OTP and the Chambers, which consider these factors to lie within the manner of commission.

The 2013, 2014, and 2016 policy papers' focus on the specific offences at hand in the assessment of the nature of the crimes was applied by the OTP on a number of occasions, with some approval by scholars.[158] It was in relation to the situation in Côte d'Ivoire, that the OTP first quoted its policy papers to such effect,[159] observing that '[t]he crimes with which Mr Blé Goudé is charged were violent by nature: murders, rapes, other inhumane acts or attempted murders causing great suffering or serious injury, and persecution'.[160] Similarly, in the assessment of sufficient gravity related to the *Mavi Marmara* incident, the prosecution noted that there was a reasonable basis to believe that the war crimes of 'wilful killing and wilfully causing serious injury to body and health

[155] OTP, *Policy Paper on Preliminary Examinations* (Nov 2013), para.63; OTP, *Policy Paper on Sexual and Gender-Based Crimes* (Jun 2014), para.44; OTP, *Policy Paper on Case Selection and Prioritisation* (15 Sep 2016), para.39.

[156] OTP, *Policy on Cyber-Enabled Crimes under the Rome Statute* (Dec 2025) para.97.

[157] OTP, *Policy on Addressing Environmental Damage through the Rome Statute* (Dec 2025), para.29.

[158] Margaret M deGuzman, 'Gravity and the Legitimacy of the International Criminal Court' (2008) 32 *FILJ* 1400, 1452.

[159] Situation of Côte d'Ivoire, *Prosecutor v Blé Goudé*, Prosecution's Response to the Defence application pursuant to Articles 19(4) and 17(1)(d) of the Rome Statute, ICC-02/11-02/11–181, 20 Oct 2014, para.33.

[160] Ibid, para.37.

under article 8(2)(a)(i) and article 8(2)(a)(iii) – both of which are grave breaches of the Geneva Conventions – as well as the war crime of committing outrages upon personal dignity under article 8(2)(b)(xxi)' had occurred even though 'the information available does not indicate that the treatment inflicted on the affected passengers amounted to torture or inhuman treatment'.[161] The OTP adopted the same approach in its 2020 report on alleged UK crimes committed in Iraq, where the OTP overturned its past 2006 position by invoking, inter alia, the fact that the alleged crimes focused on torture, inhuman treatment, and outrages upon human dignity, which have a peculiar grave nature.[162]

This trend was followed by some Chambers in subsequent assessments of sufficient gravity in relation to the nature of the crimes. For instance, PTC III, in relation to the situation in Georgia, affirmed that '[a]s for the nature of the crimes, the Chamber refers to the above analysis which demonstrates that the potential cases could encompass an array of war crimes and crimes against humanity'.[163] However, most Chambers did not engage meaningfully with the nature of the crimes in assessing sufficient gravity.

This approach to the nature of the crimes, which is seen through the lens of thematic prosecution,[164] is incorrect since it focuses on the elements of the crimes, thus conflating issues of ICC jurisdiction (elements of the crimes) with issues of admissibility once the jurisdiction has already been established (sufficient gravity). The mere enumeration of crimes punishable by the RS does not reveal anything about the nature of the crimes in relation to sufficient gravity.[165] Particularly surprising is the assertion by the OTP, in the assessment of sufficient gravity, that certain conduct in the *Mavi Marmara* assault amounted to outrages upon personal dignity (only?) but not torture or inhuman treatment.[166] PTC I read this statement as indicating that only the latter

161 Situation on Registered Vessels, OTP, Article 53(1) Report, 6 Nov 2014, para.139.

162 Situation in Iraq/UK, OTP, Final Report, 9 Dec 2020, paras 136–8.

163 Situation in Georgia, PTC I, Decision on the Prosecutor's request for authorization of an investigation, ICC-01/15-12, 27 Jan 2016, para.53.

164 See Zakerhossein, n.153, 231–8. For a broader analysis of thematic prosecution, see, for example Morten Bergsmo (ed.), *Thematic Prosecution of International Sex Crimes* (TOAEP 2012).

165 Thomas O Hansen, 'Reflections on the ICC Prosecutor's Recent "Selection Decisions"' (2013) 17 MPYUNL 125, 143; Marco Longobardo, 'Everything Is Relative, Even Gravity: Remarks on the Assessment of Gravity in ICC Preliminary Examinations, and the *Mavi Marmara* Affair' (2016) 14 JICS 1011, 1020; Priya Urs, *Gravity at the International Criminal Court: Admissibility and Prosecutorial Discretion* (OUP 2024) 65.

166 Situation on Registered Vessels, OTP, Article 53(1) Report, 6 Nov 2014, para.139.

rather than the former would have reached the gravity threshold, a reasoning that the Chamber found to be unpersuasive because it was premature at the stage of preliminary examinations;[167] accordingly, PTC I requested that the OTP assess sufficient gravity in the *Mavi Marmara* incident as if torture and/or inhuman treatment was committed on board.[168] However, irrespective of the timeliness of an assessment of the specific crimes at hand, listing crimes within the ICC jurisdiction does not contribute in any way to the assessment of sufficient gravity because this reasoning pertains to jurisdiction rather than admissibility. Accordingly, both the OTP's and PTC I's analyses of the nature of the crimes fail to assess sufficient gravity as an admissibility criterion because they focus on jurisdictional issues (with the OTP maybe alluding to, and the Chamber forcefully advocating for, an artificial hierarchy of gravity between crimes that are equally punishable under the RS).[169]

The disagreement between the OTP and PTC I in 2015 led to a reconsideration of the factor of the nature of the crimes. In 2017, again in relation to the *Mavi Marmara* incident, the OTP argued that the legal characterisation of the identified mistreatment of detainees aboard the *Mavi Marmara* had a 'neutral significance', clarifying that 'the legal label assigned to a possible crime at the preliminary examination stage is irrelevant to its gravity, given the absence of any established hierarchy of offences under the Statute'.[170] The OTP went on to affirm that 'it was the factual nature of the identified conduct … which was relevant to the gravity analysis in the Report'.[171] In other words, 'the factual, rather than legal, characteristics of the identified conduct should be of primary relevance for its gravity analysis',[172] even though the assessment of the OTP at hand did not provide significant factual analysis under the rubric of the nature of the crime.[173] In these circumstances, not only was the OTP forced to invoke

---

167 Situation on Registered Vessels, PTC I, Decision on the request of the Union of the Comoros to review the Prosecutor's decision not to initiate an investigation, ICC-01/13-34, 16 Jul 2015, paras 28–30.

168 Situation on Registered Vessels, PTC I, Decision on the 'Application for Judicial Review by the Government of the Comoros', ICC-01/13-111, 16 Sep 2020, paras 58–9.

169 Contra, Frédéric Foka Taffo, *Le pouvoir discrétionnaire du Procureur de la Cour pénale internationale* (Nomos 2018) 107 (admitting that the nature of the crimes requires an assessment of the *actus reus*).

170 Situation on Registered Vessels, OTP, Final decision of the Prosecution concerning the 'Article 53(1) Report' (ICC-01/13-6-AnxA), dated 6 Nov 2014, ICC-01/13-57-Anx1, 29 Nov 2017, para.83.

171 Ibid.

172 Ibid, para.84.

173 Longobardo, n.165, 1020.

the absence of any judicial definition of the nature of the crime in relation to sufficient gravity to justify uncertainty around this notion,[174] but more importantly, the OTP had to offer a palinode of its interpretation of the nature of the crime as based on the elements of the crimes:

> the Prosecution previously stated that the "nature" criterion refers to "the specific elements of each offence", and cited as (non-exhaustive) examples forms of conduct which, no matter their legal characterisation for the purpose of charging, may be seen as especially grave by their factual nature. The Prosecution acknowledges that the reference to "specific elements" in this context may be unclear. It thus emphasises its view that the "nature" factor encompasses the factual characteristics of the criminal conduct, and is not limited to the elements which must legally be proved to establish liability. This is consistent with the general approach of the Statute, which distinguishes between jurisdiction ratione *materiae* ("the most serious crimes of concern to the international community as a whole") and the gravity of actual or potential "cases" – it is implicit in this scheme that the gravity analysis as a whole is factdriven, and not law-driven.[175]

The OTP has since focused on factual rather than on legal elements in assessing the nature of the crimes for the purposes of Article 17(1)(d).[176] This approach may appear formally correct, since it avoids blurring jurisdiction with admissibility but, in the *Mavi Marmara* incident, it did not satisfy PTC I, which had endorsed the idea that nature should be assessed with reference to the crimes at hand. Notwithstanding such an evolution, the notion of nature of the crime for the assessment of sufficient gravity remains elusive, and scant light is provided by its incorporation in the aforementioned 2025 *Policy on Cyber-Enabled Crimes under the Rome Statute*.[177] One might wonder what the factual elements are that render certain crimes already within the ICC jurisdiction sufficiently grave due to their nature.

It is suggested here that the analysis of nature should focus on what makes a crime already punishable by the RS (jurisdictional threshold) particularly serious due to the ontological circumstances pertaining to that specific case. An example can illustrate this: wilful killing of an adult male civilian in

---

174 Situation on Registered Vessels, OTP, Final decision of the Prosecution concerning the 'Article 53(1) Report' (ICC-01/13-6-AnxA), dated 6 Nov 2014, ICC-01/13-57-Anx1, 29 Nov 2017, para.85.

175 Ibid, para.86 (emphasis added).

176 Situation on Registered Vessels, OTP, Final decision of the Prosecution concerning the 'Article 53(1) Report' (ICC-01/13-6-AnxA), dated 6 Nov 2014, as revised and refiled in accordance with the PTC's request of 15 Nov 2018 and the AC's judgment of 2 Sep 2019, ICC-01/13-99-Anx1, 2 Dec 2019, para.43.

177 OTP, *Policy on Cyber-Enabled Crimes under the Rome Statute* (Dec 2025), para.31.

good health is a war crime (jurisdictional consideration);[178] wilful killing of a newborn is the same crime, but it can be considered particularly grave in nature because the vulnerability of the victim makes it ontologically graver.[179] Accordingly, this enhanced gravity pertains to the nature of the crime. Similarly, wilful killing of a civilian because of their ethnicity is the same war crime as above, but it is particularly grave in its nature because of the discriminatory motive. It transpires that the nature of the crime should be assessed taking into consideration any discriminatory motive as well as the particular vulnerability of the victims.

Discriminatory motive and particular vulnerability are sometimes analysed by the Chambers[180] and the OTP[181] as parcels of sufficient gravity without any reference to a specific factor. On other occasions, they are mentioned in the context of the manner of commission.[182] However, as seen below, the manner of commission pertains to the *way* in which a particular crime is committed, rather than to why and against whom, both of which are relevant to the nature of a crime. Generally, the fact that vulnerability and discriminatory motive are relevant to the assessment of sufficient gravity, in particular in relation to crimes that do not include them as elements of the crimes for the purpose of jurisdiction, is supported by the need to interpret Article 17(1)(d) of the RS in

---

178 RS, Article 8(2)(a)(i).

179 Here it is possible to see some overlap with impact, since the same crime can have a more tremendous impact on a more vulnerable victim (the newborn in our example). On impact, see below, subsection 3.4.4.

180 Situation in Côte d'Ivoire, *Prosecutor v Blé Goudé*, PTC I, Decision on the Defence Challenge to the Admissibility of the Case against Charles Blé Goudé for Insufficient Gravity, ICC-02/11-02/11-185, 12 Nov 2014, para.20; Situation in Burundi, PTC III, Public redacted version of 'Decision Pursuant to Article 15 of the RS on the Authorization of an Investigation into the Situation in the Republic of Burundi', ICC-01/17-X-9-US-Exp, 25 Oct 2017, ICC-01/17-9-Red, 9 Nov 2017, para.188; Situation in Mali, *Prosecutor v Al Hassan*, PTC I, Decision on the Admissibility Challenge raised by the Defence for Insufficient Gravity of the Case, ICC-01/12-01/18-459-tENG, 27 Sep 2019, para.57.

181 Situation in Kenya, OTP, Request for authorisation of an investigation pursuant to Article 15, ICC-01/09-3, 26 Nov 2009, para.57; Situation in Afghanistan, PTC II, Public redacted version of 'Prosecution's application under article 58 for a warrant of arrest against Abdul Hakim HAQQANI', ICC-02/17-225-Red, 23 Jan 2025, para.169; Situation in Afghanistan, OTP, Public redacted version of 'Prosecution's application under article 58 for a warrant of arrest against Haibatullah AKHUNDZADA', ICC-02/17-224-Red, 23 Jan 2025, para.168.

182 Situation in Bangladesh/Myanmar, OTP, Request for authorisation of an investigation pursuant to article 15, ICC-01/19-7, 4 Jul 2019, para.284. See also below, subsection 3.4.3.

light of Article 21(3). This provision incorporates a broad ban on discrimination and refers as well to international human rights law instruments generally, which themselves include several anti-discriminatory rules, rules against hate crimes, and rules on the protection of vulnerable individuals.[183] Not belonging to the manner of commission but pertaining to the very essence of the crimes, vulnerability and discriminatory motive should be assessed in relation to the nature of the crime.

The view presented here, however, does not explicitly reflect significant judicial practice. True, in 2015, Comoros, as the state of referral of a situation, claimed that discriminatory motives should be assessed as part of the nature of the crime, but the reasoning on this point was unconvincing.[184] More significantly, in 2025, the OTP finally changed its approach by indicating that the vulnerable condition of victims (and not also discrimination) is the only relevant element to be considered in relation to nature: in the *Policy on Addressing Environmental Damage through the Rome Statute*, the assessment of the nature of the relevant crime encompasses 'whether the environmental crimes were committed against or affected particularly marginalised victims or in vulnerable situations, including but not limited to women, children, the elderly, the disabled, Indigenous People, people of African descent, and peasants'.[185] This passage focuses entirely on the vulnerable condition of victimes. It is suggested here that this is a positive direction for future assessment of the nature of crimes, which should focus on the vulnerable conditions of the victims and discriminatory motives, erroneously existing, so far, in the assessment of the manner of commission. This way, the factor of nature would finally have its autonomy without causing confusion between jurisdiction and admissibility.

3.4.3 Manner of commission

In analysing the manner of commission for the assessment of sufficient gravity, the first clarification to make pertains to whether it is relevant that the alleged crime is committed through active commission or through omission. The issue arose in judicial practice in 2011, when a defendant claimed that the alleged commission of international crimes through omission *ipso facto* demonstrated

---

183 On the interpretive value of Article 21(3) of the RS, see above, Chapter 2, subsection 3.1.

184 Situation on Registered Vessels, Comoros, Public Redacted Version with Confidential Annexes 1, 2 and 3 of Application for Review pursuant to Article 53(3)(a) of the Prosecutor's Decision of 6 Nov 2014 not to initiate an investigation in the Situation, ICC-01/13-3-Red, 29 Jan 2015, para.97 (this circumstance was considered relevant to constitute allegations of torture).

185 OTP, *Policy on Addressing Environmental Damage through the Rome Statute* (Dec 2025), para.20.

a lower level of sufficient gravity.[186] PTC II correctly noted that 'there is nothing in the Statute that can be interpreted to exclude acts by omission from the purview of the Court'.[187] The fact that there is nothing in an act of omission that renders it less grave than the active commission of a crime is the consequence of the distinction between jurisdiction and admissibility: omission and active commission pertain to the *actus reus* and modes of liability, and thus, they fall within the scope of jurisdiction. From them, nothing can be assumed as a matter of sufficient gravity.

The OTP policy papers consider that the manner of commission of the crimes should be assessed considering several sub-factors. The factors have changed slightly over time. In 2013, the OTP held that the assessment should be performed:

> in light of, *inter alia*, the means employed to execute the crime, the degree of participation and intent of the perpetrator (if discernible at this stage), the extent to which the crimes were systematic or result from a plan or organised policy or otherwise resulted from the abuse of power or official capacity, and elements of particular cruelty, including the vulnerability of the victims, any motives involving discrimination, or the use of rape and sexual violence as a means of destroying groups.[188]

However, the formulation in 2016 was slightly different, with the substantial disappearance of any reference to *mens rea* and the inclusion of concerns for the natural environment. After 2016, this assessment should be performed:

> in light of, *inter alia*, the means employed to execute the crime, the extent to which the crimes were systematic or resulted from a plan or organised policy or otherwise resulted from the abuse of power or official capacity, the existence of elements of particular cruelty, including the vulnerability of the victims, any motives involving discrimination held by the direct perpetrators of the crimes, the use of rape and other sexual or gender-based violence or crimes committed by means of, or resulting in, the destruction of the environment or of protected objects.[189]

---

[186] Situation in Kenya, *Prosecutor v Muthaura et al*, PTC II, Defence Challenge to Jurisdiction, Admissibility and Prosecution's Failure to Meet the Requirements of Article 54, ICC-01/09-02/11-338, 19 Sept 2011, paras 56–71.

[187] Situation in Kenya, *Prosecutor v Muthaura et al*, PTC II, Public Redacted Version of Decision on the Confirmation of Charges Pursuant to Article 61(7)(a) and (b) of the Rome Statute, ICC-01/09-02/11-382-Red, 23 Jan 2012, para.47.

[188] OTP, *Policy Paper on Preliminary Examinations* (Nov 2013), para.64. See also Situation in Côte d'Ivoire, *Prosecutor v Blé Goudé*, Prosecution's Response to the Defence application pursuant to Articles 19(4) and 17(1)(d) of the Rome Statute, ICC-02/11-02/11-181, 20 Oct 2014, para.34.

[189] OTP, *Policy Paper on Case Selection and Prioritisation* (15 Sept 2016), para.41.

The list of sub-factors is not homogeneous. Some of them pertain to the manner of commission *stricto sensu*, such as the use of specific means of execution characterised by brutality. The equating of manner of commission with means of execution is supported, for instance, by early judicial decisions of PTCs,[190] sometimes quoted with approval by the OTP.[191] This is the actual meaning of 'manner of commission', and it has been followed in judicial practice. For instance, in relation to Kenya, PTC II agreed with the OTP that 'the element of brutality is pertinent to the means used to execute the violence',[192] and that sufficient gravity was corroborated by 'many instances of cutting and hacking, including amputations and reports of forced circumcision and genital amputation ..., rapes ... often characterized by a degree of brutality, including high numbers of reported gang rapes, including by a group of over 20 men, and the cutting of the victims or the insertion of crude weapon and other objects in the vagina'.[193] Likewise, in the situation of Georgia, the OTP took into account 'particular cruelty ... as evidenced by patterns of close range killings and executions as well as the infliction of serious bodily injuries, together with the widespread and systematic destruction and looting of ethnic Georgian property'.[194] Cruelty was also briefly mentioned by the OTP in relation to the *Mavi Marmara* incident.[195] PTC I also mentioned the 'brutal means' of execution of the crimes allegedly committed in Georgia.[196] In relation to Burundi, PTC Chamber III emphasised that 'some crimes have been executed in a particularly cruel manner (such as torture by means of electrocution and tying of weights to genitals, as well as gang rapes)', which demonstrated that

---

[190] Situation in Kenya, PTC II, Decision Pursuant to Article 15 of the Rome Statute on the Authorization of an Investigation into the Situation in the Republic of Kenya, ICC-01/09-19-Corr, 31 Mar 2010, para.62.

[191] Situation in Côte d'Ivoire, *Prosecutor v Blé Goudé*, Prosecution's Response to the Defence application pursuant to Articles 19(4) and 17(1)(d) of the RS, ICC-02/11-02/11-181, 20 Oct 2014, para.16.

[192] Situation in Kenya, PTC II, Decision Pursuant to Article 15 of the RS on the Authorization of an Investigation into the Situation in the Republic of Kenya, ICC-01/09-19-Corr, 31 Mar 2010, para.193.

[193] Ibid.

[194] Situation in Georgia, Corrected Version of 'Request for authorisation of an investigation pursuant to article 15', 16 Oct 2015, ICC-01/15-4-Corr, ICC-01/15-4-Corr2, 17 Nov 2015, para.331.

[195] For example, Situation on Registered Vessels, OTP, Article 53(1) Report, 6 Nov 2014, para.140.

[196] Situation in Georgia, PTC I, Decision on the Prosecutor's request for authorization of an investigation, ICC-01/15-12, 27 Jan 2016, para.53.

'some crimes included elements of brutality'.[197] In relation to the situations in Bangladesh/Myanmar[198] and in Iraq/UK,[199] the OTP included in the assessment of the manner of commission the fact that some of the alleged crimes were committed with particular cruelty, with a long list of horrific practices documented.

Less persuasive is listing the degree of participation and intent as components of assessment of the manner of commission of crimes for gravity purposes. Although these elements are cited by certain judicial decisions in the assessment of sufficient gravity,[200] they pertain to the criminal responsibility of a certain individual as a matter of *mens rea* or mode of liability, more than to the realm of admissibility. Particularly when the assessment of sufficient gravity is performed at the preliminary examination stage, it would be very problematic to assess the degree of participation and intent of the suspects in the absence of any accused, merely in the context of situations and potential cases. Thus, the 2013 *Policy Paper on Preliminary Examinations* adds that the degree of participation and intent are relevant only if discernible at a certain stage.[201] In any case, the 2016 *Policy Paper on Case Selection and Prioritisation* dropped these elements from the definition of manner of commission. Although they are analysed subsequently as possible components of the most responsible criterion,[202] *mens rea* is unsuitable to be considered as part of the assessment of sufficient gravity as a matter of admissibility because it is a jurisdictional consideration: *mens rea*, indeed, is an element of the crime, whereas the factors determining gravity are external considerations pertaining to a certain situation or case.

The fact that the policy papers of the OTP mention the systematic character of the crime or the existence of a plan or policy as components of the manner

---

197 Situation in Burundi, PTC III, Public redacted version of 'Decision Pursuant to Article 15 of the Rome Statute on the Authorization of an Investigation into the Situation in the Republic of Burundi', ICC-01/17-X-9-US-Exp, 25 Oct 2017, ICC-01/17-9-Red, 9 Nov 2017, para.188.

198 Situation in Bangladesh/Myanmar, OTP, Request for authorisation of an investigation pursuant to article 15, ICC-01/19-7, 4 Jul 2019, para.285.

199 Situation in Iraq/UK, OTP, Final Report, 9 Dec 2020, paras 140–41.

200 For example, Situation in Côte d'Ivoire, *Prosecutor v Blé Goudé*, PTC I, Decision on the Defence Challenge to the Admissibility of the Case against Charles Blé Goudé for Insufficient Gravity, ICC-02/11-02/11-185, 12 Nov 2014, para.20; Situation in Mali, *Prosecutor v Al Hassan*, PTC I, Decision on the Admissibility Challenge raised by the Defence for Insufficient Gravity of the Case, ICC-01/12-01/18-459-tENG, 27 Sept 2019, para.57.

201 OTP, *Policy Paper on Preliminary Examinations* (Nov 2013), para.64.

202 See below, subsection 4.2.

of commission of the crimes is not surprising. 'Systematic' in international criminal law 'has been understood as either an organised plan in furtherance of a common policy, which follows a regular pattern and results in a continuous commission of acts or as "patterns of crimes" such that the crimes constitute a "non-accidental repetition of similar criminal conduct on a regular basis".'[203] In other words, the presence of a plan or policy is one of the ways in which the systematic character manifests.[204] In relation to the assessment of sufficient gravity, PTC I[205] and scholars, before the consolidation of the four factors, had invoked the systematicity of the crimes as one leading consideration in the assessment of sufficient gravity,[206] stressing its qualitative character.[207] The existence of a common plan or policy is now invoked as a component of the manner of commission. For instance, PTC I mentioned the systematic nature of the crimes in relation to Côte d'Ivoire[208] and Afghanistan.[209] One of the main disagreements between the OTP and PTC I over sufficient gravity in the *Mavi Marmara* incident centred on whether the alleged crimes were likely committed in pursuance of a plan or policy – as suggested by the Chamber[210] – or not – as advocated by the OTP.[211] Regardless of the fact that the two organs

---

[203] Situation in the DRC, *Prosecutor v Katanga and Ngudjolo*, PTC I, Decision on the confirmation of charges, ICC-01/04-01/07-717, 20 Sept 2008, para.397.

[204] See William A Schabas, *The International Criminal Court: A Commentary on the Rome Statute* (2nd edn, OUP 2016) 165, for further references.

[205] For example, Situation in the DRC, PTC I, Decision on the Prosecutor's Application for Warrants of Arrest, Article 58, ICC-01/04-520-Anx2, 10 Feb 2006, para.47.

[206] For example, Heller, n.52, 229–33.

[207] Ibid, 229.

[208] Situation in Côte d'Ivoire, *Prosecutor v Blé Goudé*, PTC I, Decision on the Defence Challenge to the Admissibility of the Case against Charles Blé Goudé for Insufficient Gravity, ICC-02/11-02/11-185, 12 Nov 2014, para.20.

[209] Situation in Mali, *Prosecutor v Al Hassan*, PTC I, Decision on the Admissibility Challenge raised by the Defence for Insufficient Gravity of the Case, ICC-01/12-01/18-459-tENG, 27 Sep 2019, para.57.

[210] For example, Situation on Registered Vessels, PTC I, Decision on the request of the Union of the Comoros to review the Prosecutor's decision not to initiate an investigation, ICC-01/13-34, 16 Jul 2015, paras 31–45; Situation on Registered Vessels, PTC I, Decision on the Request of the Union of the Comoros to review the Prosecutor's Decision not to Initiate an Investigation, ICC-01/13-34, 16 Jul 2015, para.21. See also Situation on Registered Vessels, PTC I, Decision on the 'Application for Judicial Review by the Government of the Comoros', ICC-01/13-111, 16 Sep 2020, paras 84–94.

[211] For example, Situation on Registered Vessels, Article 53(1) Report, 6 Nov 2014, para.140; Situation on Registered Vessels, Final decision of the Prosecution concerning the 'Article 53(1) Report' (ICC-01/13-6-AnxA), dated 6 Nov 2014,

disagreed on whether there was sufficient evidence of such a plan or policy, the fact that such a disagreement almost monopolised the assessment of the manner of commission of the crimes in that situation,[212] to the point that the OTP almost equated the analysis of the existence of a plan or policy to the entire assessment of the manner of commission of the crimes, speaks volumes.[213]

Related to this sub-factor is the fact that the 2016 *Policy Paper on Case Selection and Prioritisation* refers to the circumstance where the crimes 'otherwise resulted from the abuse of power or official capacity' as relevant for the assessment of the manner of commission.[214] One judicial decision mentions in its assessment of sufficient gravity the fact that the crimes are allegedly committed by law enforcement agents trusted with protecting citizens from violence, and the fact that they were likely committed with approval by high-level government officials.[215] Analogously, two requests for arrest warrants by the OTP in relation to Afghanistan emphasise that the alleged crime 'is carried out by the very entity – the Taliban – which now purports to claim the mantle of government for the welfare of its people'.[216] These considerations may echo the scholarly proposal to include state criminality as an autonomous

---

ICC-01/13-57-Anx1, 29 Nov 2017, paras 88–165; Situation on Registered Vessels, Final decision of the Prosecution concerning the 'Article 53(1) Report' (ICC-01/13-6-AnxA), dated 6 Nov 2014, as revised and refiled in accordance with the PTC's request of 15 Nov 2018 and the AC's judgment of 2 Sep 2019, ICC-01/13-99-Anx1, 2 Dec 2019, paras 55–86.

212 See the scant references to other components of the manner of commission in the sources cited above, n.211.

213 See the rubric of Situation on Registered Vessels, Final decision of the Prosecution concerning the 'Article 53(1) Report' (ICC-01/13-6-AnxA), dated 6 Nov 2014, as revised and refiled in accordance with the PTC's request of 15 Nov 2018 and the AC's judgment of 2 Sep 2019, ICC-01/13-99-Anx1, 2 Dec 2019, section V, entitled (certainly for brevity, but perhaps out of frustration as well) 'The manner of commission of the identified crimes (whether the crimes were committed according to a plan or policy)'.

214 OTP, *Policy Paper on Case Selection and Prioritisation* (15 Sept 2016), para.40.

215 Situation in the Philippines, Prosecution's response to the Philippine Government's Appeal Brief against 'Authorisation pursuant to article 18(2) of the Statute to resume the investigation' (ICC-01/21-65 OA), ICC-01/21-68, 4 Apr 2023, para.164.

216 Situation in Afghanistan, Public redacted version of 'Prosecution's application under article 58 for a warrant of arrest against Abdul Hakim HAQQANI', ICC-02/17-225-Red, 23 Jan 2025, para.169; Situation in Afghanistan, Public redacted version of 'Prosecution's application under article 58 for a warrant of arrest against Haibatullah AKHUNDZADA', ICC-02/17-224-Red, 23 Jan 2025, para.168.

factor in the assessment of sufficient gravity,[217] or at least as one factor to be considered along with all the others, in light of the enhanced capacity of a state apparatus to commit international crimes.[218] Indeed, official capacity in the RS is employed, in relation to a different matter, only with reference to state organs.[219] However, the emphasis on abuse of power along with official capacity is not linked to state officials only, but rather, pertains to any form of authority, state and non-state alike, that is organised (such as in the case of an organised armed group controlling a portion of territory).[220] It seems that such an abuse of authority or official capacity is relevant for the manner of commission because such a coercive environment, sanctioned by the *de jure* or *de facto* legal framework regulating a society, diminishes the possibility of the victims to defend themselves from the crimes and it grants the perpetrators the means of commission and hope of impunity.[221]

Furthermore, in relation to the manner of commission, it is patent that the fact that a crime is committed in a way that includes the use of sexual violence or environmental destruction is significant and inclusion of these considerations follows the evolution of the strategic choices of the OTP, which has now adopted relevant policy papers.[222] Indeed, crimes committed through environmental damage or sexual violence can be seen as qualitatively more serious than the same crimes committed through other means: they have a specific human rights impact that falls within the scope of human rights law conventions that constitute the interpretive framework of Article 17(1)(d) of the RS pursuant to Article 21(3). This consideration applies in particular to those crimes that do not require environmental damage or sexual violence as elements of the crimes, where, thus, environmental damage and sexual violence are components of the manner of commission rather than the *actus reus*. For instance, the Elements of the Crimes and judicial decisions recognise

---

217 Heller, n.52, 237–9.

218 Schabas, n.48, 748; Surabhi Ranganathan, *Strategically Created Treaty Conflicts and the Politics of International Law* (CUP 2014) 254; Mégret, n.59, 111–12.

219 See RS, Article 27 ('Irrelevance of official capacity').

220 Compare with the notion of authority in Article 28 of the RS ('Responsibility of commanders and other superiors').

221 See, *mutatis mutandis*, Schabas, n.48, 748; Heller, n.52, 238–9; Zakerhossein, n.153, 240.

222 OTP, *Policy on Gender-based Crimes* (2023), para.100; OTP, *Draft Policy on Environmental Crimes under the Rome Statute* (2024). See, also, Luigi Prosperi and Jacopo Terrosi, 'Embracing the "Human Factor": Is There New Impetus at the ICC for Conceiving and Prioritizing Intentional Environmental Harms as Crimes Against Humanity?' (2017) 15 JICJ 509.

that rape is a way to commit genocide[223] and torture,[224] and that it is possible to configure the commission of genocide,[225] crimes against humanity[226] and war crimes[227] through environmental destruction, even if that is not the direct intention of these crimes.[228] On the contrary, in relation to cyber-enabled international crimes, the OTP recognised that '[t]he mere fact that cyber means have been used, in isolation, will not be taken either to aggravate or mitigate the seriousness of the conduct at issue'.[229] It looks like the OTP, in this case, considered that the specific manner of commission that is analysed in its policy paper is neutral in relation to sufficient gravity.[230]

Finally, it should be recalled that the previous subsection has already argued that the vulnerability of victims and discriminatory motives are not factors for the assessment of the manner of commission.[231] Rather, they belong to the assessment of the nature of the crime, as recognised by the OTP in recent practice.

3.4.4 Impact

The factor of the impact of the crime has undergone a certain evolution in the direction of increased attention to the reverberating effect of a crime. OTP policy papers are quite consistent in tracing a trajectory from the immediate

---

223 For example, Elements of the Crimes, Article 6(b)(1)note 3; Situation in Darfur, Sudan, *Prosecutor v Al Bashir*, Second Decision on the Prosecution's Application for a Warrant of Arrest, ICC-02/05-01/09-9, 12 Jul 2010, para.30.

224 For example, ICTY, *Prosecutor v Kunarac et al*, AC, IT-96-23/1-A, 12 Jun 2002, para.150.

225 Situation in Darfur, Sudan, Public Redacted Version of the Prosecutor's Application under Article 58, ICC-02/05-157-AnxA, 14 Jul 2008, paras 174–6; OTP, *Draft Policy on Environmental Crimes under the Rome Statute* (2024), para.31.

226 Situation in Darfur, Sudan, Public Redacted Version of the Prosecutor's Application under Article 58, ICC-02/05-157-AnxA, 14 Jul 2008, para.180; OTP, *Draft Policy on Environmental Crimes under the Rome Statute* (2024), paras 32–40.

227 OTP, *Policy on Addressing Environmental Damage through the Rome Statute* (Dec 2025), paras 35–44.

228 On this topic, see, generally Matthew Gillett, *Prosecuting Environmental Harm Before the International Criminal Court* (CUP 2022) 53–133.

229 OTP, *Policy on Cyber-Enabled Crimes under the Rome Statute* (Dec 2025), para.132 (emphasis added).

230 This conclusion had been anticipated by Marco Roscini, 'Gravity in the Statute of the International Criminal Court and Cyber Conduct that Constitutes, Instigates or Facilitates International Crimes' (2019) 30 CLF 247, 266.

231 See above, subsection 3.4.2.

victim of the crime to the local community and beyond. According to the OTP in 2013, '[t]he impact of crimes may be assessed in light of, inter alia, the sufferings endured by the victims and their increased vulnerability; the terror subsequently instilled, or the social, economic and environmental damage inflicted on the affected communities'.[232] In 2016, the OTP added that '[i]n this context, the Office will give particular consideration to prosecuting [RS] crimes that are committed by means of, or that result in, *inter alia*, the destruction of the environment, the illegal exploitation of natural resources or the illegal dispossession of land'.[233] In 2025, in relation to environmental crimes, impact included:

> the extent of the damage – viewed holistically and including long-term and irreversible damage, and viewed cumulatively where there have been multiple acts of environmental damage – caused to the natural environment regardless of its anthropocentric effect; the intergenerational effect of environmental damage on human life; and the specific social, cultural, psychological, religious, spiritual, or socioeconomic harm inflicted by the environmental crimes, particularly on groups or individuals with intersecting vulnerabilities..[234]

In other words, impact accommodates the reverberating effect of a crime punishable under the RS.

The first ring of such a reverberating effect is the impact on victims, which should always be assessed in relation to sufficient gravity.[235] Rule 85 of the RPE states that '"Victims" means natural persons who have suffered harm because of the commission of any crime within the jurisdiction of the Court'. Simplifying a complex issue beyond the purview of this research, ICC case law has made a distinction between direct victims, that is, those whose harm results from the commission of the crime, and 'indirect' victims, who suffered harm as a result of the harm endured by the direct victims, such as family members.[236] The OTP attempted to define impact as a factor that:

---

232 OTP, *Policy Paper on Preliminary Examinations* (Nov 2013), para.65.

233 OTP, *Policy Paper on Case Selection and Prioritisation* (15 Sep 2016), para.41.

234 OTP, *Policy on Addressing Environmental Damage through the Rome Statute* (Dec 2025), para.20.

235 Situation on Registered Vessels, PTC I, Decision on the request of the Union of the Comoros to review the Prosecutor's decision not to initiate an investigation, ICC-01/13-34, 16 Jul 2015, para.47. Contra, Zakerhossein, n.153, 224, who considers any effect over direct victims as part of the scale.

236 Marina Lostal, 'De-objectifying Animals: Could they Qualify as Victims before the International Criminal Court?' (2021) 19 JICJ 583, 588. See generally Nema Milaninia, 'Conceptualizing Victimization at the International Criminal Court: Understanding the Causal Relationship Between Crime and

> relates primarily to the extent of the damage caused to and the harm suffered by the victims, which may be physical, psychological or material (such as physical injury, loss of a family member, psychological trauma, including as a result of witnessing and/or fearing the commission of the crimes, loss of opportunities in relation to education and/or employment, or loss of earnings).[237]

Impact, in this sense, goes beyond specific elements of the crime – which are a component of the crimes for the purposes of the ICC jurisdiction – but rather, it refers to further consequences. For instance, the OTP, in relation to the situation of Kenya, emphasised the fact that '[v]ictims of sexual violence … suffer from enormous psychological trauma, may have been infected with HIV/AIDS and/or other types of sexually transmissible diseases, are often abandoned by their husbands and/or families and suffer from social stigma'.[238] PTC II entirely mirrored these findings.[239] Likewise, in relation to the situation of Côte d'Ivoire, the OTP noted that '[t]he survivors of the crimes suffered grave physical injury, psychological trauma, and other social stigma'.[240] In relation to measures allegedly amounting to gender persecution in Afghanistan, the OTP emphasised that crime 'is intended to create an enduring regime of oppression which will afflict the targeted persons *throughout their lives*'.[241]

Harm' (2019) 50 *Columbia Human Rights Law Review* 116; Christoph Safferling and Gurgen Petrossian, *Victims Before the International Criminal Court: Definition, Participation, Reparation* (Springer 2021); Enrique Carnero-Rojo, 'Section III. Victims and Witnesses Subsection 1. Definition and General Principle Relating to Victims' in Mark Klamberg, Jonas Nilsson and Antonio Angotti (eds), *Commentary on the Law of the International Criminal Court: The Rules of Procedure and Evidence* (TOAEP 2023) 309–28.

237 Situation on Registered Vessels, PTC I, Decision on the 'Application for Judicial Review by the Government of the Comoros', ICC-01/13-111, 16 Sep 2020, para.79.

238 Situation in Kenya, OTP, Request for authorisation of an investigation pursuant to Article 15, ICC-01/09-3, 26 Nov 2009, para.59.

239 Situation in Kenya, PTC II, Decision Pursuant to Article 15 of the Rome Statute on the Authorization of an Investigation into the Situation in the Republic of Kenya, ICC-01/09-19-Corr, 31 Mar 2010, paras 195–6.

240 Situation in Côte d'Ivoire, *Prosecutor v Blé Goudé*, Prosecution's Response to the Defence application pursuant to Articles 19(4) and 17(1)(d) of the Rome Statute, ICC-02/11-02/11-181, 20 Oct 2014, para.42. See, also, Situation in Bangladesh/Myanmar, OTP, Request for authorisation of an investigation pursuant to article 15, ICC-01/19-7, 4 Jul 2019, paras 279, 288.

241 Situation in Afghanistan, Public redacted version of 'Prosecution's application under article 58 for a warrant of arrest against Abdul Hakim HAQQANI', ICC-02/17-225-Red, 23 Jan 2025, para.169 (emphasis added).

Reference to the impact of the crime on the families of the direct victims is also commonplace in the practice of the OTP[242] and in the Chambers' case law.[243] In relation to children, the OTP in the 2016 *Policy on Children* (now superseded) noted the impact that suffering and witnessing international crimes had on children's 'development and ability to reach their true potential',[244] while the 2023 *Policy on Children* now considers that 'international crimes can affect children – as witnesses, forcible perpetrators (who may also be viewed as victims), members of a targeted group or family members of direct victims. Evidence of a crime's impact on children may help demonstrate the gravity of a crime for admissibility purposes'.[245] In all these cases, the focus of impact is on the expanded consequences of the crimes regardless of how many victims can be identified, which is an element relevant for the determination of scale.[246]

The second ring of this reverberating effect encompasses the local communities to which the victims belong. This evolution has allowed the OTP and the Chambers to include in the assessment of sufficient gravity elements that, taken in isolation, would not be under the jurisdiction of the ICC, such as the displacement created by the commission of the crimes,[247] the impossibility of children receiving an education,[248] the collapse of the healthcare

---

[242] Situation on Registered Vessels, OTP, Article 53(1) Report, 6 Nov 2014, para.141; Situation on Registered Vessels, Final decision of the Prosecution concerning the 'Article 53(1) Report' (ICC-01/13-6-AnxA), dated 6 Nov 2014, ICC-01/13-57-Anx1, 29 Nov 2017, para.78; Situation in Iraq/UK, OTP, Final Report, 9 Dec 2020, para.147.

[243] For example, Situation in Darfur, Sudan, PTC I, Decision on the Confirmation of Charges, ICC-02/05-02/09-243-Red, 8 Feb 2010, para.33; Situation in Georgia, Corrected Version of 'Request for authorisation of an investigation pursuant to article 15', 16 Oct 2015, ICC-01/15-4-Corr, ICC-01/15-4-Corr2, 17 Nov 2015, paras 335–6.

[244] OTP, *Policy on Children* (Nov 2016), para.58.

[245] OTP, *Policy on Children* (Dec 2023), para.26.

[246] Situation on Registered Vessels, PTC I, Decision on the 'Application for Judicial Review by the Government of the Comoros', ICC-01/13-111, 16 Sep 2020, para.79.

[247] Situation in Kenya, OTP, Request for authorisation of an investigation pursuant to Article 15, ICC-01/09-3, 26 Nov 2009, para.59; Situation in Kenya, PTC II, Decision Pursuant to Article 15 of the Rome Statute on the Authorization of an Investigation into the Situation in the Republic of Kenya, ICC-01/09-19-Corr, 31 Mar 2010, para.195.

[248] Situation in Kenya, PTC II, Decision Pursuant to Article 15 of the Rome Statute on the Authorization of an Investigation into the Situation in the Republic of Kenya, ICC-01/09-19-Corr, 31 Mar 2010, para.196; Situation in Afghanistan,

system,[249] and the deteriorated socioeconomic conditions of a community.[250] Similarly, in relation to the gravity of cyber-enabled international crimes, the OTP claimed that it will consider 'the degree to which affected systems are relevant to services and infrastructure essential to the civilian population; the degree to which affected systems are otherwise relevant to humanitarian services'.[251] Because of this, certain negative systematic consequences of armed conflicts that usually escape comprehensive and specific legal regulation under international law, such as poverty,[252] can be taken into account insofar as they contribute to render a situation or case admissible.

From a perspective centred on the local communities it is possible to link the definition of impact suggested by the 2016 *Policy Paper on Case Selection and Prioritisation*, which emphasises focusing attention on 'crimes that are committed by means of, or that result in, inter alia, the destruction of the environment, the illegal exploitation of natural resources or the illegal dispossession of

---

OTP, Public redacted version of 'Request for authorisation of an investigation pursuant to article 15', 20 Nov 2017, ICC-02/17-7-Conf-Exp, ICC-02/17-7-Red 20-11-2017, 20 Nov 2017, para.343. See also OTP, *Policy on Children* (Dec 2023), para.29.

[249] Situation in Afghanistan, OTP, Public redacted version of 'Request for authorisation of an investigation pursuant to article 15', 20 Nov 2017, ICC-02/17-7-Conf-Exp, ICC-02/17-7-Red 20-11-2017, 20 Nov 2017, para.342. See the comments by Thomas O Hansen, 'The International Criminal Court in Kenya: Three Defining Features of a Contested Accountability Process and Their Implications for the Future of International Justice' (2012) 18 *Australian Journal of Human Rights* 187, 198–9.

[250] Situation in Kenya, OTP, Request for authorisation of an investigation pursuant to Article 15, ICC-01/09-3, 26 Nov 2009, para.59; Situation in Kenya, PTC II, Decision Pursuant to Article 15 of the Rome Statute on the Authorization of an Investigation into the Situation in the Republic of Kenya, ICC-01/09-19-Corr, 31 Mar 2010, paras 195–196; Situation in Afghanistan, OTP, Public redacted version of 'Request for authorisation of an investigation pursuant to article 15', 20 Nov 2017, ICC-02/17-7-Conf-Exp, ICC-02/17-7-Red 20-11-2017, 20 Nov 2017, para.342.

[251] OTP, *Policy on Cyber-Enabled Crimes under the Rome Statute* (Dec 2025), para.31. Also, this conclusion had been anticipated by Roscini, n.230', 268–9.

[252] See, generally, Marco Roscini, 'Il diritto internazionale umanitario si preoccupa di prevenire o ridurre la povertà?' in Massimo Starita (ed.), *La povertà nel diritto internazionale e dell'Unione europea* (Editoriale Scientifica 2025) 133; Marco Longobardo, 'Lotta alla povertà in territorio occupato: potenzialità e limiti del diritto dell'occupazione bellica', in Massimo Starita (ed.), *La povertà nel diritto internazionale e dell'Unione europea* (Editoriale Scientifica 2025) 163.

land',[253] to the often dramatic impact these crimes have on local communities. Similarly, the 2021 *Policy on Cultural Heritage* states that the assessment of gravity for these crimes should include 'the suffering of the victims and their increased vulnerability incurred as a result of the loss of, and other impact on, affected cultural heritage, the terror subsequently instilled, and the social, economic and environmental damage inflicted on the affected communities'.[254] Analogously, the 2025 *Policy on Addressing Environmental Damage through the Rome Statute* emphasises 'the specific social, cultural, psychological, religious, spiritual, or socioeconomic harm inflicted by the environmental crimes', alluding to its communitary dimension.[255] In searching for this second ring of reverberating effects, it is not necessary to perform a correct assessment of the impact of the crime under Article 17(1)(d) of the RS, rather, it is an additional layer that can reinforce the assessment of sufficient gravity.[256]

In relation to the impact on local communities, the judicial practice of the OTP and the Chambers' case law have emphasised that attacks against peacekeepers and humanitarian actors are particularly grave because they not only impact the victims of the crimes, but also the relevant local communities, which are prevented from benefiting from peacekeeping and humanitarian activities. For instance, attacks against members of the African Union Mission in Sudan (AMIS), operating under African Union and United Nations (UN) mandates, were particularly grave because 'the alleged initial suspension and ultimate reduction of AMIS activities in the area as a result of the attack had a grave impact on the local population'.[257] According to the OTP, the same principle applies to the gravity of attacks against the Joint Peacekeeping Force (JPKF) dispatched in Georgia without UN mandate: '[s]ince the JPKF tasks included the implementation of the ceasefire agreement and maintenance of

---

253 OTP, *Policy Paper on Case Selection and Prioritisation* (15 Sept 2016), para.41.

254 OTP, *Policy on Cultural Heritage* (Jun 2021), para.95.

255 OTP, *Policy on Addressing Environmental Damage through the Rome Statute* (Dec 2025), para.20.

256 Situation on Registered Vessels, PTC I, Decision on the request of the Union of the Comoros to review the Prosecutor's decision not to initiate an investigation, ICC-01/13-34, 16 Jul 2015, para.47.

257 Situation in Darfur, Sudan, PTC I, Decision on the Confirmation of Charges, ICC-02/05-02/09-243-Red, 8 Feb 2010, para.33. See also Situation in Georgia, Corrected Version of 'Request for authorisation of an investigation pursuant to article 15', 16 Oct 2015, ICC-01/15-4-Corr, ICC-01/15-4-Corr2, 17 Nov 2015, para.335; Situation on Registered Vessels, Final decision of the Prosecution concerning the 'Article 53(1) Report' (ICC-01/13-6-AnxA), dated 6 Nov 2014, ICC-01/13-57-Anx1, 29 Nov 2017, para.78.

the regime of security in South Ossetia, the alleged attack on their personnel and premises could have had a grave impact both on victims of the attack and their families as well as on the local civilian population of South Ossetia.'[258] PTC I agreed, noting that '[w]ith respect to the attacks against peacekeepers … beyond the immediate casualties or extent of immediate damage, the impact of such crimes also encompasses the detriment to their ability to execute their mission'.[259] These statements show that the relevant test is not whether the missions were dispatched under the mandate of a specific organisation, but rather, whether the activities they performed were in the service of local communities and the disruptions that the crimes could have caused to these activities.[260] Even if some authors consider this a reference to the impact on the international community as a whole – which is already considered through the inclusion of such a crime under ICC jurisdiction – the words of the OTP are more nuanced and point towards local communities as well.[261] The same reasoning behind interpreting this to refer to the impact on local communities also applies to crimes against individuals involved in humanitarian assistance,[262]

---

[258] Situation in Georgia, Corrected Version of 'Request for authorisation of an investigation pursuant to article 15', 16 Oct 2015, ICC-01/15-4-Corr, ICC-01/15-4-Corr2, 17 Nov 2015, para.336.

[259] Situation in Georgia, PTC I, Decision on the Prosecutor's request for authorization of an investigation, ICC-01/15-12, 27 Jan 2016, para.54.

[260] See Zakerhossein, n.153, 226–7 (emphasising the status of vulnerability of the population protected by the peacekeepers). See also, with reference to jurisdictional aspects of the case rather than sufficient gravity, Andrea Spagnolo, 'La criminalizzazione degli attacchi ai peacekeepers nella prospettiva della funzione della giustizia penale internazionale al fine del mantenimento della pace' (2017) 11 DUDI 151.

[261] Compare Margaret deGuzman, *Shocking the Conscience of Humanity: Gravity and the Legitimacy of International Criminal Law* (OUP 2020) 114 ('with regard to the case involving the killing of twelve peacekeepers in Sudan, the Prosecutor linked the gravity of the crime to the importance of protecting peacekeepers *around the world*' (emphasis added)) with OTP, *Eighth Report of the Prosecutor of the ICC to the UNSC pursuant to UNSC 1593 (2005)* (3 Dec 2018), para.56 (referring to the fact that 'AMIS operations were severely disrupted, thus affecting *its mission to protect millions of civilians in need of humanitarian aid and security*. … Such attacks constitute violent crimes of exceptionally serious gravity and consequences *for the victims and for the international community*' (emphasis added)).

[262] Situation on Registered Vessels, OTP, Article 53(1) Report, 6 Nov 2014, para.141; Situation on Registered Vessels, OTP, Final decision of the Prosecution concerning the 'Article 53(1) Report' (ICC-01/13-6-AnxA), dated 6 Nov 2014, ICC-01/13-57-Anx1, 29 Nov 2017, para.79.

even though the OTP was reluctant to recognise that such a factor was present in the boarding of the *Mavi Marmara*, because the Israeli authorities had offered to permit the delivery of the humanitarian supplies through a different route, as reportedly happened after the incident.[263]

The third ring of this reverberating effect pertaining to impact beyond local communities is less clearly defined and should be handled with care as a component of sufficient gravity under Article 17(1)(d). A series of examples from the OTP's practice and the Chambers' case law suffice to illustrate some possible articulations. First, in relation to the *Mavi Marmara* incident, the OTP and PTC I discussed the impact of alleged crimes that occurred on board a Comoros vessel, considering their impact on the people of the Gaza Strip, whereto the vessel was directed to deliver humanitarian supplies. Although, as noted above, the OTP considered this point moot since the supplies were in fact delivered by Israel, the point is interesting for the assessment of sufficient gravity: the people of the Gaza Strip do not qualify as the local community of the victims of the crimes, as the victims were coming from *outside* the Gaza Strip onboard the *Mavi Marmara*. Following the OTP's implied view that impact could encompass the effects on the people of the Gaza Strip,[264] one may conclude that impact extends beyond local communities.[265] But if this is the case, where does this impact stop? Since the crimes embodied in the RS 'shock the conscience of humanity'[266] and are 'of concern to the international community as a whole',[267] then the impact could hypothetically include the rippling effects of crimes on all States Parties to the RS – at a factual level, through an onerous tracing of a causal link following a butterfly effect, or at a legal level, in the name of the idea that all States Parties to a treaty embodying obligations *erga omnes partes* are affected by potential violations.[268]

Indeed, in relation to the assessment of the impact of the destruction of religious and cultural buildings in Mali, the OTP stated clearly that '[t]he destruction of religious and historical World Heritage sites in Timbuktu appears to

---

263 Situation on Registered Vessels, OTP, Article 53(1) Report, 6 Nov 2014, para.141.

264 Ibid.

265 Zakerhossein, n.153, 225; Anni Pues, 'Discretion and the Gravity of Situations at the International Criminal Court' (2017) 17 ICLR 960, 977–9.

266 RS, Preamble, para.2.

267 RS, Preamble, para.4.

268 See the discussion in Maartje Weerdesteijn and Lachezar Yanev, 'Assessing Gravity: Should the ICC Consider the Impact of Crimes on the International Community?' in Richard H Steinberg (ed.), *The International Criminal Court: Legal, Policy, and Political Challenges* (Brill 2025) 272.

have shocked the conscience of humanity',[269] mentioning a series of condemnations by international organisations.[270] PTC I also mentioned 'that the Buildings/Structures played an important role *in the life of the inhabitants of Timbuktu* and that their destruction was considered a serious matter and regarded *by the local population* as an aggression towards their faith'.[271] It is clear that the more we move away from proximity to the direct victims, the more difficult it is to contain the latitude of impact. On the other hand, with respect to the boarding of the *Mavi Marmara*, it should be noted that the humanitarian aid onboard was meant to be delivered in the Gaza Strip, creating a functional link between the alleged crimes on the vessel and the Gaza Strip; accordingly, some commentators see the population of the Gaza Strip as the local community affected by the alleged international crimes committed onboard the *Mavi Marmara*,[272] even if the geographical dimension of that situation does not extend to the Gaza Strip.[273]

Again, in relation to the *Mavi Marmara* incident, when PTC I tried to include in the assessment of impact the fact that 'the commission of the identified crimes on the *Mavi Marmara*, which were highly publicised, would have sent a clear and strong message to the people in Gaza (and beyond) that the

---

269 Situation in Mali, OTP, Article 53(1) Report, 16 Jan 2013, para.157.

270 Ibid, paras 158–9. See also Situation in Mali, *Prosecutor v Al Mahdi*, PTC I, Public redacted Decision on the confirmation of charges against Ahmad Al Faqi Al Mahdi, ICC-01/12-01/15-84-Red, 24 Mar 2016, para.39. In support of this view, but not from the perspective of sufficient gravity, see, for example, Elisa Ruozzi, 'The *Al Mahdi* Case between *Erga Omnes* Obligations and Right to Reparation: The International Community as a Victim or as a Donor?' in Alberta Fabbricotti (ed.), *Intentional Destruction of Cultural Heritage and the Law: A Research Companion* (Routledge 2025) 328; Alice Lopes Fabris, 'The Collective Interest at the ICC: International Community as a Victim of International Crimes' in Alberta Fabbricotti (ed.), *Intentional Destruction of Cultural Heritage and the Law: A Research Companion* (Routledge 2025) 355.

271 Situation in Mali, *Prosecutor v Al Mahdi*, PTC I, Public redacted Decision on the confirmation of charges against Ahmad Al Faqi Al Mahdi, ICC-01/12-01/15-84-Red, 24 Mar 2016, para.39 (emphasis added). In this sense, see also the reading of impact by Paige Casaly, '*Al Mahdi* before the ICC: Cultural Property and World Heritage in International Criminal Law' (2016) 14 JICJ 1199, 1217–18; Pierfrancesco Rossi, 'The "Al Mahdi" Trial Before the International Criminal Court: Attacks on Cultural Heritage Between War Crimes and Crimes Against Humanity' (2017) 11 DUDI 87, 99 (focusing on the effects of these crimes on individuals).

272 Russell Buchan, 'The *Mavi Marmara* Incident and the International Criminal Court' (2014) 25 CLF 465, 497–8.

273 On the definition of a situation, see above, Chapter 3, subsection 4.2.1.

blockade of Gaza was in full force and that even the delivery of humanitarian aid would be controlled and supervised by the Israeli authorities',[274] taking note of the 'international concern caused by the events at issue',[275] the OTP, correctly, refused to do so.[276] As noted above, such a vague notion of impact, with references to the expressive function of prosecutorial activities and to international concerns, is reminiscent of the rejected factor of social alarm.[277]

This enlargement and the connected risk of losing sight of sufficient gravity under Article 17(1)(d) are particularly clear in relation to those crimes that the OTP has chosen to prioritise in its policy papers. For instance, the 2021 *Policy on Cultural Heritage* stresses that, in assessing sufficient gravity 'of alleged crimes against or affecting cultural heritage, the Office will take into account the broad and severe impact that these crimes may have on individuals, affected communities, and *potentially humanity as a whole*'.[278] This formulation is redundant since all the crimes in the RS have a severe impact on the international community as a whole, and since the notion of humanity is not well defined. Accordingly, these considerations around crimes against cultural heritage, rather than being relevant under Article 17(1)(d), should be part of the further criteria that the OTP may elaborate on to guide its selection of situations and cases from the standpoint of prosecutorial discretion. Similarly, caution should be recommended in assessing the impact of environmental crimes taking into account as impact the 'intergenerational effects of environmental damage' pursuant to the 2025 *Policy on Addressing Environmental Crimes through the Rome Statute*,[279] where a semicolon separates these words from the reference to local communities: since this formulation broadens the assessment of the impact of the crimes indefinitely in the future, requiring a

---

[274] Situation on Registered Vessels, PTC I, Decision on the Request of the Union of the Comoros to Review the Prosecutor's Decision Not to Initiate an Investigation, ICC-01/13-34, 16 Jul 2015, para.48.

[275] Ibid. This point, framed from the perspective of social alarm, was anticipated, with approval, by Buchan, n.272', 497.

[276] Situation on Registered Vessels, OTP, Final decision of the Prosecution concerning the 'Article 53(1) Report' (ICC-01/13-6-AnxA), dated 6 Nov 2014, as revised and refiled in accordance with the PTC's request of 15 Nov 2018 and the AC's judgment of 2 Sep 2019, ICC-01/13-99-Anx1, 2 Dec 2019, paras 49–50. Contra, Zakerhossein, n.153, 227–230.

[277] Stegmiller, n.49, 337–8; Carsten Stahn, 'Higher Gravity Threshold? A Plea for Caution' in Richard H Steinberg (ed.), *The International Criminal Court: Legal, Policy, and Political Challenges* (Brill 2025) 258, 263. On social alarm, see above, subsection 2.2.

[278] OTP, *Policy on Cultural Heritage* (Jun 2021), para.95.

[279] OTP, *Policy on Addressing Environmental Crimes through the Rome Statute* (Dec 2025), para.20.

very difficult predictive exercise, it would be better to focus only on the effects of the crimes on local communities when assessing sufficient gravity, leaving further considerations to the realm of policy that might be relevant in the exercise of prosecutorial discretion.

3.5 Critical Considerations on the Four Factors and Preliminary Conclusions

The investigation so far has reached several conclusions in relation to the four factors determining gravity that need to be highlighted and summarised to better understand how they should be employed.

First, it is evident that the OTP and the Chambers demonstrate a well-established practice with regard to the fact that scale, nature, manner of commission, and impact are the main factors to be assessed under Article 17(1)(d) of the RS. However, it is true that, most of the time, the four factors are mentioned as if they are examples in a non-exhaustive list of factors. The reference to the rules on the determination of penalties itself allows the elaboration of further criteria beyond the four factors. Nonetheless reliance on these four factors alone has become commonplace in prosecutorial practice and judicial decisions. Factors that were previously mentioned were rejected – such as social alarm – or were incorporated into one of the four factors – such as systematicity, which became a component of the manner of commission.

Second, both the OTP and the Chambers are careful to indicate that the four factors determining sufficient gravity are external and additional to the elements of the crimes.[280] In other words, there is a strict – and correct – distinction between those elements that are necessary for the purposes of the existence of a crime (and they pertain to jurisdiction) and those elements that may or may not be present in order to determine sufficient gravity (admissibility).[281] It follows that the four factors are presented in addition to the *actus reus*, the *mens rea*, and modes of liability, which are necessary components of the ICC's

---

[280] For example, Situation in the DRC, PTC I, Decision on the Prosecutor's Application for Warrants of Arrest, Article 58, ICC-01/04-520-Anx2, 10 Feb 2006, para.42; OTP, *Report on the Activities Performed during the First Three Years (Jun 2003 – Jun 2006)* (12 Sep 2006), 6; Situation in Kenya, PTC II, Decision Pursuant to Article 15 of the Rome Statute on the Authorization of an Investigation into the Situation in the Republic of Kenya, ICC-01/09-19-Corr, 31 Mar 2010, para.56.

[281] For an endorsement of this view by a defendant, see Situation in Kenya, PTC II, *Prosecutor v Muthaura et al*, Defence Challenge to Jurisdiction, Admissibility and Prosecution's Failure to Meet the Requirements of Article 54, ICC-01/09-02/11-338, 19 Sep 2011, para.56.

subject-matter jurisdiction. As beautifully put by PTC II, sufficient gravity does not pertain to the crimes as such, but to the crimes within a specific context.[282] To quote Judge Eboe-Osuji: '"gravity" is a legal characterisation of a given circumstance *on the basis of a set of facts*.'[283] What makes the specific killing of a civilian sufficiently grave for admissibility purposes is not the voluntary causation of the death of that protected person (already considered to be sufficiently grave as to be included in the jurisdiction of the Court); rather, sufficient gravity is determined by the scale of that crime (for example, many civilians versus an isolated episode), the nature of that crime (for example, the civilian was killed for discriminatory motives), the manner of commission of that crime (for example, the civilian was tortured to death), and the impact of that crime (for example, an entire family of ten children relied upon that civilian for their sustenance). This means that certain considerations can be relevant only for certain specific crimes: for example, discriminatory motives are a jurisdictional component of the crime of persecution, a crime against humanity under Article 7(1)(h),[284] and the systematicity of an attack is a component of any crime against humanity under Article 7(1). For these crimes, these considerations should not be included in the assessment of sufficient gravity, as demonstrated by two 2023 decisions of PTC I and the AC; in these decisions, PTC I and the the AC assessed submissions on alleged lack of sufficient gravity due to the fact that there was an absence of any widespread or systematic attack directed against any civilian population or that the crimes were not committed pursuant to a state policy, and concluded that these claims were absorbed by a decision on jurisdiction about crimes against humanity.[285]

---

[282] Situation in Kenya, PTC II, Decision Pursuant to Article 15 of the Rome Statute on the Authorization of an Investigation into the Situation in the Republic of Kenya, ICC-01/09-19-Corr, 31 Mar 2010, para.61.

[283] Situation on Registered Vessels, AC, Judgment on the appeal of the Prosecutor against PTC I's 'Decision on the "Application for Judicial Review by the Government of the Union of the Comoros"', ICC-01/13-98, 2 Sept 2019, Partly Dissenting Opinion of Judge Eboe-Osuji, para.37 (emphasis added).

[284] Elements of the Crimes, Article 7(1)(h), Crime against humanity of persecution, para.2.

[285] Situation in the Philippines, PTC I, Public Redacted Version of 'Authorisation pursuant to article 18(2) of the Statute to resume the investigation', ICC-01/21-56-Red, 26 Jan 2023, para.25; Situation in the Philippines, AC, Judgment on the appeal of the Republic of the Philippines against PTC I's 'Authorisation pursuant to article 18(2) of the Statute to resume the investigation', ICC-01/21-77, 18 Jul 2023, para.229. See also Situation in Mali, *Prosecutor v Al Hassan*, Defence for Mr Al Hassan Ag Abdoul Aziz Ag Mohamed Ag Mahmoud, Public redacted version of 'Submissions for the confirmation of charges', ICC-01/12-01/18-394-Red, 4 Jul 2019, para.258.

Third, the four factors need to be assessed altogether rather than in isolation. Accordingly, one of the four factors can be less present in a specific situation or case that, nevertheless, can be sufficiently grave. However, this conclusion should not alter the imperative of considering sufficient gravity as a minimal threshold for the reasons that will be explored in the next chapter.[286]

Finally, the four factors determining gravity can be reconciled with an act of interpretation of Article 17(1)(d) of the RS. This is clear in relation to the case law of the Chambers that invokes the rules on penalties as an interpretive tool of Article 17(1)(d). The rules on penalties are part of the interpretive context that should be considered in the interpretation of Article 17(1)(d) pursuant to Article 31 of the VCLT. Providing this link between the RS (Article 78(1)) and its derivative sources (Rules 145(1)(c) and 145(2)(b) of the RPE) on the one hand, and the interpretation of sufficient gravity under Article 17(1)(d) limits the impression that the four factors are pulled out of thin air, that they are the product of a law-making process by the OTP and the Chambers. Rather, following the Chambers' approach, the four factors are linked to the process of treaty interpretation and to the applicable law mentioned in Article 21(1)(a) of the RS. Indeed, each of the four factors can be justified in light of an interpretive rule, particularly the duty to interpret the RS in a way that is 'consistent with internationally recognized human rights, and ... without any adverse distinction' as per Article 21(3).

4. THE MOST RESPONSIBLE CRITERION

4.1 The Apparent Convergence of the OTP and Chambers on the Criterion

This subsection explores whether, along with the four factors determining gravity, another element should be considered in the assessment of sufficient gravity: the fact that the alleged perpetrator is likely to be the most responsible for the commission of the crimes.

As already noted, from the beginning of the gravity discourse, the OTP has focused on the degree of responsibility of the alleged perpetrator in the commission of the crimes. For instance, in 2003, the OTP held that '[t]he concept of gravity should not be exclusively attached to the act that constituted the crime but also to the degree of participation in its commission'.[287] In the decision on the Lubanga and Ntaganda arrest warrants in 2006, PTC I interpreted

---

[286] See below, Chapter 5.

[287] OTP, *Paper on Some Policy Issues before the Office of the Prosecutor* (Sep 2003), 7.

this requirement as suggesting that gravity 'is intended to ensure that the Court initiates cases only against the *most senior leaders* suspected of being the *most responsible* for the crimes',[288] articulating a threefold test based on the accused being the most senior leader, their role, through acts or omissions, in the commission of systematic or large-scale crimes, and their role in relation to the commission of specific crimes.[289] As noted above, this conclusion sparked substantial academic criticism, was appealed by the OTP, and was ultimately rejected by the AC.[290]

It should be recalled that, in its appeals against the decision on the Lubanga and Ntaganda arrest warrants, the OTP suggested a two-pronged test in relation to the assessment of sufficient gravity under Article 17(1)(d) of the RS, based on the factors determining gravity and the most responsible criterion: '[i]f the [AC] chooses to elaborate a test under Article 17 (1) (d), ... the standard should be a basic test, taking into account as factors the gravity of the crimes and the extent of responsibility of the person.'[291] This solution met with initial support in the case law of the Chambers. For instance, PTC II, in relation to Kenya, affirmed that the assessment of sufficient gravity requires 'a generic assessment of whether such groups of persons that are likely to form the object of investigation capture those who may bear the greatest responsibility for the alleged crimes committed'.[292] The Chamber went on to affirm that what is required is:

> a generic examination of: (i) whether the persons or groups of persons that are likely to be the object of an investigation include those who may bear the greatest responsibility for the alleged crimes committed; and (ii) the gravity of the crimes allegedly committed within the incidents, which are likely to be the object of an investigation.[293]

---

[288] Situation in the DRC, PTC I, Decision on the Prosecutor's Application for Warrants of Arrest, Article 58, ICC-01/04-520-Anx2, 10 Feb 2006, para.51 (emphasis added).

[289] Ibid, paras 52–3.

[290] See above, subsection 2.2.3.

[291] Situation in the DRC, PTC I, Decision on the Prosecutor's Application for Warrants of Arrest, Article 58, ICC-01/04-520-Anx2, 10 Feb 2006, para.53.

[292] Situation in Kenya, PTC II, Decision Pursuant to Article 15 of the Rome Statute on the Authorization of an Investigation into the Situation in the Republic of Kenya, ICC-01/09-19-Corr, 31 Mar 2010, para.60.

[293] Ibid, para.188.

PTC III, in relation to the situation in the Côte d'Ivoire, was quick to follow suit.[294] Against this backdrop, in 2014, the OTP, in relation to the boarding of the *Mavi Marmara*, easily concluded that:

> [a]n evaluation of gravity includes: (i) whether the individuals or groups of persons that are likely to be the object of an investigation, include those who may bear the greatest responsibility for the alleged crimes committed; and (ii) the gravity of the crimes committed within the incidents which are likely to be the focus of an investigation.[295]

PTC I endorsed this view, in relation to the same situation, in 2015[296] and 2020,[297] while the OTP reiterated it in 2017.[298] Similarly, PTC I maintained this position in 2016 in relation to the different situation of Georgia.[299]

From the survey above, it is possible to conclude that, after 2006, the OTP and the PTCs apparently agreed on the most responsible criterion. The next subsections explore the content of this criterion and why this agreement is only apparent.

4.2 The Content of the Most Responsible Criterion

In assessing whether the focus of the investigation or prosecution is on the persons who bear the greatest responsibility for the crimes, that is, the most responsible persons, the OTP and the Chambers have resorted to multiple factors. An overview of some judicial practice and case law suffices to show that there is no uniformity of approach.

A small group of judicial decisions and prosecutorial documents refer to the seniority of the persons that are likely to be the objects of an investigation, are

---

294 Situation in Côte d'Ivoire, PTC III, Corrigendum to 'Decision Pursuant to Article 15 of the RS on the Authorisation of an Investigation into the Situation in the Republic of Côte d'Ivoire', ICC-02/11-14-Corr, 15 Nov 2011, para.204.

295 Situation on Registered Vessels, OTP, Article 53(1) Report, 6 Nov 2014, para.135.

296 Situation on Registered Vessels, PTC I, Decision on the request of the Union of the Comoros to review the Prosecutor's decision not to initiate an investigation, ICC-01/13-34, 16 Jul 2015, para.21.

297 Situation on Registered Vessels, PTC I, Decision on the 'Application for Judicial Review by the Government of the Comoros', ICC-01/13-111, 16 Sept 2020, para.19.

298 Situation on Registered Vessels, OTP, Final decision of the Prosecution concerning the 'Article 53(1) Report' (ICC-01/13-6-AnxA), dated 6 Nov 2014, ICC-01/13-57-Anx1, 29 Nov 2017, para.166.

299 Situation in Georgia, PTC I, Decision on the Prosecutor's request for authorization of an investigation, ICC-01/15-12, 27 Jan 2016, paras 51–2.

investigated, or are accused. For instance, in 2010, commenting on the persons likely to be the object of an investigation in the situation in Kenya, PTC II mentioned with approval 'their high-ranking positions'[300] as a relevant factor in assessing sufficient gravity. Similarly, in 2015, in relation to Georgia, PTC I noted 'rank in political or command positions' as relevant for the assessment of sufficient gravity.[301] However, this reference to high-ranking position is misplaced, as explained by the AC in 2006, when it found a similar conclusion in relation to the Lubanga and Ntaganda arrest warrants to be incorrect, as detailed above.[302] In fact, every time these considerations have resurfaced over the years, they have been judged to be irrelevant by the Chambers, as demonstrated by the 2020 decision of PTC I in relation to the boarding of the *Mavi Marmara*: 'this factor did not relate to the seniority or hierarchical position of the persons likely to be the object of the investigation, but to the Prosecutor's ability to investigate those most responsible.'[303]

A second group of judicial decisions and prosecutorial documents mentions the capacity of the persons that likely will be the objects of an investigation, are investigated, or are accused, to induce the commission of the crimes. For instance, in 2010, again in relation to the situation in Kenya, PTC II observed that 'their alleged role in the violence, namely inciting, planning, financing, colluding with criminal gangs, and otherwise contributing to the organization of the violence ... renders the first constituent element of gravity satisfied'.[304] Likewise, in relation to Côte d'Ivoire in 2014, PTC I took note of the fact that:

---

300 Situation in Kenya, PTC II, Decision Pursuant to Article 15 of the Rome Statute on the Authorization of an Investigation into the Situation in the Republic of Kenya, ICC-01/09-19-Corr, 31 Mar 2010, para.198.

301 Situation in Georgia, OTP, Corrected Version of 'Request for authorisation of an investigation pursuant to article 15', 16 Oct 2015, ICC-01/15-4-Corr, ICC-01/15-4-Corr2, 17 Nov 2015, para.335.

302 See above, subsection 2.2.3. For criticism of the most responsible criterion, on the basis of the fact that it overlaps with seniority, see Dondé Matute, n.68, 60–62.

303 Situation on Registered Vessels, PTC I, Decision on the 'Application for Judicial Review by the Government of the Comoros', ICC-01/13-111, 16 Sept 2020, para.36. However, the OTP had not openly advocated for a seniority approach to this point, as requested by the Comoros: see Situation on Registered Vessels, OTP, Final decision of the Prosecution concerning the 'Article 53(1) Report' (ICC-01/13-6-AnxA), dated 6 Nov 2014, ICC-01/13-57-Anx1, 29 Nov 2017, para.169; Situation on Registered Vessels, Comoros, Application for Review pursuant to Article 53(3)(a) of the Prosecutor's Decision of 6 Nov 2014 not to initiate an investigation in the Situation, ICC-01/13-3-Red, 29 Jan 2015, paras 86 and 88.

304 Situation in Kenya, PTC II, Decision Pursuant to Article 15 of the Rome Statute on the Authorization of an Investigation into the Situation in the Republic

> Charles Blé Goudé was a member of the inner circle of Laurent Gbagbo and played a key role in the very conception and implementation of the plan that resulted in the commission of the crimes charged, and was a prominent member of that group of people that also conceived, adopted and implemented the policy to commit the widespread and systematic attack against the civilian population, in the framework of which the crimes charges were perpetrated.[305]

Similarly, in 2015, PTC I noted that the information available in relation to the situation in Georgia 'indicate[d] … their alleged role in the violence in ordering, facilitating or otherwise contributing to the commission of alleged crimes'. [306]

It looks as though both PTC I and PTC II gave significant weight to the fact that the persons likely to be investigated were not the direct perpetrators, but rather accessories; not those who allegedly committed the crimes under Article 25(3)(a) of the RS, but those who ordered, solicited, or induced the commission of the crimes under Article 25(3)(b) of the RS, those who aided, abetted, or otherwise assisted in the commission under Article 25(3)(c) of the RS, and those who in any other way contributed to the commission or attempted commission of the crimes by a group of persons acting with a common purpose under Article 25(3)(d) of the RS.[307]

However, the weight attributed to this factor runs contrary to the past judicial practice of both the OTP and the Chambers. In 2011, when a defendant

---

of Kenya, ICC-01/09-19-Corr, 31 Mar 2010, para.198.

305 Situation in Côte d'Ivoire, *Prosecutor v Blé Goudé*, PTC I, Decision on the Defence Challenge to the Admissibility of the Case against Charles Blé Goudé for Insufficient Gravity, ICC-02/11-02/11-185, 12 Nov 2014, para.21(v).

306 Situation in Georgia, Corrected Version of 'Request for authorisation of an investigation pursuant to article 15', 16 Oct 2015, ICC-01/15-4-Corr, ICC-01/15-4-Corr2, 17 Nov 2015, para.335.

307 On the different modes of participation in international crimes, see, among many others, Elies van Sliedregt, *Individual Criminal Responsibility in International Law* (OUP 2012); Gerhard Werle and Boris Burghardt, 'Establishing Degrees of Responsibility: Modes of Participation in Article 25 of the ICC Statute' in Elies van Sliedregt and Sergey Vasiliev (eds), *Pluralism in International Criminal Law* (OUP 2014) 301; Neha Jain, *Perpetrators and Accessories in International Criminal Law* (Hart 2014); Giulia Lanza, *Indirect Perpetration and Organisationscherrschaftslehre: An Analysis of Article 25(3) of the Rome Statute in Light of the German Differentiated and Italian Unitarian Models of Participation in a Crime* (D&H 2021); Aleksandra Nieprzecka, *Participation in Crime Falling Within the Subject-Matter Jurisdiction of the International Criminal Court* (TMC Asser 2024).

claimed that, depending on the relevant mode of liability, the sufficient gravity of the case may vary,[308] the OTP opposed this view by arguing:

> that the case is not grave enough if the mode of liability is based on accessorial conduct' is an interpretation that 'would lead to the absurd result that charging a person with grave crimes, but under the "wrong" mode of liability, would convert the otherwise grave (and thus admissible) case into one that is necessarily inadmissible.[309]

PTC II correctly noted that, with regard to 'the argument that only cases brought against principals or direct perpetrators are of sufficient gravity to justify action by the Court, the Chamber considers that this argument is legally unfounded, for the reason that it would, as a matter of principle, deprive article 25(3)(d) of the Statute of any meaning'.[310] This conclusion is sound as it preserves the distinction between subject-matter jurisdiction (the alleged crime, with all its elements, including modes of liability) and admissibility.

A third limited set of judicial decisions refers to the extent of the *mens rea* of the suspect or accused as an element relevant for sufficient gravity, particularly when defendants have challenged the admissibility of a case for lack of sufficient gravity. For instance, PTC I noted 'the degree of [Charles Blé Goudé's] intent and participation in the charged crimes'.[311] In relation to Mali, the same Chamber took 'note of Mr Al Hassan's degree of intent and degree of participation in these crimes'.[312] The fact that the degree of intent, which pertains to *mens rea*, is mentioned alongside the degree of participation may suggest that they are components of the most responsible criterion, even though, as mentioned above, in 2013, it was considered to be part of the manner of commission of the crime.[313] However, the Chamber offered no thorough elaboration on this. In reality, as *mens rea* is an element of an international crime, as such,

---

[308] Situation in Kenya, PTC II, *Prosecutor v Muthaura et al*, Defence Challenge to Jurisdiction, Admissibility and Prosecution's Failure to Meet the Requirements of Article 54, ICC-01/09-02/11-338, 19 Sept 2011, paras 56–71.

[309] Situation in Kenya, OTP, *Prosecutor v Muthaura et al*, Prosecution's Response to the Defence Challenges to Jurisdiction, ICC-01/09-02/11-356, 14 Oct 2011, para.50.

[310] Situation in Kenya, PTC II, *Prosecutor v Muthaura et al*, Public Redacted Version of Decision on the Confirmation of Charges Pursuant to Article 61(7)(a) and (b) of the Rome Statute, ICC-01/09-02/11-382-Red, 23 Jan 2012, para.47.

[311] Situation in Côte d'Ivoire, PTC I, *Prosecutor v Blé Goudé*, Decision on the Defence Challenge to the Admissibility of the Case against Charles Blé Goudé for Insufficient Gravity, ICC-02/11-02/11-185, 12 Nov 2014, para.20.

[312] Situation in Mali, PTC I, *Prosecutor v Al Hassan*, Decision on the Admissibility Challenge raised by the Defence for Insufficient Gravity of the Case, ICC-01/12-01/18-459-tENG, 27 Sept 2019, para.57.

[313] See above, subsection 3.4.3.

it should be considered part of the existence of the crime for jurisdictional purposes rather than for admissibility ones.

A fourth group of decisions and prosecutorial documents seems to interpret the reference to those who bear the greatest responsibility in a pragmatic way, alluding to the causal link between the alleged perpetrator and crime rather than relying on seniority or on a specific mode of participation. For instance, in 2010, a policy paper of the OTP claimed that 'the Office will select for prosecution those situated at the highest echelons of responsibility, including those who ordered, financed, or otherwise organized the alleged crimes'.[314] Similarly, PTC III noted in the assessment of sufficient gravity that 'high-ranking officials of the Burundian government, the police, the intelligence service and the military services, but also the Imbonerakure, appear to be the most responsible for the most serious crimes'.[315] PTC I, in relation to the situation of Mali, took note of:

> the significant role that the Prosecutor attributes to Mr Al Hassan in the execution of said crimes, not least through his contribution to the Islamic Police, an organ of repression established by the armed groups to cement their power and control over the civilian population of the city of Timbuktu and its region and thereby to impose on it their own ideological and religious vision by any means.[316]

Very clearly, in relation to the *Mavi Marmara* incident, the OTP affirmed that:

> the assessment of whether the potential objects of any investigation "may bear the greatest responsibility for the identified crimes" is fact-sensitive. It may be informed by factors including: the potential legal characterisation(s) of the conduct relevant to the potential case(s) under consideration (including whether the identified crime was perpetrated individually or with others); and whether or not other persons may potentially be involved in the relevant conduct, and the manner in which that involvement might be legally characterised (as accessories, superiors, etc); and so on.[317]

---

[314] OTP, *Report on Prosecutorial Strategy (2009–2012)* (1 Feb 2010), para.18.

[315] Situation in Burundi, PTC III, Public redacted version of 'Decision Pursuant to Article 15 of the RS on the Authorization of an Investigation into the Situation in the Republic of Burundi', ICC-01/17-X-9-US-Exp, 25 Oct 2017, ICC-01/17-9-Red, 9 Nov 2017, para.187.

[316] Situation in Mali, PTC I, *Prosecutor v Al Hassan*, Decision on the Admissibility Challenge raised by the Defence for Insufficient Gravity of the Case, ICC-01/12-01/18-459-tENG, 27 Sept 2019, para.57.

[317] Situation on Registered Vessels, OTP, Final decision of the Prosecution concerning the 'Article 53(1) Report' (ICC-01/13-6-AnxA), dated 6 Nov 2014, as

In all these cases, there is a refusal to define the most responsible criterion, emphasising the factual contribution of the alleged perpetrator to the commission of the crimes, irrespective of the type of contribution and regardless of any seniority. This pragmatic approach, though well suited to a case-by-case application, makes it difficult to formulate a precise definition of the most responsible criterion.

All in all, it is impossible to distil a singular definition of the most responsible criterion under Article 17(1)(d) from the practice of the OTP and judicial decisions. Simply, the practice of the OTP and of the Chambers is too fragmented, radiating in diverse directions. The following subsection demonstrates that this criterion does not belong to the gravity assessment.

4.3 Why the Most Responsible Criterion Does Not Belong to Sufficient Gravity

In relation to the most responsible criterion, it has been noted that the OTP and Chambers have converged on its relevance for sufficient gravity, despite the fact that its content is not easy to grasp. This subsection explains why there has never been a real agreement between ICC organs on the fact that the most responsible criterion belongs to sufficient gravity.

A careful analysis of relevant prosecutorial practice demonstrates that the OTP considers the most responsible criterion to be additional to, rather than a primary component of, the assessment of sufficient gravity under Article 17(1)(d) of the RS. As mentioned above, the first time the OTP articulated the criterion in 2006, PTC I observed that for 'a test under Article 17 (1) (d), … the standard should be a basic test, taking into account as factors the gravity of the crimes and the extent of responsibility of the person'.[318] Although here the extent of responsibility is anchored to Article 17(1)(d), in fact, the OTP did not consider it to be a component of sufficient gravity, but rather, a factor to be assessed in addition to the gravity of the crimes. In its appeal against this decision, the OTP observed that 'more stringent standards, such as "persons most responsible", or "those bearing the greatest responsibility" may be appropriate for case selection among serious cases, *but should not be legal preconditions for admissibility'*.[319]

---

revised and refiled in accordance with the PTC's request of 15 Nov 2018 and the AC's judgment of 2 Sept 2019, ICC-01/13-99-Anx1, 2 Dec 2019, para.21.

[318] Situation in the DRC, PTC I, Decision on the Prosecutor's Application for Warrants of Arrest, Article 58, ICC-01/04-520-Anx2, 10 Feb 2006, para.53.

[319] Situation in the DRC, Public Redacted Version of the Prosecutor's Document in Support of the Appeal, ICC-01/04-120-Red, 3 Mar 2006, para.30 (emphasis added).

Relevant policy papers are also ambiguous on whether the most responsible criterion is a component of sufficient gravity. In the *Report on Prosecutorial Strategy (2009–2012)*, the OTP addressed the topic of 'Focused investigations and prosecutions', claiming that the Office has to 'take into account the gravity of the crime when deciding on the initiation of investigations'.[320] The immediately following paragraph, mentioning the most responsible criterion, reads:

> the Office consolidated a policy of focused investigations and prosecutions, meaning it will investigate and prosecute those who bear the greatest responsibility for the most serious crimes, based on the evidence that emerges in the course of an investigation. Thus, the Office will select for prosecution those situated at the highest echelons of responsibility, including those who ordered, financed, or otherwise organized the alleged crimes.[321]

This statement is not directly linked to the assessment of sufficient gravity, which is explored in the subsequent paragraph with reference to the four previously discussed factors.[322]

Similarly, the 2013 *Policy Paper on Preliminary Examinations* addresses the most responsible criterion in its overall assessment of admissibility, stating that '[t]he Office will assess complementarity and gravity in relation to the most serious crimes alleged to have been committed and those most responsible for those crimes'.[323] Although the Policy Paper goes on to quote the PTCs' views on the relevance of the most responsible criterion, this is done in relation to the definition of what amounts to a 'potential case' rather than to gravity specifically.[324] Indeed, the policy paper clarifies that, in past cases, the OTP 'considered admissibility in the *light of its stated policy* of focussing on those bearing the greatest responsibility for the most serious crimes'.[325] Unsurprisingly, the analysis of gravity in the policy paper centres almost entirely on the four factors,[326] with only the following reference at the end to the most responsible criterion:

> The gravity assessment is an important consideration in the opening of investigations, bearing in mind the potential cases that are likely to arise from an investigation. The principle of impartiality … requires the Office to focus its efforts objectively on those most responsible for the most serious crimes within the

---

[320] OTP, *Report on Prosecutorial Strategy (2009–2012)* (1 Feb 2010), para.19.

[321] Ibid.

[322] Ibid, para.20.

[323] OTP, *Policy Paper on Preliminary Examinations* (Nov 2013), para.42.

[324] Ibid, paras 43 and 45.

[325] Ibid, para.45.

[326] Ibid, paras 59–65.

> situation in a consistent manner, irrespective of the States or parties involved or the person(s) or group(s) concerned.[327]

Clearly, the gravity assessment, in this statement, is separate from the most responsible criterion. It is pursued as a matter of policy, and it allegedly derives from the principle of impartiality rather than from Article 17(1)(d).

Even more unquestionable is the OTP's position in its 2016 *Policy Paper on Case Selection and Prioritisation*. Under the rubric 'case selection criteria', the OTP distinguishes between 'gravity' (which is based only on the four determining factors),[328] '[d]egree of responsibility of alleged perpetrators'[329] and 'charges'.[330] Unsurprisingly, the most responsible criterion is addressed under the section on the degree of responsibility of alleged perpetrators rather than under gravity,[331] thus demonstrating that it does not belong to the gravity assessment. Similarly, the most responsible criterion does not appear in the 2025 *Policy on Addressing Environmental Damage through the Rome Statute*, which, in relation to sufficient gravity, refers to scale, nature, and impact only.[332] Unequivocally, the 2025 Policy on Cyber-Enabled Crimes under the Rome Statute refers to them as two discrete considerations:

> one key consideration is the gravity of the alleged conduct, having regard to all the relevant circumstances. *Another* is the degree of responsibility of the alleged perpetrators, bearing in mind that this does not necessarily equate with *de jure* hierarchical status within a structure but rather is to be assessed on a case-by-case basis depending on the evidence.[333]

Indeed, the most responsible criterion is not mentioned in Regulation 29(2) of the Regulations of the OTP, which lists only the four gravity-determining factors as those relevant for the assessment of sufficient gravity.[334] Under Regulation 33, the OTP must 'identify the most serious crimes committed within the situation' taking into account 'jurisdiction, admissibility (including gravity), as well as the interests of justice'. The Regulations mention the most responsible criterion only in Regulation 34(1) that reads: '[t]he joint

---

[327] Ibid, para.66.

[328] OTP, *Policy Paper on Case Selection and Prioritisation* (15 Sept 2016), paras 35–41.

[329] Ibid, paras 42–4.

[330] Ibid, paras 45–6.

[331] Ibid, paras 42–3.

[332] OTP, *Policy on Addressing Environmental Damage through the Rome Statute* (Dec 2025), para.20.

[333] OTP, *Policy on Cyber-Enabled Crimes under the Rome Statute* (Dec 2025), para.129 (emphasis added).

[334] OTP, *Regulations of the OTP*, 23 Apr 2009.

team shall review the information and evidence collected and shall determine a provisional case hypothesis (or hypotheses) identifying the incidents to be investigated and the person or persons who appear to be the most responsible.' This provision identifies two elements to be assessed: incidents and persons. It seems that gravity pertains to the identification of the incidents, while the most responsible criterion pertains to the identification of the persons, which, together, form a potential case. In other words, although not straightforwardly, the Regulations of the OTP do not mention the most responsible criterion as a component of sufficient gravity, but only separately, in relation to the selection of accused.

In practice, the OTP has often treated the most responsible criterion as a matter of policy rather than as a component of sufficient gravity. For instance, in 2013, in relation to the situation in Mali, the OTP noted that 'admissibility requires an assessment of complementarity and gravity. *Pursuant to its prosecutorial strategy*, the Office assesses complementarity and gravity in relation to the most serious crimes allegedly committed by those who appear to bear the greatest responsibility.[335] Moreover, in 2015, the OTP issued a statement explaining why affiliates of Daesh, who were nationals of ICC States Parties, would not have been investigated and prosecuted for alleged international crimes committed in Syria and Iraq under the principle of personal jurisdiction.[336] The OTP noted that:

> The information gathered indicates that several thousand foreign fighters have joined the ranks of ISIS in the past months alone, including significant numbers of State Party nationals ... Some of these individuals may have been involved in the commission of crimes against humanity and war crimes. A few have publicised their heinous acts through social media. The information available to the Office also indicates that ISIS is a military and political organisation primarily led by nationals of Iraq and Syria. Thus, at this stage, the prospects of my Office investigating and prosecuting those most responsible, within the leadership of ISIS, appear limited.[337]

Notwithstanding the fact that some commentators have analysed this statement discussing the most responsible criterion as part of sufficient gravity,[338] the OTP never mentions sufficient gravity. Rather, the OTP affirms that 'the jurisdictional basis for opening a preliminary examination into this situation

---

335 Situation in Mali, OTP, Article 53(1) Report, 16 Jan 2013, para.134.

336 OTP, *Statement of the Prosecutor of the International Criminal Court, Fatou Bensouda, on the Alleged Crimes Committed by ISIS* (8 Apr 2015).

337 Ibid.

338 deGuzman, n.261, 103.

is too narrow'.[339] This conclusion sparked significant criticism because either the jurisdiction of the Court exists – due to the fact that some alleged perpetrators are nationals of a State Party – or it does not exist: the most responsible criterion does not pertain to jurisdiction.[340] However, for the purposes of sufficient gravity, it is necessary to note that the OTP claimed to have reached this conclusion after the 'Office took into account the scope of its *policy*, which is to focus on those most responsible for mass crimes'.[341] Accordingly, it is patent that the most responsible criterion is linked to policy considerations, rather than to legal reasons pertaining to admissibility.[342]

Navanethem Pillay, when she was United Nations High Commissioner for Human Rights, explained the origins of the most responsible criterion. She observed that this criterion was adopted by the OTP *as a matter of policy*, following the activity of the Prosecutor of the Special Court for Sierra Leone (SCSL).[343] Indeed, Article 15(1) of the 2002 Statute of the SCSL provides that '[t]he Prosecutor shall be responsible for the investigation and prosecution of persons who bear the greatest responsibility for' the crimes within the SCSL jurisdiction.[344] Similarly, Rule 28(A) of the RPE of the ICTY, as amended in 2004, provided that '[t]he President shall refer the matter to the Bureau

339 OTP, *Statement of the Prosecutor of the International Criminal Court, Fatou Bensouda, on the Alleged Crimes Committed by ISIS* (8 Apr 2015) (emphasis added).

340 See the criticisms by Mohammad Hadi Zakerhossein, 'To Bury a Situation Alive - A Critical Reading of the ICC Prosecutor's Statement on the ISIS Situation' (2016) 16 ICLR 613, 624–7; Cóman Kenny, 'Prosecuting Crimes of International Concern: Islamic State at the ICC?' (2017) 33 *Utrecht Journal of International and European Law* 120, 125.

341 OTP, *Statement of the Prosecutor of the International Criminal Court, Fatou Bensouda, on the Alleged Crimes Committed by ISIS* (8 Apr 2015) (emphasis added).

342 Zakerhossein, n.340, 627; Zakerhossein, n.153, 249; Pues, n.265, 979–8; Darryl Robinson et al, *An Introduction to International Criminal Law and Procedure* (5th edn, CUP 2024) 151–2; Urs, n.165, 71. See also Xabier Agirre Aranburu, 'Gravity of Crimes and Responsibility of the Suspect' in Morten Bergsmo (ed.), *Criteria for Prioritizing and Selecting Core International Crimes Cases* (3rd edn, TOAEP 2024) 417, 433 (referring to the criterion as a policy choice).

343 Assembly of States Parties, Review Conference of the Rome Statute of the International Criminal Court Kampala, 31 May–11 Jun 2010, Annex V(c), *Report of the Bureau on Stocktaking: Complementarity (Taking Stock of the Principle of Complementarity: Bridging the Impunity Gap)*, para.12. The criterion has been used even before: see Aranburu, ibid, 429–433.

344 Emphasis added.

which shall determine whether the indictment, *prima facie*, concentrates on one or more of *the most senior leaders* suspected of being *most responsible* for crimes within the jurisdiction of the Tribunal'.[345] Likewise, Article 19 of the 219 Estatutaria de la Administración de Justicia en la Jurisdicción Especial para la Paz, provides that 'La Sala de Definición de Situaciones Jurídicas y la Sala de Reconocimiento de Verdad y Responsabilidad de la JEP, aplicarán criterios para concentrar el ejercicio de la acción penal en quienes tuvieron *participación determinante* en los hechos más graves y representativos'.[346] Transplanting these subsequent rules into the RS cannot be justified as an act of interpretation of Article 17(1)(d), nor is the Statute of the SCSL applicable to the activities of the OTP as a matter of applicable law under Article 21 of the RS. Correctly, Navanethem Pillay mentioned that the OTP adopted the approach of the Statute of the SCSL as a matter of policy.[347]

All these sources, taken together, suggest not only that there is no actual convergence of the OTP and the Chambers in relation to the content of the most responsible criterion, but, more significantly, that the most responsible criterion is not a component of the assessment of sufficient gravity under Article 17(1)(d). Sure, the OTP refers to the most responsible criterion as a driving force in the selection and prioritisation of situations and cases, but this practice is determined by a policy consideration that explicitly falls outside the scope of sufficient gravity.

5. CONCLUSIONS

This chapter has reconstructed the practice of the OTP and Chambers in relation to the identification and determination of the factors that are relevant to assess sufficient gravity. After an initial period of lack of interest in this topic, the OTP first suggested that mainly quantitative factors should govern the assessment of sufficient gravity. In 2006, PTC I introduced a test based on three main quantitative and qualitative factors that was rapidly overturned by the AC, which, nevertheless, did not provide an authoritative list of factors to use in future cases. This circumstance paved the way for the OTP and the Chambers to determine the factors relevant to gravity in their practice from 2006 to the present day. The OTP did so both in policy papers and judicial practice, crystallising these factors in the Regulations of the OTP that refer to

345 Emphasis added.

346 Emphasis added.

347 See also Stegmiller, n.49, 349 (arguing that 'individual circumstances of the accused (such as planning, form of participation, motive, and position and role)' pertain to 'subjective considerations [that] must be left aside when legal gravity is looked at' and should be assessed under the notion of interests of justice).

scale, nature, manner of commission, and impact. The Chambers, in response, embraced the approach of the OTP regarding these four factors, stressing, however, that they derive from the rules on the determination of penalties in the RS and RPE. Both organs identified these factors in light of circumstances that are external to the elements of the crimes, marking a correct distinction between those elements that are relevant to assess the jurisdiction of the Court and those that pertain to admissibility.

Both the OTP and the Chambers converged on the four factors, which crystallised and developed in judicial practice over time. Scale has a mainly quantitative dimension that pertains to the number of victims and special and temporal considerations. Although nature was first interpreted as a reference to the intrinsic gravity of certain acts that constitute certain crimes, recently, the OTP has suggested a different approach, focusing correctly on the vulnerable conditions of the victims; discriminatory motives should be included in the assessment of nature as well. Manner of commission encompasses brutality, systematicity, abuse of power, and the resort to sexual violence or harm to the environment as a means to commit international crimes. Finally, impact refers to consequences upon the victims, their families, and local communities beyond the crime itself, with an unconvincing attempt to widen the scope to encompass effects on the international community as a whole.

Although some practice by the OTP and the Chambers has included consideration of the role of the suspect/accused/defendant (here called the most responsible criterion) within the assessment of sufficient gravity, there is no real convergence between the two organs. In fact, the most responsible criterion has been invoked and applied in addition to sufficient gravity to justify some prosecutorial choices. As such, regardless of what the legal basis of this criterion is, it cannot be considered a component of the assessment of sufficient gravity. This conclusion is reinforced by the uncertain content of the most responsible criterion, which has been interpreted very differently over time by the OTP and the Chambers.

In conclusion, the OTP and the Chambers agree that sufficient gravity must be assessed taking into account the scale of the crimes, their nature, manner of commission, and impact.

5. Article 17(1)(d) and sufficient gravity as a threshold

> 'It is true that, in order to succeed, the OTP must connect the ends it wishes to achieve with the means it has available to achieve them. This is the hard reality. It must also meet this challenge within the framework of the [RS] and the mandate it has been given.'[1]

1. INTRODUCTION

This chapter explores Article 17(1)(d), demonstrating its nature as a minimal threshold. This means that cases and potential cases within situations should be analysed by the organs of the International Criminal Court (ICC) to determine whether they meet this threshold and are therefore admissible. The fact that other situations, cases, and potential cases within the ICC jurisdiction might be more grave is irrelevant to passing this threshold.

This chapter argues that the object and purpose of the Rome Statute (RS), the preparatory work of Article 17(1)(d), and the judicial practice of the Office of the Prosecutor (OTP) and the Chambers concur that Article 17(1)(d) should be interpreted as providing a minimal threshold of sufficient gravity, rather than a high one (section 2). The chapter also concludes that the assessment of this threshold is different when deciding whether to open an investigation from the assessment performed when deciding whether to launch a prosecution: in the former scenario, the assessment is generic in nature, while in the latter, it is more specific due to the OTP's investigative powers (section 2.4).

The chapter moves on to argue that this minimal threshold also applies when sufficient gravity governs the activity of the OTP under Article 53(1)(b) (directly or through Rule 49 of the Rules of Procedure and Evidence (RPE) when the OTP acts *proprio motu*) and (2)(b) (section 3). Indeed, the chapter

1 Overall Response of the International Criminal Court to the 'Independent Expert Review of the International Criminal Court and the Rome Statute System – Final Report', Preliminary Analysis of the Recommendations and Information on Relevant Activities Undertaken by the Court (14 Apr 2021), para.404.

demonstrates that, in these cases, the OTP must merely assess *ex ante* whether an investigation or prosecution would be likely deemed inadmissible by the Chambers; if so, the OTP must decide not to open an investigation or not to launch a prosecution for lack of sufficient gravity. However, the OTP invokes sufficient gravity to justify the selection of the allegedly gravest situations and cases, and decisions not to open investigations and not to launch prosecutions of situations and cases that cross the threshold of Article 17(1)(d) but are not the gravest when compared to others. This practice, which has given rise to a robust scholarly debate on the existence of a so-called relative gravity, is not in line with the RS. This chapter discusses whether decisions taken in pursuance of so-called prosecutorial discretion should be presented as decisions based on sufficient gravity. Not only is this legally incorrect, but also, this blurs the line of sufficient gravity beyond the intention of the drafters. The open-ended and discretionary notion of interests of justice should be employed by the OTP to justify the decision not to select situations and cases that cross the minimal threshold of Article 17(1)(d).

The chapter concludes that the imperative to interpret Article 17(1)(d) as a minimal threshold should be combined with the interpretive value of OTP practice and the case law of the Chambers in identifying the four factors determining sufficient gravity (scale, nature, manner of commission, and impact), discussed in the previous chapter. It is argued here that every time a situation or case presents as demonstrating these factors, then it should be presumed to be admissible under Article 17(1)(d) (section 4).

2. ARTICLE 17(1)(D) AS A MINIMAL THRESHOLD

This section explains why sufficient gravity should be considered a legal threshold, why such a threshold is minimal, and why comparative reasoning between situations and cases should not be used to determine the threshold. The analysis will refer to those factors determining gravity discussed in the previous chapter.

2.1 Sufficient Gravity as a Threshold

The standard of sufficient gravity provided by Article 17(1)(d) is a legal threshold.[2] When the RS posits that a case is inadmissible if '[t]he case is not of suf-

---

[2] See, for example, Margaret M deGuzman, 'Gravity and the Legitimacy of the International Criminal Court' (2008-2009) 32 FILJ 1400; Jacopo Governa, *Rethinking the Prosecutor's Discretion at the International Criminal Court: Substantive Limitations and Judicial Control* (D&H 2023) 206–10; Todd F Buchwald, 'The Aperture of the ICC: More than Just the Issue of Gravity' in

ficient gravity to justify further action by the Court', it creates a legal barrier that renders a case either admissible or not. The concept of threshold can be defined as 'the level or point at which you start to experience something, or at which something starts to happen'.[3] The notion of threshold is helpful to describe how sufficient gravity operates because it provides only two options: admissible or inadmissible. From a legal perspective,[4] there is no graduation, no need to resort to a hierarchy between different levels of gravity. As demonstrated by the very text of Article 17(1)(d), the only relevant thing is that the situation or case at hand crosses that threshold.[5]

This view is confirmed by the case law of the Chambers. According to the Appeals Chamber (AC), 'the gravity requirement must be assessed on a case-by-case basis, having regard to the specific facts of a given case. The purpose of this requirement is to *exclude from the purview of the Court* some cases.[6] On this premise, Pre-Trial Chamber (PTC) I stated that 'gravity under article 17(1)(d) of the Statute is not a criterion for the *selection* of the most serious situations and cases, as argued by the Prosecutor, but rather, is a requirement for the exclusion of (potential) cases of *marginal gravity*'.[7] Visualising the threshold as a gate, either a situation or case is in, or it is out.

To explain how such a legal threshold operates, it is helpful to compare Article 17(1)(d) with the role played by the gravity of the crimes in the penalty determination.[8] Irrespective of the fact that the assessment factors might be similar, the two exercises are fundamentally different. In relation to the determination of penalties, gravity is employed to articulate, nuance, and tailor the penalty in respect to certain specific cases that, in principle, can be punished very differently: basically, the judges have to decide between 0 and 30 years

---

Richard H Steinberg (ed.), *The International Criminal Court*: Legal, Policy, and Political Challenges (Brill 2025) 211.

3 'Threshold' in https://dictionary.cambridge.org/dictionary/english/threshold.

4 In non-legal studies, on the contrary, thresholds are sometimes considered as areas of 'queerness', irreconcilable with an in or out dichotomy. See, for example, Michela Murgia, *God Save the Queer: Catechismo femminista* (Einaudi 2022).

5 deGuzman, n.2, 1432.

6 Situation in Mali, *Prosecutor v Al Hassan*, AC, Judgment on the appeal of Mr Al Hassan against the decision of PTC I entitled 'Décision relative à l'exception d'irrecevabilité pour insuffisance de gravité de l'affaire soulevée par la défense', ICC-01/12-01/18 OA, 19 Feb 2020, para.53 (emphasis added).

7 Situation on Registered Vessels, PTC I, Decision on the 'Application for Judicial Review by the Government of the Comoros', ICC-01/13-111, 16 Sep 2020, para.96.

8 See above, Chapter 3, subsection 4.5.

of imprisonment, with the exceptional possibility of life imprisonment, on the basis of several factors, including the gravity of the crimes. This exercise is not an in or out situation as in relation to a threshold, but rather the result of a balancing process that happens in the framework of a case that is already above the sufficient gravity threshold of Article 17(1)(d). In other words, a specific human conduct can be grave enough to be criminalised by the RS (Articles 1 and 5 on jurisdiction); it can constitute a sufficiently grave case to be admissible under Article 17(1)(d); and, in addition, it can present certain particular gravity that provides for the determination of a specific penalty. For this reason, decisions on penalties may refer to the perceived lower gravity of certain crimes[9] without rendering the cases on those crimes less admissible. While the determination of penalties requires a graduation of gravity to decide between 0 years and life imprisonment, the determination of admissibility of a case under Article 17(1)(d) is an in or out exercise, a threshold, where, in principle, all the crimes may be at the centre of an admissible case (and where, accordingly, there is no room for wondering whether certain crimes are inherently graver or less grave). It is not by chance that the determination of the penalty under gravity comes at the end of the trial, when all elements have been properly scrutinised and it is possible to assess the degree of gravity granularly, whereas gravity as an admissibility criterion is assessed in more abstract terms when deciding whether to start an investigation or launch a prosecution.[10]

The problem of sufficient gravity is that Article 17(1)(d) does not set the threshold through a rule, but rather, through a standard. To recall an example provided earlier in this book, we are dealing with a provision that sounds more like 'drive with reasonable care' rather than 'speed limit at 50 km/h'.[11] However, it is clear that either the driver is using reasonable care (and then, we are below the threshold) or is not (and then we are above the threshold). The next subsection explains how treaty interpretation demands that such a threshold is interpreted as a minimal one.

2.2 Treaty Interpretation and the Imperative of a Minimal Threshold

Applying the rules on treaty interpretation embodied in the Vienna Convention on the Law of Treaties (VCLT), it is manifest that the RS demands that Article 17(1)(d) is interpreted as providing a minimal threshold. Textual, contextual,

---

9 For example, Situation in Mali, *Prosecutor v Al Mahdi*, TC VII, Judgment and Sentence, ICC-01/12-01/15-171, 27 Sep 2016, para.77.

10 Pierre Jouette, 'La gravité en droit international pénal' (2022) 67 *McGill Law Journal* 407, 449.

11 See above, Chapter 2, subsection 2.1.

and teleological interpretations all point in this direction, along with the preparatory work of Article 17(1)(d).

Article 17(1)(d) provides that 'the Court shall determine that a case is inadmissible where: ... [t]he case is not of sufficient gravity to justify further action by the Court'. As discussed in Chapter 2, textual interpretation of the word 'sufficient' in multiple authentic languages suggests that Article 17(1)(d) identifies 'sufficient gravity' as a degree of seriousness that is adequate to grant further actions by the Court in the exercise of its jurisdiction.[12] Accordingly, the object and purpose of the RS, chiefly emphasised in its Preamble, should guide the evaluation of which cases deserve further action in the exercise of the Court's jurisdiction, as mandated by the need to include teleological considerations when interpreting a treaty. As discussed, the main objects and purposes of the RS are accountability and justice, but other purposes such as truth-telling and reconciliation play a role as implied purposes.[13] The idea of accountability and justice, including their preventive and deterrent effects, indicates that the gravity threshold is low; if the gravity threshold were a high bar, there would be a broad zone of impunity for less grave cases of international crimes that would weaken the aims of accountability and justice, sending the wrong message to potential perpetrators in the sense that, under certain circumstances, they can commit international crimes under ICC jurisdiction with impunity.

That the imperative of pursuing accountability and justice, with the aim of deterring the future commission of international crimes, mandates an interpretation of sufficient gravity as a lower threshold is confirmed by contextual interpretation. Article 17 of the RS mentions, along with sufficient gravity, two other inadmissibility grounds: complementarity[14] and *ne bis in idem*.[15] Neither of those other grounds is interpreted as granting impunity to the perpetrators of international crimes, but rather, both admissibility grounds are based on the fact that accountability and justice for those crimes are provided elsewhere: in relation to complementarity, the same person is investigated or prosecuted for the same crime by a domestic court; in the case of *ne bis in idem*, the same person has been tried for the same conduct before a court. Since these two inadmissibility grounds are explicitly premised on a division of labour between courts with jurisdiction to prosecute international crimes, rather than on not prosecuting them at all, then sufficient gravity, with the potential outcome that an international crime is not prosecuted by any court, must be exceptional and must be considered a very low threshold.

---

12 See above, Chapter 2, subsection 3.2.1.

13 See above, Chapter 2, subsection 3.2.1.

14 RS, Article 17(1)(a)–(b).

15 RS, Article 17(1)(c). See also Article20(3).

Additionally, from a contextual perspective, it is worth mentioning Article 77(1) of the RS, according to which the Court can impose a sentence of between 0 and 30 years of imprisonment, with the possibility of imposing life imprisonment in consideration of the 'extraordinary gravity of the crimes'. This provision is relevant for the interpretation of *sufficient* gravity of a case under Article 17(1)(d) insofar as cases that are admissible under Article 17(1)(d) are not only those that are *extraordinarily* grave. True, Article 77(1) pertains only to cases in which the defendant is convicted, whereas Article 17(1)(d) pertains to all situations and cases that deserve further action from the Court – which may end in acquittal. Nevertheless, Article 77(1) is an important interpretive element militating against Article 17(1)(d) imposing a particularly high threshold of gravity.

Moreover, the preparatory work of the RS, which is a supplementary means of interpretation under Article 32 of the VCLT, clearly indicates that the gravity that is sufficient under Article 17(1)(d) of the RS is particularly low. This is strikingly evident from the discussions among the members of the International Law Commission (ILC), which provide helpful insights on the reason why the sufficient gravity threshold was inserted into the RS, and on the meaning of the word 'sufficient'. For instance, Special Rapporteur James Crawford noted that, absent a provision on sufficient gravity 'the court might be swamped by *peripheral complaints* involving minor offenders, possibly in situations where the major offenders were going free'.[16] This statement clearly explains that sufficient gravity was included in the Statute to avoid the Court's time being mired in minor cases. Indeed, at the time, the subject-matter jurisdiction of the Court was still being debated; with some proposals to include jurisdiction for treaty-based transnational crimes as well, providing such an admissibility criterion was considered necessary to avoid the Court spending its resources on trivial cases.[17] This view was shared by other members of the ILC, such as Robert Rosenstock, who affirmed that the Court should be provided the power 'to decline to accept a particular case on specific grounds – for instance, that it did not consider the case of sufficient gravity to merit a trial at international level or that the existing national tribunals could handle the matter expeditiously', cautioning that this need was linked to 'the concerns raised with regard to the inclusion … of crimes under national law, such as drug-related crimes and, for that matter, the "terrorism" conventions',[18] which ultimately were not included in ICC jurisdiction. Similarly, upon adoption,

---

16 ILC, *Summary record of the 2330th meeting*, A/CN.4/SR.2330, para.9 (emphasis added).

17 deGuzman, n.2, 1421–2; William A Schabas, *The International Criminal Court: A Commentary on the Rome Statute* (2nd edn, OUP 2016) 462.

18 ILC, *Summary record of the 2332nd meeting*, A/CN.4/SR.2332, para.59.

James Crawford noted that 'Article 35 provided for discretion not to exercise jurisdiction' in cases not pertaining to the most serious crimes.[19]

The views of the states that drafted the RS on the basis of the works of the ILC support the idea that the gravity threshold must be interpreted as a low one. For instance, a proposal of including 'exceptional gravity' rather than 'sufficient gravity' was advanced, but not adopted,[20] thus suggesting a rejection of too high a threshold. At the Rome Conference,[21] Croatia, during the negotiations, emphasised: that 'there must also be guarantees that cases brought before the Court [are] of sufficient gravity and significance. The Court must not be burdened with *minor* violations.'[22] Zimbabwe observed that 'the concern that inclusion of *minor breaches* might undermine the Court's effectiveness was covered by the reference in article 15, paragraph 1 (d), to cases not of sufficient gravity to justify further action by the Court'.[23] Both statements suggest that only minor situations falling within the ICC's jurisdiction are inadmissible because they lack sufficient gravity.

Accordingly, the preparatory work indicates that this admissibility ground was created for purposes of judicial economy, to avoid the ICC (the entire organisation, rather than just the OTP) wasting its limited resources on trivial cases, rather than to create a high threshold for admissibility.[24] Although some scholars consider these two takes to be contradictory,[25] they can be construed as supporting each other: only trivial cases should be dismissed because of insufficient gravity given that the object and purpose of the RS – the preven-

19 ILC, *Summary record of the 2356th meeting*, A/CN.4/SR.2356, para.60.

20 *Summary of the proceedings of the Preparatory Committee during the period 25 Mar – 12 Apr 1996*: Preparatory Committee on the Establishment of an ICC, Annex III, A compilation of proposals made in the course of discussion for amendment of the ILC draft statute, A/AC.249/1, 7.

21 See Susana SáCouto and Katherine Cleary, 'The Gravity Threshold of the International Criminal Court' (2008) 23 AUILR 807, 821, n.28.

22 UN Diplomatic Conference of Plenipotentiaries on the Establishment of an ICC, Rome, Italy 15 Jun–17 Jul 1998, A/CONF.183/SR.5, *Summary Record of the 5th Plenary Meeting*, para.45 (emphasis added).

23 UN Diplomatic Conference of Plenipotentiaries on the Establishment of an ICC, Rome, Italy 15 Jun–17 Jul 1998, A/CONF.183/C.1/SR.36, *Summary Record of the 36th Meeting of the Committee of the Whole*, para.32 (emphasis added).

24 See, for example, Héctor Olásolo, *The Triggering Procedure of the International Criminal Court* (Brill 2005) 185; deGuzman, n.2, 1425; Gerhard Werle and Florian Jessberger, *Principles of International Criminal Law* (4th edn, OUP 2020) 130.

25 Farid Mohammed Rashid, *Prosecutorial Discretion in the International Criminal Court: Legitimacy and the Politics of Justice* (Routledge 2021) 131.

tion and repression of international crimes – demand the admissibility of all other cases.[26]

2.3 The Practice of the OTP and of the Chambers Regarding a Minimal Threshold

A similar conclusion can be reached by looking at the practices of the OTP and of the Chambers, which amount to acts of interpretation and have interpretive value as discussed above.[27] With regard to the OTP, it suffices to say that, as early as 2006 it stated that 'Article 17 (1) (d) is intended to establish a *basic standard* for gravity, excluding *minor offenders and minor crimes* that *clearly do not warrant the exercise of jurisdiction*'[28] and that '[i]t would be more appropriate to maintain Article 17 (1) (d) as a mechanism allowing the judiciary to screen out *clearly minor cases*'.[29] It is clear that the OTP considers the gravity threshold to be minimal.

As examined in the previous chapter, PTC I offered the first detailed judicial analysis of sufficient gravity in the 2006 decision on the arrest warrants against Lubanga and Ntaganda, where the Chamber provided for a high threshold of sufficient gravity.[30] According to the Chamber, 'the relevant conduct must present particular features which render it *especially* grave',[31] with an emphasis on the word 'especially' rather than 'sufficient' to connote the gravity assessment. The Chamber reached this result specifically by articulating the requirement of focusing on 'the *most senior leaders* suspected of being the *most responsible* for the crimes within the jurisdiction of the Court allegedly committed in any given situation under investigation'.[32] Irrespective of whether this factor

---

[26] In this sense, see the position of Al Hassan, claiming that the case against him did not reach sufficient gravity, in Situation in Mali, *Prosecutor v Al Hassan*, Defence for Mr Al Hassan Ag Abdoul Aziz Ag Mohamed Ag Mahmoud, Public redacted version of 'Submissions for the confirmation of charges', ICC-01/12-01/18-394-Red, 4 Jul 2019, para.262 ('[t]he acts attributed to Mr Al Hassan, … are not of a magnitude that would justify the Court's action').

[27] See above, Chapter 2, subsection 3.3.

[28] Situation in the RDC, Public Redacted Version of the Prosecutor's Document in Support of the Appeal, ICC-01/04-120-Red, 3 Mar 2006 (public redacted on 28 Jan 2011), para.50 (emphasis added).

[29] Ibid, para.41.

[30] See above, Chapter 4, subsection 2.2.1.

[31] Situation in the RDC, *Prosecutor v Lubanga and Ntaganda*, PTC I, Decision on the Prosecutor's Application for Warrants of Arrest, Article 58, ICC-01/04-520-Anx2, 10 Feb 2006, para.46 (emphasis added).

[32] Ibid, para.51 (emphasis added).

was linked to the content of sufficient gravity,[33] it created an impunity gap for atrocities committed by less senior figures. This gap was not reduced by the principle of complementarity because, if domestic courts with jurisdiction are unwilling and unable to prosecute the less senior alleged perpetrator, then no court will exercise its jurisdiction.[34] Accordingly, PTC I attempted to provide a high threshold of sufficient gravity by creating a specific gravity factor that almost every commentator criticised as being too strict.[35]

The OTP reacted to the imposition of such a high threshold of sufficient gravity in its appeal against the decision, wherein it affirmed that sufficient gravity under Article 17(1)(d) of the RS 'is intended to establish a basic standard for gravity, excluding minor offenders and minor crimes that clearly do not warrant the exercise of jurisdiction'.[36] Consequently, the threshold identified by PTC I was considered to be too restrictive.[37] The AC shared the concerns of the OTP and rejected the gravity factors articulated by the PTC;[38] in doing so, the AC did not elaborate on the gravity threshold explicitly, but it implicitly rejected a high threshold by recalling the preparatory work of the RS (and by the dismissal of 'exceptional' gravity in place of sufficient gravity),[39] as well as by rejecting the most senior leaders factor.[40] Indeed, in a subsequent individual opinion, Judge Silvia Fernández de Gurmendi interpreted this dictum

33 See the criticisms above, Chapter 4, subsections 2.2.2 and 2.2.3.

34 Stephen Eliot Smith, 'Inventing the Laws of Gravity: The ICC's Initial *Lubanga* Decision and Its Regressive Consequences' (2008) 8 ICLR 331, 340–41.

35 Unanimously: Ray Murphy, 'Gravity Issues and the International Criminal Court' (2006) 17 CLF 281, 291; Matthew Happold, '*Prosecutor v Thomas Lubanga*, Decision of PTC I of the International Criminal Court, 29 Jan 2007' (2007) 56 ICLQ 713, 716; SáCouto and Cleary, n.21, 845; Smith, n.34, 346; deGuzman, n.2, 1428–9, Dov Jacobs, 'Arrest Warrants and Admissibility - Commentary' in André Klip and Göran Sluiter (eds), *Annotated Leading Cases of International Criminal Tribunals, vol XXIII: The International Criminal Court 2005 2007* (Intersentia 2010) 113, 122; Ignaz Stegmiller, *The Pre-Investigation Stage of the ICC: Criteria for Situation Selection* (D&H 2011) 350.

36 Situation in the DRC, Public Redacted Version of the Prosecutor's Document in Support of the Appeal, ICC-01/04-120-Red, 3 Mar 2006, para.23. See also paras 41 and 50.

37 Ibid, para.24.

38 Situation in the DRC, AC, Judgment on the Prosecutor's appeal against the decision of PTC I entitled 'Decision on the Prosecutor's Application for Warrants of Arrest, Article 58', ICC-01/04-169, 13 Jul 2006.

39 Ibid, para.81.

40 Ibid, paras 73–9.

as meaning that the AC 'has rejected the application of a high threshold in defining gravity'.[41]

The individual opinion of Judge Pikis, attached to the 2006 AC decision, provides for granular elaboration on this minimal threshold. According to Judge Pikis: '"[s]ufficient" is an adjective determinative of a given level, quality or quantity. In the context we are dealing with, it signifies a case of sufficient weightiness to merit consideration by the Court … [Article 17(1)(d)] is confined to cases that merit no "further action by the Court".'[42] He went on to argue that the 'case would have to be such as to qualify as a matter unworthy of consideration by the Court' to be inadmissible.[43] The judge went on to elaborate on this threshold in a statement that deserves to be quoted in full:

> Which cases are unworthy of consideration by the International Criminal Court? The answer is cases insignificant in themselves; where the criminality on the part of the culprit is wholly marginal; *borderline cases*. A crime is insignificant in itself if, notwithstanding the fact that it satisfies the formalities of the law, i.e. the insignia of the crime, bound up with the *mens rea* and the *actus reus*, the acts constituting the crime are *wholly peripheral* to the objects of the law in criminalising the conduct. Both, the inception and the consequences of the crime must be *negligible*. In those circumstances the Court need not concern itself with the crime nor will it assume jurisdiction for the trial of such an offence, when national courts fail to do so. Any other construction of Article 17 (1) (d) of the Statute *would neutralize its avowed objects and purposes and to a large extent empty it of content*. The subject-matter must be minimal, so much so that it can be ignored by the Court.[44]

Although this statement has been criticised as unhelpful because of its obscurity,[45] it deserves careful attention. Judge Pikis is not providing a magic number to measure the gravity threshold, simply because such a measurement is not compatible with the nature of evaluative conceptual term providing a standard of sufficient gravity.[46] Rather, correctly, Judge Pikis looks to treaty

---

41 Situation in the DRC, *Prosecutor v Mbarushimana*, AC, Judgment on the appeal of the Prosecutor against the decision of PTC I of 16 Dec 2011 entitled 'Decision on the confirmation of charges', ICC-01/04-01/10-514, Separate Opinion of Judge Silvia Fernández de Gurmendi, para.10.

42 Situation in the DRC, AC, Judgment on the Prosecutor's appeal against the decision of PTC I entitled 'Decision on the Prosecutor's Application for Warrants of Arrest, Article 58', ICC-01/04-169, 13 Jul 2006, Separate and partly dissenting opinion of Judge Georghios M Pikis, para.39.

43 Ibid.

44 Ibid, para.40 (emphasis added).

45 Jacobs, n.35, 120, n.69: Kai Ambos, *Treatise on International Criminal Law: Vol.III; International Criminal Procedure* (2nd edn, OUP 2024) 285.

46 See above, Chapter 2, subsection 2.1.

interpretation to find direction on how to limit the discretion in ascertaining the content of such a standard in relation to a concrete situation or case.[47] In doing so, Judge Pikis employs textual interpretation and teleological interpretation to conclude that only 'borderline cases', 'peripheral crimes', with 'negligible' consequences do not meet the gravity threshold. This clearly leaves the door open for wondering which potential case within a situation or which case is actually borderline, peripheral, or with negligible consequence, but it is patent that it points towards a presumption of sufficient gravity of situations and cases within the ICC's jurisdiction.

Clearly, this formulation is embodied in an individual opinion rather than in the majority opinion of the AC: nevertheless, there is no contradiction between the reasoning of the AC – demolishing the PTC's high threshold – and Judge Pikis' proposal – attempting to construct the boundaries of a lower threshold. Accordingly, it is not possible to consider that the AC disagreed with Judge Pikis' view, forcing him to include it in a separate opinion. Rather, even if Judge Pikis' opinion is called a '[s]eparate and partly dissenting opinion', Judge Pikis only openly dissents 'from the decision of the majority that the case should be sent back to the [PTC]'.[48] As the AC noted, 'Judge Georghios M Pikis appends a separate opinion *concurring in part* and dissenting in part'.[49] It seems likely that the strong indication of a very low gravity threshold forms part of the concurring opinion of Judge Pikis and, as such, it does not conflict with the majority decision; rather, it illuminates the reasoning of the majority on that point.[50] The fact that his elaboration has not been included in the majority decision could be explained for other reasons – for instance, in relation to the task of the AC to respond to PTC I's assessment rather than elaborate further in abstract terms – and nothing suggests that the majority of the AC disagreed with Judge Pikis.

Subsequent case law and judicial practice followed this minimal approach. For instance, PTC II in 2010 and PTC III in 2011 affirmed that 'the reference

---

47 See above, Chapter 2, subsection 2.2.

48 Situation in the DRC, AC, Judgment on the Prosecutor's appeal against the decision of PTC I entitled 'Decision on the Prosecutor's Application for Warrants of Arrest, Article 58', ICC-01/04-169, 13 Jul 2006, Separate and partly dissenting opinion of Judge Georghios M Pikis, para.48.

49 Ibid, 2 (emphasis added).

50 On individual opinions as tools to interpret the decisions of the majority (albeit in relation to the International Court of Justice), see, for example, Joint Inspection Unit, *Publications of the International Court of Justice, Annex II: Observations of the International Court of Justice*, A/41/591/Add.1, 5 Dec 1986, para.8; Rainer Hofmann, 'Separate Opinion: International Court of Justice (ICJ)' in *MPEIPL* (2018) para.48.

to the insufficiency of gravity is actually an additional safeguard, which prevents the Court from investigating, prosecuting and trying peripheral cases'.[51] Indeed, the entire *Al Mahdi* case, turning on the destruction of religious and historical property, was handled with scant specific assessment of sufficient gravity as a matter of admissibility: once the OTP assessed that the totality of the potential cases within the situation in Mali met the gravity threshold (rather than the specific attacks performed by Al Mahdi)[52] the opening of an investigation was justified.[53] No assessment of sufficient gravity was provided in the arrest warrant decision,[54] only a perfunctory reference was present in the decision on confirmation of charges,[55] and no examination of admissibility was included in the trial judgment[56] (which focuses on gravity only in relation to the determination of the penalty).[57] Accordingly, this entire trial suggests a low gravity threshold to render the case admissible, with no need for any occurrence of physical harm to human beings.[58]

---

[51] Situation in Kenya, PTC II, Decision Pursuant to Article 15 of the Rome Statute on the Authorization of an Investigation into the Situation in the Republic of Kenya, ICC-01/09-19-Corr, 31 Mar 2010, para.56 (emphasis added); Situation in Côte d'Ivoire, PTC III, Corrigendum to 'Decision Pursuant to Article 15 of the RS on the Authorisation of an Investigation into the Situation in the Republic of Côte d'Ivoire', ICC-02/11-14-Corr, 15 Nov 2011, para.201 (emphasis added).

[52] Karolina Wierczyńska and Andrzej Jakubowski, 'Individual Responsibility for Deliberate Destruction of Cultural Heritage: Contextualizing the ICC Judgment in the *Al-Mahdi* Case' (2017) 16 Chinese JIL 695, 711.

[53] Situation in Mali, OTP, Article 53(1) Report, 16 Jan 2013, paras 142–70. See the commentary by Musab Talha Günay, 'Looking Humanity in the Eye and Seeing its Loss in the Eyes of the ICC: An Evaluation of Daesh's Destruction of Palmyra using the Gravity Assessment Made by the ICC Prosecutor in the *Al Mahdi* Case' (2019) 5 *Santander Art & Culture Law Review* 245.

[54] Situation in Mali, PTC I, Version publique expurgée Mandat d'arrêt à l'encontre d'Ahmad AL FAQI AL MAHDI, ICC-01/12-01/15-1-Red, 18 Sep 2015, para.12.

[55] Situation in Mali, *Prosecutor v Al Mahdi*, PTC I, Public redacted Decision on the confirmation of charges against Ahmad Al Faqi Al Mahdi, ICC-01/12-01/15-84-Red, 24 Mar 2016, para.39. See, also, Situation in Mali, *Prosecutor v Al Mahdi*, OTP, Hearing for the Confirmation of Charges, ICC-01/12-01/15, 1 Mar 2016, 91.

[56] Situation in Mali, *Prosecutor v Al Mahdi*, TC VII, Judgment and Sentence, ICC-01/12-01/15-171, 27 Sep 2016. This is not unusual since challenges to admissibility should generally be brought before the beginning of a trial under Article 19(4). See below, Chapter 6, subsection 3.2.

[57] Ibid, paras 71–82.

[58] See the reference to this case in Situation in Burundi, PTC III, Public redacted version of 'Decision Pursuant to Article 15 of the RS on the Authorization

Furthermore, in 2019, again in the situation of Mali, Al Hassan, claiming that his case did not reach sufficient gravity, observed that his 'case is precisely the type of "peripheral case" that the drafters of the [RS] did not want the Court to pursue',[59] arguing that '[t]he Court's mandate should not *be trivialised by taking on cases of minor importance*'.[60] In denying this claim, PTC I concurred on the minimal threshold of sufficient gravity by noting that 'the purpose of article 17(1)(d) of the Statute is *not to oblige the Court to choose only the most serious cases*, but merely to oblige it *not to prosecute cases of marginal gravity*'.[61] In response to Al Hassan's challenge on alleged lack of sufficient gravity, in 2020, the AC pronounced the final word on the requirement of a minimal threshold. In its rich reasoning based on treaty interpretation, the AC stated that '[t]he gravity requirement under article 17(1)(d) of the Statute aims at excluding those rather unusual cases where the specific facts of a given case technically qualify as crimes under the jurisdiction of the Court, but are nonetheless not of sufficient gravity to justify further action'.[62] This conclusion takes into account a textual interpretation of Article 17(1)(d) of the RS, which, if worded through a negative formulation, indicates that, in principle, sufficient gravity for cases involving international crimes is warranted.[63] The AC went on to argue that teleological interpretation, based on the object

of an Investigation into the Situation in the Republic of Burundi', ICC-01/17-X-9-US-Exp, 25 Oct 2017, ICC-01/17-9-Red, 9 Nov 2017, para.184 ('even those [cases] dealing exclusively with the destruction of buildings dedicated to religion have been considered to be sufficiently grave not only to justify an investigation but even actual prosecutions'). See also Marina Lostal, 'The Misplaced Emphasis on the Intangible Dimension of Cultural Heritage in the *Al Mahdi* Case at the ICC' (2017) 1 *Inter Gentes* 45, 52; Milena Sterio, 'Individual Criminal Responsibility for the Destruction of Religious and Historic Buildings: The *Al Mahdi* Case' (2017) 49 Case Western Reserve JIL 63, 71–2; Gilbert Bitti, 'La jurisprudence de la Cour pénale internationale en 2015: le développement de nouveaux contentieux' (2015) 2 *Annuaire de Justice Pénale Internationale et Transitionnelle* 393, 399.

59 Situation in Mali, *Prosecutor v Al Hassan*, Defence for Mr Al Hassan Ag Abdoul Aziz Ag Mohamed Ag Mahmoud, Public redacted version of 'Submissions for the confirmation of charges', ICC-01/12-01/18-394-Red, 4 Jul 2019, para.262.

60 Ibid, para.286 (emphasis added).

61 Situation in Mali, *Prosecutor v Al Hassan*, PTC I, Decision on the Admissibility Challenge raised by the Defence for Insufficient Gravity of the Case, ICC-01/12-01/18-459-tENG, 27 Sep 2019, para.50 (emphasis added).

62 Situation in Mali, *Prosecutor v Al Hassan*, AC, Judgment on the appeal of Mr Al Hassan against the decision of PTC I entitled 'Décision relative à l'exception d'irrecevabilité pour insuffisance de gravité de l'affaire soulevée par la défense', ICC-01/12-01/18 OA, 19 Feb 2020, para.1. See also para.53.

63 Ibid, para.55.

and purpose of the RS as formulated in the Preamble, 'demonstrates that the purpose of the gravity requirement is to exclude those unusual cases in which the specific facts are only of marginal gravity'.[64] Finally, the AC provided an accurate analysis of the preparatory work of the RS – akin to that provided above in the previous subsection – noting that sufficient gravity is a remnant of a time when the ICC should have had jurisdiction on treaty-based crimes as well, when states were concerned that core crimes plus treaty crimes would have produced an unmanageable workload for the Court.[65] With the decision not to include treaty-based crimes in the RS, the risk of overloading the Court was lower and, accordingly, sufficient gravity should now be interpreted as a minimal threshold. Accordingly, the AC concluded that PTC I was correct in considering that Article 17(1)(d) does not provide for a threshold of special gravity, but rather, merely excludes marginal cases from the exercise of the ICC's jurisdiction.[66] The OTP endorsed this view in subsequent judicial practice.[67]

Furthermore, looking at the activity of the ICC from a wider perspective, it is clear that the Court, so far, has not addressed extreme cases. Looking only at convictions, which are not the sole legitimate outcome of an ICC trial,[68] it is easy to see that, in most of the cases, relatively mild penalties have been inflicted so far, with no life imprisonment imposed for the extreme gravity of the relevant crimes.[69] Although Article 17(1)(d) pertains to cases regardless of whether they will eventually result in a conviction or an acquittal, the practice pertaining to the determination of penalties suggests that cases that are sufficiently grave can nonetheless focus on offences that are not extremely serious.

---

64 Ibid, para.56.

65 Ibid, paras 57–8.

66 Ibid, para.59 (quoting Situation in Mali, *Prosecutor v Al Hassan*, PTC I, Decision on the Admissibility Challenge raised by the Defence for Insufficient Gravity of the Case, ICC-01/12-01/18-459-tENG, 27 Sep 2019, para.50).

67 Situation in the Philippines, Prosecution's response to the Philippine Government's Appeal Brief against 'Authorisation pursuant to article 18(2) of the Statute to resume the investigation' (ICC-01/21-65 OA), ICC-01/21-68, 4 Apr 2023, para.163. See also para.164.

68 Richard Goldstone, 'Acquittals by the International Criminal Court', *EJIL:Talk!* (18 Jan 2019), https://www.ejiltalk.org/acquittals-by-the-international-criminal-court/.

69 Penalties ranged from 9–30 years. See the overview of case law offered by Roger S Clark and Beti Hohler, 'Sentencing at the ICC: Is It Time for Sentencing Guidelines?' in Róisín Mulgrew and Mikkel Jarle Christens (eds), *Research Handbook on the Punishment of Atrocity Crimes* (Edward Elgar Publishing 2024) 120, 128–32 (to which must be added Situation in Mali, *Prosecutor v Al Hassan*, TC, ICC-01/12-01/18-2662, 20 Nov 2024 (10 years)).

Additional support on the fact that Article 17(1)(d) incorporates a minimal threshold of sufficient gravity can be found in some documents pertaining to the ongoing review of ICC policies and practices. In 2020, the *Final Report of the Independent Expert Review of the International Criminal Court and the Rome Statute System* noted a 'concern that the threshold of sufficient gravity is pitched too low',[70] recommending that the OTP 'might well consider the application of a higher gravity threshold in deciding whether to open or continue a [preliminary examination], with a view to allocating the limited resources of the OTP to the situations that are the most serious, and for those most responsible for the commission of the crimes'.[71] This suggestion implies that, at the moment, sufficient gravity is interpreted as a low threshold and that it must be increased as a matter of policy.[72] The ICC response to this suggestion, which received significant criticism by scholars,[73] is particularly interesting as well: in its tepid rejection of the proposal, the response argued that 'the question of gravity, insofar as it is applied as a legal threshold under the Statute, cannot be addressed unilaterally by the OTP, since it will be subject to judicial review'.[74] Accordingly, it demonstrates that a higher threshold would be in line neither with current practice nor with the RS.

All in all, although the nature of an evaluative conceptual term providing a standard of sufficient gravity prevents the predetermination of the gravity threshold through a numerical formula, in favour of assessment on a case-by-case analysis, it is possible to conclude that the correct interpretation of the threshold of sufficient gravity under Article 17(1)(d) of the RS revolves around the indication of a minimal threshold excluding only peripheral cases. This is the product of the application of the interpretive criteria embodied in Article 31 of the VCLT, in light of the text of Article 17(1)(d) of the RS, its context, and its object and purpose, taking into account the preparatory work of the RS and the practice of the OTP and Chambers (including the AC).

---

[70] *Independent Expert Report of the International Criminal Court and the Rome Statute System, Final Report* (30 Sep 2020), para.634.

[71] Ibid, para.650.

[72] Erroneously, the document claims that 'there is no formal threshold for gravity assessment' (ibid, para.649), obliterating the fact that it is Article 17(1)(d), a legal parameter, that demands such an assessment.

[73] See, for example, Buchwald, n.2; Carsten Stahn, 'Higher Gravity Threshold? A Plea for Caution' in Richard H Steinberg (ed.), *The International Criminal Court: Legal, Policy, and Political Challenges* (Brill 2025) 258.

[74] Overall Response of the International Criminal Court to the 'Independent Expert Review of the International Criminal Court and the Rome Statute System – Final Report'' Preliminary Analysis of the Recommendations and Information on Relevant Activities Undertaken by the Court (14 Apr 2021), para.405.

2.4 Different Assessments of the Minimal Gravity Threshold at Different Stages?

This subsection explores whether there are multiple gravity thresholds that should be applied depending on the stage of the proceedings at which gravity is assessed. In particular, the subsection examines whether the sufficient gravity threshold applied in opening an investigation under Article 53(1)(b) of the RS (and Article 15(3) when the OTP acts *proprio motu*) is different from that applied under Article 53(2)(b). As already noted, since both provisions incorporate a reference to Article 17, the factors at the basis of sufficient gravity are always the same. However, the different circumstances of the assessment, which depend on the different stages of the proceedings, might suggest a different approach to the gravity threshold. Indeed, the assessment under Article 53(1)(b) is generic in nature, since there is no proper investigation yet that allows for more specific determinations.

The object of the gravity assessment in deciding whether to open an investigation is different from the object of the gravity assessment in deciding whether to launch a prosecution. As recalled in Chapter 3, although Article 17(1)(d) of the RS refers to the sufficient gravity of a 'case', when the OTP evaluates whether or not to open an investigation under Article 53(1)(b) or Article 15(3) (depending on the triggering mechanisms, according to the AC's case law), the object of the gravity assessment is determining sufficient gravity of *potential* cases arising within a certain situation, since at that stage there is not yet a *case* in technical terms.[75] On the other hand, when sufficient gravity is assessed under Article 53(2)(b) to decide whether or not to launch a prosecution, its focus is on a specific case.

One might wonder whether the assessment of sufficient gravity of potential cases arising from situations has a different threshold (compared to the assessment of sufficient gravity pertaining to specific cases), particularly because, in the former scenario, the OTP has not yet started proper investigations. As the AC observed in relation to considerations on the interests of justice: 'the information that the Prosecutor must provide at this stage is of a limited and very general nature. This is consistent with the preliminary stage of proceedings when the Prosecutor has not had the opportunity to gather evidence and ascertain the facts in the course of an investigation.'[76] At this stage, it is obvious that the OTP's understanding of how grave the potential case may be is less detailed than the its appreciation of the sufficient gravity of an actual case.

---

[75] See above, Chapter 3, subsection 4.2.1.

[76] Situation in Afghanistan, AC, Judgment on the appeal against the decision on the authorisation of an investigation into the situation in the Islamic Republic of Afghanistan, ICC-02/17-138, 5 Mar 2020, paras 39–40

In the former scenario, the OTP has to ascertain sufficient gravity without having performed any investigation, speculating on which cases could materialise if an investigation were to be initiated and successfully undertaken; on the other hand, in the latter scenario, the OTP has already collected evidence and performed other investigative activities that have informed its understanding of the gravity of the case.

Logically, one could argue not only that, absent any actual case, the assessment of sufficient gravity of a case is impossible, but further that, absent any investigation, the assessment of sufficient gravity is impossible as well. This conclusion, however, is not in line with OTP practice which demonstrates intense information gathering activity at the preliminary examination stage before the opening of a formal investigation.[77] More relevantly, this conclusion runs contrary to Article 53(1)(b) of the RS, which unequivocally requires a gravity assessment before deciding whether or not to open an investigation in cases of referrals, and to Rule 49 of the RPE, which renders the criteria of Article 53(1)(b) of the RS applicable to the *proprio motu* requests for authorisation under Article 15(3).

The case law of the Chambers shows awareness of these difficulties and attempts to overcome them by invoking the need for a 'generic assessment' of sufficient gravity at this stage. For instance, in 2010, PTC II noted that the examination of sufficient gravity: 'involves a *generic assessment* of whether such groups of persons that are likely to form the object of investigation capture those who may bear the greatest responsibility for the alleged crimes committed. Such assessment should be *general in nature and compatible with the pre-investigative stage into a situation*.'[78] Clearly, this conclusion and similar subsequent positions by the Chambers and OTP[79] refer to the most respon-

---

[77] See, for example, Stegmiller, n.35, 215–23; Mohammad Hadi Zakerhossein, *Situation Selection Regime at the International Criminal Court: Law, Policy, Practice* (Intersentia 2017) 111–29; Dov Jacobs and Jennifer Naouri, 'Making Sense of the Invisible: The Role of the "Accused" during Preliminary Examinations' in Morten Bergsmo and Carsten Stahn (eds), *Quality Control in Preliminary Examination: Vol.2*(TOAEP 2018) 469, 474–7

[78] Situation of Kenya, PTC II, Decision Pursuant to Article 15 of the Rome Statute on the Authorization of an Investigation into the Situation in the Republic of Kenya, ICC-01/09-19-Corr, 31 Mar 2010, para.60 (emphasis added).

[79] See, for example, Situation in Afghanistan, OTP, Public redacted version of 'Request for authorisation of an investigation pursuant to article 15', 20 Nov 2017, ICC-02/17-7-Red 20-11-2017, 20 Nov 2017, para.336; Situation in Burundi, PTC III, Public redacted version of 'Decision Pursuant to Article 15 of the Rome Statute on the Authorization of an Investigation into the Situation in the Republic of Burundi', ICC-01/17-X-9-US-Exp, 25 Oct 2017, ICC-01/17-9-Red, 9 Nov 2017,

sible criterion, which this author does not consider to be part of the gravity assessment, as discussed in the previous chapter.[80] Nevertheless, the idea that the assessment of sufficient gravity (even in relation to a component that this author does not consider to be relevant) should be generic at the pre-investigation stage (that is, during preliminary examination) is clear. Indeed, the OTP argued in 2011 that the entire assessment of sufficient gravity – rather than the most responsible criterion only – is generic at this stage, involving 'a generic examination of (i) [the most responsible criterion]; and (ii) the gravity of the crimes allegedly committed within the incidents, which are likely to be the object of an investigation'.[81] PTC III concurred, affirming that '[t]his assessment must be carried out following a quantitative as well as a qualitative approach. However, *the assessment should be general in nature and compatible with the pre-investigative stage of a situation'*.[82]

The reference to an assessment 'general in nature' at this stage suggests that the gravity threshold at the preliminary examination phase, for example, when deciding whether to open an investigation, is even lower that that required to start prosecution.[83] The impression is that, in cases in which the OTP believes that sufficient gravity is present to open an investigation, Chambers are happy to defer to the OTP on the matter. There is almost a presumption that sufficient gravity is met if the OTP wants to open an investigation. For instance, PTC III, in relation to the situation in Burundi, summarily ascertained that sufficient gravity was demonstrated by observing that 'cases encompassing a limited number of casualties or even those dealing exclusively with the destruction of buildings dedicated to religion *have been considered to be sufficiently grave not only to justify an investigation but even actual prosecutions*',[84] thus

para.184; Situation in Bangladesh/Myanmar, OTP, Request for authorisation of an investigation pursuant to article 15, ICC-01/19-7, 4 Jul 2019, para.279.

80 See above, Chapter 4, subsection 4.3.

81 Situation in Côte d'Ivoire, OTP, Request for authorisation of an investigation pursuant to article 15, ICC-02/11-3, 23 Jun 2011, para.55.

82 Situation in Côte d'Ivoire, PTC III, Corrigendum to 'Decision Pursuant to Article 15 of the Rome Statute on the Authorisation of an Investigation into the Situation in the Republic of Côte d'Ivoire', ICC-02/11-14-Corr, 15 Nov 2011, para.203 (emphasis added).

83 Situation on Registered Vessels, Public Redacted Version of ICC-01/13-27-Conf Observations on behalf of victims in the proceedings for the review of the Prosecutor's decision not to initiate an investigation, ICC-01/13-27-Red, 23 Jun 2015, paras 21–2.

84 Situation in Burundi, PTC III, Public redacted version of '"Decision Pursuant to Article 15 of the Rome Statute on the Authorization of an Investigation into the Situation in the Republic of Burundi', ICC-01/17-X-9-US-Exp, 25 Oct 2017, ICC-01/17-9-Red, 9 Nov 2017, para.184.

alluding to the fact that the threshold for prosecution is higher than that for investigation.

It is, however, difficult to find reference to this issue within case law because, most of the time, the Chambers do not perform judicial review of the assessment of sufficient gravity undertaken by the OTP in deciding whether to open an investigation.[85] Indeed, when the OTP activates the jurisdiction of the ICC *proprio motu*, it must request permission from a PTC to open an investigation under Article 15(3). However, if the OTP believes that sufficient gravity is not met, no request will be issued and no judicial review of that assessment would be conducted; if the OTP believes that sufficient gravity is met, the PTCs are precluded from examining admissibility because of the interpretation of Article 15(4) offered by the AC.[86] When the activity of the OTP is triggered by a referral from a State Party or the United Nations Security Council (UNSC), its decision to open an investigation is not subject to judicial review (so no discussion of sufficient gravity would result); only its decision *not to open an investigation* in cases of referrals can be subject to reconsideration under Article 53(3)(a).

This quite unlikely scenario has materialised only once, in relation to the *Mavi Marmara* incident which, as discussed in this book, has sparked the most judicial debate on sufficient gravity. In this affair, PTC I, disagreeing with the statement of the OTP that sufficient gravity was not met, observed:

> The question that is asked of the Prosecutor by article 53(1) of the Statute is merely whether or not an investigation should be opened. The Prosecutor's assessment of the criteria listed in this provision *does not necessitate any complex or detailed process of analysis*. In the presence of several plausible explanations of the available information, the *presumption* of article 53(1) of the Statute, as reflected by the use of the word "shall" in the chapeau of that article, and of common sense, is that the Prosecutor investigates in order to be able to properly assess the relevant facts. Indeed, *it is precisely the purpose of an investigation to provide clarity*. Making the commencement of an investigation contingent on the information available at the pre-investigative stage being already clear, univocal or not contradictory creates a short circuit and deprives the exercise of any purpose.[87]

In the view of PTC I, then, the threshold of sufficient gravity under Article 53(1)(b) is even lower than that in Article 53(2)(b) because of the absence of

---

[85] On these procedural issues, see extensively below, Chapter 6.

[86] Situation in Afghanistan, AC, Judgment on the appeal against the decision on the authorisation of an investigation into the situation in the Islamic Republic of Afghanistan, ICC-02/17-138, 5 Mar 2020, para.40.

[87] Situation on Registered Vessels, PTC I, Decision on the request of the Union of the Comoros to review the Prosecutor's decision not to initiate an investigation, ICC-01/13-34, 16 Jul 2015, para.13 (emphasis added).

extensive investigative powers during preliminary examinations. Obviously, the OTP vehemently disagreed with this conclusion, but its fierce response did not question the fact that Article 53(1)(b) presents a threshold that is lower than that of Article 53(2)(b); rather, it only considered that PTC I's reading basically obliterated any meaningful gravity threshold (and any prosecutorial discretion) in the assessment of sufficient gravity.[88] In any case, the AC later confirmed that the OTP, in similar instances, is bound by the legal determinations of the PTCs, even in relation to relevant procedural standards.[89]

Rather than invoking 'common sense' to justify a lower threshold in Article 53(1)(b) (directly or through Rule 49 of the RPE for *proprio motu* investigations) as PTC I does,[90] treaty interpretation suggests that the threshold under Article 53(1)(b) is lower. Article 53(1), in its chapeau, requires that the OTP assesses the subsistence of 'a reasonable basis to proceed under this Statute', which is articulated in 'a reasonable basis to believe that a crime within the jurisdiction of the Court has been or is being committed',[91] admissibility of the (potential) case under Article 17,[92] and the interests of justice based on 'the gravity of the crime and the interests of victims'.[93] On the other hand, Article 53(2), in its chapeau, requires the OTP to assess the subsistence of 'a sufficient basis for a prosecution', which is articulated in 'a sufficient legal or factual basis to seek a warrant or summons'[94] (that is 'reasonable grounds to believe

88 Situation on Registered Vessels, OTP, Final decision of the Prosecution concerning the 'Article 53(1) Report' (ICC-01/13-6-AnxA), dated 6 Nov 2014, ICC-01/13-57-Anx1, 29 Nov 2017, paras 14–35.

89 Situation on Registered Vessels, AC, Judgment on the appeal of the Prosecutor against PTC I's 'Decision on the "Application for Judicial Review by the Government of the Union of the Comoros"', ICC-01/13 OA 2, 2 Sep 2019, para.78. Different is the conclusion of the AC in relation to the evaluation of facts in light of those legal determinations, which is controversially left to the OTP, as discussed below, Chapter 6, subssection 2.3.2. The OTP, forced to oblige this decision, reserved its right to adopt a different interpretation in different situations (Situation on Registered Vessels, OTP, Final decision of the Prosecution concerning the 'Article 53(1) Report' (ICC-01/13-6-AnxA), dated 6 Nov 2014, as revised and refiled in accordance with the PTC's request of 15 Nov 2018 and the AC's judgment of 2 Sep 2019, ICC-01/13-99-Anx1, 2 Dec 2019, para.14, n.20).

90 Situation on Registered Vessels, PTC I, Decision on the request of the Union of the Comoros to review the Prosecutor's decision not to initiate an investigation, ICC-01/13-34, 16 Jul 2015, para.13.

91 RS, Article 53(1)(a).

92 RS, Article 53(1)(b).

93 RS, Article 53(1)(c).

94 RS, Article 53(2)(a).

that the person has committed a crime'),[95] admissibility of the case under Article 17,[96] and the interests of justice based on 'all the circumstances, including the gravity of the crime, the interests of victims and the age or infirmity of the alleged perpetrator, and his or her role in the alleged crime'.[97] The chapeau of Article 53(1), when compared to that of Article 53(2), demonstrates that the entire articulation of the test of whether to open an investigation ('a reasonable basis to proceed') is lower than that which is necessary to start a prosecution ('a sufficient basis for a prosecution').[98] True, Article 53(2) is strictly linked to Article 58(1)(a), which mentions 'reasonable grounds' to believe that a person has committed a crime in order to request an arrest warrant. Since the scope of Article 58(1)(a) is too narrow compared to that of Article 53(2) (which includes also admissibility and interests of justice), it is not possible to concur with those authors who consider that Article 58(1)(a) forces Article 53(2) to be reinterpreted in line with Article 53(1).[99] Indeed, this difference in the thresholds is explicit in relation to subject-matter jurisdiction of the Court (a 'reasonable basis' versus a 'sufficient' basis). This difference, however, should also be read in the admissibility test, including sufficient gravity, which should be interpreted in Article 53(1) and (2) in light of the different chapeaux, as part of the interpretive context.

All in all, since the chapeau in Article 53(1) presents a lower threshold than the corresponding elements in Article 53(2), it is reasonable to conclude that the assessment of both jurisdiction and admissibility[100] in Article 53(1) (including

---

[95] RS, Article 58(1)(a).

[96] RS, Article 53(2)(b).

[97] RS, Article 53(2)(c).

[98] See, for example, Stegmiller, n.35, 253–4; Karel De Meester, *The Investigation Phase in International Criminal Procedures: In Search of Common Rules* (Intersentia 2015) 141; Schabas, n.17, 839; Azé Kerté Amoulgam, 'Examens préliminaires à la Cour pénale internationale: fondements juridiques, pratique du Bureau de la Procureure et développements judiciaires' (2019) 32 RQDI 173, 181; Gilbert Bitti, 'Article 53 – Ouverture d'une enquête' in Julian Fernandez, Xavier Pacreau and Muriel Ubéda-Saillard (eds), *Statut de Rome de la Cour Pénale Internationale: Commentaire Article par Article* (2nd edn, Pedone 2019) 1447, 1485; Morten Bergmso and Olympia Bekou, 'Article 53 – Initiation of an investigation' in Kai Ambos (ed.), *Rome Statute of the International Criminal Court: Article-by-Article Commentary* (4th edn, Beck-Hart-Nomos 2022) 1623, 1630.

[99] For example, Zakerhossein, n.77, 126.

[100] An exception is interests of justice under Article 53(1)(c), which includes a separate threshold ('substantial reasons to believe'). See Matthew E Cross, 'The Standard of Proof in Preliminary Examinations' in Morten Bergsmo and Carsten Stahn (eds), *Quality Control in Preliminary Examination: Vol.2* (TOAEP 2018), 213, 218.

sufficient gravity under Article 53(1)(b)) should be interpreted as lower than those corresponding assessments in Article 53(2).[101] Indeed, as noted above, case law has corrected the reference to Article 53(1)(b) to 'cases' to include 'potential cases' in order to rectify poor drafting, forcing the interpreter to lower the threshold at the preliminary examination phases (invoking a 'general assessment') because of the lack of proper investigative powers.

Finally, it should be noted that the principle of presumption of innocence under Article 66 of the RS, which is part of the interpretive context of the RS, plays different roles at different stages of the proceedings. Article 66(1) protects 'everyone', while Article 66(2) mentions 'the accused'. The accused is defined as a person for whom charges have been confirmed; before the confirmation of charges, the person for whom a warrant of arrest or a summons to appear is issued is technically identified as a suspect.[102] Clearly, when the OTP decides to open an investigation under Article 53(1), there is no accused yet that can be protected by this principle; similarly, when the OTP decides to launch a prosecution under Article 53(2), although technically there is no accused yet, there is a suspect who has already been identified as a potential accused and for whom an arrest warrant is about to be requested (the first step in a chain of events that might lead to discussing their guilt at trial). If one considers that the reference to 'everyone' in Article 66(1) covers suspects before the trial, as suggested by some case law,[103] then it is possible to identify the principle of the

---

[101] Marco Longobardo, 'Everything Is Relative, Even Gravity: Remarks on the Assessment of Gravity in ICC Preliminary Examinations, and the *Mavi Marmara* affaire' (2016) 14 JICJ 1011, 1023; Cross, n.100, 218–19; Rosario Salvatore Aitala, *Diritto internazionale penale* (Le Monnier 2021) 277. Contra, see Governa, n.2, 206, n.283 (arguing, tautologically and without elaboration, that '[t]his assumption should be rejected because the evidentiary threshold for commencing an investigation or a prosecution does not affect the required gravity threshold for the case (actual or potential) to be admissible').

[102] Situation in the DRC, *Prosecutor v Lubanga*, PTC I, Transcript, ICC-01/04-01/06-T-32-EN, 10 Nov 2006, 36, lines 15–22. See generally Schabas, n.17, 492; Daniel D Ntanda Nsereko and Manuel J Ventura, 'Article 19: Challenges to the Jurisdiction of the Court or the Admissibility of a Case' in Kai Ambos (ed.), *Rome Statute of the International Criminal Court: Article-by-Article Commentary* (4th edn, Beck-Hart-Nomos 2022) 1033, 1054–5.

[103] In favour of this position, and for references to relevant case law, see Michelle Coleman, *The Presumption of Innocence in International Human Rights Law and Criminal Law* (Routledge 2021) 100. See also William A Schabas and Yvonne McDermott, 'Article 66: Presumption of Innocence' in Kai Ambos (ed.), *Rome Statute* of the International Criminal Court: Article-by-Article Commentary (4th edn, Beck-Hart-Nomos 2022) 1949, 1953 (noting, however, that Article 66 is included in Part 6 of the RS, concerning trials).

presumption of innocence as an interpretive framework influencing the gravity threshold at Article 53(2). On the contrary, in an Article 53(1) situation, since 'it is not possible to have a concrete case involving an identified suspect for the purpose of prosecution, prior to the commencement of an investigation',[104] in no way would the principle of the presumption of innocence influence the determination of the gravity threshold, which, as a result, is lower.

3. LEGAL THRESHOLD VERSUS RELATIVE GUIDANCE IN THE SELECTION OF SITUATIONS AND CASES

This section examines the OTP practice of considering sufficient gravity as a comparative tool for the selection of situations and cases. Similarly, the academic debate on the existence of relative gravity as contraposed to sufficient gravity is analysed here. Although these diversifications of gravity might be helpful to describe the approach of different ICC organs, ultimately, they do not reflect a correct interpretation of the RS. Indeed, this section closes with demonstrating that sufficient gravity is a threshold that should not be determined through comparison in the search for the gravest situation or the gravest case. Rather, the OTP must perform an *ex ante* assessment of sufficient gravity considering the minimal threshold of Article 17(1)(d) to determine whether or not to open investigations or prosecute cases. OTP decisions not to open investigations or launch prosecutions where situations and cases meet this minimal threshold cannot be justified on the application of sufficient gravity, though they can be justified by other considerations, such as the interests of justice.

3.1 The Ambiguous Approach of the OTP to Sufficient Gravity

The practice of the OTP has been inconsistent in relation to treating sufficient gravity as a legal threshold or as a consideration allowing the Office to compare different situations and cases in order to choose which to investigate and prosecute. This subsection reconstructs the position of the OTP by arguing that only certain considerations regarding sufficient gravity as a threshold fall within Article 17(1)(d) as incorporated by Article 53(1)(b) and (2)(b); relative considerations of gravity are simply outside the scope of these provisions and should be kept separate to avoid blurring the distinction between admissibility and other grounds for exercising prosecutorial discretion.

---

104 Situation in Kenya, PTC II, Decision Pursuant to Article 15 of the Rome Statute on the Authorization of an Investigation into the Situation in the Republic of Kenya, ICC-01/09-19-Corr, 31 Mar 2010, para.48.

The OTP has presented Article 17(1)(d) as a legal threshold that requires a comparative analysis to ascertain which situations, potential cases, and cases are sufficiently grave. Behind this reasoning is the perspective of the OTP that, since too many grave situations, cases, and potential cases fall within the jurisdiction of the Court, the assessment of sufficient gravity 'is necessary as the Court is faced with multiple situations involving hundreds or thousands of crimes and must select situations in accordance with the Article 53 criteria'.[105] In other words, the absence of a pre-identified threshold forces the OTP to use comparison to select the gravest potential cases within situations to investigate and the gravest cases to prosecute.

Accordingly, the OTP holds that the reference to admissibility in Article 53(1)(b) and (2)(b) entitles the Office to select the gravest situations and cases in light of the practical impossibility of the OTP allocating resources to investigate all grave situations and to prosecute all grave cases within the ICC's jurisdiction. To select the gravest situations and cases, the OTP compares them. This is particularly evident in the first years in which, as explored in the previous chapter, the OTP assessed sufficient gravity, primarily taking into account quantitative factors (such as the number of alleged victims).[106] For instance, in 2005, Prosecutor Luis Moreno Ocampo, in relation to the situation in Uganda, justified the decision to request arrest warrants only for members of the Lord's Resistance Army (LRA), rather than for governmental forces as well, as a decision driven by gravity considerations.[107] The Prosecutor presented a comparison between the two, noting that '[c]rimes committed by the LRA were *much more numerous* and of *much higher gravity* than alleged crimes committed by' governmental forces.[108]

The OTP employed comparative considerations the following year in its assessment of sufficient gravity by stating that the situation in Iraq was comparably less grave than other situations where investigations were opened, and thus refused to request the authorisation to open an investigation under Article 15(3):

> The *number of potential victims of crimes* within the jurisdiction of the Court in this situation – 4 to 12 victims of wilful killing and a limited number of victims of

---

105 OTP, *Prosecutor's Letter*, 9 Feb 2006, 8 .

106 See above, Chapter 4, subsection 2.1.

107 OTP, *Statement by the Chief Prosecutor on the Uganda Arrest Warrants*, The Hague (14 Oct 2005), 2–3; OTP, *Statement of the Prosecutor at the Informal meeting of Legal Advisors of Ministries of Foreign Affairs New York* (24 Oct 2005), 6; OTP, *Statement of the Prosecutor at the Fourth Session of the Assembly of States Parties 28 Nov – 3 Dec 2005*, The Hague (28 Nov 2005), 1–2.

108 OTP, *Statement by the Chief Prosecutor on the Uganda Arrest Warrants*, The Hague (14 Oct 2005), 2–3 (emphasis added).

> inhuman treatment – was of *a different order than the number of victims found in other situations* under investigation or analysis by the Office. It is worth bearing in mind that the OTP is currently investigating three situations involving long-running conflicts in Northern Uganda, the [DRC] and Darfur. Each of the three situations under investigation involves thousands of wilful killings as well as intentional and large-scale sexual violence and abductions. Collectively, they have resulted in the displacement of more than 5 million people. Other situations under analysis also feature hundreds or thousands of such crimes.[109]

Here, the comparison was between different situations under current investigation, which, apparently, were graver than the situation of Iraq. This mere fact, without further elaboration or reference to Article 17(1)(d), was employed by the OTP in deciding not to request authorisation to open an investigation. Curiously, years later, Moreno Ocampo claimed that this decision pertained to a lack of gravity as a jurisdictional element imposed by the chapeau of Article 8(1).[110] However, leaving aside the fact that large-scale commission is not a jurisdictional requirement under Article 8(1),[111] the OTP's communication explicitly referred to Article 53(1)(b) on admissibility, and thus, sufficient gravity. Furthermore, one could wonder whether the decision would have been the same if the situation of Iraq had materialised before those in Northern Uganda, the DRC and Darfur; in other words, not only did the OTP imply that a comparison is always available, though this is not always the case, but also it implied that the situations under current investigation, rather than the drafters of the RS, were the determining factor in relation to the gravity threshold. Unsurprisingly, this statement raised significant criticism among scholars, with one commentator noting that comparing different situations is like comparing apples and oranges,[112] and another observing that each situation should be assessed on its own merit.[113]

Similarly, in considering sufficient gravity in relation to the *Mavi Marmara* boarding of 31 May 2010, the OTP noted that the vessel boarded by the Israel Defense Forces was carrying over 500 passengers, 10 of whom died as a result

109 OTP, *Prosecutor's Letter*, 9 Feb 2006, 9 (emphasis added).

110 Luis Moreno Ocampo, *War and Justice in the 21st Century: A Case Study on the International Criminal Court and its Interaction with the War on Terror* (OUP 2022) 276–7.

111 See above, Chapter 3, subsection 4.2, on the basis of the words 'in particular' in this provision.

112 William A Schabas, 'Prosecutorial Discretion v Judicial Activism at the International Criminal Court' (2008) 6 JICJ 731, 741.

113 Carsten Stahn, *A Critical Introduction to International Criminal Law* (CUP 2019) 330.

of the alleged crimes, and around 50–55 of whom were injured,[114] concluding that 'the total number of victims of the flotilla incident reached *relatively limited proportions as compared, generally, to other cases investigated by the Office*'.[115] As a result, the OTP decided not to open an investigation. Commentators criticised this decision because the situation involving the *Mavi Marmara* boarding could not be compared to those pertaining to large-scale armed conflicts on land: as suggested, the comparison would have held water only if the *Mavi Marmara* boarding was compared to other situations exclusively focusing on alleged crimes committed on vessels.[116]

In further elaborations, the OTP explained that practical reasons demand the OTP focus only on certain situations and cases, which requires selection based on relative gravity:

> A policy of focused investigations also means that cases inside a situation are selected according to gravity .... A limited number of incidents are selected. This allows the Office to carry out short investigations; to limit the number of persons put at risk by reason of their interaction with the Office; and to propose expeditious trials while aiming to represent the entire range of victimization. While the Office's mandate does not include production of comprehensive historical records for a given conflict, incidents are selected to provide *a sample that is reflective of the gravest incidents and the main types of victimization*.[117]

All this practice suggests an attempt to interpret sufficient gravity under Article 17(1)(d), thanks to its incorporation in Article 53(1)(b) and (2)(b), as allowing – and even demanding – that the OTP compare situations and cases to decide which should be investigated or prosecuted. It is anticipated that this is incorrect, not because the OTP does not enjoy such discretion, but simply because this discretion cannot be built upon a sound interpretation of Articles 17(1)(d), 53(1)(b), and (2)(b).

Unsurprisingly, the relative approach quickly backfired. In 2014, Charles Blé Goudé's defence challenged the admissibility of the case brought against him in relation to the situation in Côte d'Ivoire by arguing that the case was comparatively less grave than others in the ICC's docket.[118] Boldly, the application noted that the OTP

---

114 Situation on Registered Vessels, OTP, Article 53(1) Report, 6 Nov 2014, para.138.

115 Ibid (emphasis added).

116 Victor Kattan, 'The ICC and the Saga of the Mavi Marmara' (2015) 18 Palestine YIL 53, 86–7 and 90; Longobardo, n.101, 1027.

117 OTP, *Prosecutorial Strategy 2009–2012* (1 Feb 2010), para.20 (emphasis added).

118 Situation in Côte d'Ivoire, *Prosecutor v Blé Goudé*, Defence application pursuant to Articles 19(4) and 17(1)(d) of the Rome Statute, ICC-02/11-02/11-171,

made one notable pronouncement on gravity in his decision on an Article 15 communication concerning Iraq. In this decision, the Prosecutor decided that his office would not initiate, proprio motu, an investigation when the casualties were not of the "order" of those affected by the "long-running conflicts in Northern Uganda, the [RDC] and Darfur"; i.e., upwards of thousands of deaths and rapes conducted over years with a large geographical span. In the present case, after filtering out those incidents which may be attributed to "pro-Gbagbo youth", and thus to the Suspect on a prima facie basis alone, the number of casualties is extremely limited.[119]

In response to the challenge brought by Blé Goudé, the OTP was forced to go back to the comparative approach adopted in Iraq, claiming that:

That letter compared the limited number of potential victims of crimes within the jurisdiction of the Court – four to 12 victims of wilful killing and a limited number of victims of inhuman treatment – with the number of victims found in other situations under investigation or analysis by the OTP, which included long-running conflicts in Northern Uganda, the DRC and Darfur, each involving thousands of wilful killings as well as intentional and large-scale sexual violence and abductions, and large-scale displacement. The Prosecutor's illustration through these examples of the difference between the scale of the crimes attributable to State Party nationals in Iraq with other situations under investigation does not mean that only crimes reaching the magnitude described above meet the Prosecution's definition of gravity.[120]

In other words, the OTP defended the comparative approach but undermined its decisiveness in relation to determining sufficient gravity. Correctly, PTC I dismissed the challenge by noting that all the factors determining gravity, rather than only scale, should be assessed, and that the mere comparison of the scale of the crimes is inconducive.[121] This conclusion is correct because the assessment of sufficient gravity moved from exclusively quantitative considerations to a mix of qualitative and quantitative elements based on four factors. Moreover, such an approach aligns with considering sufficient gravity as a minimal threshold.

Similarly, in 2019, Al Hassan's defence challenged the sufficient gravity of the case brought against him by noting that '[i]n comparison to other similar cases, it is clear that Mr. Al Hassan's actual conduct does not justify the

27 Sep 2014.

[119] Ibid, paras 33–4.

[120] Situation in Côte d'Ivoire, *Prosecutor v Blé Goudé*, Prosecution's Response to the Defence application pursuant to Articles 19(4) and 17(1)(d) of the Rome Statute, ICC-02/11-02/11-181, 20 Oct 2014, para.30.

[121] Situation in Côte d'Ivoire, *Prosecutor v Blé Goudé*, PTC I, Decision on the Defence Challenge to the Admissibility of the Case against Charles Blé Goudé for Insufficient Gravity, ICC-02/11-02/11-185, 12 Nov 2014, para.19.

Court's action'.[122] Mimicking the approach of the OTP's letter in relation to Iraq, Al Hassan's defence observed that:

> [t]hese figures are well below other cases found to be of sufficient gravity to be tried before the ICC. For example, the case against Mr. Blé Goudé was related to five alleged incidents resulting in 'at least 184 deaths, 38 rapes, 126 cases of serious bodily harm, and 348 cases of religious or political persecution.' In the Situation in the Republic of Kenya, the Prosecution alleged that over 1,000 people were killed, that 900 acts rape and sexual violence were documented, that around 350,000 people were displaced, and over 3,500 were seriously injured. Clearly, the Al Hassan case does not reach the gravity of previous cases before the Court in quantitative terms.[123]

Al Hassan's defence was also prudent in dismissing the relevance of the comparison with the *Al Mahdi* case, wherein no bodily harm to human victims occurred, claiming that the lack of granular assessment of sufficient gravity under Article 17 because of the defendant plea agreement made the case unsuitable for comparison.[124] In its response, the OTP mentioned, inter alia, the fact that it was possible to identify some cases which were considered to be sufficiently grave and which were comparatively less grave than the case against Al Hassan.[125]

Overall, the impression is that the OTP employs both arguments in favour and arguments against a relative approach to sufficient gravity, depending on whether the assessment of sufficient gravity pertains to the admissibility of a specific case before the Court under Article 17(1)(d), or the activity of the OTP under Article 53(1)(b) (directly or through Rule 49 of the RPE for *proprio motu* investigations) and (2)(b). Before the Chambers, in discussing the admissibility of a specific case that the Office considers to be sufficiently grave, not only is the OTP quick to dismiss comparisons between different cases that might undermine its gravity assessment, but it also advocates the primacy of its own assessment of sufficient gravity over that of the Chambers.

This reasoning was already fully articulated in 2006, when PTC I considered, in relation to the request for an arrest warrant against Ntaganda and Lubanga, that sufficient gravity should have been assessed, by taking into

122 Situation in Mali, *Prosecutor v Al Hassan*, Defence for Mr Al Hassan Ag Abdoul Aziz Ag Mohamed Ag Mahmoud, Public redacted version of 'Submissions for the confirmation of charges', ICC-01/12-01/18-394-Red, 4 Jul 2019, para.279.

123 Ibid, para.264.

124 Ibid, paras 283–6.

125 Situation in Mali, *Prosecutor v Al Hassan*, Public redacted version of 'Prosecution's observations in response to the Defence's admissibility challenge', 25 Jul 2019, ICC-01/12-01/18-432-Conf, ICC-01/12-01/18-432-Red, 1 Aug 2019, paras 15 and 17.

account, inter alia, the seniority of the suspect.[126] Leaving aside analysis of the factors determining gravity identified by the Chamber, which are discussed in the previous chapter,[127] the rejection of the criterion based on seniority by the OTP should be emphasised. The OTP noted that:

> the Decision appears to conceive Article 17 (1) (d) not as a basic threshold but rather as a means of directing the policy of case selection among grave cases. This not only eclipses any scope for case selection, but in addition, hardening a restrictive case selection policy into a legal requirement would erect a fixed and permanent legal barrier.[128]

What was the problem with this threshold? That, according to the OTP, this threshold was so high that it reduced its latitude of selection among grave cases: '[i]t would be more appropriate to maintain Article 17 (1) (d) as a mechanism allowing the judiciary to screen out clearly minor cases, and allow the Prosecution to do the additional case selection among the grave cases.'[129] In other words, the OTP was unsatisfied by the predetermination of a gravity threshold that would have resulted in a strong limitation of its capacity to select for itself potential cases within situations and cases, reserving its right to compare the gravity of situations and cases with limited scrutiny. The problem soon became moot because the AC overturned the decision at hand.[130]

All in all, it appears that the OTP considers that sufficient gravity is both a threshold set by Article 17(1)(d) – which should be considered minimal as discussed below – and the product of a comparative assessment of available situations and cases that it can perform with limited scrutiny under Article 53(1)(b) (directly or through Rule 49 of the RPE for *proprio motu* investigations) and (2)(c). Noting this discrepancy, scholars have been quick to discuss sufficient gravity as split into different kinds.

---

126 Situation in the DRC, PTC I, Decision on the Prosecutor's Application for Warrants of Arrest, Article 58, ICC-01/04-520-Anx2, 10 Feb 2006, paras 50–54.

127 See above, Chapter 4, subsection 2.2.

128 Situation in the DRC, Public Redacted Version of the Prosecutor's Document in Support of the Appeal, ICC-01/04-120-Red, 3 Mar 2006 (public redacted on 28 Jan 2011), para.26.

129 Ibid, para.41.

130 Situation in the DRC, AC, Judgment on the Prosecutor's appeal against the decision of PTC I entitled 'Decision on the Prosecutor's Application for Warrants of Arrest, Article 58', ICC-01/04-169, 13 Jul 2006.

3.2 The Academic Debate About 'Legal' or 'Absolute' Gravity versus 'Relative Gravity'

The approach of the OTP in alluding to sufficient gravity as a threshold under Article 17(1)(d) as contraposed to the Office's own assessment of sufficient gravity through comparison under Article 53(1)(b) and (2)(b) has generated significant legal debate concerning the existence of different conceptions of sufficient gravity, usually labelled as 'legal gravity' and 'relative gravity'. Although it is possible to anticipate that this terminology does not reflect the content of the RS, let alone that of Articles 17(1)(d) and 53, such terminology is so pervasive in the scholarly discourse on sufficient gravity that it warrants attention in order to dispel any possible confusion. Accordingly, this subsection explores how the two notions of legal gravity and relative gravity emerged, how they have been used by scholars, and what – if any – practical utility they have.

To the best knowledge of this author, the first discussion on relative gravity belongs to Susana SáCouto and Katherine Cleary, who considered the 'relative gravity' of crimes as one of the potential factors governing the selection of situations and cases.[131] Subsequently, in a seminal article published in 2009, Margaret deGuzman elaborated on the distinction between the expressions 'relative gravity' and 'absolute gravity'.[132] According to deGuzman:

> Gravity plays two important and distinct roles in the ICC regime. First, the concept of gravity provides a legal and normative basis for the Court's jurisdiction as well as the exercise of that jurisdiction; and second, consideration of relative gravity is an important factor in the Prosecutor's discretionary selection of situations and cases to pursue. The first function is embedded in the [RS]'s provisions regarding jurisdiction and its exercise, including admissibility. Nothing in Statute addresses, however, whether or when the Prosecutor should consider *relative gravity* in making selection decisions.[133]

In a later work, the distinction between relative and absolute gravity was refined as follows:

> Absolute gravity is an abstract determination of weight: a case or situation has a certain importance irrespective of that of other cases or situations. The [RS]'s gravity threshold requires an absolute gravity judgment: a situation or case is either grave enough to meet the threshold or is not. Relative gravity, on the other hand,

---

131 SáCouto and Cleary, n.21.

132 deGuzman, n.2, 1440. For further elaboration, see Margaret deGuzman, *Shocking the Conscience of Humanity: Gravity and the Legitimacy of International Criminal Law* (OUP 2020) 15.

133 deGuzman, n.2, 1405–1406 (emphasis added).

requires a comparison between the situation or case under consideration and other comparable situations or cases to determine their relative importance.[134]

According to this view, relative gravity coincides with prosecutorial discretion[135] but does not overlap with the interests of justice since Article 53(1)(c) and (2)(c) applies only after the gravity threshold is assessed under Article 53(1)(b) and (2)(b).[136] In the absence of a specific provision in the RS, deGuzman situates relative gravity in the decision of the OTP to open or not open an Article 15 *proprio motu* investigation, conceding that it is 'much less clear that such discretion is available to [the OTP] when situations are referred'.[137] DeGuzman refers to 'relative' gravity because the OTP has often compared the gravity of certain situations to justify its decision whether or not to open an investigation, as demonstrated by the approach taken in 2006 in relation to alleged crimes committed in Iraq.[138] However, correctly, deGuzman notes that the OTP does not make a clear distinction between sufficient gravity under Article 17(1)(d), which pertains to a threshold rather than a comparison,[139] and its alleged discretionary power not to investigate a situation or not to select a case because of gravity considerations.[140]

Ignaz Stegmiller articulated the distinction between relative gravity and legal gravity slightly differently. He first introduced the distinction in 2009, noting that legal gravity is a purely legal admissibility test based on Articles 53(1)(b) and 17(1)(d), whereas relative gravity is a discretionary test based on Article 53(1)(c), the provision applying the interests of justice as a justification for not opening an investigation.[141] In his opinion, following a textual interpretation, legal gravity should be wider than relative gravity because Article 53(1)(b) refers to the gravity of the entire case (including the role of the individual), whereas Article 53(1)(c) pertains only to the gravity of the crime (only the conduct, rather than the individual).[142] However, this conclusion conflicts with the aforementioned jurisprudential debate about the necessity to interpret Article 53(1)(b) as referring to the gravity of the situation rather than the case at the

134 deGuzman, n.132, 15.

135 deGuzman, n.2, 1413.

136 Ibid, 1413.

137 Ibid, 1415

138 Ibid, 1432. See OTP, *Prosecutor's Letter*, 9 Feb 2006, 9.

139 deGuzman, n.2, 1432; deGuzman, n.132, 15.

140 deGuzman, n.2, 1432–5.

141 Ignaz Stegmiller, 'The Gravity Threshold under the ICC Statute: Gravity Back and Forth in *Lubanga* and *Ntaganda*' (2009) 9 ICLR 547, 562–3. See, more in detail, Stegmiller, n.35, 331–5.

142 Stegmiller, n.141, 563.

preliminary examination stage.[143] Accordingly, Stegmiller contends that the gravity of the crime under Article 53(1)(c), that is, relative gravity according to the interests of justice, should be considered to be broader than legal gravity, that is, sufficient gravity as per admissibility.[144]

The same reasoning can be applied to legal gravity in the assessment of a case (under Article 53(2)(b)) and relative gravity in the assessment of a case (under Article 53(2)(c) on the interests of justice).[145] Stegmiller advocates for the introduction of the terminology of legal gravity as a synonym of gravity of cases and situations, with relative gravity being employed in relation to the interests of justice.[146] This proposal met with agreement among scholars who already commonly referred to legal gravity as a matter of admissibility and relative gravity as a matter of interests of justice.[147] Like deGuzman, Stegmiller sees relative gravity as an assessment coloured by prosecutorial discretion, which should be anchored in Article 53(1)(c) or (2)(c) on the interests of justice in order to find a proper basis in the RS.

With due respect to these important contributions, different labels that suggest different gravity thresholds should be rejected since they do not contribute to clarification of the assessment of sufficient gravity; rather, they introduce further layers of unnecessary complexity that are not embodied in the RS and are unhelpful in understanding sufficient gravity. First, as seen, the two main views on relative gravity versus absolute/legal gravity clash in their content and legal sources. Simply, relative gravity means different things for different authors, and the RS is silent on the discretionary powers of the OTP to decide whether to open an investigation or to launch a prosecution when the requirements under Article 53(1) and (2) are met. Accordingly, if the one and only sufficient gravity threshold mentioned by the RS is met (under Article

143 See above, Chapter 3, subsection 4.2.2.

144 Stegmiller, n.141, 563.

145 Ibid, 563–4.

146 Ibid.

147 See, for example, De Meester, n.98, 256; Claire Magnoux, '*The Sound of Silence*: le pouvoir discrétionnaire du Procureur de la Cour pénale internationale à travers l'utilisation des critères d'intérêts de la justice et de gravité lors de l'ouverture d'une enquête' (décembre 2017 - hors-série) RQDI 9, 24–7; Marco Roscini, 'Gravity in the Statute of the International Criminal Court and Cyber Conduct that Constitutes, Instigates or Facilitates International Crimes' (2019) 30 CLF 247; Farid Mohammed Rashid, 'The Hidden Discretionary Capacity of the ICC Prosecutor: Revisiting the Analysis of Legal and Relative Gravity' (2020) 24 *The International Journal of Human Rights* 773; Oriola O Oyewole, 'Unveiling the Powers of the ICC Prosecutor: Promoting Access to Justice and Accountability through Sustainable Development Goal 16' (2024) 15 *The Journal of Sustainable Development, Law and Policy* 422, 439; Ambos, n.45, 289–92.

17(1)(d), which is incorporated by Article 53(1)(c) and (2)(c)), then the OTP can only invoke the interests of justice to justify a decision not to open an investigation or launch a prosecution. In this, Stegmiller is correct, but it is unclear why interests of justice should be called relative gravity, as this creates confusion between two different legal concepts. Indeed, as already explained, the interests of justice assessment balances the gravity of the crime against other factors,[148] thus, labelling interests of justice as relative gravity would erase its autonomous, and multifaceted, nature, as recognised by deGuzman who, rightly, steers away from conflating the concepts of relative gravity and the interests of justice.

3.3 Against the Employment of Article 17(1)(d) to Compare and Select Situations and Cases

3.3.1 The OTP must provide a prognostic assessment of sufficient gravity to minimise declarations of inadmissibility of situations and cases under the minimal threshold of Article 17(1)(d)

This subsection argues that, since there is only one correct interpretation on how to assess sufficient gravity as a minimal threshold under Article 17(1)(d), via Articles 53, and 15(3) (thanks to Rule 49 of the RPE), nothing in the RS allows for the creation of two separate assessments of sufficient gravity, one based on a threshold, the other based on a comparison between different situations and cases. The OTP has articulated several criteria to justify its prosecutorial decisions in relation to selection and prioritisation of situations and cases, proposing an updated set of criteria that include 'gravity of the alleged crime; complementarity with national jurisdictions; representativeness of the cases; crime prevention; degree of responsibility of the alleged perpetrators; and feasibility of investigations and prosecutions'.[149] Although sympathetic to the fact that the OTP cannot investigate and prosecute all sufficiently grave situations and cases, the search for a legal basis for its discretion cannot result in a manipulation of the notion of sufficient gravity.

Article 17(1)(d) is incorporated by Article 53(1)(b) and (2)(b) for obvious reasons of judicial economy: why should the OTP – which is the first organ activated by the triggering of the ICC's jurisdiction – waste time and resources on situations and cases that would be deemed inadmissible by the Court? Starting an investigation or a prosecution that would likely result in a declaration of inadmissibility would not only have a negative impact on the OTP and

---

148 See above, Chapter 3, subsection 4.3.

149 ICC, *Progress in the Assessment of the Independent Expert Report Recommendations Submitted Pursuant to Resolution ICC-ASP/20/Res.3*, para.11, *Matrix*, 6 Sep 2024, 28.

Chambers (as a matter of time and resource), but also on the suspect or accused, who would face investigation and even prosecution without sound reasons, and the victims, whose legitimate expectations would be frustrated by a doomed investigation or prosecution. Accordingly, the RS asks the OTP to assess *ex ante* whether the situation will be inadmissible (and, if so, no investigation will be opened) or whether a potential case will be inadmissible (and, if so, no prosecution will be launched). The determination of admissibility by the Chambers is exceptional in the sense that it is allowed only if a Chamber opposes the *ex ante* assessment of the OTP, or if another interested party (for example, the accused or the referring state, depending on the cases)[150] disagrees.

However, it is undisputed that Article 53(1)(b) and (2)(b) refer to the ascertainment of sufficient gravity in relation to admissibility only, rather than as a vehicle for other (whether legitimate or inappropriate is irrelevant here) considerations. Not only is this in the texts of the two provisions, which mention admissibility and incorporate Article 17 without any indication of a different function, but it is also evident in the corresponding mechanism in place for determining jurisdiction. The OTP must consider jurisdiction before opening an investigation into a situation or before launching a prosecution of a case under Articles 15(3), 53(1)(a) and(b). This requirement is clearly set forth to avoid the possibility of the OTP wasting time and resources on investigating situations or prosecuting cases outside the Court's jurisdiction, when these situations/cases would be struck out by the Chambers anyway. Significantly, most mechanisms to challenge admissibility (including sufficient gravity) are available to challenge jurisdiction as well,[151] the only exception being Article 18 on admissibility which, as explored subsequently, aims to protect state sovereignty rather than judicial economy.[152] To the best knowledge of this author, the OTP has never claimed that jurisdiction should be assessed on a comparative basis, or that the Office has a degree of discretion over jurisdiction beyond the rules embodied in the RS. Why should a different test apply to admissibility?

All in all, the impression is that the OTP has misunderstood the role of all the rules mandating an assessment of sufficient gravity, such as Article 53(1)(b), directly or through Rule 49 of the RPE for *proprio motu* requests, and (2)(b). These rules are embodied in the RS and RPE to preclude the OTP from opening investigations or bringing cases that would be considered inadmissible by the Chambers. These rules are not there to guide the selection of situations and cases among many admissible ones. If situations and cases are above

---

150 See below, Chapter 6, subsection 3.3.

151 See RS, Articles 19 and 53(3)(a).

152 See below, Chapter 6, subsection 2.2.

the minimal threshold of sufficient gravity under Article 17(1)(d), then Article 53(1)(b) and (2)(b) cannot be invoked as bases for not opening an investigation or not launching a prosecution.

This conclusion, however, is usuallydevoid of legal consequences since the OTP's determinations on sufficient gravity are seldom contested. Each time the OTP decides to open an investigation into a situation or to launch a prosecution, believing that sufficient gravity is met, the Chambers do not comment on the issue or wholeheartedly agree with the assessment. Being that the gravity threshold is minimal, it is indeed an almost speculative occurrence that the Chambers might reject the ascertainment made by the OTP on the fact that a certain situation or case meets the threshold.[153] As explored below, in most of the instances where the OTP decided not to open an investigation or not to launch prosecution because of lack of sufficient gravity, there has been no way to challenge this.[154] Perhaps unexpectedly, and with ample resonance among scholars and practitioners, this de facto freedom of the OTP to interpret and reinterpret sufficient gravity in the selection of situations and cases was exposed and challenged only in the circumstance where a decision not to investigate because of lack of sufficient gravity was brought to the attention of PTCs: when the OTP decided not to open an investigation in relation to the *Mavi Marmara* incident, the referring state, the Comoros, activated the process of judicial review under Article 53(3)(b) that shed much needed light in relation to the assessment of sufficient gravity.

3.3.2 Disentangling sufficient gravity from other considerations pertaining to the selection of situations and cases

The general absence of judicial mechanisms for scrutinising the OTP's assessment of sufficient gravity has resulted in the idea that the relevant practice of the Office – including the alleged relative character of the assessment of sufficient gravity and the right of the Office to decide, with scant interference, which situations and cases should be selected allegedly on the basis of their sufficient gravity – was correct and in line with the RS. But, as demonstrated here, Article 53(1)(b) and (2)(b) only demand a prognostic assessment of admissibility under Article 17(1)(d), rather than the selection of only the gravest situations and cases. In this context, the aforementioned scholarly attempts

[153] This happened only in relation to the aforementioned request for an arrest warrant against Ntaganda, first rejected by PTC I for alleged lack of sufficient gravity, a decision that was subsequently overturned by the AC because it was rendered at the wrong stage (as discussed below, Chapter 6, subsection 3.1) and because it applied the wrong factors (as discussed above, Chapter 4, subsection 2.2.3).

[154] See below, Chapter 6.

to identify two different types of gravity, one absolute or legal threshold under Article 17(1)(d) and one relative assessment under Article 53(1)(b) and (2)(b), have the merit of presenting an adequate snapshot of the practice of the OTP. However, since said practice does not have its basis in the RS, the distinction between legal and relative gravity must be rejected so as not to muddy the waters surrounding the correct interpretation of Article 17(1)(d) as a minimal threshold.

There are several reasons why sufficient gravity has been misinterpreted by the OTP, some of them supported by practical necessities, others open to manipulation. First, the RS does not include any mechanism to review the activity of the OTP in its entirety, only some of its decisions. Concretely, this means that certain aspects of OTP activity are outside any form of judicial control, such as decisions prioritising certain situations or potential cases, and decisions as to which suspects investigations should focus on: even when justified by invoking gravity considerations or undertaken under severe political pressure, these choices are not usually subject to judicial review.[155] Second, it is undeniable that the number of situations and cases potentially within the ICC's jurisdiction and above the gravity threshold set by Article 17(1)(d) is unmanageable for the Office (and the Chambers) as a matter of time and resource (judicial economy). The principle of complementarity tries to deflate the workload of the ICC by favouring domestic prosecution and punishment, but this might not be sufficient. Accordingly, the entire history of international criminal law is indeed characterised by selectivity: mass atrocities can only be answered for by the prosecution and punishment of certain crimes, of certain

---

[155] See, for example OTP, *Statement of the Prosecutor of the ICC, Karim A A Khan QC, Following the Application for an Expedited Order under Article 18(2) Seeking Authorisation to Resume Investigations in the Situation in Afghanistan* (27 Sep 2021). For the context of US extraordinary political pressures on prosecutorial activities in Afghanistan, see, for example, Daphne Psaledakis and Michelle Nichols, 'U.S. Blacklists ICC Prosecutor over Afghanistan War Crimes Probe', *Reuters* (2 Sep 2020), https://www.reuters.com/world/us-blacklists-icc-prosecutor-over-afghanistan-war-crimes-probe-2020-09-02/. See, among many scholars, Aldo Zammit Borda, 'The Situation in Afghanistan, US Sanctions and the Historical Narratives Emerging from the ICC', *EJIL:Talk!* (24 Jun 2020), https://www.ejiltalk.org/the-situation-in-afghanistan-us-sanctions-and-the-historical-narratives-emerging-from-the-icc/; Jennifer Trahan, 'Prosecutor De-Prioritizes ICC Investigation of US Torture Program', *Opinio Juris* (1 Oct 2021), https://opiniojuris.org/2021/10/01/prosecutor-de-prioritizes-icc-investigation-of-us-torture-program/; Kate Leisner, 'Prioritizing the Taliban at the ICC: Is the Court Able to Curb Political Prosecutions?' (2022) 37 Maryland JIL 93.

perpetrators.[156] In the framework of the ICC, the selection of situations does not rest only with the OTP, it can be activated by states or the UNSC by referral; however, the decision whether or not to open an investigation or launch a prosecution is entirely left to the Office.

The RS is not particularly helpful in guiding the OTP's decisions. Two potential solutions could have been included by the drafters: provision for explicit prosecutorial discretion or provision of specific criteria to guide the OTP in its application of discretion. However, the RS does not contain either of these. On the one hand, explicit prosecutorial discretion simply does not exist in the RS, which instead refers to prosecutorial independence.[157] Prosecutorial independence safeguards the OTP from external influence, rather than from judicial review,[158] which is a function that protects the legality, impartiality, independence, legitimacy, and credibility of the ICC in its entirety.[159] On the basis of the practice of other international criminal tribunals and of some domestic legal systems, prosecutorial discretion has emerged in ICC practice as an interstitial rule:[160] for sure the OTP enjoys some margin of discretion in performing its duties, but this margin is not always defined by the RS in relation to what the OTP can do; rather, it is identified in the lack of judicial review over certain discretionary choices made by the Office. This author appreciates that it is a matter of perspective: if the activity of the ICC was a family picture, one could consider that the explicit rules of the RS are the persons captured in the picture, while prosecutorial discretion is the invisible air in the spaces between those persons. Which one is the focus of the picture is a matter that different observers might interpret differently and, sure enough, the OTP might remind

---

156 For a minimal background on this, see, at the very least, Robert Cryer, *Prosecuting International Crimes: Selectivity and the International Criminal Law Regime* (CUP 2005); Harmen van der Wilt, 'Selectivity in International Criminal Law: Asymmetrical Enforcement as a Problem for Theories of Punishment' in Florian Jessberger and Julia Geneuss (eds), *Why Punish Perpetrators of Mass Atrocities?* (CUP 2020) 305.

157 RS, Article 42(1).

158 Situation on Registered Vessels, AC, Judgment on the appeal of the Prosecutor against PTC I's 'Decision on the "Application for Judicial Review by the Government of the Union of the Comoros"', ICC-01/13-98, 2 Sep 2019, Separate and Partly Dissenting Opinion of Judge Luz del Carmen Ibáñez Carranza, paras 69–70; Aitala, n.101, 223.

159 Ibid.

160 The notion of interstitial rule is employed here in a sense different from that of interstitial rules provided by Vaughan Lowe, 'The Politics of Law-Making: Are the Method and Character of Norm Creation Changing?' in Michael Byers (ed.), *The Role of Law in International Politics: Essays in International Relations and International Law* (OUP 2000) 207, 219–21.

us that it is that invisible air (prosecutorial discretion) that keeps those people (the rules of the RS) alive.

The interstitial nature of prosecutorial discretion in the RS and the desire to avoid the perception of bias and double standards have made it unpalatable for the OTP to justify its decisions in relation to opening an investigation and launching a prosecution on purely discretionary grounds. Rather, the OTP has preferred to present its decisions under Article 53(1) and (2) as driven mainly by predetermined legal criteria.[161] These criteria were primarily identified as jurisdiction, admissibility, and interests of justice, as demanded by Article 53(1) and (2).[162] A closer scrutiny of Article 53 criteria demonstrates that they allow for very little discretion. Whether the situation or case falls within the ICC's jurisdiction is largely a matter of fact, easily verifiable objectively. Similarly, whether the situation or case passes the complementarity test and the *ne bis in idem* bar is ascertained on the basis of facts, in an objective way (the existence of past or ongoing proceedings at the domestic level). Sufficient gravity, being an evaluative concept providing a standard with no definition in the RS, is a better anchorage for prosecutorial discretion. Although the OTP proposed and agreed with the Chambers certain objective factors determining gravity that have been explored in the previous chapter,[163] it considered that the weight of these factors, the determination of the relevant threshold, and the use of comparisons between situations and cases to find the gravest ones should be left to the appreciation of the OTP. Clearly, in the few instances where the Chambers have disagreed with the OTP's discretion, a judicial struggle as to the nature of sufficient gravity has ensued.

---

[161] See, for example, recently, Matilde E Gawronski, 'The Legalistic Function of Preliminary Examinations: Quality Control as a Two-Way Street' in Morten Bergsmo and Carsten Stahn (eds), *Quality Control in Preliminary Examination: Vol.2*(TOAPB 2018) 179. For merciless criticism of attempting to reach this result through policy papers, see William A Schabas, 'Feeding Time at the Office of the Prosecutor', *International Criminal Justice Today* (23 Nov 2026).

[162] For an updated list, see, for example, ICC, *Progress in the Assessment of the Independent Expert Report Recommendations Submitted Pursuant to Resolution ICC-ASP/20/Res.3*, para.11, *Matrix*, 6 Sep 2024, 28 ('the new selection and prioritization criteria will include, inter alia, gravity of the alleged crime; complementarity with national jurisdictions; representativeness of the cases; crime prevention; degree of responsibility of the alleged perpetrators; and feasibility of investigations and prosecutions.').

[163] See above, Chapter 4, section 3.

3.3.3 The potential role of the interests of justice to justify the selection of situations and cases

Since sufficient gravity under Article 17(1)(d) is the same as sufficient gravity under Article 53(1)(b) and (2)(b), it is important to disentangle sufficient gravity from prosecutorial discretion or, at least, to understand how much sufficient gravity can be affected by this interstitial rule. Going back to Article 53(1) and (2), it appears that the OTP could have focused on a different ground explicitly provided by the RS to justify its exercise of prosecutorial discretion: the interests of justice.

Under Article 53(1)(c) and (2)(c), decisions not to investigate admissible situations and not to prosecute admissible cases can be justified on a discretionary basis. As recalled above, under Article 53(1)(c), '[i]n deciding whether to initiate an investigation, the Prosecutor shall consider whether: … [t]aking into account the gravity of the crime and the interests of victims, there are nonetheless *substantial reasons* to believe that an investigation would not serve the interests of justice';[164] under Article 53(2)(c), a prosecution should not be launched '[i]f, upon investigation, the Prosecutor concludes that there is not a sufficient basis for a prosecution because: … [a] prosecution is not in the interests of justice, taking into account *all the circumstances*, including the gravity of the crime, the interests of victims and the age or infirmity of the alleged perpetrator, and his or her role in the alleged crime'.[165] The formulation of Article 53(1)(c) is particularly relevant here: the RS allows the OTP to balance the gravity of the crime(s) and the interests of the victim(s) with unnamed substantial reasons that would render an admissible investigation contrary to the interests of justice. It is in this provision, and the slightly differently wording in Article 53(2)(c), that the RS provides the OTP with the power to balance different considerations and to decide not to proceed with potential cases (within situations) or cases which are above the gravity threshold of Article 17(1)(d). The notion of the interests of justice is quintessentially discretionary, as is any balancing test that considers different interests and factors. As such, it has been considered the brightest exemplification of prosecutorial discretion in the RS.[166]

Accordingly, the decision not to open an investigation because there are more grave situations available, or not to launch a prosecution because there are graver cases available, is not an application of sufficient gravity as

164 Emphasis added.

165 Emphasis added.

166 See, for example, Schabas, n.17, 834; Lovisa Bådagård and Mark Klamberg, 'The Gatekeepers of the ICC: Prosecutorial Strategies for Selecting Situations and Cases at the International Criminal Court' (2017) 48 Georgetown JIL 639, 698.

incorporated by Article 53(1)(b) or (2)(b), but rather, based on an application of the interests of justice under Article 53(1)(c) or (2)(c), which are the appropriate provisions to support discretionary choices.[167] Referring to an exercise of the power conferred to the OTP under Article 53(1)(c) or (2)(c) would have been a more solid anchor to the RS and would have preserved the need to interpret sufficient gravity as a minimal threshold.

If the interests of justice offer such an easy legal basis for the exercise of prosecutorial discretion, why has the OTP never invoked the interests of justice, instead of turning sufficient gravity into a relative, discretionary ground? One could speculate that one of the reasons lies in the fact that the drafters of the RS provided a strong balance against this clear manifestation of prosecutorial discretion: under Article 53(3)(b), the PTC 'may, *on its own initiative*, review a decision of the Prosecutor not to proceed if it is based solely on paragraph 1 (c) or 2 (c). In such a case, the decision of the Prosecutor *shall be effective only if confirmed by the [PTC].*'[168] This means that, in relation to negative decisions based on lack of interests of justice, a PTC can issue a binding decision forcing the OTP to open an investigation or launch a prosecution.[169] In cases of lack of sufficient gravity, judicial review is only available when there is a referral by a state, as in relation to the *Mavi Marmara* boarding, or by the UNSC, under Article 53(3)(a).[170] If there is no referral or the referring entity does not invite the review, the determination of the OTP on sufficient gravity escapes judicial review. Moreover, the review under Article 53(3)(a), applicable to decisions allegedly taken for lack of sufficient gravity, does not bind the OTP in relation to the final assessment of sufficient gravity,[171] contrary to what

---

167 Situation on Registered Vessels, PTC I, Decision on the 'Application for Judicial Review by the Government of the Comoros', ICC-01/13-111, 16 Sep 2020, para.15. See, also, Claudia Cárdenas Aravena, 'Revisión crítica del criterio "interés de la justicia" como razón para no abrir una investigación o no iniciar un enjuiciamiento ante la Corte Penal Internacional' (2011) 18 *Revista de Derecho Universidad Católica del Norte* 21; Anni Pues, 'Discretion and the Gravity of Situations at the International Criminal Court' (2017) 17 ICLR 960, 975; Magnoux, n.147; Ambos, n.45, 291.

168 Emphasis added.

169 Jan Wouters, Sten Verhoeven and Bruno Demeyere, 'The International Criminal Court's Office of the Prosecutor: Navigating between Independence and Accountability?' in José Doria, Hans-Peter Gasser and M Cherif Bassiouni (eds), *The Legal Regime of the International Criminal Court: Essays in Honour of Professor Igor Blishchenko* (Martinus Nijhoff 2009) 345, 372; Bitti, n.98, 1508–511; Bergmso and Bekou, n.98, 1644–5. See, however, the doubts on how this binding power could work in practice expressed by Schabas, n.17, 843.

170 RS, Article 53(3)(a).

171 See below, Chapter 6, subsection 2.3.2.

happens under Article 53(3)(b) in relation to reviews pertaining to the interests of justice. In light of these different mechanisms of judicial review, why should the OTP invite judicial review on the PTC's initiative, with a potentially binding outcome, by mentioning the interests of justice? It is far easier to invoke sufficient gravity.[172]

The OTP, for practical reasons and to maximise prosecutorial discretion, has constructed the interests of justice very narrowly, deciding not to invoke it, but rather, present it as an *extrema ratio*.[173] The ontological discretionary nature of the interests of justice may lead to accusations of double standards and bias; its built-in system of judicial review may lead to judicial confrontations with the PTC. On the other hand, sufficient gravity is presented by the OTP as based on objective factors, those explored in the previous chapter. Such proclaimed objectivity might have been seen as a tool to reduce the perception of double standards and bias, even if the attempt has not been particularly successful.[174] However, the fact that sufficient gravity is invoked instead of the interests of justice also reduces the risk of judicial review. These considerations may explain why the interests of justice assessment has been interpreted by the OTP as such a discretionary and extreme solution that it has never been invoked in practice (and is almost a taboo), while sufficient gravity, under the pretence of being an objective, legalistic assessment, has been interpreted as allowing the OTP to perform relative comparisons, and, ultimately, make decisions not directly based in the content of Article 17(1)(d).[175]

All in all, the need for the OTP to exercise discretion as to which investigations should be opened, and which prosecutions should be launched, is understandable. This need should be linked to the practical functioning of the ICC organs. Although, especially in the initial phases of ICC activity, decisions explicitly based on the interests of justice might have led to disagreements with PTCs, invocation of the interests of justice could have led to the establishment

---

172 See, for example, Bitti, n.98, 1507–508; Catherine Maia and Ghislain Poissonnier, 'Cour pénale internationale: de la signification des «intérêts de la justice»' in Catherine Maia and Jean-Baptiste Harelimana (eds), *Réenchanter la justice internationale pénale: perspectives universelles et africaines* (Éditions du Net 2022) 61, 62.

173 OTP, *Policy Paper on the Interests of Justice* (Sep 2007).

174 Governa, n.2, 204. See, for example, Frédéric Mégret, 'Beyond "Gravity": For a Politics of International Criminal Prosecutions' (2013) *107* ASIL Proceedings 428, 430; Valentina Azarova and Triestino Mariniello, 'Why the ICC Needs a "Palestine Situation" (More than Palestine Needs the ICC): On the Court's Potential Role(s) in the Israeli-Palestinian Context' (2017) 11 DUDI 115, 127–8.

175 See the rigorous study by Magnoux, n.147.

of a robust case law, which could then have reduced the perception of bias or double standards when invoked. It should be recalled that judicial review under Article 53(3)(b) is optional, as clarified by the use of the word 'may'.[176]

Moreover, according to some commentators[177] and to the AC,[178] Article 53(3)(b) does not apply to *proprio motu* decisions not to open an investigation. Indeed, Rule 105(2) of the RPE posits that Rule 49 applies if the OTP decides not to request authorisation to open an investigation in *proprio motu* scenarios; since Rule 49 does not mention any notification or other role for PTCs, one could interpret Rule 105(2) as providing *lex specialis* to Rule 105(4), so that no involvement of PTCs in *proprio motu* decisions under Article 53(1)(c) would be available. Although the RPE cannot derogate from the RS under Article 21, this result is reached by the AC disconnecting the procedure under Article 15 from that under Article 53(1).[179] Following this reasoning,[180] judicial examination of decisions not to open an investigation because of the interests of justice is limited to cases of referrals – where a state or the UNSC voices a concern over a certain situation, thus activating the discretion of the OTP – or when the OTP itself has already requested and obtained authorisation to open a *proprio motu* investigation but decides not to launch a prosecution. In other words, judicial review is available only when a state or the UNSC, or the OTP and the Chamber, has already expressed their views on the need to investigate or prosecute alleged crimes committed in a certain situation or case.

Considering the above, it is possible to conclude that sufficient gravity can be used by the OTP to select situations and cases only in an extremely limited way: the OTP must perform a prognostic exercise and must refrain from selecting those potential cases within situations and cases that are likely to be inadmissible for lack of sufficient gravity. Nothing in the RS allows the OTP to compare situations and cases in light of their perceived gravity to decide which to investigate and which to prosecute. Contrary to what has been claimed by some authors,[181] sufficient gravity is not inherently political, but rather,

---

176 Giuliano Turone, 'Powers and Duties of the Prosecutor' in Antonio Cassese, Paola Gaeta and John R W D Jones (eds), *The Rome Statute of the International Criminal Court: A Commentary* (OUP 2002) 1137, 1156–8; Schabas, n.17, 842. Contra, Bekou and Bergsmo, n.98, 1644–5.

177 Schabas, n.17, 842.

178 Situation in Afghanistan, AC, Judgment on the appeal against the decision on the authorisation of an investigation into the situation in the Islamic Republic of Afghanistan, ICC-02/17-138, 5 Mar 2020, para.30, n.52.

179 Ibid, para.30.

180 The impact of this reasoning on judicial review of the OTP's assessment of sufficient gravity is discussed below in Chapter 6, subsection 2.1.

181 See above, Chapter 2, subsection 2.4.

its incorrect employment as a tool to select situations and cases has cast a political shadow on it, especially when gravity assessment has been performed by ICC organs under significant political pressure.[182] Certainly, the OTP needs to select situations and cases; however, this is not the function assigned to sufficient gravity. The interests of justice provide a more solid ground on which to base non-selection in cases of referrals and non-prosecution even if cases are within ICC jurisdiction and admissible. In doing so, the correct interpretation of sufficient gravity would be preserved without the need to invoke an artificial distinction between different types of gravity, and the transparency of the reasoning guiding OTP decisions would be enhanced. The interstitial nature of prosecutorial discretion cannot result in the alteration of an explicit rule embodied in the RS.

4. THE ABSENCE OF GRAVITY FACTORS AS AN INDICATION THAT A CASE IS BELOW THE GRAVITY THRESHOLD

The detailed case law on the four factors determining gravity analysed in the previous chapter, coupled with the need to interpret sufficient gravity as a minimal threshold described in this chapter, suggests that every time the factors of scale, nature, manner of commission, and impact are present, the gravity threshold is presumed to be met. Indeed, although the gravity threshold should be interpreted to be minimal and not encompassing a comparative search for the gravest situation or case, this conclusion does not dispel all doubts in relation to whether a specific situation or case is above the threshold – and thus admissible – or below the threshold – and thus inadmissible. This is in line with the nature of sufficient gravity as a standard rather than a rule. However, the practice of the OTP and Chambers in ascertaining the four factors determining constitutes significant interpretive practice that suggests that, when all these factors are present, a situation or case is admissible. It is the presence of these factors that demonstrates that the threshold is crossed; their absence makes a situation or case peripheral, and thus inadmissible.

The consistent practice of the OTP and the case law of the Chambers have presented the four factors as objective elements that are present in relation to each case but that are additional to the elements of the crimes. Chambers consider the four factors to be objective in nature. Although this may appear to be wishful thinking and certain authors have criticised this attempt to depoliticise

182 For a contraposition between political decisions and decisions based on gravity, see Mark A Drumbl, *Atrocity, Punishment, and International Law* (CUP 2007) 152.

sufficient gravity,[183] the words of the AC in rejecting the subjective factor of social alarm are unequivocal: 'the criterion of "social alarm" depends upon subjective and contingent reactions to crimes rather than upon their objective gravity ... The subjective criterion of social alarm therefore is not a consideration that is necessarily appropriate.'[184] Moreover, as already noted, these four factors are factual in nature: the scale of the crimes, their nature (as interpreted with reference to factual circumstances), their manner of commission, and their impact, all refer to components of the facts that, combined, constitute the case. When the OTP and the Chambers assess sufficient gravity, they discuss whether these factors are present in relation to a specific situation, potential case, or case. This is the consolidated practice of the ICC organs tasked with the interpretation and application of the RS, which has significant interpretive value in and of itself.

In light of these considerations, a situation or a case is below the gravity threshold, that is, it is peripheral or minor, only if it is not possible to ascertain the presence of the four factors determining gravity. Equally, every time the four factors are present, the situation or case cannot be considered peripheral and, thus, inadmissible, because of lack of sufficient gravity. In other words, a situation or case deserves further action in the exercise of ICC jurisdiction every time all four factors are present, as crystallised in ICC case law and the practice of the OTP. Only in those cases in which the four factors are not objectively present is further action by the Court undeserved.

Two objections should be immediately addressed. First, the four factors are not defined with 100 per cent precision, and it is unclear how they should be weighed against one another. This is the undeniable consequence of the precise choice made by the drafters of the RS when they decided to impose a standard rather than a rule. However, whether the factors are present or not is, often, easy to ascertain factually. If certain facts are established during the activity of the ICC organs, it is difficult to downplay their role: if the factors determining gravity exist, the imperative to interpret the gravity threshold as minimal renders a finding of insufficient gravity very difficult. This is illustrated by the *Al Hassan* case discussed above: admittedly, as a matter of policy, the crimes committed by Al Hassan are not the most serious *if compared to other crimes punished by the RS*. However, as explained above,[185] the gravity threshold does not require such a comparison and the AC, correctly, considered the case to be

183 deGuzman, n.132, 14–15, 105–106.

184 Situation in the DRC, AC, Judgment on the Prosecutor's appeal against the decision of PTC I entitled 'Decision on the Prosecutor's Application for Warrants of Arrest, Article 58', ICC-01/04-169, 13 Jul 2006, para.72. This is also the reading by De Meester, n.98, 251–2.

185 See above, subsection 3.3.

admissible because of the presence of the factors irrespective of the gravity of other cases before the ICC.

The same reasoning could have been applied in relation to the *Mavi Marmara* affair: the alleged international crimes committed onboard the vessel are, probably, not as serious as other situations under ICC scrutiny; nevertheless, Article 17(1)(d) does not require a comparison, and the factual presence of the four factors in relation to the *Mavi Marmara* affair caused it to cross the gravity threshold.[186] Accordingly, in the assessment of sufficient gravity, the presence of the four factors makes a situation, case, or potential case sufficiently grave as a matter of Article 17(1)(d), in line with the need to construct this threshold as a minimal one. However, Article 17(1)(d) provides a threshold that is not identified by a rule but, rather, by a standard, thus making it impossible (and, more relevantly, against the RS) to obliterate any discretion of the ICC's organs in ascertaining that threshold.

The second objection concerns how to reconcile a minimal gravity threshold with the need to identify factual circumstances that are additional to the elements of the crimes in order to ascertain the existence of the factors determining gravity. In other words, is there any conflict between a minimal threshold and additional factors? The answer is no: international crimes occur in violent, brutal settings; they are often motivated by political or ethnic hatred; they usually involve commission through policy and plan, often by governmental officials; and they almost always have a devastating impact on the victims and the local communities. In other words, it is very difficult to identify the commission of an international crime that does not present the four factors. They are almost always there, and as such, considering these factors as additional to the elements of the crimes is not only correct under the distinction between jurisdiction and admissibility, but also in line with the minimal threshold provided by Article 17(1)(d).

It is difficult to even imagine a case in which the commission of an international crime does not meet the gravity threshold due the absence of the four factors. However, crimes with just one victim might not cross the threshold. One could envisage a wilful killing of one adult enemy civilian, with a single shot, during an assault on an enemy military objective in an armed conflict, which allows the perpetrator to steal civilian property. This fictional case would likely amount to the war crime of wilful killing, and probably pillage as well,[187] and surely would be extremely serious for the victim and their family; however, the very limited scale of the crime, the relatively non-brutal manner

---

[186] As this author explained in Marco Longobardo, 'Factors Relevant for the Assessment of Sufficient Gravity in the ICC. Proceedings and the Elements of International Crimes' (2016) 33 Zoom-In QIL 21.

[187] Respectively, RS, Article 8(2)(a)(i) and (b)(xvi).

of commission, the absence of discriminatory intent or of a plan in relation to the nature of the crime, and the limited impact would probably render this case as insufficiently grave – and thus inadmissible – under the minimal threshold provided by Article 17(1)(d). Since the most responsible factor does not belong to sufficient gravity, this conclusion would stand even if the perpetrator were the most responsible for the crime because, for example, they were the leader of that military unit or a senior officer.

5. CONCLUSIONS

The RS imposes a threshold of sufficient gravity under Article 17(1)(d). A threshold means that situations, cases, and potential cases are either sufficiently grave enough to deserve further action by the Court or they are not. There is nothing in the RS and other applicable rules that allows the determination of sufficient gravity to be based on comparison. The RS does not provide for the admissibility of the gravest cases, but rather, as demonstrated by the correct interpretation of Article 17(1)(d), in light of its preparatory work, the object and purpose of the RS, and relevant judicial practice, sufficient gravity should be considered as a minimal threshold, excluding only peripheral cases. The assessment of this threshold is generic in nature before the decision to open an investigation, at the preliminary examination stage, due to the lack of specific investigative powers.

The chapter has demonstrated that the features of sufficient gravity apply every time the RS incorporates Article 17(1)(d) in relation to the activity of the OTP. This incorporation is explicit in Article 53(1)(b) and (2)(b), as well as in Rule 49 of the RPE that applies to the *proprio motu* request for authorisation of investigation under Article 15(3). In all these cases, sufficient gravity should be interpreted as in Article 17(1)(d): as a minimal threshold, excluding only peripheral cases. The OTP must conduct a prognostic assessment of sufficient gravity when deciding whether to open investigations or launch prosecutions, and adopting negative decisions if that investigation or prosecution would likely focus on a case that is ultimately inadmissible. The RS does not justify the OTP's use of sufficient gravity as a justification for selecting certain situations and cases, deciding not to investigate or not to prosecute just because they may not be the gravest in comparison to others under the ICC jurisdiction. Although the RS affords some discretion to the OTP in the selection of situations and cases, this discretion cannot result in blurring the contours of sufficient gravity. Rather, the RS offers the OTP the instrument of the interests of justice to substantiate the decision not to investigate or not to prosecute situations and cases which are above the minimal gravity threshold offered by Article 17(1)(d).

Finally, the chapter demonstrated that every time the four factors determining gravity described in the previous chapter are present in relation to a situation or case, the minimal gravity threshold is crossed, and the situation or case is admissible. This is the product of the convergence of the imperative to interpret Article 17(1)(d) as a minimal threshold not requiring a comparative search for the gravest situation or case, and the practices of the OTP and Chambers that have coalesced into the four factors.

6. Judicial review of sufficient gravity

'Those who argued against granting *proprio motu* powers to the Prosecutor feared an overzealous or politically motivated prosecutor targeting, unfairly or in bad faith highly sensitive political situations.[1]'

1. INTRODUCTION

The previous chapters have examined the theoretical framework pertaining to the assessment of sufficient gravity, reconstructed the four well-established factors determining gravity, and concluded that Article 17(1)(d) imposes a minimal threshold. This chapter explores the avenues for judicial review of sufficient gravity in the Rome Statute (RS). It demonstrates that the RS provides for only limited judicial review of the assessment of sufficient gravity by the Office of the Prosecutor (OTP). Sometimes, this limit is the product of the application of the RS itself, which does not provide for an organic system of judicial review; other times, limitations on judicial review are the product of decisions of the Appeals Chamber (AC), which are examined here in detail.

Not all of the mechanisms discussed here pertain solely to sufficient gravity, some of them apply to any ground of inadmissibility, and some apply to both admissibility and jurisdiction. In line with the scope of this book, only issues relevant to sufficient gravity are fully explored. Similarly, procedural issues that do not bear significantly on the assessment of sufficient gravity are not discussed here in detail.

This chapter is articulated in four parts: first, it addresses the mechanisms for judicial review of sufficient gravity of potential cases within a situation (section 2). Then, it discusses the mechanisms for judicial review pertaining to cases (section 3). Subsequently, the chapter focuses on the mechanisms common to both (section 4). Finally, it offers some conclusions on how the limited judicial review of sufficient gravity has affected the way in which the concept has been interpreted and applied (section 5).

---

[1] Silvia Fernández de Gurmendi, 'The Role of the Prosecutor' in Mauro Politi and Giuseppe Nesi (eds), *The Rome Statute of the International Criminal Court: A Challenge to Impunity* (Ashgate 2001) 55, 56.

2. AVENUES FOR JUDICIAL REVIEW OF THE ASSESSMENT OF SUFFICIENT GRAVITY PERTAINING TO POTENTIAL CASES

2.1 No Judicial Review of Authorising a *Proprio Motu* Investigation under Article 15(4)

This subsection explores whether in the authorisation of *proprio motu* investigations under Article 15(4), a Pre-Trial Chamber (PTC) can review the assessment of sufficient gravity provided by the OTP. While a robust series of judicial decisions militate in favour of such scrutiny, the AC barred this trend in 2019 with arguments that are not fully persuasive.

For a decade, PTCs have assessed sufficient gravity when authorising *proprio motu* investigations under Article 15(4). Under this provision:

> [i]f the [PTC], upon examination of the request and the supporting material, considers that there is a reasonable basis to proceed with an investigation, and that the case appears to fall within the jurisdiction of the Court, it shall authorise the commencement of the investigation, without prejudice to subsequent determinations by the Court with regard to the jurisdiction and admissibility of a case.

In 2010, PTC I noted that this provision echoes Article 53(1), according to which, '[t]he Prosecutor shall, having evaluated the information made available to him or her, initiate an investigation unless he or she determines that there is *no reasonable basis to proceed* under this Statute' in light of jurisdiction, admissibility (including sufficient gravity), and interests of justice.[2] Accordingly, PTC I concluded that 'the Chamber must equally consider whether the requirements set out in article 53(l)(a) - (c) of the Statute are satisfied for the sake of meeting the "reasonable basis to proceed" test before deciding whether to authorize the Prosecutor to commence an investigation'.[3] This position has been followed by numerous similar decisions of the PTCs who assessed sufficient gravity in authorising investigations under Article 15(3).[4]

---

[2] Situation in Kenya, PTC II, Decision Pursuant to Article 15 of the Rome Statute on the Authorization of an Investigation into the Situation in the Republic of Kenya, ICC-01/09-19-Corr, 31 Mar 2010, para.21 (emphasis added).

[3] Ibid, para.24.

[4] See Situation in Côte d'Ivoire, PTC III, Corrigendum to 'Decision Pursuant to Article 15 of the Rome Statute on the Authorisation of an Investigation into the Situation in the Republic of Côte d'Ivoire", ICC-02/11-14-Corr, 15 Nov 2011, paras 16–17; Situation in Burundi, PTC III, Public redacted version of 'Decision Pursuant to Article 15 of the Rome Statute on the Authorization of an Investigation into the Situation in the Republic of Burundi', ICC-01/17-X-9-US-Exp, 25 Oct

The vast majority of scholars have agreed with this interpretation without raising serious concerns.[5]

This well-established case law has provided valuable insight into the assessment of sufficient gravity, as discussed above.[6] Notwithstanding the support of the OTP for such a review,[7] however, in 2020, the AC, in relation to the situation in Afghanistan, stated that the OTP is not bound by Article 53(1) in requesting authorisation to open an investigation under Article 15(3), and thus, in authorising investigations under Article 15(4), the PTCs can only scrutinise whether 'there is a reasonable factual basis to proceed with an investigation, in the sense of whether crimes have been committed, and whether potential case(s) arising from such investigation appear to fall within the Court's jurisdiction'.[8] The AC reached this conclusion in answer to an appeal on whether a PTC could order the OTP not to open an investigation because of lack of interests of justice in its authorisation under Article 15(4). To answer this question, the AC could have merely noted that the RS allows a PTC to intervene on the basis of interests of justice only when the OTP invokes the interests of justice as a reason not to open an investigation or not to launch an investigation, rather than when the Office is persuaded that there is no obstacle linked to the interests of justice. Instead, the AC removed interests of justice from the entire procedure

---

2017, ICC-01/17-9-Red, 9 Nov 2017, para.28; Situation in Bangladesh/Myanmar, PTC III, Decision Pursuant to Article 15 of the Rome Statute on the Authorisation of an Investigation into the Situation in Bangladesh/Myanmar, ICC-01/19-27, 14 Nov 2019, para.125.

5 See, for example, Fabricio Guariglia, '*Propio Motu* Powers of the Prosecutor to Commence Investigations' in Andraž Zidar and Olympia Bekou (eds), *Contemporary Challenges for the International Criminal Court* (BIICL 2014) 93, 100; William A Schabas, *The International Criminal Court: A Commentary on the Rome Statute* (2nd edn, OUP 2016) 404; Gerhard Werle and Florian Jessberger, *Principles of International Criminal Law* (4th edn, OUP 2020) 133; Morten Bergsmo and Dan Zhu, 'Article 15 – Prosecutor' in Kai Ambos (ed.), *Rome Statute of the International Criminal Court: Article-by-Article Commentary* (4th edn, Beck-Hart-Nomos 2022) 881, 894; Ignaz Stegmiller, 'Article 15' in Mark Klamberg, Jonas Nilsson and Antonio Angotti (eds), *Commentary on the Law of the International Criminal Court: The Statute Vol.1* (2nd edn, TOAEP 2023) 543, 557. For an isolated contrary position, see Héctor Olásolo, *The Triggering Procedure of the International Criminal Court* (Brill 2005) 72.

6 See above, Chapters 4 and 5.

7 For example, Situation in Afghanistan, Prosecution Appeal Brief, ICC-02/17-74, 30 Sep 2019, paras 19–33.

8 Situation in Afghanistan, AC, Judgment on the appeal against the decision on the authorisation of an investigation into the situation in the Islamic Republic of Afghanistan, ICC-02/17-138, 5 Mar 2020, para.34.

under Article 15(4), stating that this procedure does not mirror all the requirements under Article 53(1), that is, jurisdiction, admissibility, and interests of justice, but that only jurisdiction should be assessed.

A rigorous separate dissenting opinion and plenty of scholarly commentary have pointed out that this conclusion is incorrect, unnecessary to answer the specific appeal at hand at the time (*ultra petita*), and counterproductive because it bars the PTCs from controlling the assessment of admissibility (including sufficient gravity) in *proprio motu* procedures.[9] Interpreting Article 15 as providing a procedure that is completely disconnected from Article 53(1) runs contrary to the very heading of Article 53 ('Initiation of an Investigation') and that of Part 5 of the RS (under which Article 53 falls) ('Investigation and Prosecution'). Nothing in these headings refers to the fact that they apply only to two triggering mechanisms (state referral and United Nations Security Council (UNSC) referral) out of the three available. Moreover, when the OTP has received authorisation under Article 15(4), its activity falls back under Article 53(2), which provides the criteria that the OTP must consider before starting a prosecution. It is contradictory to deem that Article 15 replaces Article 53(1), while it does not replace Article 53(2): true, Article 15 pertains only to the opening of investigations, but, absent any express provision, it is difficult to understand how Article 53 can be parted in two separate paragraphs that apply differently depending on the triggering mechanisms.

Moreover, the need for authorisation to open an investigation under Article 15(4) is a clear balance to an overzealous OTP: absent any political backing by a State Party or the UNSC through a referral, drafting states permitted a *proprio motu* investigation only as long as it was subject to mandatory judicial authorisation.[10] Limiting judicial review only to jurisdiction, as held by the AC, dramatically truncates the strength of such a review. It is quite unlikely that the OTP, as politically motivated as it can be, would be able to manipulate the fixed parameters of ICC jurisdiction; more likely, admissibility, both in rela-

9 Ibid, separate opinion of Judge Luz del Carmen Ibáñez Carranza. See, also, Kevin Jon Heller, 'The Appeals Chamber Got One Aspect of the Afghanistan Decision Very Wrong', *Opinio Juris* (9 Mar 2020), https://opiniojuris.org/2020/03/09/the-appeals-chamber-got-one-aspect-of-the-afghanistan-decision-very-wrong/; Michael A Newton, 'Absolutist Admissibility at the ICC: Revalidating Authentic Domestic Investigations' (2021) 54 IsLR 143,163; Lloyd T Chigowe, 'The ICC and the Situation in Afghanistan: A Critical Examination of the Role of the PTCs in the Initiation of Investigations *Proprio Motu*' (2022) 35 LJIL 699. For more favourable consideration, see Aude Brejon, 'Cour Pénale Internationale' (2020) 124 RGDIP 419; Kai Ambos, *Treatise on International Criminal Law: Vol. III: International Criminal Procedure* (2nd edn, OUP 2025) 292.

10 Bergsmo and Zhu, n.5, 885–6.

tion to complementarity and sufficient gravity, could be weaponised in a way as to require judicial authorisation as a check. In practice, the only time a PTC has decided not to authorise such an investigation, as mentioned above, was in relation to the situation in Afghanistan, the request was denied for alleged lack of interests of justice,[11] with the decision subsequently overturned by the AC.[12] The final line of Article 15(4), providing that the determination of PTC is 'without prejudice to subsequent determinations by the Court with regard to the jurisdiction and admissibility of a case', also militates in favour of assessing admissibility and sufficient gravity in the authorisation: what prejudice to admissibility could come by a decision that does not address admissibility? This specification would be meaningless without considering that Article 15(4) allows a PTC to determine admissibility. Finally, the preparatory work of the Rules of Procedure and Evidence (RPE) demonstrates that drafting states assumed that PTCs could deny authorisation for an investigation because of admissibility.[13]

Notwithstanding these objections, for the purposes of this book, it must be noted that, at the moment, this is the very controversial final word on this topic, and thus, it is difficult to imagine that, in the future, PTCs will defy the AC and review the assessment of sufficient gravity provided by the OTP when authorising an investigation under Article 15(3). For instance, in 2021, in authorising an investigation in the Philippines, PTC I affirmed that 'the [AC] has held explicitly that a decision under Article 15(4) does not involve determinations on admissibility and interests of justice'[14] but, nevertheless, noted that 'as declared in the Article 15(3) Request, the Prosecutor … has concluded that potential cases which would likely arise from an investigation into the situation would be both admissible and sufficiently grave to justify further action by

11 Situation in Afghanistan, PTC II, Decision Pursuant to Article 15 of the Rome Statute on the Authorisation of an Investigation into the Situation in Afghanistan, ICC-02/17-33, 12 Apr 2019.

12 Situation in Afghanistan, AC, Judgment on the appeal against the decision on the authorisation of an investigation into the situation in Afghanistan, ICC-02/17-138, 5 Mar 2020.

13 Preparatory Commission for the ICC, Working Group on Rules of Procedure and Evidence, 23 Nov 1999, Proposal submitted by France concerning part 2 of the Rome Statute of the International Criminal Court, concerning jurisdiction, admissibility and applicable law, Rule 2.11(c) ('If the negative decision of the [PTC] is based wholly or partly on the lack of competence of the Court or the inadmissibility of the case, the parties to the proceedings may appeal to the [AC] in accordance with article 82 and rules X to XX.').

14 Situation in the Philippines, PTC I, Decision on the Prosecutor's request for authorisation of an investigation pursuant to Article 15(3) of the Statute, ICC-01/21-12, 5 Sep 2021, para.15.

the Court'.[15] No judicial review thus transpired, but rather, a quiet endorsement of the conclusion of the OTP. Clearly, the opposite, that is, a disagreement with the assessment provided by the Office, would have run contrary to the AC's decision.[16]

2.2 Potential Judicial Review under Article 18 upon Request of a State with Jurisdiction

This subsection addresses the complex mechanism provided by Article 18, thanks to which the state that would normally exercise jurisdiction over alleged crimes can ask the OTP to defer an investigation; both that state and the OTP can end up litigating the admissibility of a situation before a PTC under Article 18, which pertains mainly to complementarity. However, since judicial practice has considered this provision to be applicable to sufficient gravity as well, it must be analysed here along with other available means of judicial review.

Article 18 provides a mechanism to allow a state with jurisdiction over the alleged crimes to defer an investigation by the OTP by activating its domestic courts. Under Article 18(1):

> [w]hen a situation has been referred to the Court pursuant to article 13 (a) and the Prosecutor has determined that there would be a reasonable basis to commence an investigation, or the Prosecutor initiates an investigation pursuant to articles 13 (c) and 15, the Prosecutor shall notify all States Parties and those States which, taking into account the information available, would normally exercise jurisdiction over the crimes concerned.[17]

In cases of *proprio motu* activity by the OTP, while most scholars consider that such a notification should be rendered before the authorisation of a PTC under Article 15(4), Chambers consider that such a notification must be issued after the authorisation.[18] Either way, under Article 18, this procedure occurs at a stage when there is not yet a case, but only potential cases within situations.[19]

---

15 Ibid.

16 See the concerns by Heller, n.9.

17 Article 18(1) does not mention referrals by the UNSC, which are thus excluded from the scope of Article 18. See William A Schabas, *An Introduction to the International Criminal Court* (6th edn, CUP 2020) 293.

18 See the persuasive criticism of Daniel D Ntanda Nsereko and Manuel J Ventura, 'Article 18: Preliminary Rulings Regarding Admissibility' in Kai Ambos (ed.), *Rome Statute of the International Criminal Court: Article-by-Article Commentary* (4th edn, Beck-Hart-Nomos 2022) 1009, 1022–3; Chigowe, n.9, 709–16.

19 Schabas, n.17, 293.

Article 18(2) triggers a particular kind of judicial review. Under Article 18(2), 'a State may inform the Court that it is investigating or has investigated its nationals or others within its jurisdiction' for the same facts, asking the OTP to defer its investigation, 'unless the PTC, on the application of the Prosecutor, decides to authorize the investigation'. This latter sentence means that the OTP can ask a PTC to rule on the admissibility of the situation, thus authorising the Office to proceed, while the state can oppose this application.[20] Indeed, Article 18(3) provides that '[t]he Prosecutor's deferral to a State's investigation shall be open to review by the Prosecutor six months after the date of deferral or at any time when there has been a significant change of circumstances based on the State's unwillingness or inability genuinely to carry out the investigation'. Article 18(4) provides that a ruling of a PTC under Article 18(2) can be appealed by both the state and the OTP.[21]

It is doubtful whether the concerned state can invoke lack of sufficient gravity when asking the AC to bar the OTP from resuming the investigation. There is no doubt that Article 18 was included in the RS in order to address concerns of complementarity and consequently, it is usually discussed in scholarship as a mechanism for challenging the respect of the principle of complementarity in relation to a situation.[22] As stated by the OTP in 2025: 'Article 18 was introduced to ensure that States would be aware of the commencement of the Court's investigation in order to avoid duplication of proceedings.'[23] Indeed, the original US proposal behind Article 18 is crystal-clear:

> [a]t the request of that State, the Prosecutor shall defer to the State's investigation of such persons unless the Prosecutor determines that *there has been a total or partial collapse or unavailability of the State's national judicial system, or the State*

---

20 Ibid, 294.

21 The ruling must decide whether the situation is admissible or not. A decision on whether the OTP had to issue a new notice under Article 18(2) is not subject to appeal (see Situation in Palestine, AC, Decision on the admissibility of the appeal of the State of Israel against PTC I's 'Decision on Israel's request for an order to the Prosecution to give an Article 18(1) notice', ICC-01/18-423, 24 Apr 2025, para.33).

22 For example, David J Scheffer, 'The United States and the International Criminal Court' (1999) 93 AJIL 12, 15; Mohamed El Zeidy, *The Principle of Complementarity in International Criminal Law: Origin, Development and Practice* (Brill 2008) 222; Christoph Safferling, *International Criminal Procedure* (OUP 2012) 195 and 201; Schabas, n.17, 294; Ntanda Nsereko and Ventura, n.18, 1015.

23 Situation in Palestine, Prosecution Response to Israel's 'Appeal of "Decision on Israel's request for an order to the Prosecution to give an Article 18(1) notice" (ICC-01/18–375)', ICC-01/18-440, 9 Jun 2025, para.37.

> *is unwilling or unable genuinely to carry out the investigation and prosecutions.* Before the Prosecutor may commence investigation of such persons, the Prosecutor must obtain a preliminary ruling from a [PTC] confirming the Prosecutor's determination.[24]

Similar language appeared in the Preparatory Committee Draft of the Statute discussed in Rome.[25] The language resonates verbatim with the principle of complementarity as articulated in Article 17(a) and (b) of the RS. As noted by a leading scholar, Article 18's 'presence was reassuring to some States who were nervous about the operation of the complementarity regime'.[26]

In light of the object and purpose of the RS, Article 18 itself as part of the interpretive context, and its preparatory work, this author would not hesitate to consider that Article 18 applies only to complementarity rather than to sufficient gravity as well.[27] Indeed, if Article 18 pertained to sufficient gravity, why would the activation of domestic jurisdiction matter? Why would only the states normally exercising jurisdiction over the alleged crimes be able to activate Article 18? Sufficient gravity prescinds considerations of state sovereignty (which matters under the principle of complementarity), and focuses on the common values at the centre of the activity of the International Criminal Court (ICC), shared, at least, by the parties of the RS. The fact that Article 18 refers to 'admissibility' in general would not be an obstacle, since the text of a treaty must be balanced against its context and object and purpose under Article 31(1) of the Vienna Convention on the Law of Treaties (VLCT).

Contrary to the correct interpretation suggested above, Rule 53(2) of the RPE, governing proceedings under Article 18(2) of the RS, provides that '[t]he [PTC] shall examine the Prosecutor's application and any observations submitted by a State that requested a deferral in accordance with article 18,

---

24 Proposal submitted by the US, Article 11 bis, Preliminary rulings regarding admissibility, Preparatory Committee on the Establishment of an ICC, 16 Mar–3 Apr 1998, Working Group on Complementarity and Trigger Mechanism, A/AC.249/1998/WG.3/DP.2, 25 Mar 1998, Article 11bis(2) (emphasis added). For more on the preparatory work of Article 18, see Ntanda Nsereko and Ventura, n.18, 1011–15.

25 Report of the Preparatory Committee on the Establishment of an ICC, A/CONF.183/2/Add.1 14 Apr 1998, Article 16.

26 Schabas, n.17, 293.

27 Contrary views are rare and usually cursory. See, for example, the brief notation by Flavia Lattanzi, 'Concurrent Jurisdictions between Primacy and Complementarity' in Roberto Bellelli (ed.), *International Criminal Justice: Law and Practice from the Rome Statute to Its Review* (Ashgate 2010) 181, 196, n.35, who, however, discusses the substance of this article only in relation to complementarity (ibid, 198–202).

paragraph 2, and shall *consider the factors in article 17* in deciding whether to authorize an investigation'.[28] Although the Rule does not state 'all the factors', it does not even provide for 'some factors'. The impression is that, unless other indications are available, this provision of the Rules should be interpreted as referring to 'all the factors', including sufficient gravity. Although the RPE cannot derogate from the RS, the fact that the factors in Article 17 (including, apparently, sufficient gravity) are mentioned within the Rules in this respect is telling. Between an interpretation creating a normative conflict between the RS and the RPE (the one purported above on the exclusion of sufficient gravity by the review under Article 18(2)), and one that reconciles the RS and the RPE (based on the fact that Article 18 only mentions 'admissibility'), interpreters may tend to choose the interpretation that avoids a normative conflict. Yet, such an interpretation would conflict with the context of Article 18(2) as well as with its drafting history.

Judicial practice is inconsistent on whether Article 18(2) applies to all the admissibility criteria (including sufficient gravity) or to complementarity only. Indeed, until 2022, no case law on Article 18(2) was available. Since then, though, the Chambers have expressed the opinion that the review under Article 18(2) encompasses sufficient gravity, while the OTP has usually opposed this view. For instance, in 2022, in relation to the situation in Afghanistan, PTC II considered that all the factors under Article 17 should be assessed.[29] This pronouncement was unnecessary since the OTP had requested authorisation to resume an investigation under Article 18(2) for issues pertaining to complementarity only.[30] Similarly, in 2022, the OTP asked for authorisation under Article 18(2) to resume an investigation in the situation of the Philippines, citing only complementarity as the relevant admissibility test.[31] However, the Philippines opposed the OTP's request by invoking alleged lack of sufficient gravity.[32] PTC I addressed the issue by considering, on the one hand,

---

28 Emphasis added.

29 Situation in Afghanistan, PTC II, Decision pursuant to Article 18(2) of the Statute authorising the Prosecution to resume investigation, ICC-02/17-196, 31 Oct 2022, paras 43–4.

30 Situation in Afghanistan, OTP, Request to authorise resumption of investigation under Article 18(2) of the Statute, ICC-02/17-161, 27 Sep 2021.

31 Situation in the Philippines, Prosecution's request to resume the investigation into the situation in the Philippines pursuant to Article 18(2), ICC-01/21, 24 Jun 2022, paras 44–9.

32 Situation in the Philippines, Philippine Government's Observation on the OTP's Request, CC-01/21-51, 8 Sep 2022, paras 6, 33–4, 38–48. See also Philippine Government's Appeal Brief against 'Authorisation pursuant to Article

that Article 18 encompasses sufficient gravity,[33] but, on the other, that the Philippines' submissions on sufficient gravity in reality pertained to the jurisdiction of the Court[34] and, thus, were outside the scope of Article 18 but within that of Article 15.[35]

On appeal, the OTP offered a robust argument, under the rules on treaty interpretation, that assessment of sufficient gravity should be excluded under Article 18.[36] The AC discussed Article 18 mainly from the perspective of complementarity, affirming that, when involved in this procedure:

> a State is required to demonstrate an advancing process of domestic investigations and prosecutions of the same groups or categories of individuals in relation to the relevant criminality, including the patterns and forms of criminality, within a situation. The domestic criminal proceedings must sufficiently mirror the scope of the Prosecutor's intended investigation.[37]

However, the AC cautiously accepted that, in principle, sufficient gravity can be assessed in proceedings under Article 18, confirming that the PTC correctly reclassified the Philippines' observations as pertaining to jurisdiction rather than admissibility.[38] Thus, not only did the AC miss an opportunity to rectify the interpretation of Article 18 in the sense suggested here (sufficient gravity being of no relevance), it also walked a dangerous line: the submissions on lack of sufficient gravity by the Philippines were recharacterised by the PTC and the AC as pertaining to jurisdiction rather than admissibility,

---

18(2) of the Statute to resume the investigation', ICC-01/21-65, 13 Mar 2023, paras 154–60.

33 Situation in the Philippines, PTC I, Public Redacted Version of 'Authorisation pursuant to Article 18(2) of the Statute to resume the investigation', ICC-01/21-56-Red, 26 Jan 2023, para.10.

34 The submission is on Article 7 on crimes against humanity, on whether there has been any widespread or systematic attack directed against any civilian population or whether the crimes were committed pursuant to a state policy (ibid).

35 Ibid, para.25.

36 Situation in the Philippines, Prosecution's response to the Philippine Government's Appeal Brief against 'Authorisation pursuant to article 18(2) of the Statute to resume the investigation' (ICC-01/21-65 OA), ICC-01/21-68, 4 Apr 2023, paras 158–60. See also the less persuasive argument in Situation in the Philippines, OPCV, Observations on behalf of victims on the Philippines Government Appeal against the Decision authorising the resumption of the investigation, ICC-01/21-71, 18 Apr 2023, para.70

37 Situation in the Philippines, AC, Judgment on the appeal of the Republic of the Philippines against PTC I's 'Authorisation pursuant to Article 18(2) of the Statute to resume the investigation', ICC-01/21-77, 18 Jul 2023, para.106.

38 Ibid, paras 229–30.

and thus were placed in the framework of proceedings under Article 15. However, regardless of whether such a recharacterisation, in express opposition to the Philippines' submission, was correct, genuine points of sufficient gravity that do not pertain to jurisdiction cannot be addressed in proceedings under Article 15, according to the very same AC's decision on Afghanistan discussed above.[39] For all these reasons, it would have been better if the AC had addressed the point more straightforwardly.

The same uncertainties materialised in relation to the situation in Venezuela. In 2022, the OTP requested authorisation to resume an investigation under Article 18(2), without mentioning sufficient gravity.[40] Venezuela opposed the request by claiming, *inter alia*, that the sufficient gravity threshold, which is allegedly relevant under Article 18(2), was not met in the situation at hand.[41] PTC I decided that:

> [i]n relation to the requirement of sufficient gravity under article 17(1)(d) of the Statute, it is recalled that rule 55 of the Rules stipulates that, when examining an application by the Prosecution under article 18(2) of the Statute, the Chamber 'shall consider the factors in article 17 in deciding whether to authorize an investigation'. While *in some situations it may be necessary to consider the gravity requirement set out in article 17(1)(d) of the Statute in the context of an article 18(2) assessment*, given the determinations reached below, there is no need to consider the gravity requirement in these proceedings.[42]

The 'determination reached below', though, pertains to the existence of the crimes, the identity of the potential accused, and domestic proceedings. It does not address sufficient gravity as an admissibility threshold. Moreover, it is completely unclear what situations might render an assessment of sufficient gravity under Article 18(2) necessary. The impression is that PTC I tried not to contradict the ambiguous (and far from straightforward) reasoning of the AC in the situation of the Philippines, thus providing an obscure pronunciation

---

39 See above, subsection 2.1.

40 Situation in Venezuela I, Prosecution request to resume the investigation into the situation in the Bolivarian Republic of Venezuela I pursuant to article 18(2), ICC-02/18-18, 1 Nov 2022.

41 Situation in Venezuela I, PTC I, Corrigendum to the Public redacted version of 'Observations of the Government of the Bolivarian Republic of Venezuela to the Prosecution request to resume the investigation (ICC-01/18-18)' with Annexes 4, 5, 6, 7 and 8 PUBLIC and Annexes 1, 2, 3, 9 to 13 CONFIDENTIAL EX PARTE only available to the OTP, ICC-02/18-30-AnxII-Red-Corr, 27 Mar 2023, paras 171–81.

42 Situation in Venezuela I, PTC I, Decision authorising the resumption of the investigation pursuant to Article 18(2) of the Statute, ICC-02/18-45, 27 Jun 2023, para.54 (emphasis added).

on the point. Surprisingly, Venezuela did not address this issue in its appeal,[43] which ended with the recognition of the admissibility of the situation for the purposes of Article 18(2).[44]

In light of the above, the role of Article 18 in relation to judicial review of sufficient gravity is still open to debate. The correct interpretation of Article 18(2) should exclude this procedure from being employed to challenge the assessment of sufficient gravity performed by the OTP. The OTP, as prompt as ever to push back against judicial scrutiny of its assessment of sufficient gravity, of course agrees wholeheartedly. However, without solid arguments, a PTC and the AC have concluded that sufficient gravity could potentially play a role in proceedings under Article 18(2), even if, in practice, they have never scrutinised the assessment of sufficient gravity by the OTP under this provision. The unconvincing position of the Chambers, which leaves room for speculation on what conditions would allow for scrutiny of sufficient gravity under Article 18(2), might be seen as counterbalancing the case law, discussed above, according to which the assessment of sufficient gravity is not possible under Article 15(4).[45] However, this solution is not fully convincing because it is not in line with the *raison d'être* of Article 18(2), as evidenced by the entirety of Article 18 and its preparatory work.

2.3 Judicial Review of Decisions Not to Open an Investigation or Not to Launch Prosecution under Article 53(3)(a)

2.3.1 Overview and triggering of the mechanism

Article 53(3)(a) permits PTCs to scrutinise the decisions of the OTP not to open an investigation or not to launch prosecution for lack of sufficient gravity. This is a unique feature of this mechanism, as all the others examined so far permit judicial review of an affirmative assessment of sufficient gravity.

Under Article 53(3)(a), '[a]t the request of the State making a referral under article 14 or the [UNSC] under article 13, paragraph (b), the [PTC] may review

43 Situation in Venezuela I, AC, The Bolivarian Republic of Venezuela's Appeals Brief against the Pre-Trial I's 'Decision authorizing the resumption of the investigation pursuant to Article 18(2) of the Statute (ICC-02/18-45)', ICC-02/18-59-AnxII-Red, 14 Aug 2023.

44 Situation in Venezuela I, AC, Judgment on the appeal of the Bolivarian Republic of Venezuela against PTC I's 'Decision authorising the resumption of the investigation pursuant to Article 18(2) of the Statute', ICC-02/18-89, 1 Mar 2024.

45 Again, in the background, there is the idea that the proceedings are the same if the scholarly interpretation according to which the information under Article 18(1), in *proprio motu* activities by the OTP, should be issued before the authorisation under Article 15(4), is correct. See again Chigowe, n.9.

a decision of the Prosecutor under paragraph 1 or 2 not to proceed and may request the Prosecutor to reconsider that decision'. The reference to paragraph 1 pertains to the considerations that the OTP must take account of in order to open an investigation, namely whether 'there is [a] reasonable basis to proceed under this Statute' in light of the existence of 'a reasonable basis to believe that a crime within the jurisdiction of the Court has been or is being committed', admissibility, and the interests of justice. The reference to paragraph 2 pertains to a similar assessment in relation to 'a sufficient basis for a prosecution', considering whether there is 'a sufficient legal or factual basis to seek a warrant or summons under article 58', admissibility, and interests of justice.

Article 53(3)(a) applies only when the ICC's jurisdiction is activated through a referral by a State Party or the UNSC. Accordingly, there is no similar mechanism available when the OTP operates *proprio motu* under Article 15. The reason behind this disparity is clearly political: if a State Party or the UNSC considers that a situation needs to be investigated, the contrary determination of the OTP that no investigation or no prosecution should be started is subject to further scrutiny. Remember that the drafters of the Statute in Rome were worried about an 'overzealous' OTP,[46] but equally clearly did not like the idea that the OTP might not do the job they assigned to it. Accordingly, the referring state or the UNSC can trigger Article 53(3)(a). Interestingly, this possibility is not reserved for the victims of the alleged crimes, who can only submit observations once the procedure is triggered in relation to admissibility issues,[47] nor to states that have issued ad hoc declarations of acceptance of the ICC's jurisdiction but cannot issue referrals.[48] Article 53(3)(a) includes the word 'may'. This suggests that there might be circumstances in which a PTC refuses to review the decision by the OTP.[49] No similar case has occurred in practice, and it is unclear from the RS and other relevant sources what circumstances might give rise to a PTC refusing such a review.

---

46 Fernández de Gurmendi, n.1, 56.

47 See Rule 107(5) of the RPE, which makes it applicable to procedures under Article 53(3)(a) and Rule 59 of the RPE (including Rule 59(1)(b) about the participation of victims).

48 William Schabas and Giulia Pecorella, 'Article 13 – Exercise of Jurisdiction' in Kai Ambos (ed.), *Rome Statute of the International Criminal Court: Article-by-Article Commentary* (4th edn, Beck-Hart-Nomos 2022) 834, 840.

49 For example, Frédéric Foka Taffo, *Le pouvoir discrétionnaire du Procureur de la Cour pénale internationale* (Nomos 2018) 96; Morten Bergmso and Olympia Bekou, 'Article 53 – Initiation of an Investigation' in Kai Ambos (ed.), *Rome Statute of the International Criminal Court: Article-by-Article Commentary* (4th edn, Beck-Hart-Nomos 2022) 1623, 1641.

This mechanism of review under Article 53(3)(a) is limited to OTP decisions not to proceed. Indeed, Rules 105 and 106 of the RPE provide that the OTP must notify decisions not to open an investigation or not to launch a prosecution to the referring entities. If the OTP decides not to proceed, then Article 53(3)(a) applies. However, the RS is silent on what can be done if the OTP simply does not make any decision on these matters:[50] preliminary examinations and investigations do not have a time limit, potentially leaving the OTP free to dither indefinitely.[51]

All three elements included in Article 53(1) and 3(2), that is, jurisdiction, admissibility, and the interests of justice, can be scrutinised by the Court under this provision. Indeed, since Article 53(3)(b) pertains to the review of decisions based on the interests of justice, most commentators argue that Article 53(3)(a) is available only in relation to jurisdiction (Article 53(1)(a) and (2)(a)) and admissibility (Article 53(1)(b) and (2)(b)).[52] This is incorrect since Article 53(3)(b) is introduced by the words 'in addition', which make it impossible to consider it as a derogation to Article 53(3)(a).[53] The plain text of Article 53(3)(a), which does not impose any limitation, along with the different triggering mechanisms of Article 53(3)(a) and (b), makes it possible to consider that it may also apply in cases where a referring entity asks for the review of a decision not to investigate based on the interests of justice.[54] So far, the only time

---

50 In 2006, a PTC requested information from the OTP about lengthy preliminary examinations (Situation in the CAR, PTC III, Decision Requesting Information on the Status of Preliminary Examinations, ICC-01/05-6, 30 Nov 2006) but the lack of a decision to open an investigation was not equated with a decision not to open it (see Sarah M H Nouwen, *Complementarity in the Line of Fire: The Catalysing Effect of the International Criminal Court in Uganda and Sudan* (CUP 2013) 94; Lovisa Bådagård and Mark Klamberg, 'The Gatekeepers of the ICC: Prosecutorial Strategies for Selecting Situations and Cases at the International Criminal Court' (2017) 48 Georgetown JIL 639, 673).

51 See the discussion in Gilbert Bitti, 'Article 53 – Ouverture d'une enquête' in Julian Fernandez and Xavier Pacreau (eds), *Statut de Rome de la Cour Pénale Internationale: Commentaire Article par Article* (Pedone 2019) 1447, 1489–93.

52 For example, Jan Wouters, Sten Verhoeven and Bruno Demeyere, 'The International Criminal Court's Office of the Prosecutor: Navigating between Independence and Accountability?' in José Doria, Hans-Peter Gasser and M Cherif Bassiouni (eds), *The Legal Regime of the International Criminal Court: Essays in Honour of Professor Igor Blishchenko* (Martinus Nijhoff 2009) 345, 371; Ignaz Stegmiller, *The Pre-Investigation Stage of the ICC: Criteria for Situation Selection* (D&H 2011) 447; Taffo, n.49, 96.

53 Florian Razesberger, *The International Criminal Court: The Principle of Complementarity* (Peter Lang 2006) 109.

54 Ibid. See also Bitti, n.51, 1493; Bergmso and Bekou, n.49, 1641.

this provision has been applied was in relation to sufficient gravity, in the often mentioned *Mavi Marmara* affair, when the OTP decided not to open an investigation into the boarding of the *Mavi Marmara* for alleged lack of sufficient gravity, triggering the Comoros' request for a review of the decision by a PTC.

2.3.2 The scope and effects of a PTC's review: the *Mavi Marmara* saga

Some thorny issues pertain to PTCs' task under Article 53(3)(a), particularly in relation to the scope of the review, the parameters of the review, and the legal effects of the review. The litigation triggered by the OTP's decision not to open an investigation in relation to the *Mavi Marmara* affair provides some answers to these questions, but not all of them are persuasive.

In relation to the scope of the PTC's review, PTC I observed that the procedure under Article 53(3)(a) is triggered by a disagreement between the referring entity and the OTP.[55] Accordingly, it is upon the referring state or the UNSC to identify the grounds for scrutiny that the PTC has to apply under Article 53(3)(a).[56] Some scholars disagree with this interpretation, arguing that Article 53(3)(a) focuses on the entire decision not to investigate, rather than on the disagreement.[57] However, this conclusion would leave the referring entity with a very limited role (merely triggering the mechanism), rather than making it the protagonist of the disagreement with the OTP that the PTC is being asked to resolve.

Another issue is whether the PTC should show deference to the OTP's assessment, in the name of prosecutorial discretion. PTC I considered that:

> there is also no valid argument for the proposition that in order not to encroach on the independence of the Prosecutor, the Chamber should knowingly tolerate and not request reconsideration of decisions under article 53(1) of the Statute which are erroneous, but within some field of deference. The role of the Chamber in the present proceedings is to exercise independent judicial oversight.[58]

This conclusion was opposed forcefully by Judge Kovács, who advocated for a deferential approach to the assessment performed by the OTP.[59] PTC

55 Situation on Registered Vessels, PTC I, Decision on the request of the Union of the Comoros to review the Prosecutor's decision not to initiate an investigation, ICC-01/13-34, 16 Jul 2015, para.9.

56 Ibid, paras 3 and 9–10.

57 Bitti, n.51, 1496.

58 Situation on Registered Vessels, PTC I, Decision on the request of the Union of the Comoros to review the Prosecutor's decision not to initiate an investigation, ICC-01/13-34, 16 Jul 2015, para.15.

59 Ibid, partly dissenting opinion of Judge Péter Kovács, para.8. See, also, Priya Urs, *Gravity at the International Criminal Court: Admissibility and Prosecutorial Discretion* (OUP 2024) 107–10.

I's view is correct because it preserves the legal nature of the assessment of a decision not to open an investigation or launch a prosecution: it is based on legal parameters and, as such, not inherently subjective and subject to judicial review. This resonates with the approach followed by the Chambers and the OTP in identifying the factors determining gravity.[60] However, as seen below, some deference to prosecutorial discretion is maintained by the AC in the form of a limitation on the scope of the review that a PTC can perform.

Another issue is the type of review performed by the PTC under Article 53(3)(a). The RS does not provide any express insight on this topic. According to PTC I, in relation to the boarding of the *Mavi Marmara*, 'the Chamber must request the Prosecutor to reconsider her decision not to investigate if it concludes that the validity of the decision is materially affected by an error, whether it is an error of procedure, an error of law, or an error of fact'.[61] Judge Kovács[62] and the OTP[63] dissented, arguing, erroneously, that PTC I echoed the standard that is appropriate for appeals, thus providing for a *de novo* review of the entire decision.[64] Some authors argued that PTC I erred insofar as it performed a criminal law review of the merits of the OTP's decision, rather than merely an administrative review[65] that, on the model of some national legislation cited, should only focus on whether the decision of the Office is 'patently unreasonable'.[66] The AC did not clarify the point directly as to what standard of review is to be applied, but rather discussed this issue in relation to the legal effects of the PTC's decision under Article 53(3)(a), examined below.

The most contentious issue likely pertains to the legal effects of a PTC's determinations under Article 53(3)(a). The provision states that a PTC 'may request the Prosecutor to reconsider that decision'. Rule 108(2) of the RPE

60 See above, Chapter 4, subsection 3.5.

61 Situation on Registered Vessels, PTC I, Decision on the request of the Union of the Comoros to review the Prosecutor's decision not to initiate an investigation, ICC-01/13-34, 16 Jul 2015, para.12.

62 Ibid, partly dissenting opinion of Judge Péter Kovács, paras 6–7.

63 Situation on Registered Vessels, Final decision of the Prosecution concerning the 'Article 53(1) Report' (ICC-01/13-6-AnxA), dated 6 Nov 2014, ICC-01/13-57-Anx1, 29 Nov 2017, paras 38–9.

64 See also Geert-Jan Alexander Knoops and Tom Zwart, 'The Flotilla Case before the ICC: The Need to Do Justice While Keeping Heaven Intact' (2015) 15 ICLR 1069, 1077–81.

65 Ibid, 1077. See also Situation on Registered Vessels, AC, Judgment on the appeal of the Prosecutor against PTC I's 'Decision on the "Application for Judicial Review by the Government of the Union of the Comoros"', ICC-01/13-98, 2 Sep 2019, separate and partly dissenting opinion of Judge Luz del Carmen Ibáñez Carranza, para.23.

66 Knoops and Zwart, n.64, 1079.

provides that: '[w]here the [PTC] requests the Prosecutor to review, in whole or in part, his or her decision not to initiate an investigation or not to prosecute, the Prosecutor shall reconsider that decision as soon as possible.' Rule 108(3) adds that: '[o]nce the Prosecutor has taken a final decision, he or she shall notify the [PTC] in writing. This notification shall contain the conclusion of the Prosecutor and the reasons for the conclusion. It shall be communicated to all those who participated in the review.' In interpreting this legal framework in 2015, the AC opined that 'the [PTC]'s review under this provision cannot lead to a determination of admissibility that would have the effect of obliging the Prosecutor to initiate an investigation, the final decision in this regard being reserved for the Prosecutor'.[67] This conclusion was reached to justify the fact that – according to the AC – decisions under Article 53(3)(a) cannot be appealed under Article 82(1)(a) of the RS pertaining to '[a] decision with respect to jurisdiction or admissibility'. The AC argued that since decisions under Article 53(3)(a) do not determine the jurisdiction or admissibility of a case, but rather, only ask the OTP to reconsider its findings, they are not decisions on jurisdiction or admissibility.[68] This conclusion was reached on the basis of several considerations: a) the absence of any reference to a right to appeal the PTC's decision;[69] b) the fact that Article 53(3)(a) can only be triggered by the referring entity;[70] c) the fact that Rule 108(3) of the RPE men-

67 Situation on Registered Vessels, AC, Decision on the admissibility of the Prosecutor's appeal against the 'Decision on the request of the Union of the Comoros to review the Prosecutor's decision not to initiate an investigation' ICC-01/13-51 06-11-2015 1/31 EC PT OA, ICC-01/13-51, 16 Nov 2015, para.64. See also Giuliano Turone, 'Powers and Duties of the Prosecutor' in Antonio Cassese, Paola Gaeta and John R W D Jones (eds), *The Rome Statute of the International Criminal Court: A Commentary* (OUP 2002) 1137, 1157–8.

68 Situation on Registered Vessels, AC, Decision on the admissibility of the Prosecutor's appeal against the 'Decision on the request of the Union of the Comoros to review the Prosecutor's decision not to initiate an investigation' ICC-01/13-51 06-11-2015 1/31 EC PT OA, ICC-01/13-51, 16 Nov 2015, para.50. Approval for this conclusion can be found, for example, in Giulia Pecorella, 'The Comoros Situation, the PTC and the Prosecutor: The Rome Statute's System of Checks and Balances Is in Good Health', *International Law Blog* (30 Nov 2015), https://internationallaw.blog/2015/11/30/the-comoros-situation-the-pre-trial-chamber-and-the-prosecutor-the-rome-statutes-system-of-checks-and-balances-is-in-good-health/.

69 Situation on Registered Vessels, AC, Decision on the admissibility of the Prosecutor's appeal against the 'Decision on the request of the Union of the Comoros to review the Prosecutor's decision not to initiate an investigation' ICC-01/13-51 06-11-2015 1/31 EC PT OA, ICC-01/13-51, 16 Nov 2015, para.55.

70 Ibid, para.56.

tions a 'final' decision of the OTP after the PTC's decision;[71] d) the fact that mechanisms to challenge jurisdiction and/or admissibility under Articles 18 and 19 include explicit references to a right to appeal;[72] e) the fact that under Article 53(3)(a) there is no explicit power for the PTC to confirm a decision of the OTP, contrary to what is provided for by Article 53(3)(b) when the decision not to open an investigation or not to launch prosecution is based allegedly on the interests of justice;[73] and f) the preparatory work of Article 53(3)(b),[74] and, particularly, the circumstance that the International Law Commission's (ILC's) draft provided for the final decision to be left to the OTP[75] and the fact that a French proposal to make decisions under Article 53(3)(a) explicitly appealable under Article 82(1)(a) through a specific rule of the REP was not adopted due disagreement among states.[76]

Upon closer scrutiny, the arguments provided by the AC do not hold water. Preliminarily, the reasoning appears convoluted: the AC had to answer the question whether a decision under Article 53(3)(a) was appealable, rather than determining the legal effects of that decision. The AC, unnecessarily, considered that, to answer the former question, it had to entertain the latter, offering reasoning that jumps from the two points without analytical rigour.

Coming to the substance of the AC's reasoning, some arguments advanced are inconclusive. For instance, the fact that only referring entities can trigger the procedure under Article 53(3)(a) does not bear on the bindingness of judicial review. Similarly, the absence of an explicit reference to the possibility of appealing the decision under Article 53(3)(a) does not make it unappealable as long as one takes into account the general scope of Article 81(1)(a); rather, this general provision could be the reason why states dropped the idea of specifying in the RPE that decisions under Article 53(3)(a) can be appealed.[77] The

71 Ibid.

72 Ibid, para.57.

73 Ibid, paras 58–9.

74 Ibid, paras 61–5.

75 *Report of the International Law Commission on the work of its forty-sixth session 2 May-22 Jul 1994*, GAOR, Forty-ninth Session Supplement No 10 (A/49/10), 93, para.7.

76 Preparatory Commission for the ICC, 16–26 Feb 1999, Proposal by France on RPE: Part 3, Trial proceedings; Section 3, Pre-trial phase; Subsection 1, Commencement of investigation and proceedings, 12 Feb 1999, PCNICC/1999/DP.6, 3–4: Proposed rule 55.2 (c).

77 Situation on Registered Vessels, AC, Decision on the admissibility of the Prosecutor's appeal against the 'Decision on the request of the Union of the Comoros to review the Prosecutor's decision not to initiate an investigation' ICC-01/13-51 06-11-2015 1/31 EC PT OA, ICC-01/13-51, 16 Nov 2015, joint dissenting

reference to a presumed difference between determinations of admissibility under Articles 18 and 19 on the one hand (which are binding and thus can be appealed) and Article 53(3)(a) on the other (which, for the AC, is not binding and thus not appealable) does not make sense, since all these provisions refer to admissibility under Article 17.[78] Moreover, Articles 18 and 19 provide mechanisms to challenge positive determinations of admissibility (such as the fact that sufficient gravity is met) rather than negative determinations of admissibility (such as the fact that sufficient gravity is not met); there could be an argument that the two mechanisms of judicial review have the same effects on the OTP so there is a symmetry in the judicial review of positive and negative determinations. Additionally, judicial review is premised on the idea that the judiciary imposes checks and balances on the OTP: leaving the OTP free to ignore the determination of the PTC to the extent that the final determination rests with the Office would make the OTP the appellate body of the determination of the PTC, an absurd conclusion in the framework of any judicial institution.[79] Finally, the analysis of the preparatory work by the AC is incomplete and does not take into account contrary voices that suggested, during the drafting process, that judicial review of decisions not to investigate was an appropriate solution.[80]

Other arguments offered by the AC, albeit not conclusive in and of themselves, deserve more attention. Coming to the differences between Article 53(3)(a) and (b), it is indisputable that the latter provides for more robust intervention by the PTCs. This is also confirmed by the fact that Article 53(3)(a) includes a 'request' rather than an 'order' to reconsider.[81] However, not only is the RS often inconsistent with regard to terminology,[82] but there is inconsistency between different authentic texts as well: while the Spanish text employs

opinion of Judge Silvia Fernández De Gurmendi and Judge Christine Van Den Wyngaert, paras 22 and 30.

[78] Bitti, n.51, 1500.

[79] See the vigorous arguments ibid, 1498.

[80] See the forceful reconstruction in Situation on Registered Vessels, AC, Judgment on the appeal of the Prosecutor against PTC I's 'Decision on the "Application for Judicial Review by the Government of the Union of the Comoros"', ICC-01/13-98, 2 Sep 2019, separate and partly dissenting opinion of Judge Luz del Carmen Ibáñez Carranza, paras 49–55.

[81] Schabas, n.17, 258–9.

[82] Situation on Registered Vessels, AC, Judgment on the appeal of the Prosecutor against PTC I's 'Decision on the "Application for Judicial Review by the Government of the Union of the Comoros"', ICC-01/13-98, 2 Sep 2019, partly dissenting opinion of Judge Eboe-Osuji, para.35.

similar non-mandatory language ('pedir'), the French text sounds mandatory ('demander').

The question returned to the AC, in a different composition, in 2019, again in relation to the boarding of the *Mavi Marmara*; some context is needed to untangle what happened. In response to the 2015 PTC's decision that the OTP should reconsider, in 2017 the OTP confirmed its decision not to investigate;[83] this latter decision (called 'final decision' to echo Rule 108(3) of the RPE) was challenged again by the Comoros under Article 53(3)(a), leading to another PTC decision inviting the OTP to again reconsider its decision.[84] The latter PTC's decision was appealed by the OTP under Article 82(1)(d) ('[a] decision that involves an issue that would significantly affect the fair and expeditious conduct of the proceedings or the outcome of the trial, and for which, in the opinion of the PTC or Trial Chamber, an immediate resolution by the AC may materially advance the proceedings') rather than Article 82(1)(a), and reached the AC.[85]

In this instance, the AC had to decide whether the OTP, in carrying out a reconsideration under Article 53(3)(a), has a duty to follow the conclusions of law or fact contained in the PTC's request, and whether the PTC can scrutinise the decision of the OTP a second time if it believes that the Office has not followed the Chamber's determination.[86] First, the AC held that, once the OTP has reconsidered its determination following the PTC's request, this 'final decision' under Rule 108(3) of the RPE can again be subject to the scrutiny of a PTC under Article 53(3)(a): as noted by the AC, 'if the [PTC] lacked such power, the Prosecutor could simply decide to ignore the basis for the [PTC]'s request for reconsideration. This would in turn negate the effectiveness of the

83 Situation on Registered Vessels, Final decision of the Prosecution concerning the 'Article 53(1) Report' (ICC-01/13-6-AnxA), dated 6 Nov 2014, ICC-01/13 57 Anx1, 29 Nov 2017.

84 Situation on Registered Vessels, PTC I, Decision on the 'Application for Judicial Review by the Government of the Union of the Comoros', ICC-01/13-68, 15 Nov 2018.

85 Situation on Registered Vessels, OTP, Request for Leave to Appeal the 'Decision on the "Application for Judicial Review by the Government of the Union of the Comoros"', ICC-01/13-69, 21 Nov 2018; Situation on Registered Vessels, PTC I, Decision on the Prosecutor's request for leave to appeal the 'Decision on the "Application for Judicial Review by the Government of the Union of the Comoros"', ICC-01/13-73, 18 Jan 2019; Situation on Registered Vessels, Prosecution Appeal Brief, ICC-01/13-85, 11 Feb 2019.

86 Situation on Registered Vessels, AC, Judgment on the appeal of the Prosecutor against PTC I's 'Decision on the "Application for Judicial Review by the Government of the Union of the Comoros"', ICC-01/13-98, 2 Sep 2019, para.32.

procedure under article 53(3)(a) of the Statute as a whole'.[87] However, such a review should be 'limited to establishing whether the Prosecutor carried out the reconsideration in accordance with the [PTC]'s request for reconsideration'.[88]

Having concluded that the OTP's 'final decision' could be scrutinised again, the AC moved on to analyse whether the OTP had to follow the determination of the PTC in reaching its final decision. To answer this question, the AC had first to describe the effects of the PTC's determination under this provision. The AC proceeded in two directions, apparently contradicting itself. First, the AC considered that the OTP cannot ignore the PTC's request for a revision; otherwise, the entire procedure under Article 53(3)(a) would be pointless.[89] Accordingly:

> when the Prosecutor is reconsidering her decision not to investigate upon a request by the [PTC], it will not suffice for the Prosecutor to do so in a perfunctory manner such that the authenticity of the exercise could be questioned. Rather, the Prosecutor is required to demonstrate how she addressed the relevant issues in light of the [PTC]'s directions.[90]

The AC went on to elaborate a distinction between questions of law and questions of fact. For questions of law,

> *the only authoritative interpretation of the relevant law is that espoused by the Chambers of this Court and not the Prosecutor.* It is therefore *not open to the Prosecutor*, despite the margin of appreciation that she enjoys in deciding whether to initiate an investigation or not, *to disagree with, or fail to adopt, a legal interpretation of the [PTC]* that is contained in a request for reconsideration. This applies both to the [PTC]'s interpretation of the *substantive law as well as of the procedural law*, for instance, in respect of the legal standards to be applied to the evaluation of evidence etc. In the view of the [AC], article 53(3)(a) of the Statute does not support the view that the Prosecutor is not required to *correct any legal errors that the [PTC] has identified.* To assume, based solely on the terms used in that provision, that the Prosecutor may simply ignore legal errors identified by the [PTC] would lead to an unreasonable result, which cannot be countenanced.[91]

So, as a matter of law, both substantial and procedural, the OTP cannot invoke any discretion but must follow the PTC's directions. This means not only that the statements of the PTCs under Article 53(3)(a) are legally binding in relation to the law, but also that the review under this procedure pertains to both substantial and procedural legal aspects.

---

87 Ibid, para.59.
88 Ibid, para.60. See also para.61.
89 Ibid, para.77
90 Ibid.
91 Ibid, para.78 (emphasis added).

The two main points made by the AC are slightly distinct (one pertains to the standards of review, the other to the effects of the determination), but overall, the AC seems to veer towards robust support for judicial review. However, the AC went on to state that, nevertheless, under Article 53(3)(a), 'the final decision as to whether to initiate an investigation will always be for the Prosecutor'.[92] It is indeed possible that, once the OTP has corrected a legal error following the PTC's determination, '[d]epending on the circumstances and given that a decision on whether to initiate an investigation will be based on a variety of factors, … the Prosecutor may still arrive at the same conclusion as before, namely not to initiate an investigation'.[93] In brief, the AC alluded to an alleged distinction between the assessment of law – which would be entirely under the scope of the review of the PTC – and the assessment of facts, where a more nuanced partition of responsibility exists.

Following this reasoning, the AC noted that the PTC is not mandated to 'direct the Prosecutor as to how to assess this information and which factual findings she should reach. Rather, it is primarily for the Prosecutor to evaluate the information made available to her and apply the law (where relevant, as interpreted by the [PTC]) to the facts found'.[94] Somewhat confusingly, the AC went on to suggest that the PTCs have the power to request the OTP to take certain facts into account, but the way in which these facts are assessed is left to the Office. Specifically, the AC considered, by majority, that the assessment of sufficient gravity requires

> the evaluation of numerous factors and information relating thereto, which the Prosecutor has to balance in reaching her decision … [T]he Prosecutor enjoys a margin of appreciation, which the [PTC] has to respect when reviewing the Prosecutor's decision … it is not the role of the [PTC] to direct the Prosecutor as to what result she should reach in the gravity assessment or what weight she should assign to the individual factors. The [PTC] may, however, oblige the Prosecutor to take into account certain factors and/or information relating thereto when reconsidering her decision not to initiate an investigation.[95]

In other words, the AC concluded that the PTC's decision under Article 53(3)(a) only binds the OTP in performing a reconsideration in light of a certain interpretation of relevant law and in light of certain facts to be considered. However, it does not impose a duty to reach a particular result.[96]

92 Ibid, para.79.
93 Ibid.
94 Ibid, para.80.
95 Ibid, para.81.
96 The AC thus summarised its findings: ibid, para.82.

The AC's conclusion is unpersuasive because it creates an artificial distinction between law and fact. Indeed, Article 53(3)(a) does not make any distinction between law and fact.[97] This distinction does not exist in any other source pertaining to the powers of the judiciary under the RS. Nor is there any convincing basis in the AC's reasoning for why PTCs can direct the OTP to certain facts but are prevented from questioning how those facts are assessed. Simply, this distinction does not make any sense, as noted in a dissenting opinion, because law does not operate in a factual vacuum.[98] Rather, as noted by another judge: 'applying law to facts is purely a legal exercise. As such, it is a judicial prerogative.'[99] Either the revision under Article 53(3)(a) is not binding in its entirety for the OTP or it is binding in its entirety. A judge argued that the conclusion of the AC was motivated by the desire not to contradict the 2015 finding that decisions under Article 53(3)(a) are not appealable as decisions on jurisdiction and admissibility, a wrong conclusion in that judge's view that should have been overturned.[100] Similarly, the idea that prosecutorial discretion – a rule that, as such, does not exist in the RS[101] – should be used as an interpretive tool for Article 53(3)(a) is incorrect since Article 53(3)

---

[97] Ibid, separate and partly dissenting opinion of Judge Luz del Carmen Ibáñez Carranza, para.24 ('according to the plain wording of this provision, there are no express limitations on the [PTC]'s powers).

[98] Situation on Registered Vessels, AC, Judgment on the appeal of the Prosecutor against PTC I's 'Decision on the "Application for Judicial Review by the Government of the Union of the Comoros"', ICC-01/13-98, 2 Sep 2019, partly dissenting Opinion of Judge Eboe-Osuji, paras 36 and 46. See also Situation on Registered Vessels, PTC I, Decision on the 'Application for Judicial Review by the Government of the Comoros', ICC-01/13-111, 16 Sep 2020, paras 108–109. See, also, Juan-Pablo Pérez-León-Acevedo, 'Application for Judicial Review of OTP Decision not to Open an Investigation and Authorisation of Investigation at the ICC' in André Klip and Steven Freeland (eds), *Annotated Leading Cases of International Criminal Tribunals, .VolLXXVI* (Intersentia 2025) 339, 344.

[99] Situation on Registered Vessels, AC, Judgment on the appeal of the Prosecutor against PTC I's 'Decision on the "Application for Judicial Review by the Government of the Union of the Comoros"', ICC-01/13-98, 2 Sep 2019, separate and partly dissenting opinion of Judge Luz del Carmen Ibáñez Carranza, para.62.

[100] Situation on Registered Vessels, AC, Judgment on the appeal of the Prosecutor against PTC I's 'Decision on the "Application for Judicial Review by the Government of the Union of the Comoros"', ICC-01/13-98, 2 Sep 2019, partly dissenting opinion of Judge Eboe-Osuji, para.27.

[101] See above, Chapter 5, subsection 3.3.2.

(a) is explicitly an exception to prosecutorial discretion.[102] Moreover, the AC's interpretation bars any judicial review of the decision not to investigate or not to launch a prosecution by the OTP, arguably in contrast with the human right to access to justice which, thanks to Article 21(3) of the RS, is the relevant interpretive context of Article 53(3)(a).[103]

This entire saga – which, it should be borne in mind, revolved around a negative assessment of sufficient gravity – demonstrates a Solomonic attitude[104] of the AC that cannot be reconciled with the RS. Caught in an ongoing power struggle between the OTP and the PTCs over who has the last word on a negative determination on sufficient gravity,[105] the AC artificially split the issue in two, assigning half of it (law) to the PTCs, the other half (facts) to the Office. Yet, not only can the two not be disentangled so easily, there is also no basis in the RS for such a distinction which ultimately results in accepting the possibility, *arguendo*, of the OTP making a decision openly in defiance of the RS and relevant case law.[106]

A simpler solution would be to consider that PTCs can bind the OTP in relation to the assessment of sufficient gravity when acting under Article 53(3)(a) both in relation to facts and law. This would mean – as a consequence, rather than as a precondition! – that PTCs would perform a determination of sufficient gravity in the form of a review of the correctness of the OTP's assessment when acting under Article 53(3)(a). Indeed, Article 81(1)(a) does not limit appealability to decisions *on* admissibility, but *with respect to* admissibility, a broader formulation (confirmed by another authentic text)[107] that does not require the PTC to substitute its assessment for that of the OTP. Such a determination should then be appealable under Article 82(1)(a). This interpretation would preserve the possibility of a judicial review of admissibility (includ-

---

[102] Situation on Registered Vessels, AC, Judgment on the appeal of the Prosecutor against PTC I's 'Decision on the "Application for Judicial Review by the Government of the Union of the Comoros"', ICC-01/13-98, 2 Sep 2019, partly dissenting opinion of Judge Eboe-Osuji, para.9.

[103] The point is made, persuasively, in ibid, separate and partly dissenting opinion of Judge Luz del Carmen Ibáñez Carranza, paras 34–9.

[104] Ibid, partly dissenting opinion of Judge Eboe-Osuji, para.36. See, also, Rosario Salvatore Aitala, *Diritto internazionale penale* (Le Monnier 2021) 277–8 (concluding that the PTC should have the power to force the OTP to open an investigation).

[105] Schabas, n.17, 259.

[106] Bitti, n.51, 1501.

[107] The Spanish text mentions 'decisión relativa a la competencia o la admisibilidad'. However, the French text refers to 'décision sur la compétence ou la recevabilité'.

ing sufficient gravity) when the OTP acts upon a referral but decides not to open an investigation or not to launch a prosecution; otherwise, there would be no opportunity for a Chamber to scrutinise the admissibility of the case where, clearly, a State Party or the UNSC considers that a situation or case is admissible.

To be clear, the language of Article 53(3)(a) of the RS and Rule 108 of the RPE does not permit a conclusion that the PTC can order the OTP to open an investigation or to launch prosecution. Irrespective of the normative desirability of this outcome, the relevant rules cannot be stretched so far through interpretation. However, besides enhancing the transparency of the OTP's decision-making process,[108] the fact that the OTP is bound by the legal interpretation and the appreciation of facts performed by the PTC – contrary to the AC's view – has important consequences on the reconsideration performed by the OTP. If the OTP must reconsider its decision in light of the facts and law stated by the PTC (eventually, after an appeal), it would be extremely difficult to justify the maintenance of a decision not to investigate or not to launch a prosecution. What could be the basis that the Office could invoke besides law and fact? Moreover, as noted by a judge, the OTP is a party before the PTC and, as such:

> failure of the Prosecutor to abide by a judicial decision, particularly from the Court's understanding and application of the law, could amount to misconduct under article 71(1) of the Statute based on the Prosecutor's deliberate refusal to duly follow the [PTC]'s orders and directions when she should have appropriately implemented a judicial decision.[109]

The confusion left by the determination of the AC had further repercussions on the *Mavi Marmara* saga. When Comoros once again requested a review[110] of the renewed OTP decision not to investigate,[111] PTC I found that the OTP

---

[108] Salvatore Zappalà, 'Il procuratore della Corte penale internazionale: luci e ombre' (1999) 82 RDI 39, 57 (with reference to Article 53(3)(b), but the reasoning is applicable to Article 53(3)(a) too).

[109] Situation on Registered Vessels, AC, Judgment on the appeal of the Prosecutor against PTC I's 'Decision on the "Application for Judicial Review by the Government of the Union of the Comoros"', ICC-01/13-98, 2 Sep 2019, separate and partly dissenting opinion of Judge Luz del Carmen Ibáñez Carranza, para.67.

[110] Situation on Registered Vessels, Comoros, Application for Judicial Review by the Government of the Comoros, ICC-01/13-100, 2 Mar 2020.

[111] Situation on Registered Vessels, Notice of Prosecutor's Final Decision under rule 108(3), as revised and refiled in accordance with the PTC's request of 15 Nov 2018 and the AC's judgment of 2 Sep 2019, ICC-01/13-99, 2 Dec 2019.

had not genuinely reconsidered its decision.[112] Nevertheless, PTC I decided not to request the OTP to conduct another reconsideration, arguing that 'it is unclear to the Chamber, based on the guidance received from the [AC], whether and to what extent it may request the Prosecutor to correct errors related to questions of law and the application of the law to the facts',[113] and that 'it is unclear to the Chamber, based on the guidance received from the [AC], whether and to what extent it may request the Prosecutor to correct errors related to her assessment of the factors relevant to the gravity requirement'.[114] This conclusion, that some scholars considered to be surprising,[115] demonstrates the profound unhappiness of PTC I with the AC's conclusions,[116] and the difficulties in understanding how such conclusions can apply practically to the relationship between PTCs and OTP in the assessment of sufficient gravity.

2.3.3 Interim conclusions

Some nuanced considerations are needed to better situate this debate in the framework of different conceptions of criminal procedure. Two different visions of criminal procedure influence the way in which states, judges, and commentators address this point: civil law and common law. States and individuals trained in civil law would see no scandal in the judiciary directing the OTP, even contradicting its determination and demanding a different course of action. However, common law states as well as judges and scholars trained in common law would more likely see such an intervention by the judiciary as an interference with prosecutorial discretion. As noted by one judge, this distinction colours the way in which this problem is addressed.[117] More relevantly, the drafters of the RS had these different models in mind when they created the

---

112 Situation on Registered Vessels, PTC I, Decision on the 'Application for Judicial Review by the Government of the Comoros', ICC-01/13-111, 16 Sep 2020, para.102.

113 Ibid, para.107.

114 Ibid, para.110.

115 For example, Rémy Prouvèze, 'Cour Pénale Internationale' (2020) 124 RGDIP 699, 701.

116 Situation on Registered Vessels, PTC I, Decision on the 'Application for Judicial Review by the Government of the Comoros', ICC-01/13-111, 16 Sep 2020, para.114 ('The Chamber considers that the current jurisprudence of the [AC] does not establish with sufficient clarity the exact distribution of prerogatives between the Prosecutor and the [PTC] in article 53(3)(a) proceedings').

117 Situation on Registered Vessels, AC, Judgment on the appeal of the Prosecutor against PTC I's 'Decision on the "Application for Judicial Review by the Government of the Union of the Comoros"', ICC-01/13-98, 2 Sep 2019, partly dissenting opinion of Judge Eboe-Osuji, para.6.

rules governing the OTP and the powers of PTCs.[118] These different visions coalesced into an often ambiguous RS that allows for divergent interpretations. These pages have attempted to provide the most correct interpretation of these issues, to the best knowledge of this author, attempting to interpret the RS as it is, rather than in light of any specific legal tradition. However, it is important to be aware of biases and preconceptions.

3. AVENUES FOR JUDICIAL REVIEW OF THE ASSESSMENT OF SUFFICIENT GRAVITY PERTAINING TO CASES

3.1 No Judicial Review in Deciding on an Application for an Arrest Warrant under Article 58(1)

The first time that judicial review of sufficient gravity of a case was discussed related to a decision on a request for an arrest warrant. Technically, a case materialises only when an arrest warrant is issued,[119] so a negative determination of sufficient gravity by the Chambers bars the emergence of a case. However, since the object of the Chambers' judicial review is the positive assessment of sufficient gravity of the case prepared by the OTP, the possibility for the judiciary to review sufficient gravity when assessing a request for an arrest warrant is discussed here. On the contrary, a negative assessment of sufficient gravity by the OTP at this stage prevents a case from materialising, and its judicial review was discussed in the previous subsection on potential cases.

At the onset of the activity of the ICC, PTCs performed a cursory assessment of admissibility in their decisions to issue arrest warrants. In particular, on 13 October 2005, PTC II issued five arrest warrants concerning the situation in Uganda, which included the following paragraph: the Court approved the applications for arrest warrants 'BEING SATISFIED that, on the basis of the application, the evidence and other information submitted by the Prosecutor, and without prejudice to subsequent determination, the case against [specific person] falls within the jurisdiction of the Court and appears

---

118 See, for example, Claus Kreß, 'The Procedural Law of the International Criminal Court in Outline: Anatomy of a Unique Compromise' (2003) 1 JICJ 603; George P Fletcher, 'The Influence of the Common Law and Civil Law Traditions on International Criminal Law' in Antonio Cassese (ed.), *The Oxford Companion to International Criminal Justice* (OUP 2009) 104; Hanna Kuczyńska, *The Accusation Model Before the International Criminal Court: Study of Convergence of Criminal Justice Systems* (Springer 2015); Bertram Schmitt, 'Legal Diversity at the International Criminal Court: Reflections of a Judge' (2021) 19 JICJ 485.

119 See above, Chapter 3, subsection 4.2.1.

to be admissible.'[120] This is far from a detailed analysis of admissibility and no explicit reference to sufficient gravity can be found, in line with the scant attention that sufficient gravity received at that time.[121]

However, the situation changed in 2006. In response to the OTP's application for an arrest warrant against Lubanga and Ntaganda, PTC I scrutinised the gravity of the case against them, concluding that an arrest could only be issued against Lubanga, as the case against Ntaganda lacked sufficient gravity.[122] PTC I articulated its power to review sufficient gravity at this stage in three points: first, it mentioned the fact that Article 19(1) provides that '[t]he Court may, on its own motion, determine the admissibility of a case';[123] second, it mentioned past decisions by PTCs wherein admissibility was assessed in deciding on applications for arrest warrants;[124] third, it considered that the lack of assessment of admissibility by the OTP in the application for arrest warrants made it necessary for the PTC to rule on admissibility.[125] The first ground, pertaining to Article 19(1), is addressed in the subsequent section in the framework of *proprio motu* judicial review of sufficient gravity by the Chambers.[126]

In response to PTC I's decision on the Lubanga and Ntaganda arrest warrants, the AC articulated a robust decision on why PTC I had erred in deciding on sufficient gravity at the stage of an application for an arrest warrant. In this respect, the AC recalled that Article 58(1) contains an exhaustive list of factors that a PTC must assess in relation to an application for an arrest warrant: none of these factors mention admissibility.[127] The fact that Article 58(1) employs

---

120 Situation in Uganda, PTC II, Warrant of Arrest for Joseph Kony issued on 8 Jul 2005 as amended on 27 Sep 2005, ICC-02/04-01/05-53, 13 Oct 2005, para.38; Situation in Uganda, PTC II, Warrant of Arrest for Vincent Otti, ICC-02/04-01/05-54, 13 Oct 2005, para.38; Situation in Uganda, PTC II, Warrant of Arrest for Raska Lukwiya, ICC 02/04-01/05-55, 13 Oct 2005, para.26; Situation in Uganda, PTC II, Warrant of Arrest for Okot Odhiambo, ICC-02/04-01/05-56, 13 Oct 2005, para.28; Situation in Uganda, PTC II, Warrant of Arrest for Dominic Ongwen, ICC-02/04-01/05-57, 13 Oct 2005, para.26.

121 See above, Chapter 4, section 2.

122 Situation in the DRC, PTC I, Decision on the Prosecutor's Application for Warrants of Arrest, Article 58, ICC-01/04-520-Anx2, 10 Feb 2006, paras 75–6 and 89.

123 Ibid, para.17.

124 Ibid, para.18.

125 Ibid, para.19.

126 See below, subsection 3.2.

127 Situation in the DRC, AC, Judgment on the Prosecutor's appeal against the decision of PTC I entitled 'Decision on the Prosecutor's Application for Warrants of Arrest, Article 58', ICC-01/04-169, 13 Jul 2006, paras 42–5.

the word 'shall' makes the issuance of an arrest warrant by the OTP mandatory when these factors – and only these factors – are met.[128] Accordingly, Article 58(1) does not require an assessment of sufficient gravity.[129]

PTCs have not consistently followed the AC's view on the possibility of assessing admissibility, including sufficient gravity, in the decision on an application for an arrest warrant. Most of the time, PTCs have refused to assess admissibility, sometimes for reasons linked to the limitations of their discretionary power under Article 19(1) discussed below,[130] or simply omitting any reference to admissibility altogether.[131] In a few instances, PTCs have made a cursory determination that the case was admissible, with no reference to any specific circumstances of the case.[132] What is missing is any determination of inadmissibility for lack of sufficient gravity in a decision on an application for an arrest warrant or any significant challenge to the reasoning that Article 58(1) does not require an analysis of admissibility. In other words, the 2006 AC's decision has had the effect of deterring any explicit disagreement between the OTP and the Chambers on sufficient gravity at this stage. This has led one commentator to wonder whether the attempt to avoid such a disagreement amounts to a decision to abandon all oversight of prosecutorial assessment of sufficient gravity.[133]

3.2 *Proprio Motu* Judicial Review under Article 19(1)

A different question is, according to the AC, whether it is possible for a PTC to invoke its discretionary power under Article 19(1) to determine admissibility

---

128 Ibid, para.44.

129 Dov Jacobs, 'Arrest Warrants and Admissibility - Commentary' in André Klip and Göran Sluiter (eds), *Annotated Leading Cases of International Criminal Tribunals, Vol.XXIII: The International Criminal Court 2005–2007* (Intersentia 2010) 113, 116.

130 See below, subsection 3.2.

131 For example, Situation in the CAR, PTC II, Warrant of arrest for Jean-Pierre Bemba Gombo, Aimé Kilolo Musamba, Jean-Jacques Mangenda Kabongo, Fidèle Babala Wandu and Narcisse Arido, ICC-01/05-01/13-1-Red2-tENG, 20 Nov 2013; Situation in Kenya, PTC II, Decision on the 'Prosecution's Application under Article 58(1) of the RS', ICC-01/09-01/15-1-Red, 10 Sep 2015.

132 For example, Situation in the DRC, PTC I, *Prosecutor v Katanga*, Warrant of Arrest for Mathieu Ngudjolo Chui, ICC-01/04-01/07-260-tENG, 6 Jul 2007, 3; Situation in the CAR, PTC III, *Prosecutor v Bemba Gombo*, Warrant of Arrest for Jean-Pierre Bemba Gombo, ICC-01/05-01/08-1-tENG, 24 May 2008, para.8; Situation in Côte d'Ivoire, *Prosecutor v Gbagbo*, PTC III, Warrant of Arrest for Simone Gbagbo, ICC-02/11-01/12-1, 29 Feb 2012, para.4.

133 Jacobs, n.129, 122.

when deciding on an application for arrest warrant. Under this provision, '[t]he Court may, on its own motion, determine the admissibility of a case in accordance with article 17'. This provision applies to any Chamber at any stage when a case exists. Significant case law has focused on the employment of this power.

Article 19(1) provides for a discretionary power, rather than a duty, to assess admissibility, including sufficient gravity. Although Article 17(1) employs the word 'shall', the Chambers have no duty to positively assess the admissibility of a case under Article 17(1)(d) if the OTP or the defence does not raise the matter.[134] Indeed, Article 19(1) replaces 'shall' with 'may', thus indicating that the Chambers have no obligation to determine admissibility *proprio motu* in relation to every case at hand.[135] In relation to sufficient gravity, this happened in the *Al Mahdi* case, where no assessment of sufficient gravity was provided in the decision on issuing an arrest warrant,[136] only a cursory reference was inserted in the decision of confirmation of charges (with no mention of Article 17(1)(d)),[137] and no discussion of admissibility was included in the trial judgment[138] (which focused on gravity only in relation to the determination of the penalty).[139] In this case, the defendant had not challenged the admissibility of the case, but rather, he had entered a plea agreement, a consideration that significantly coloured the entire process, which was characterised by unusual speed.[140] The mandatory nature of the word 'shall' in Article 17(1) can be

---

[134] See Situation in the CAR, AC, *Prosecutor v Yekatom and Ngaïssona*, Public redacted version of 'Judgment on Mr Yekatom's appeal against Trial Chamber V's Decision on the Yekatom Defence's Admissibility Challenge', 11 Feb 2021, ICC-01/14-01/18-678-Red, para.41; Schabas, n.17, 181.

[135] Situation in the DRC, AC, Judgment on the Prosecutor's appeal against the decision of PTC I entitled 'Decision on the Prosecutor's Application for Warrants of Arrest, Article 58', ICC 01/04 169, 13 Jul 2006, para.48.

[136] Situation in Mali, PTC I, Version publique expurgée Mandat d'arrêt à l'encontre d'Ahmad AL FAQI AL MAHDI, ICC-01/12-01/15-1-Red, 18 Sep 2015, para.12.

[137] Situation in Mali, *Prosecutor v Al Mahdi*, PTC I, Public redacted Decision on the confirmation of charges against Ahmad Al Faqi Al Mahdi, ICC-01/12-01/15-84-Red, 24 Mar 2016, para.39. See, also, Situation in the Republic of Mali, *Prosecutor v Al Mahdi*, OTP, Hearing for the Confirmation of Charges, ICC-01/12-01/15, 1 Mar 2016, 91.

[138] Situation in Mali, *Prosecutor v Al Mahdi*, TC VII, Judgment and Sentence, ICC-01/12-01/15-171, 27 Sep 2016.

[139] Ibid, paras 71–82.

[140] Among the significant academic debate on this case, see, for example Paige Casaly, '*Al Mahdi* before the ICC: Cultural Property and World Heritage in International Criminal Law' (2016) 14 JICJ 1199; Marina Lostal, 'The Misplaced

preserved by emphasising that the Chambers have an explicit duty to declare inadmissibility for lack of sufficient gravity under this provision, whereas they have discretion whether or not to confirm *proprio motu* that a case is admissible because of sufficient gravity under Article 19(1).

The first time the power under Article 19(1) was discussed in relation to sufficient gravity occurred with regard to the request for an arrest warrant against Lubanga and Ntaganda. In 2006, PTC I referred to this provision to justify its assessment of sufficient gravity, which led to a denial of the request for an arrest warrant against Ntaganda for supposed lack of sufficient gravity.[141] This conclusion was overturned by the AC, which held that the discretionary power under Article 19(1) must be exercised only when this 'is appropriate in the circumstances'.[142] Since procedures for requesting arrest warrants under Article 58 are held *ex parte*, a determination of admissibility at this stage would also be rendered without the participation of the suspect. This had the potential to create a prejudice against the suspect. Although the PTC held that the determination on admissibility in deciding on an arrest warrant was rendered without prejudice to subsequent determinations on admissibility,[143] according to the AC:

> if the [PTC] makes a determination that the case against a suspect is admissible without the suspect participating in the proceedings, and the suspect at a later stage seeks to challenge the admissibility of a case pursuant to article 19 (2) (a) of the Statute, he or she comes before a [PTC] that has already decided the very same

---

Emphasis on the Intangible Dimension of Cultural Heritage in the *Al Mahdi* Case at the ICC' (2017) 1 *Inter Gentes* 45; Vittorio Mainetti, 'La Cour pénale internationale face à la destruction du patrimoine culturel: réflexions à propos de l'Affaire al-Mahdi' (2017) 39 *Ethnologies* 213; Tullio Scovazzi, 'La prima sentenza della Corte penale internazionale in tema di distruzione di beni culturali' (2017) 11 DUDI 77; Pierfrancesco Rossi, 'The "Al Mahdi" Trial Before the International Criminal Court: Attacks on Cultural Heritage Between War Crimes and Crimes Against Humanity' (2017) 11 DUDI 87; Milena Sterio, 'Individual Criminal Responsibility for the Destruction of Religious and Historic Buildings: The *Al Mahdi* Case' (2017) 49 Case Western Reserve JIL 63; Karolina Wierczyńska and Andrzej Jakubowski, 'Individual Responsibility for Deliberate Destruction of Cultural Heritage: Contextualizing the ICC Judgment in the *Al-Mahdi* Case' (2017) 16 CJIL 695.

141 Situation in the DRC, PTC I, Decision on the Prosecutor's Application for Warrants of Arrest, Article 58, ICC-01/04-520-Anx2, 10 Feb 2006, para.17.

142 Situation in the DRC, AC, Judgment on the Prosecutor's appeal against the decision of PTC I entitled 'Decision on the Prosecutor's Application for Warrants of Arrest, Article 58', ICC-01/04-169, 13 Jul 2006, para.52.

143 Situation in the DRC, PTC I, Decision on the Prosecutor's Application for Warrants of Arrest, Article 58, ICC-01/04-520-Anx2, 10 Feb 2006, para.20.

> issue to his or her detriment. A degree of predetermination is inevitable. If, on the other hand, the [PTC] decides that the case against the suspect is inadmissible, the situation for the suspect could be even worse: pursuant to article 82 (1) (a) of the Statute, decisions with respect to admissibility can be appealed by the Prosecutor as matter of right; the present appeal is an appeal of this kind. If the [AC] overturns the [PTC]'s decision and determines that the case is admissible, the suspect would be faced with a decision by the [AC] that the case is admissible. The right of the suspect to challenge the admissibility of the case before the Pre-Trial and – potentially – the [AC] thus would be seriously impaired.[144]

The AC's concern was thus to prevent a determination of admissibility adopted by a PTC without the participation of the suspect, but with the participation of the OTP, thus indicating that it might be better not to have any judicial pronouncement on admissibility at this stage.

The AC considered that the disadvantages for the accused and judicial (in) economy of issuing an arrest warrant for a case that would be inadmissible are mitigated by the ability of the person against whom the arrest warrant is issued to challenge the admissibility of the case against them under Article 19(2)(a) before the beginning of the trial.[145] However, this conclusion is not fully persuasive since it does not adequately consider the interest of the suspect in not being indicted nor that of the ICC as an institution in trying to operate efficiently.[146] Moreover, one could wonder why an *ex parte* determination on admissibility at the issuance of an arrest warrant would be detrimental for the suspect (who could challenge that admissibility again but would face an uphill battle), whereas the same reasoning does not apply to the fact that the accused will have to challenge again the *ex parte* determination that '[t]here are reasonable grounds to believe that [they have] committed a crime within the jurisdiction of the Court'.[147] Arguably, the AC's reasoning could be used to question the legitimacy of all *ex parte* determinations without the suspect present as potentially prejudicial to the rights of defence.[148]

Moreover, the AC did not accurately specify the cases in which a PTC could decide to exercise its discretion to assess admissibility under Article 19(1) in

---

144 Situation in the DRC, AC, Judgment on the Prosecutor's appeal against the decision of PTC I entitled 'Decision on the Prosecutor's Application for Warrants of Arrest, Article 58', ICC-01/04-169, 13 Jul 2006, para.50.

145 Ibid, para.51. See below, subsection 3.3.

146 Jacobs, n.129, 116–17.

147 Article 58(1)(a) of the RS. As noted by Jacobs, n.129, 117, n.34, the challenge at the confirmation of charges would be based on the more stringent test of Article 61(7), based on 'whether there is sufficient evidence to establish substantial grounds to believe that the person committed each of the crimes charged'.

148 Jacobs, n.129, 117. See, also, Urs, n.59, 150–52.

deciding on an application for an arrest warrant. The AC mentioned, as examples, 'instances where a case is based on the established jurisprudence of the Court, uncontested facts that render a case clearly inadmissible or an ostensible cause impelling the exercise of proprio motu review' as circumstances where the PTC may decide to exercise its discretion 'bearing in mind the rights of other participants'.[149] Yet, it is unclear what the 'ostensible cause[s]' and 'self-evident factor[s]' are that would allow for the exercise of such a discretionary power at this stage.[150]

As a result, in subsequent decisions on requests for arrest warrants, PTCs have been cautious in invoking their discretionary power to perform judicial review. Typically, PTCs have not performed any assessment of admissibility, noting that there was no ostensible cause or self-evident factor to justify the exercise of that discretionary power.[151] On other occasions, PTCs have justified their decision to exercise this discretionary power on the basis of the specific circumstances of the situation at hand.[152]

Outside procedures pertaining to requests for arrest warrants, the AC has demonstrated more flexibility in relation to *proprio motu* judicial review of

---

[149] Situation in the DRC, AC, Judgment on the Prosecutor's appeal against the decision of PTC I entitled 'Decision on the Prosecutor's Application for Warrants of Arrest, Article 58', ICC-01/04-169, 13 Jul 2006, para.52.

[150] Jacobs, n.129, 117.

[151] See, for example, Situation in Darfur, Sudan, PTC I, Decision on the Prosecution's Application for a Warrant of Arrest against Omar Hassan Ahmad Al Bashir, ICC-02/05-01/09-3, 4 Mar 2009, paras 46–51; Situation in Kenya, PTC II, Decision on the Prosecutor's Application for Summonses to Appear for Francis Kirimi Muthaura, Uhuru Muigai Kenyatta and Mohammed Hussein Ali, ICC-01/09-02/11-1, 8 Mar 2011, para.12; Situation in Libya, PTC I, Warrant of Arrest for Muammar Mohammed Abu Minyar Gaddafi, ICC-01/11-01/11-2, 27 Jun 2011, para.4; Situation in the Republic of Côte d'Ivoire, PTC III, Decision on the Prosecutor's Application Pursuant to Article 58 for a warrant of arrest against Charles Blé Goudé ICC-02/11-02/11-3, 6 Jan 2012, para.12; Situation in Georgia, PTC I, Public redacted version of 'Arrest warrant for David Georgiyevich Sanakoev', ICC-01/15-42-Red, 30 Jun 2022, para.3; Situation in Libya, PTC I, Corrected version of the 'Warrant of Arrest for Mr Osama Elmasry/Almasri Njeem' dated 18 Jan 2025 (ICC- 01/11-149-US-Exp), including dissenting opinion of Judge Socorro Flores Liera, ICC-01/11, 18 Jan 2025, para.12; Situation in the Philippines, PTC I, Warrant of Arrest for Mr Rodrigo Roa Duterte, ICC-01/21, 7 Mar 2025, para.8.

[152] For example, Situation in Mali, PTC I, Decision on the Prosecutor's Application for the Issuance of a Warrant of Arrest for Al Hassan Ag Abdoul Aziz Ag Mohamed Ag Mahmoud, ICC-01/12-01/18-35-Red2-tENG, 22 May 2018, para.23.

admissibility. Probably to mitigate the intrusiveness of its intervention curtailing the discretionary power of Chambers to assess admissibility (including sufficient gravity) under Article 19(1), in 2009, the AC clarified that such an intervention must be limited to cases when this is strictly necessary. According to the Court, 'the [AC] will not interfere with the [PTC]'s exercise of discretion under article 19 (1) of the Statute to determine admissibility, save where it is shown that that determination was vitiated by an error of law, an error of fact, or a procedural error, and then, only if the error materially affected the determination'.[153] The interference with the Chambers' exercise of discretion in this field is only justified by the existence of legal errors but the AC also explicitly states that 'the [AC] will interfere with a discretionary decision *only under limited conditions*'.[154]

3.3 Judicial Review under Article 19(2)

Article 19(2) also provides the possibility of challenging the admissibility of a case. According to this provision, challenges to jurisdiction and to admissibility under Article 17 can be brought by:

> (a) An accused or a person for whom a warrant of arrest or a summons to appear has been issued under article 58; (b) A State which has jurisdiction over a case, on the ground that it is investigating or prosecuting the case or has investigated or prosecuted; or (c) A State from which acceptance of jurisdiction is required under article 12.

In line with the scope of this book, only aspects pertaining to the admissibility of a case are analysed here. In this respect, the case law of the Chambers concurs in considering that only cases in a technical sense can be challenged under Article 19(2),[155] leaving aside the possibility of challenging the admissibility of situations.

The main issue to be addressed here is whether Article 19(2) provides an avenue for reviewing sufficient gravity, and to whom. The provision mentions challenges to admissibility under Article 17, making no distinction between

---

[153] Situation in Uganda, *Prosecutor v Kony et al*, AC, Judgment on the Ad Hoc Defence's Appeal on the Admissibility of the Case, ICC-02/04-01/05-408 OA3, 16 Sep 2009, para.80.

[154] Ibid (emphasis added).

[155] Situation in Palestine, PTC I, Decision on the 'Prosecution request pursuant to article 19(3) for a ruling on the Court's territorial jurisdiction in Palestine', ICC-01/18-143, 5 Feb 2021, para.73; PTC I, Situation in Venezuela I, Decision authorising the resumption of the investigation pursuant to article 18(2) of the Statute, ICC-02/18-45, 27 Jun 2023, para.35.

different grounds. This indicates that all the grounds of admissibility, including sufficient gravity, can be challenged. However, the provision is articulated differently depending on who can bring the challenge.

There is little doubt that '[a]n accused or a person for whom a warrant of arrest or a summons to appear' can challenge sufficient gravity under Article 19(2). As mentioned above, an 'accused' can be identified only after confirmation of charges; before, the person for whom a warrant of arrest or a summons to appear is requested should be identified as a 'suspect'.[156] For both the accused and suspects, there is no limitation to grounds for admissibility that can be invoked under Article 19(2).[157] This is confirmed by a number of challenges to sufficient gravity that have been submitted by suspects and accused which have been dealt with by the Court with no objection.[158]

One might wonder what the interest of the accused or suspect is in challenging lack of sufficient gravity: as seen before, sufficient gravity really pertains to the protection of judicial function, the avoidance of the ICC wasting resources and time on prosecuting peripheral cases. The suspect or accused of a crime within the ICC's jurisdiction has no autonomous interest in relation to the protection of the judicial function of the ICC, which affects States Parties (who bear the costs for the functioning of the Court). Different is the situation in relation to complementarity and *ne bis in idem*, where the accused or suspect could claim to be or have been the object of a different but similar criminal procedure.[159] Nevertheless, the need to protect the rights of accused and

[156] Situation in the DRC, *Prosecutor v Lubanga*, PTC I, Transcript, ICC-01/04-01/06-T-32-EN, 10 Nov 2006, 36, lines 15–22. See above, subsection 3.2.

[157] This has already been foreshadowed by Giorgio Gaja, 'Issues of Admissibility in Case of Self-referrals' in Mauro Politi and Federica Gioia (eds), *The International Criminal Court and National Jurisdictions* (Routledge 2008) 49, 52 (where the reference to Article 18 instead of Article 19 is clearly a typo).

[158] For example, Situation in Kenya, *Prosecutor v Muthaura et al*, PTC II, Public Redacted Version Decision on the Confirmation of Charges Pursuant to Article 61(7)(a) and (b) of the RS, ICC-01/09-02/11-382-Red, 23 Jan 2012; Situation in Côte d'Ivoire, *Prosecutor v Blé Goudé*, PTC I, Decision on the Defence Challenge to the Admissibility of the Case against Charles Blé Goudé for Insufficient Gravity, ICC-02/11-02/11-185, 12 Nov 2014; Situation in Mali, *Prosecutor v Al Hassan*, PTC I, Decision on the Admissibility Challenge raised by the Defence for Insufficient Gravity of the Case, ICC-01/12-01/18-459-tENG, 27 Sep 2019; Situation in Mali, *Prosecutor v Al Hassan*, AC, Judgment on the appeal of Mr Al Hassan against the decision of PTC I entitled 'Décision relative à l'exception d'irrecevabilité pour insuffisance de gravité de l'affaire soulevée par la défense', ICC-01/12-01/18 OA, 19 Feb 2020.

[159] The legal interest of the suspect or the accused in challenging complementarity, which is a principle protecting states, has been discussed extensively

suspects renders it always permissible for them to challenge the admissibility of a case, for any ground, irrespective of any specific interest.[160]

Different is the situation in relation to '[a] State which has jurisdiction over a case, on the ground that it is investigating or prosecuting the case or has investigated or prosecuted' it. This state can either be a State Party or a state that is not a party to the RS.[161] The reference to the fact that this state is investigating or prosecuting the case mirrors the test for complementarity.[162] Complementarity, besides safeguarding judicial economy by helping to ensure that the ICC does not waste time and resources on investigating and prosecuting cases that are addressed by domestic courts, clearly protects the sovereignty of the state that is investigating or prosecuting the case and does not want the ICC to intervene.[163] Accordingly, Article 19(2)(b) provides standing to challenge admissibility to those states who can render the case inadmissible because of their own investigation or prosecution. Indeed, the suspensive effect, under Article 19(7), of investigations because of challenges of admissibility brought by states under Article 19(2)(b) and (c) has been explained by a PTC as a means to avoid a conflict between the ICC and domestic jurisdictions.[164] These domestic investigations and prosecutions, however, do not bear on sufficient gravity. Accordingly, most scholars correctly agree that Article 19(2)(b) does not encompass challenges on sufficient gravity,[165] which, indeed, have never been presented. It is thus regrettable that a PTC, in addressing a

---

by Markus Benzing, 'The Complementarity Regime of the International Criminal Court: International Criminal Justice between State Sovereignty and the Fight against Impunity' (2003) 7 MPYUNL 591, 595–600; Muzit Iyasu and Joshua N Aston, 'Admissibility of the International Criminal Court' (2011) 53 *Journal of the Indian Law Institute* 626, 644–9.

160 See the comments by Iyasu and Aston, n.159, 645; Enrico Amati et al, *Introduzione al diritto penale internazionale* (4th edn, Giappichelli 2020) 42.

161 Daniel D Ntanda Nsereko and Manuel J Ventura, 'Article 19: Challenges to the Jurisdiction of the Court or the Admissibility of a Case' in Kai Ambos (ed.), *Rome Statute of the International Criminal Court: Article-by-Article Commentary* (4th edn, Beck-Hart-Nomos 2022) 1033, 1055.

162 Schabas, n.5, 492–493.

163 Benzing, n.159, 595–600; El Zeidy, n.22, 256; Iyasu and Aston, n.159, 647; Ambos, n.9, 265. On the growing role of this function of complementarity, albeit in a different context, see Nouwen, n.50, 82.

164 Situation in Palestine, PTC I, Decision on the State of Israel's request to have arrest warrants withdrawn, vacated, or declared of no force or effect and to suspend the Prosecutor's investigation, ICC-01/18-457, 16 Jul 2025, para.35.

165 For example, Jean Paul Pierini, 'Le contestazioni della giurisdizione della Corte e dell'ammissibilità del caso' in Giorgio Lattanzi and Vito Monetti (eds), *La Corte Penale Internazionale: Organi – competenza – reati – processo*

challenge on complementarity under Article 19(2)(b), totally unnecessarily, noted that: '[a]s to the second limb (gravity), since the Government of Kenya does not contest this element, the Chamber shall confine its examination to the subject-matter defined in the Application, namely whether there are actually ongoing domestic proceedings (complementarity).'[166]

Finally, there is no textual indication in Article 19 as to whether '[a] State from which acceptance of jurisdiction is required under article 12' can challenge sufficient gravity under Article 19(2)(c). Some authors have considered that the lack of reference to the complementarity terminology, contrary to Article 19(2)(b), means that all grounds of inadmissibility can be invoked by a state whose acceptance of jurisdiction is required by Article 12.[167] However, this conclusion is unreasonable since it grants a broader standing to states that are not parties to the RS than to States Parties. Moreover, the suspensive effect of challenges to admissibility, as per Article 19(7), applies explicitly to challenges under Article 19(2)(b) as well.[168] Accordingly, it appears more correct to interpret Article 19(2)(c) in light of Article 19(2)(b), concluding that both groups of states can only challenge the admissibility of a case under the principle of complementarity. In relation to the state under Article 19(2)(c), it must be noted that Israel considers itself that state in relation to the situation in Palestine since it does not recognise the right of Palestine to join the RS and confer jurisdiction to the Court;[169] this conclusion is untenable in light of the ICC case law on jurisdiction over alleged international crimes committed in

(Giuffrè 2006) 159, 163: El Zeidy, n.22, 260; Ntanda Nsereko and Ventura, n.161, 1057.

[166] Situation in Kenya, *Prosecutor v Muthaura et al*, PTC II, Decision on the Application by the Government of Kenya Challenging the Admissibility of the Case Pursuant to Article 19(2)(b) of the Statute, ICC-01/09-02/11-96, 30 May 2011, para.45. See also Situation in Kenya, *Prosecutor v Ruto et al*, PTC II, Decision on the Application by the Government of Kenya Challenging the Admissibility of the Case Pursuant to Article 19(2)(b) of the Statute, ICC-01/09-01/11-101, 30 May 2011, para.49.

[167] Gideon Boas et al, *International Criminal Law Practitioner Library, vol III: International Criminal Procedure* (CUP 2011) 91; Ntanda Nsereko and Ventura, n.161, 1058.

[168] Situation in Palestine, PTC I, Decision on the State of Israel's request to have arrest warrants withdrawn, vacated, or declared of no force or effect and to suspend the Prosecutor's investigation, ICC-01/18-457, 16 Jul 2025, para.35.

[169] Situation in Palestine, Public Redacted Version of 'Israel's challenge to the jurisdiction of the Court pursuant to article 19(2) of the Rome Statute', ICC-01/18-354-AnxII-Corr, 23 Sep 2024, paras 38–45.

the territory of Palestine,[170] and thus the Chambers have considered Israel to be a state under Article 19(2)(b).[171]

Article 19 governs the timing of challenges pertaining to sufficient gravity. As a rule, sufficient gravity under Article 19 should be challenged as soon as possible before the beginning of the trial. According to Article 19(4), challenges to admissibility should be brought 'prior to or at the commencement of the trial'. The same provision clarifies that '[c]hallenges to the admissibility of a case, at the commencement of a trial, or subsequently with the leave of the Court, may be based only on article 17, paragraph 1 (c)' (that is, *ne bis in idem*), thus excluding challenges based on lack of sufficient gravity. Since the challenge at hand pertains to cases, it cannot be presented before the issuance of an arrest warrant.[172]

The RS provides a bar to challenges to the admissibility of cases under Article 19(2). The bar is embodied in Article 18(7), according to which '[a] State which has challenged a ruling of the [PTC] under this article may challenge the admissibility of a case under article 19 *on the grounds of additional significant facts or significant change of circumstances*'.[173] Article 18, as noted above, pertains to potential cases within situations, thus the overlap with Article 19 is not complete. However, the drafters of the RS attempted to limit

---

170 Situation in Palestine, PTC I, Decision on the 'Prosecution request pursuant to article 19(3) for a ruling on the Court's territorial jurisdiction in Palestine', ICC-01/18-143, 5 Feb 2021.

171 Situation in Palestine, PTC I, Decision on Israel's challenge to the jurisdiction of the Court pursuant to article 19(2) of the Rome Statute, ICC-01/18–374, 21 Nov 2024, para.16. Note that the AC ordered the PTC 'to rule on the substance of the jurisdictional challenge', noting that: 'it is for the [PTC] to determine the applicable legal basis under article 19(2) of the Statute for addressing Israel's jurisdictional challenge at the present stage of the proceedings, and to provide any required further instructions on the procedure to be followed.' (Situation in Palestine, AC, Judgment on the appeal of the State of Israel against PTC I's 'Decision on Israel's challenge to the jurisdiction of the Court pursuant to article 19(2) of the RS', ICC-01/18-422, 24 Apr 2025, para.64.)

172 Situation in Palestine, PTC I, Decision on Israel's challenge to the jurisdiction of the Court pursuant to article 19(2) of the Rome Statute, ICC-01/18-374, 21 Nov 2024, para.17. The AC did not overturn this conclusion in Situation in Palestine, AC, Judgment on the appeal of the State of Israel against PTC I's 'Decision on Israel's challenge to the jurisdiction of the Court pursuant to article 19(2) of the Rome Statute', ICC-01/18-422, 24 Apr 2025, para.64 (where it states that 'it is for the PTC to determine the applicable legal basis under article 19(2) of the Statute for addressing Israel's jurisdictional *challenge at the present stage of the proceedings*' (emphasis added)).

173 Emphasis added.

the potential delay created by challenges under Articles 18 and 19 by imposing that 'additional significant facts or significant change of circumstances' should be demonstrated in order to challenge the admissibility of a case where a state has already challenged the sufficient gravity of the situation from which that case arose. Clearly, this bar applies only to challenges brought by states, since individuals have no standing under Article 18. In any case, as argued above, it is doubtful that Article 18 applies to sufficient gravity rather than complementarity only. This bar to challenges under Article 19 applies to sufficient gravity only if it is accepted that sufficient gravity can be challenged under Article 18.

4. JUDICIAL REVIEW MECHANISMS APPLICABLE TO BOTH SITUATIONS AND CASES

Under Article 19(3): '[t]he Prosecutor may seek a ruling from the Court regarding a question of jurisdiction or admissibility. In proceedings with respect to jurisdiction or admissibility, those who have referred the situation under article 13, as well as victims, may also submit observations to the Court.' This procedure aims at avoiding the OTP wasting resources on investigating situations or prosecuting cases that would be outside the jurisdiction of the Court or that would be inadmissible.[174]

So far, this procedure has never been invoked in relation to admissibility (including sufficient gravity). Rather, the OTP has activated this procedure only on two occasions, when asking the Chambers to rule on whether the ICC had jurisdiction over alleged international crimes committed in Myanmar[175] and Palestine.[176] The judicial determination of jurisdiction is, however, outside the scope of this book.

According to the case law of the Chambers, the procedure under Article 19(3) applies to both potential cases within situations and cases. Indeed, in

---

174 Ntanda Nsereko and Ventura, n.161', 1062.

175 Situation in Bangladesh/Myanmar, Application under Regulation 46(3), OTP, Prosecution's Request for a Ruling on Jurisdiction under Article 19(3) of the Statute, ICC-RoC46(3)-01/18-1, 9 Apr 2018. PTC I addressed the request under Article 119(1) rather than under Article 19(3) (see Situation in Bangladesh/Myanmar, PTC I, Decision on the 'Prosecution's Request for a Ruling on Jurisdiction under Article 19(3) of the Statute', ICC-RoC46(3)-01/18-37, 6 Sep 2018, para.28).

176 Situation in Palestine, Prosecution Request Pursuant to Article 19(3) for a Ruling on the Court's Territorial Jurisdiction in Palestine, ICC-01/18-12, 22 Jan 2020; Situation in Palestine, PTC I, Decision on the 'Prosecution request pursuant to Article 19(3) for a ruling on the Court's territorial jurisdiction in Palestine, ICC-01/18-143, 5 Feb 2021.

contrast to Article 19(1) and (2), which explicitly mention the word 'case', Article 19(3) is silent on the object of the ruling on questions of admissibility. As noted by PTC I in 2018: '[t]he absence of such references in article 19(3) of the Statute confirms, *a contrario*, that this mechanism extends beyond a case.'[177] This view was confirmed subsequently in 2021[178] and is supported by some scholars.[179] However, this conclusion is challenged by some judges in their individual opinions and by other scholars, who argue that other paragraphs in Article 19, referring only to cases, should be used as an interpretive tool in relation to the scope of Article 19(3).[180] Indeed, Rule 58(2) of the RPE mentions cases as the object of the procedures under both Article 19(2) and (3).

It is debatable whether a decision under Article 19(3) has the power of *res judicata*. In relation to Palestine, PTC I considered that a decision under Article 19(3) does not bar challenges of jurisdiction under Article 19(2).[181] However, in 2024, PTC I rejected the possibility of entertaining a jurisdictional challenge

---

177 Situation in Palestine, PTC I, Decision on the 'Prosecution request pursuant to Article 19(3) for a ruling on the Court's territorial jurisdiction in Palestine', ICC-01/18-143, 5 Feb 2021, para.73. See also, Situation in Venezuela I, PTC I, Decision authorising the resumption of the investigation pursuant to Article 18(2) of the Statute, ICC-02/18-45, 27 Jun 2023, para.35; Ntanda Nsereko and Ventura, n.161, 1062.

178 Situation in Palestine, PTC I, Decision on the 'Prosecution request pursuant to Article 19(3) for a ruling on the Court's territorial jurisdiction in Palestine', ICC-01/18-143, 5 Feb 2021, paras 68–86.

179 For example, Laurent Trigeaud, 'Article 19: Contestation de la Compétence de la Cour ou de la Recevabilité d'une Affaire' in Julian Fernandez, Xavier Pacreau and Muriel Ubeda-Saillard (eds), *Statut de Rome de la Cour Pénale Internationale: Commentaire Article par Article* (2nd edn, Pedone 2019) 919, 930; Ntanda Nsereko and Ventura, n.161, 1062.

180 Situation in Bangladesh/Myanmar, PTC I, Decision on the 'Prosecution's Request for a Ruling on Jurisdiction under Article 19(3) of the Statute', ICC-RoC46(3)-01/18-37, 6 Sep 2018, partially dissenting opinion of Judge Marc Perrin De Brichambaut, paras 7–13 (a position softened in Situation in Palestine, PTC I, Decision on the 'Prosecution request pursuant to article 19(3) for a ruling on the Court's territorial jurisdiction in Palestine', ICC-01/18-143, 5 Feb 2021, partly separate opinion of Judge Perrin De Brichambaut). For academic views, see El Zeidy, n.22, 265–6; Safferling, n.22, 209; Michail Vagias, 'The Prosecutor's Request Concerning the Rohingya Deportation to Bangladesh: Certain Procedural Questions' (2018) 31 LJIL 981, 990–94; Caleb H Wheeler, 'Human Rights Enforcement at the Borders: International Criminal Court Jurisdiction over the Rohingya Situation' (2019) 17 JICJ 609, 613–18; Aitala, n.104, 282.

181 Situation in Palestine, PTC I, Decision on the 'Prosecution request pursuant to article 19(3) for a ruling on the Court's territorial jurisdiction in Palestine', ICC-01/18-143, 5 Feb 2021, para.131.

brought by Israel under Article 19(2) on the basis that any decision on this issue would result in a revision of the 2021 decision under Article 19(3), which should be considered *res judicata*.[182] In responding to an Israeli appeal on this decision, in 2025, the AC ordered the PTC to answer the Israeli challenge on the merits, clarifying why and to what extent the 2021 decision under Article 19(3) amounted to *res judicata* and on the Israeli standing to bring the claim under Article 19(2).[183]

For the purposes of this book, it must be emphasised that, in principle, Article 19(3) offers the OTP the possibility of obtaining a ruling on sufficient gravity in relation to a case and, following the interpretation offered by the Chambers, potential cases within a situation as well. However, no corresponding practice exists.

5. CONCLUSIONS

The RS provides for multiple avenues for judicial review of sufficient gravity. No mechanism for review is specific to sufficient gravity, but rather, all of them pertain to admissibility in general or, sometimes, to both admissibility and jurisdiction. The lack of a specific mechanisms for reviewing sufficient gravity might signal that the drafters did not consider this ground of admissibility important enough to deserve a specific mechanism. This consideration is strengthened by the idea that some mechanisms exist to challenge complementarity only, such as Article 18, which, in the interpretation offered above, does not apply to sufficient gravity. However, more likely, it made more sense for reasons of drafting economy to create nearly identical venues for reviewing all grounds for admissibility together.

From the overview offered here, it is clear that the assessment of sufficient gravity, initially performed by the OTP, can be subject to judicial review. This consideration alone supports the idea, discussed in detail in a previous chapter, that sufficient gravity is a legal notion subject to legal interpretation rather

182 Situation in Palestine, PTC I, Decision on Israel's challenge to the jurisdiction of the Court pursuant to Article 19(2) of the Rome Statute, ICC-01/18-374, 21 Nov 2024, paras 15–18.

183 Situation in Palestine, AC, Judgment on the appeal of the State of Israel against PTC I's "'Decision on Israel's challenge to the jurisdiction of the Court pursuant to Article 19(2) of the Rome Statute', ICC-01/18-422, 24 Apr 2025, paras 57–60, 64. See the commentary by Kevin Jon Heller, 'The Appeals Chamber Decides Israel's Appeals – And Refuses to Suspend the Arrest Warrants', *Opinio Juris* (25 Apr 2025), https://opiniojuris.org/2025/04/25/the-appeals-chamber-decides-israels-appeals-and-refuses-to-suspend-the-arrest-warrants/.

than an inherently political or subjective notion.[184] To this end, it is necessary to recall that legal interpretation demands that sufficient gravity is interpreted as a minimal threshold, and that the four factors determining gravity – scale, nature, manner of commission, and impact – coalesced in the practice of the ICC organs as the elements by which to interpret sufficient gravity. This minimal threshold and these four factors are the instruments that should be used any time judicial review is available.

The RS, however, does not articulate a comprehensive and rigorous system of judicial review of sufficient gravity. True, Article 19(1) provides the Chambers with the discretionary power to review the sufficient gravity of a case, but there is no parallel generalised mechanism to review sufficient gravity of situations. More generally, the intervention of the Chambers is exceptional in relation to negative determinations of sufficient gravity by the OTP, which can be challenged only under Article 53(3)(a). However, this provision is drafted in a way that suggests that the final word on sufficient gravity is left to the OTP even when a PTC requests it to reconsider its determination. The AC confirmed this view with reasoning that is unpersuasive for many reasons. However, ultimately, no robust mechanisms to challenge decisions on lack of sufficient gravity are available, especially when compared to the mechanisms that are available to challenge decisions not to open an investigation or launch prosecution due to the interests of justice, which are subject to the far more stringent judicial review provided for by Article 53(3)(b). Undesirable as this reality may be from a normative point of view, and at odds with the judicial traditions of some civil law countries that allow the judiciary to force the prosecution to open an investigation or launch a prosecution, this is the reality of the RS as it stands currently, and as interpreted by the AC.

In this regard, one might wonder what the reasons are for such an lack of judicial review of sufficient gravity. Why did the drafting states include so many mechanisms to review positive determinations of sufficient gravity, and only one feeble mechanism to review negative determinations? The answer lies in the quote that opens this chapter and that has been reproduced deliberately more than once in this book: the drafting states feared an overzealous Prosecutor and, consequently, included in the RS several mechanisms for blocking the activity of the OTP, including through review of its positive determinations of sufficient gravity. States, on the other hand, had less interest in forcing the OTP to act in relation to a certain situation or case, as demonstrated by the weak role of referrals in relation to specific situations and cases, and the lack of judicial mechanisms to review negative determinations of sufficient gravity.

[184] See above, Chapter 2, section 2.

The fact that only positive determinations of sufficient gravity are subject to robust judicial scrutiny should not give the impression that the OTP must fight an uphill battle to have its assessment of sufficient gravity accepted by the Chambers. Rather, the imperative to interpret sufficient gravity as a minimal threshold has ensured the Chambers agree with the assessment of the OTP on most occasions, including when, such as in the case against Al Mahdi, no proper assessment of sufficient gravity was offered. Similarly, all attempts by defendants to challenge sufficient gravity have been dismissed by the Chambers. Contrary to complementarity, which impacts the sovereignty of states and is often forcefully litigated by those same states, positive determinations of sufficient gravity are usually easy wins for the OTP.

As discussed, the only time a PTC has disagreed with the OTP's positive assessment of sufficient gravity, in relation to the request for an arrest warrant against Ntaganda in 2006, the AC was prompt in blocking the possibility of such a judicial review. Although the AC's reasoning on why the discretionary power under Article 19(1) should not normally be exercised when PTCs decide on a request for an arrest warrant is far from persuasive, this is only one example in a constant limitation of the avenues for review of the OTP's determination of sufficient gravity by the AC. When, in 2015, the AC affirmed that the PTC's decision to request that the OTP reconsider its decision not to investigate under Article 53(3)(a) was not appealable, the AC was not protecting the determination of the PTC: rather, it was saying that it was not appealable because the OTP retained the last word on the assessment of sufficient gravity, as the AC confirmed later in 2019 with an artificial distinction between law and fact in the PTC's decisions under Article 53(3)(a). The overall impression is that, on the one hand, PTCs are eager to exercise judicial review over the OTP's assessment of sufficient gravity, following a civil law attitude towards the relationship between prosecution and judiciary, while, on the other hand, the AC prefers to leave the ultimate decisions to the OTP.

The limited mechanisms available to review the OTP's assessment of sufficient gravity and the limited powers of PTCs in relation to negative assessments, whether in-built in the RS or the product of questionable interpretations by the AC, have not discouraged litigation of sufficient gravity. Rather, judicial review of sufficient gravity occurs in relation to many cases and some situations, either at the request of referring states, states with jurisdiction over the situation, the defendants, or the Chambers *proprio motu*. It is possible that, in the future, more litigation will occur. Accordingly, it is crucial to understand how sufficient gravity should be assessed and how its assessment can be challenged, as this book has sought to do.

7. General conclusions on the assessment of sufficient gravity

> 'It is a mistake to regard these norms as simply blank checks for discretion, as though the most they told the person that they were addressed to was to prepare yourself for the arbitrary imposition of a value judgment by those in power. In fact, the use of standards clearly represents an exercise in legal guidance.'[1]

> 'It is doubtful whether a higher gravity threshold for situations or selection of cases is the proper remedy to address the underlying problems. It might do more harm than good.'[2]

This book has explored the content of sufficient gravity under Article 17(1)(d), how this criterion should be assessed, and the conditions governing its judicial review. The investigation has applied principles and rules of international law, in particular those pertaining to treaty interpretation, and has explored the practical functioning of the International Criminal Court (ICC) in light of the practice of the Office of the Prosecutor (OTP) and the case law of the Chambers. Agreeing with the ICC organs on some occasions and disagreeing on others, this text has sought to describe the rules that apply to an assessment of sufficient gravity – a process that, far from being extra-legal, is a highly legalised component of ICC procedure. It is this author's hope that this work will serve as a reminder to those organs that might think that, when specific judicial review is not available, no legal rules should govern the assessment of sufficient gravity.

Sufficient gravity might have been a moot problem in the practice of the ICC. Introduced in the preparatory work of the Rome Statute (RS) at a time when the subject-matter jurisdiction of the Court included treaty-based transnational

---

1 Jeremy Waldron, 'How to Do Things with Standards' in Upendra Baxi, Christopher McCrudden and Abdul Palowala (eds), *Law's Ethical, Global and Theoretical Contexts: Essays in Honour of William Twining* (CUP 2015) 335, 349.

2 Carsten Stahn, 'Higher Gravity Threshold? A Plea for Caution' in Richard H Steinberg (ed.), *The International Criminal Court: Legal, Policy, and Political Challenges* (Brill 2025) 258, 260.

crimes, it survived every round of negotiation ultimately finding its way into Article 17(1)(d) of the RS. After a few years of scant attention, sufficient gravity has, however, become the epicentre of disagreement between the OTP and the Chambers: on the one hand, the OTP claims that sufficient gravity should be used as a tool to select situations and cases, and that its ultimate assessment rests with the Office; on the other, the Chambers consider sufficient gravity to be a legal threshold for admissibility, sometimes subject to judicial review. Disagreement between the two organs, in practice, is rare: the Chambers usually rubber-stamp the assessment of sufficient gravity provided by the OTP. Every time a defendant has challenged this assessment, the Chambers have confirmed that sufficient gravity was satisfied.

The only instances, so far, in which the OTP and the Chambers have disagreed, however, were momentous: the saga concerning the arrest warrants against Lubanga and Ntaganda demonstrated that the OTP was not willing to accept a predetermined gravity threshold imposed by the Chambers, rather, that there is a minimum gravity threshold to be assessed on a case-by-case basis; the saga pertaining to the boarding of the *Mavi Marmara* centred the assessment of sufficient gravity on prosecutorial discretion, with acrobatic distinctions between fact and law by the Appeals Chamber (AC), and an extremely politicised background because of the potential involvement of Israeli soldiers in the affair.

In this framework, this book's primary contribution to the existing scholarship on the subject lies in its critical exploration of how sufficient gravity under Article 17(1)(d) of the RS should be assessed. Chapter 1 introduced the topic of the book, demonstrating that the assessment of sufficient gravity is an area that both needs more scholarly engagement and is vital for the practical life of the ICC. The relative paucity of monograph-length works on this topic, its constant centrality for states, defendants, victims, prosecutors and judges, as well as the challenges in trying to define what has no definition triggered this author's scholarly interest in this project. The ongoing process of reviewing ICC policies and practices, indeed, has involved ongoing discussion concerning sufficient gravity, its usage, and its limits.

Coherently with the background of this author, Chapter 2 laid down the theoretical framework that has been employed throughout the book to analyse how sufficient gravity should be assessed, discussing both jurisprudence and treaty interpretation. Borrowing from jurisprudence, this book reconstructed sufficient gravity as a combined evaluative concept that embodies a standard. The fact that a standard rather than a rule is provided means that it is impossible to identify with 100 per cent accuracy a numeric formula to identify situations, cases, and potential cases that meet sufficient gravity. The drafters of the RS, in providing a standard, left some discretion to the ICC organs in relation to the assessment of sufficient gravity in specific cases.

However, the nature of a standard of sufficient gravity does not mean that the notion is inherently political or inherently subjective. Rather, Article 17(1)(d) is a treaty provision, and the RS allows challenges to the determination of sufficient gravity by the ICC organs. On these bases, Chapter 2 argued that sufficient gravity is subject to legal interpretation, the conceptual tool that can be used to reduce the discretion of the ICC organs in assessing this standard. In relation to the RS, such rules encompass both rules on interpretation provided by the RS itself (such as Article 21(3) on the duty to take into account internationally recognised human rights and non-discrimination) and those rules on treaty interpretation provided by Articles 31, 32, and 33 of the Vienna Convention on the Law of Treaties (VCLT). In particular, Chapter 2 explored how the entire RS is an interpretive context for the notion of sufficient gravity; how its object and purpose can lead to the interpretation of sufficient gravity; and why the preparatory work is important. Furthermore, taking into account the constitutive nature of the RS, the chapter argued that the interpretive criteria embodied in the VCLT demand particular attention in the practice of the ICC organs tasked with the interpretation and application of sufficient gravity. Accordingly, the practice of the OTP and the case law of the Chambers (which are the organs tasked with the final word on the interpretation of the RS) should be considered important elements in the interpretation of the RS in relation to sufficient gravity.

Chapter 3 explored the notion of gravity in international law, international criminal law, and in the RS. Indeed, gravity is not a feature specific to the admissibility of cases and potential cases under Article 17(1)(d); rather, it is a notion commonly employed in several areas of international law. Beyond international criminal law, gravity has attracted limited scholarly attention, with scant efforts to try to provide an overarching notion of gravity in favour of a sectoral approach. Nevertheless, it is evident that gravity is often employed in international law in relation to a perceived value centred approach to issues. This conclusion is particularly apparent with regard to the employment of the notion of gravity in relation to state responsibility.

In parallel, Chapter 3 also reconstructed the emergence of the notion of gravity in international criminal law. The entire history of this discipline is drenched in gravity considerations, from the attempt to put the German Kaiser on trial at the end of World War I to Nuremberg, the United Nations (UN) ad hoc tribunals, and the preparatory work of the RS. It is commonplace to see gravity as the driving force behind criminalisation, at the international level, of certain acts that are considered so harmful for the international community as a whole as to deserve international criminalisation. Although this conclusion is correct, the rhetoric behind gravity-driven international criminalisation should not overshadow the limits that such a process encounters, including those pertaining to the imbalance of power between states in the Global North

– in favour of a narrow understanding of international crimes based on the London Charter of the International Military Tribunal in Nuremberg – and states in the Global South – fighting to include additional crimes linked to centuries of colonial exploitation.

Coming to the RS, Chapter 3 discussed the notion of gravity in many different areas, bearing in mind that the entire RS is part of the interpretive context of Article 17(1)(d). First, the chapter delineated the object of this book by exploring the role of Article 17(1)(d) as an admissibility criterion, clarifying the relevant terminology for situation, case, and potential case, and providing a very brief overview of the stages of the proceedings where sufficient gravity may be discussed in order to guide the reader in understanding the analysis of subsequent chapters. The chapter went on to explore the notion of gravity in relation to different areas of the RS, such as gravity as a component of the jurisdiction of the ICC over certain crimes, gravity and the interim release of individuals, and gravity and the functioning of ICC organs in relation to misconduct and miscarriage of justice. The analyses of gravity as a component of the interests of justice and as a criterion for the determination of penalties were particularly relevant for the topic of this book: on the one hand, there is often confusion between sufficient gravity and the interests of justice, thanks to the sometimes flippant use of sufficient gravity by the OTP; on the other, the criteria for the determination of penalties have been invoked by the Chambers as tools to interpret Article 17(1)(d).

Chapter 4 provided a detailed analysis of which factors the OTP and Chambers have considered to be decisive in assessing the sufficient gravity of situations, cases, and potential cases. After an initial period in which quantitative considerations prevailed, the practice of the OTP and the case law of the Chambers (mediated by reference to some factors for the determination of penalties) coalesced around four factors: scale, nature, manner of commission, and impact. The chapter analysed the relevant practice and case law to correctly define these four factors. These factors can be reconstructed as additional to the elements of the crimes (*actus reus*, *mens rea*, modes of liability), which pertain to jurisdiction rather than to admissibility. They are seen as external factual considerations surrounding a case or potential case that render it sufficiently grave.

The chapter discarded the proposal that the contribution of the alleged perpetrator to the commission of the crimes (the so-called 'most responsible criterion') is a relevant factor in determining gravity. Although some judicial practice refers to it, upon closer scrutiny it is evident that the OTP focuses on the most responsible criterion as a matter of policy rather than as an act of interpretation of sufficient gravity. Indeed, usually, the most responsible criterion is mentioned in addition to sufficient gravity.

Chapter 5 explored the idea that sufficient gravity is a threshold, answering the question of when the presence of the factors determining gravity is sufficient under Article 17(1)(d). In light of the object and scope of the RS, its preparatory work, and judicial practice, the chapter concluded that Article 17(1)(d) does not mandate the investigation and prosecution of the most grave or peculiarly grave cases and potential cases, but only those cases and potential cases which are sufficiently grave to justify further action by the ICC. The consequences of this conclusion are twofold. First, sufficient gravity is a threshold that does not require a comparative analysis of situations, cases, and potential cases to decide which investigation or prosecution to pursue. This conclusion demonstrates that the practice of the OTP, largely based on alleged comparisons between situations and cases in search of the gravest, is not based on Article 17(1)(d); rather, it can be justified under other rules of the RS. Indeed, the OTP can legitimately decide to select or prioritise some situations or cases, but such assessment does not pertain to Article 17(1)(d), which only imposes on the OTP, through Article 53, the obligation not to open an investigation and not to launch a prosecution that likely will be inadmissible.

Second, the application of the aforementioned interpretive criteria demonstrated that sufficient gravity is a minimal threshold, which allows the ICC organs to consider inadmissible only cases and potential cases that are truly peripheral. How can these peripheral cases and potential cases be identified in the absence of a more specific indication in the RS? The final part of Chapter 5 argued that the presence of the four factors determining gravity described in Chapter 4 imposes a presumption of admissibility of cases and potential cases. In other words, the discretion provided in the assessment of sufficient gravity by the fact that it is a standard rather than a rule (discussed in Chapter 2) is reduced by the application of correct interpretive criteria (identified in Chapter 3), according to which gravity is based on four factors (provided in Chapter 4), which should be assessed against a minimal threshold (identified in Chapter 5). Every time the four factors are present, admissibility is met.

The fact that the four gravity criteria are based on factual circumstances should render it easy to ascertain them. Nevertheless, sometimes, ICC organs, states, and defendants have divergent views on whether situations, cases, or potential cases cross the gravity threshold under Article 17(1)(d). Chapter 6 discussed the mechanisms available in the RS to provide judicial review of the assessment of sufficient gravity performed by the OTP. When these mechanisms are available, they are usually generic mechanisms to challenge positive determinations of admissibility by the OTP (often alongside the possibility of challenging findings on jurisdiction). In relation to potential cases within a situation, Chapter 6 argued that the mechanism under Article 18 does not apply to sufficient gravity but only to complementarity, and that the AC has barred any possibility of assessing sufficient gravity when a PTC authorises a *proprio motu* investigation under Article 19(4). In relation to cases, these mechanisms pertain to the discretional power of the Chambers to determine the admissibility of a case *proprio motu* under Article 19(1), the possibility for the accused to challenge sufficient gravity under Article 19(2), and the faculty of the OTP to seek a preliminary ruling on admissibility under Article 19(3) (which is interpreted by the Chambers as applying to both potential cases within situations and cases).

In relation to judicial review of negative assessments of sufficient gravity, Chapter 6 explored the mechanism provided by Article 53(3)(a), which has been applied only once in relation to sufficient gravity when the OTP decided not to open an investigation into the *Mavi Marmara* boarding. In relation to this, the chapter analysed the ensuing judicial saga, criticising the AC's stance that concluded that PTCs cannot bind the OTP in relation to the assessment of sufficient gravity concerning specific facts; however, in doing so, it must be acknowledged that the mechanism under Article 53(3)(a) lacks the binding features of the mechanism under Article 53(3)(b).

Overall, this author hopes to have provided the reader with a better understanding of how sufficient gravity should be assessed under the RS. In doing so, the reader might be better equipped to evaluate whether the ICC organs have assessed sufficient gravity correctly, especially in relation to situations and cases that are particularly delicate from a political perspective. At a time when the ICC, its Prosecutor, and its judges are at the centre of intense political pressures from powerful states, it is important to reinforce the legitimacy of the Court's activities through adherence to its legal mandate under the RS. Clarifying contested issues such as sufficient gravity might not save the ICC project from political turmoil and radical geopolitical changes, but it could nevertheless contribute to reinforcing the ICC project.

Selected Bibliography

Abass, Ademola, 'Historical and Political Background to the Malabo Protocol' in Gerhard Werle and Moritz Vormbaum (eds), *The African Criminal Court: A Commentary on the Malabo Protocol* (Springer 2017) 11

Abbott, Kenneth W, Keohane, Robert O, Moravcsik, Andrew, Slaughter, Anne-Marie and Snidal, Duncan, 'The Concept of Legalization' (2000) 54 *International Organization* 401

Abi-Saab, Georges, 'The Uses of Article 19' (1999) 10 EJIL 339

Ainis, Michele, *La legge oscura: come e perché non funziona* (Laterza 1997)

Aitala, Rosario Salvatore, *Diritto internazionale penale* (Le Monnier 2021)

Akande, Dapo, 'The Jurisdiction of the International Criminal Court over Nationals of Non-Parties: Legal Basis and Limits' (2003) 1 JICJ 618

Alland, Denis, 'L'interprétation du droit international public' (2014) 362 RdC 41

Amati, Enrico, Caroli Paolo, Costi Matteo, Fronza Emanuela, Maculan Elena, Pizzuti Alessandro and Vallini, Antonio, *Introduzione al diritto penale internazionale* (4th edn, Giappichelli 2020)

Ambos, Kai, *Treatise on International Criminal Law: Vol.I: Foundations and General Part* (2nd edn, OUP 2021)

Ambos, Kai, *Treatise on International Criminal Law: Vol.II, Crimes and Sentencing* (2nd edn, OUP 2022)

Ambos, Kai, *Treatise on International Criminal Law: Vol.III, International Criminal Procedure* (2nd edn, OUP 2025)

Amerasinghe, Chittharanjan F, *Principles of the Institutional Law of International Organizations* (2nd edn, CUP 2005)

Amoroso, Daniele, *Insindacabilità del potere estero e diritto internazionale* (Editoriale Scientifica 2012)

Amoulgam, Azé Kerté, 'Examens préliminaires à la Cour pénale internationale: fondements juridiques, pratique du Bureau de la Procureure et développements judiciaires' (2019) 32 RQDI 173

Annoni, Alessandra, 'Il rapporto fra pace e giustizia nella prassi applicativa dello Statuto di Roma' in Alessandra Annoni, Serana Forlati and Pietro Franzina (eds), *Il diritto internazionale come sistema di valori: scritti in onore di Francesco Salerno* (Jovene 2021) 31

Aranburu, Xabier Agirre, 'Gravity of Crimes and Responsibility of the Suspect' in Morten Bergsmo (ed.), *Criteria for Prioritizing and Selecting Core International Crimes Cases* (3rd edn, TOAEP 2024) 417

Arcarazo, Diego Acosta, Buchan, Russell and Urueña, Rene, 'Beyond Justice, Beyond Peace? Colombia, the Interests of Justice, and the Limits of International Criminal Law' (2015) 26 CLF 291

Arcari, Maurizio, 'Alla ricerca di gravità: le conseguenze delle gravi violazioni del diritto internazionale' in Paolo Benvenuti (ed.), *L'accertamento delle gravi violazioni del diritto internazionale: Dalle proposte di Gaetano Arangio-Ruiz alla prassi contemporanea* (RomaTre Press 2025) 97

Arsanjani, Mahnoush H and Reisman, W Michael, 'The International Criminal Court and the Congo: From Theory to Reality' in Leila Nadya Sadat and Michael P Scharf (eds), *The Theory and Practice of International Criminal Law: Essays in Honor of M Cherif Bassiuni* (Martinus Nijhoff 2008) 325

Ascensio, Harvé, 'La motivation des decisions des jurisdictions penales internationales' in Hélène Ruiz Fabri and Jan-Marc Sorel (eds), *La motivation des decisions des jurisdictions internationals* (Pedone 2008) 207

Azarova, Valentina and Mariniello, Triestino, 'Why the ICC Needs a "Palestine Situation" (More than Palestine Needs the ICC): On the Court's Potential Role(s) in the Israeli-Palestinian Context' (2017) 11 DUDI 115

Ba, Oumar, 'Constructing an International Legal Order under the Shadow of Colonial Domination' (2023) 22 *Journal of Human Rights* 4

Ba, Oumar, 'International Justice and the Postcolonial Condition' (2017) 63 *Africa Today* 44

Ba, Oumar, Bluen, K Jo and Owiso, Owiso, 'The Geopolitics of Race, Empire, and Expertise at the ICC' in *Oxford Research Encyclopedias of International Studies Online* (2023)

Bådagård, Lovisa and Klamberg, Mark, 'The Gatekeepers of the ICC: Prosecutorial Strategies for Selecting Situations and Cases at the International Criminal Court' (2017) 48 Georgetown JIL 639

Bassiouni, M Cherif, *Introduction to International Criminal Law* (2nd edn, Brill 2013)

Bassiouni, M Cherif and Schabas, William A (eds), *The Legislative History of the International Criminal Court* (2nd edn, Brill 2016)

Bellelli, Roberto, 'The Establishment of the System of International Criminal Justice' in Roberto Bellelli (ed.), *International Criminal Justice: Law and Practice from the Rome Statute to Its Review* (Ashgate 2010) 5

Bennouna, Mohamed, 'The Statute's Rules on Crimes and Existing or Developing International Law' in Antonio Cassese, Paola Gaeta and John RWD Jones (eds), *The Rome Statute of the International Criminal Court: A Commentary* (OUP 2002) 1101

Benvenuti, Paolo, 'Complementarity of the International Criminal Court to National Criminal Jurisdictions' in Flavia Lattanzi and William A Schabas (eds), *Essays on the Rome Statute of the International Criminal Court,* Vol.I (il Sirente 1999) 21

Bergsmo, Morten (ed.), *Thematic Prosecution of International Sex Crimes* (TOAEP 2012)

Bergsmo, Morten and Bekou, Olympia, 'Article 53 – Initiation of an investigation' in Kai Ambos (ed.), *Rome Statute of the International Criminal Court: Article-by-Article Commentary* (4th edn, Beck-Hart-Nomos 2022) 1623

Bergsmo, Morten, Buis, Emiliano J and Song, Tianying (eds), *Philosophical Foundations of International Criminal Law: Legally-Protected Interests* (TOAEP 2022)

Bergsmo, Morten, Cheah, Wui Ling, Song, Tianying and Yi Ping (eds), *Historical Origins of International Criminal Law,* Vols I–IV (TOAEP 2014–2015)

Bergmso, Morten and Stahn, Carsten (eds), *Quality Control in Preliminary Examination: Vols 1 and 2* (TOAPB 2018)

Bergsmo, Morten and Zhu, Dan, 'Article 15 – Prosecutor' in Kai Ambos (ed.), *Rome Statute of the International Criminal Court: Article-by-Article Commentary* (4th edn, Beck-Hart-Nomos 2022) 881

Berman, Franklin, 'International Treaties and British Statutes' (2005) 26(1) *Statute Law Review* 1

Bernard, Diane, *Juger et juger encore les crimes internationaux* (Bruylant 2014)

Bianchi, Andrea, 'Textual Interpretation and (International) Law Reading: The Myth of (In)Determinacy and the Genealogy of Meaning' in Pieter H F Bekker, Rudolf Dolzer and Michael Waibel (eds), *Making Transnational Law Work in the Global Economy: Essays in Honour of Detlev Vagts* (CUP 2010) 34

Bianchi, Andrea and Zarbiyev, Fuad, *Demystifying Treaty Interpretation* (CUP 2024)

Billis, Emmanouil, 'The Limits of Discretion in the Investigation and Prosecution of War Crimes at the International Level: The *Mavi Marmara* Saga' (2022) 10 *Bergen Journal of Criminal Law and Criminal Justice* 1

Bitti, Gilbert, 'Article 53 – Ouverture d'une enquête' in Julian Fernandez, Xavier Pacreau and Muriel Ubéda-Saillard (eds), *Statut de Rome de la Cour Pénale Internationale: Commentaire Article par Article* (2nd edn, Pedone 2019) 1447

Bitti, Gilbert, 'La jurisprudence de la Cour pénale internationale en 2015: le développement de nouveaux contentieux' (2015) 2 *Annuaire de Justice Pénale Internationale et Transitionnelle* 393

Bjørge, Eirik, 'The Convergence of the Methods of Treaty Interpretation: Different Regimes, Different Methods of Interpretation?' in Mads Andenas and Eirik Bjørge (eds), *A Farewell to Fragmentation: Reassertion and Convergence in International Law* (CUP 2015) 498

Bjørge, Eirik, *The Evolutionary Interpretation of Treaties* (OUP 2014)

Blokker, Niels, 'Legal Facets of the Practice of International Organizations' (2024) 435 RdC 73

Boas, Gideon, Bischoff, James L, Reid, Natalie L and Taylor III, B Don, *International Criminal Law Practitioner Library, Vol.III: International Criminal Procedure* (CUP 2011)

Boister, Neil, *Introduction to Transnational Criminal Law* (2nd edn, OUP 2018)

Boister, Neil and Cryer, Robert, *The Tokyo International Military Tribunal: A Reappraisal* (OUP 2008)

Boister, Neil, Gless, Sabine and Jeßberger, Florian (eds), *Histories of Transnational Criminal Law* (OUP 2021)

Book, Jan Philipp, *Appeal and Sentence in International Criminal Law* (Verlag 2011)

Bosco, David, 'Discretion and State Influence at the International Criminal Court: The Prosecutor's Preliminary Examinations' (2017) 111 AJIL 395

Bosco, David, 'The International Criminal Court and Crime Prevention: Byproduct or Conscious Goal?' (2011) 19 Michigan State JIL 163

Bourdon, William and Duverger, Emmanuelle, *La Cour pénale internationale: Le statut de Rome* (Editions du Seuil 2000)

Bozbayındır, Emrah Ali, 'The Venture of the Comoros Referral at the Preliminary Examination Stage' in Morten Bergsmo and Carsten Stahn (eds), *Quality Control in Preliminary Examination: Vol.1* (TOAEP 2018) 555

Brejon, Aude, 'Cour Pénale Internationale' (2020) 124 RGDIP 419

Buchan, Russell, 'The *Mavi Marmara* Incident and the International Criminal Court' (2014) 25 CLF 465

Buchwald, Todd F, 'The Aperture of the ICC: More than Just the Issue of Gravity' in Richard H Steinberg (ed.), *The International Criminal Court: Legal, Policy, and Political Challenges* (Brill 2025) 211

Bufalini, Alessandro, *I rapporti tra la Corte penale internazionale e il Consiglio di sicurezza* (Editoriale Scientifica 2018)

Caflisch, Lucius, 'Règles générales du droit des cours d'eau internationaux' (1989) 219 RdC 9
Cançado Trindade and Antônio Augusto, *International Law for Humankind: Towards a New Jus Gentium* (3rd edn, Brill 2020)
Carcano, Andrea, 'Sentencing and the Gravity of the Offence in International Criminal Law' (2002) 51 ICLQ 583
Cárdenas Aravena, Claudia, 'Revisión crítica del criterio "interés de la justicia" como razón para no abrir una investigación o no iniciar un enjuiciamiento ante la Corte Penal Internacional' (2011) 18 *Revista de Derecho Universidad Católica del Norte* 21
Carella, Gabriella, *La responsabilità dello Stato per crimini internazionali* (Jovene 1985)
Carnelutti, Francesco, *Teoria Generale del diritto* (Foro Italiano 1940)
Carnero-Rojo, Enrique, 'Section III. Victims and Witnesses Subsection 1. Definition and General Principle Relating to Victims' in Mark Klamberg, Jonas Nilsson and Antonio Angotti (eds), *Commentary on the Law of the International Criminal Court: The Rules of Procedure and Evidence* (TOAEP 2023) 309
Casaly, Paige, '*Al Mahdi* before the ICC: Cultural Property and World Heritage in International Criminal Law' (2016) 14 JICJ 1199
Casanovas, Oriol, *Unity and Pluralism in Public International Law* (Brill 2001)
Cassese, Antonio, *Self-Determination of Peoples: A Legal Reappraisal* (CUP 1995)
Cassese, Antonio, 'The Statute of the International Criminal Court: Some Preliminary Reflections' (1999) 10 EJIL 144
Cassese, Antonio and Gaeta, Paola (eds), *Cassese's International Criminal Law* (3rd edn, OUP 2013)
Chigowe, Lloyd T, 'The ICC and the Situation in Afghanistan: A Critical Examination of the Role of the Pre-Trial Chambers in the Initiation of Investigations *Proprio Motu*' (2022) 35 LJIL 699
Clarenc Bicudo, Nathalie, 'Article 21' in Julian Fernandez, Xavier Pacreau and Muriel Ubéda-Saillard (eds), *Statut de Rome del la Cour Pénale Internationale: Commentaire Article par Article* (2nd edn, Pedone 2019) 957
Clark, Roger S and Hohler, Beti, 'Sentencing at the ICC: Is It Time for Sentencing Guidelines?' in Róisín Mulgrew and Mikkel Jarle Christens (eds), *Research Handbook on the Punishment of Atrocity Crimes* (Edward Elgar Publishing 2024) 120
Coleman, Michelle, *The Presumption of Innocence in International Human Rights Law and Criminal Law* (Routledge 2021)
Collins Concise Dictionary (3rd edn, Harper Collins 1995)
Cormier, Monique, *The Jurisdiction of the International Criminal Court Over Nationals of Non-States Parties* (CUP 2020)
Cornu, Gérard (ed.), *Vocabulaire juridique* (10th edn, PUF 2014)
Costelloe, Daniel, *Legal Consequences of Peremptory Norms in International Law* (CUP 2017)
Côté, Luc, 'Independence and Impartiality' in Luc Reydams, Jan Wouters and Cedric Ryngaert (eds), *International Proesecutors* (OUP 2012) 319
Crawford, James, *State Responsibility: The General Part* (CUP 2013)
Crawford, James, 'The Drafting of the Rome Statute' in Philippe Sands (ed.), *From Nuremberg to The Hague: The Future of International Criminal Justice* (CUP 2003) 109
Cross Dillard, Hardy, 'Some Aspects of Law and Diplomacy' (1957) 91 RdC 445

Cross, Matthew E, 'The Standard of Proof in Preliminary Examinations' in in Morten Bergsmo and Carsten Stahn (eds), *Quality Control in Preliminary Examination: Vol.2* (TOAEP 2018) 213

Cryer, Robert, *Prosecuting International Crimes: Selectivity and the International Criminal Law Regime* (CUP 2005)

Cryer, Robert, 'Royalism and the King: Article 21 of the Rome Statute and the Politics of Sources' (2009) 12 *New Criminal Law Review* 390

D'Ascoli, Silvia, *Sentencing in International Criminal Law* (Hart 2011)

d'Aspremont, Jean, *After Meaning: The Sovereignty of Forms in International Law* (Edward Elgar Publishing 2021)

d'Aspremont, Jean, 'The Multidimensional of Interpretation' in Andrea Bianchi, Daniel Peat and Matthew Windsor (eds), *Interpretation in International Law* (OUP 2015) 111

Dascalopoulou-Livada, Phani, 'The Principle of Complementarity and Security Council Referrals' in Mauro Politi and Federica Gioia (eds), *The International Criminal Court and National Jurisdictions* (Ashgate 2008) 57

David, Eric, *Droit des organisations internationals* (Bruylant 2016)

David, Eric, 'La Cour Pénale Internationale' (2005) 313 RdC 325

David, Eric, 'Préambule' in Julian Fernandez, Xavier Pacreau and Muriel Ubéda-Saillard (eds), *Statut de Rome del la Cour Pénale Internationale: Commentaire Article par Article* (2nd edn, Pedone 2019) 441

Davidson, Caroline, 'How to Read International Criminal Law: Strict Construction and the Rome Statute of the International Criminal Court' (2017) 91 *St John's Law Review* 37

Davis, Cale, *Prosecutorial Discretion in International Criminal Justice* (Edward Elgar Publishing 2025)

de Casadevante, Romaní and Carlos Fernández, *La Interpretación de las Normas Internacionales* (Aranzadi 1996)

de Hoogh, André, *Obligations Erga Omnes and International Crimes* (Brill 1996)

De Meester, Karel, *The Investigation Phase in International Criminal Procedures: In Search of Common Rules* (Intersentia 2015)

de Souza Dias, Talita, '"Interests of Justice": Defining the Scope of Prosecutorial Discretion in Article 53(1)(c) and (2)(c) of the Rome Statute of the International Criminal Court' (2017) 30 LJIL 731

de Souza Dias, Talita and Akande, Dapo, 'Peace Negotiations as "Interests of Justice"' in Richard H Steinberg (ed.), *The International Criminal Court: Contemporary Challenges and Reform Proposals* (Brill 2020) 344

de Vos, Christian M, Complementarity, Catalysts, *Compliance: The International Criminal Court in Uganda, Kenya, and the Democratic Republic of Congo* (CUP 2020)

de Wet, Erika and Vidmar, Jure (eds), *Hierarchy in International Law: The Place of Human Rights* (OUP 2012)

Degan, VD, *L'interprétation des accords end droit international* (Martinus Nijhoff 1963)

deGuzman, Margaret, 'Gravity and the Legitimacy of the International Criminal Court' (2008-2009) 32 FILJ 1400

deGuzman, Margaret, 'How Serious Are International Crimes? The Gravity Problem in International Criminal Law' (2012-2013) 51 CJTL 18

deGuzman, Margaret, *Shocking the Conscience of Humanity: Gravity and the Legitimacy of International Criminal Law* (OUP 2020) deGuzman, Margaret, 'The International Criminal Court's Gravity Jurisprudence at Ten' (2013) 12 *Washington University Global Studies Law Review* 475

Della Morte, Gabriele, 'Potestà giurisdizionale della Corte penale internazionale: complementarità, condizioni di procedibilità, soggetti legittimati a richiedere l'esercizio dell'azione penale e *ne bis in idem*' in Gaetano Carlizzi, Gabriele Della Morte, Siliana Laurenti and Antonio Marchesi (eds), *La Corte Penale Internazionale: problemi e prospettive* (Vivarium 2003) 1

Deprez, Christophe, *L'applicabilité des droits humains à l'action de la Cour pénale internationale* (Bruylant 2016)

Di Bernardini, Igor, '"Mavi Marmara": Crimini di Guerra senza responsabili? La decisione del Procuratore della Corte Penale Internazionale sull'attacco israeliano alla Freedom Flottilla per Gaza' (2020) 31 *Diritti Umani: Cronache e Battaglie* 167

Djeffal, Christian, *Static and Evolutive Treaty Interpretation: A Functional Reconstruction* (CUP 2016)

Donat Cattin, David, 'Il diritto applicabile' in Giorgio Lattanzi and Vito Monetti (eds), *La Corte Penale Internazionale: Organi – competenza – reati – processo* (Giuffrè 2006) 269

Dondé Matute, Javier, 'La política criminal de la Fiscalíade la Corte Penal Internacionalpara el inicio de investigaciones' (2014) 14 AMDI 31

Dörr, Oliver, 'Articles 31-33' in Oliver Dörr and Kirsten Schmalenbach (eds), *Vienna Convention on the Law of Treaties: A Commentary* (2nd edn, Springer 2018) 559

Drumbl, Mark A, Atrocity, Punishment, *and International Law* (CUP 2007)

El Zeidy, Mohamed M, 'The Gravity Threshold under the Statute of the International Criminal Court' (2008) 19 CLF 35

El Zeidy, Mohamed M, *The Principle of Complementarity in International Criminal Law: Origin, Development and Practice* (Brill 2008)

Errol P, Mendes, *Peace and Justice at the International Criminal Court: A Court of Last Resort* (Edward Elgar Publishing 2010)

Estupiñan Silva, Rosmerlin, 'La gravité dans la jurisprudence de la Cour Pénale Internationale à propos des crimes de guerre' (2011) 82 RIDP 541

Falzea, Angelo, *Introduzione alle scienze giuridiche: Parte prima: Il concetto di diritto* (4th edn, Giuffrè 1996)

Farrell, Norman, 'Seriousness' in Antonio Cassese (ed.), *The Oxford Companion to International Criminal Justice* (OUP 2009) 511

Ferdinandusse, Ward N, *Direct Application of International Criminal Law in National Courts* (TMC Asser 2006)

Ferdinandusse, Ward N and Whiting, Alex, 'Prosecute Little Fish at the ICC' (2021) 19 JICJ 759

Fernández de Gurmendi, Silvia, 'The Role of the Prosecutor' in Mauro Politi and Giuseppe Nesi (eds), *The Rome Statute of the International Criminal Court: A Challenge to Impunity* (Ashgate 2001) 55

Fisher, Kirsten J, *Moral Accountability and International Criminal Law* (Routledge 2012)

Fitzmaurice, Malgosia, Elias, Olufemi and Merkouris, Panos (eds), *Treaty Interpretation and the Vienna Convention on the Law of Treaties: 30 Years On* (Brill 2010)

Fletcher, George P, 'The Influence of the Common Law and Civil Law Traditions on International Criminal Law' in Antonio Cassese (ed.), *The Oxford Companion to International Criminal Justice* (OUP 2009) 104

Fletcher, George P and Ohlin, Jens David, 'The ICC – Two Courts in One?' (2006) 4 JICJ 428, 431

Foka Taffo, Frédéric, *Le pouvoir discrétionnaire du Procureur de la Cour pénale internationale* (Nomos 2018)

Ford, Stuart, 'The Meaning of Gravity at the International Criminal Court: A Survey of Attitudes about the Seriousness of Mass Atrocities' (2018) 24 UC Davis JILP 210

Ford, Stuart, 'Understanding Crime Gravity: Exploring the Views of International Criminal Law Experts' (2019) 27 *William & Mary Bill of Rights Journal* 659

Ford, Stuart, 'What Investigative Resources Does the International Criminal Court Need to Succeed? A Gravity-Based Approach' (2017) 16 *Washington University Global Studies Law Review* 1

Gaeta, Paola, 'Grave Breaches of the Geneva Conventions' in Andrew Clapham, Paola Gaeta and Marco Sassòli (eds), *The 1949 Geneva Conventions: A Commentary* (OUP 2015) 615

Gaja, Giorgio, 'Issues of Admissibility in Case of Self-referrals' in Mauro Politi and Federica Gioia (eds), *The International Criminal Court and National Jurisdictions* (Routledge 2008) 49

Galand, Alexandre Skander, *UN Security Council Referrals to the International Criminal Court* (Brill 2018)

Gardiner, Richard, *Treaty Interpretation* (2nd edn, OUP 2015)

Garner, Bryan A (ed.), Black's Law Dictionary (11th edn, Thomson Reuters 2019)

Gawronski, Matilde E, 'The Legalistic Function of Preliminary Examinations: Quality Control as a Two-Way Street' in Morten Bergsmo and Carsten Stahn (eds), *Quality Control in Preliminary Examination: Vol.2* (TOAEP 2018) 179

Gillett, Matthew, *Prosecuting Environmental Harm Before the International Criminal Court* (CUP 2022)

Głogowska, Sonia, 'The Complexities of Law Interpretation with Regard to the International Criminal Court' (2018) 24 *Comparative Law Review* 175

Goldstone, Richard, 'Acquittals by the International Criminal Court', *EJIL:Talk!*, 18 Jan 2019, https://www.ejiltalk.org/acquittals-by-the-international-criminal-court/

Gourgourinis, Anastasios, 'The Distinction between Interpretation and Application of Norms in International Adjudication' (2011) 2 JIDS 31

Governa, Jacopo, *Rethinking the Prosecutor's Discretion at the International Criminal Court: Substantive Limitations and Judicial Control* (D&H 2023)

Gradoni, Lorenzo, 'Regole di interpretazione difficili da interpretare e frammentazione del principio di integrazione sistemica' (2010) 93 RDI 809

Grey, Rosemary and Wharton, Sara, 'The Full Picture. Preliminary Examinations at the International Criminal Court' (2019) 56 Canadian YIL 1

Grover, Leena, *Interpreting Crimes in the Rome Statute of the International Criminal Court* (CUP 2014)

Guariglia, Fabricio, 'Algunas reflexiones sobre el proyecto de estatuto para un Tribunal Penal Internacional Permanente' (1996) 23 *Revista Instituto Interamericano de Derechos Humanos* 57

Guariglia, Fabricio, '*Propio Motu* Powers of the Prosecutor to Commence Investigations' in Andraž Zidar and Olympia Bekou (eds), *Contemporary Challenges for the International Criminal Court* (BIICL 2014) 93

Guastini, Roberto, *Interpretare e argomentare* (Giuffrè 2011)

Günay, Musab Talha, 'Looking Humanity in the Eye and Seeing its Loss in the Eyes of the ICC: An Evaluation of Daesh's Destruction of Palmyra using the Gravity Assessment Made by the ICC Prosecutor in the *Al Mahdi* Case' (2019) 5 *Santander Art and Culture Law Review* 245

Hafner, Gerhard and Binder, Christina, 'The Interpretation of Article 21 (3) ICC Statute Opinion Reviewed' (2004) 9 ARIEL 163
Hall, Jérémy, 'CPI: Les ambiguïtés de l'obligation de motivation des charges: L'illustration par l'affaire Ongwen', Institut des Hautes Études Sur La Justice, 2016
Hansen, Thomas O, 'Reflections on the ICC Prosecutor's Recent "Selection Decisions"' (2013) 17 MPYUNL 125
Hansen, Thomas O, 'The International Criminal Court in Kenya: Three Defining Features of a Contested Accountability Process and Their Implications for the Future of International Justice' (2012) 18 *Australian Journal of Human Rights* 187
Happold, Matthew, '*Prosecutor v Thomas Lubanga*, Decision of Pre-Trial Chamber I of the International Criminal Court, 29 January 2007' (2007) 56 ICLQ 713
Haque, Adil Ahmad, 'Indeterminacy in the Law of Armed Conflict' (2019) 95 ILS 118
Hart, H L A, *The Concept of Law* (3rd edn, OUP 2012)
Hegel, G W F, *Philosophy of Right* (originally 1821), English trans. by SW Dyde (Bell and Sons 1896)
Heller, Kevin Jon, 'A Dissenting Opinion on the ICC and Burundi', *Opinio Juris*, 29 Oct 2017, https://opiniojuris.org/2017/10/29/does-the-icc-still-have-jurisdiction-over-crimes-in-burundi
Heller, Kevin Jon, 'Situational Gravity under the Rome Statute' in Carsten Stahn and Larissa Van den Herik (eds), *Future Perspectives in International Criminal Justice* (TMC Asser Press 2010) 227
Heller, Kevin Jon, 'The Appeals Chamber Decides Israel's Appeals – And Refuses to Suspend the Arrest Warrants', *Opinio Juris*, 25 Apr 2025, https://opiniojuris.org/2025/04/25/the-appeals-chamber-decides-israels-appeals-and-refuses-to-suspend-the-arrest-warrants/
Heller, Kevin Jon, 'The Appeals Chamber Got One Aspect of the Afghanistan Decision Very Wrong', *Opinio Juris*, 9 Mar 2020, https://opiniojuris.org/2020/03/09/the-appeals-chamber-got-one-aspect-of-the-afghanistan-decision-very-wrong/
Heller, Kevin Jon, 'The Most Distressing Paragraph in the Comoros Review Decision', *Opinio Juris*, 19 July 2015, https://opiniojuris.org/2015/07/19/the-most-distressing-paragraph-in-the-comoros-review-decision/
Hexner, Ervin P, 'Teleological Interpretation of Basic Instruments of Public International Organizations' in Salo Engel and Rudolf A Métall (eds), *Law, State, And International Legal Order: Essays in Honor of Hans Kelsen* (University of Tennessee Press 1964) 120
Hofmann, Rainer, 'Separate Opinion: International Court of Justice (ICJ)' in MPEIPL (February 2018)
Holmes, John T, 'Complementarity: National Courts versus the ICC' in Antonio Cassese, Paola Gaeta and John R W D Jones (eds), *The Rome Statute of the International Criminal Court: A Commentary* (OUP 2002) 667
Holmes, John T, 'The Principle of Complementarity' in Roy S Lee (ed.), *The International Criminal Court: The Making of the Rome Statute* (Kluwer 1999) 41
Imoedemhe, Ovo Catherine, *The Complementarity Regime of the International Criminal Court: National Implementation in Africa* (Springer 2016)
Iyasu, Muzit and Aston, Joshua N, 'Admissibility of the International Criminal Court' (2011) 53 *Journal of the Indian Law Institute* 626
Jacobs, Dov, 'Arrest Warrants and Admissibility - Commentary' in André Klip and Göran Sluiter (eds), *Annotated Leading Cases of International Criminal Tribunals, Vol.XXIII: The International Criminal Court: 2005-2007* (Intersentia 2010) 113

Jacobs, Dov and Naouri, Jennifer, 'Making Sense of the Invisible: The Role of the "Accused" during Preliminary Examinations' in Morten Bergsmo and Carsten Stahn (eds), *Quality Control in Preliminary Examination: Vol.2* (TOAEP 2018) 469

Jain, Neha, *Perpetrators and Accessories in International Criminal Law* (Hart 2014)

Jalloh, Charles C, 'A Classification of the Crimes in the Malabo Protocol' in Charles C Jalloh, Kamari M Clarke and Vincent O Nmehielle (eds), *The African Court of Justice and Human and Peoples' Rights in Context Development and Challenges* (CUP 2019) 225

Jalloh, Charles C, 'The ICC Reform Process and the Failure to Address the African State Concerns on the Sequencing of Peace with Criminal Justice under Article 53 of the Rome Statute' (2022) 54 NYU JILP 809

Jørgensen, Nina H B, *The Responsibility of States for International Crimes* (OUP 2000)

Jouette, Pierre, 'La gravité en droit international pénal' (2022) 67 *McGill Law Journal* 407

Jurdi, Nidal Nabil, *The International Criminal Court and National Courts: A Contentious Relationship* (Routledge 2016)

Kalpouzos, Ioannis and Mann, Itamar, 'Banal Crimes Against Humanity: The Detention of Asylum Seekers in Greece' (2015) 16 Melbourne JIL 1

Karagiannakis, Magda, 'Article 46' in Kai Ambos (ed.), *Rome Statute of the International Criminal Court: Article-by-Article Commentary* (4th edn, Beck-Hart-Nomos 2022) 1547

Kattan, Victor, 'The ICC and the Saga of the Mavi Marmara' (2015) 18 Palestine YIL 53

Keenan, Patrick J, 'The Slippery Concept of "Object and Purpose" in International Criminal Law' (2023) 37 AUILR 799

Kelsen, Hans, *Pure Theory of Law* (2nd edn, originally 1960), English trans. by Max Knight (University of California Press 1967)

Kelsen, Hans, *The Law of United Nations: A Critical Analysis of Its Fundamental Problems* (Stevens & Sons 1950)

Kenny, Cóman, 'Prosecuting Crimes of International Concern: Islamic State at the ICC?' (2017) 33 *Utrecht Journal of International and European Law* 120

Kim, Young Sok, *The Law of the International Criminal Court* (2nd edn, William Hein & Co 2019)

Kittrie, Orde F, *Lawfare: Law as a Weapon of War* (OUP 2016)

Kiyani, Asad G, 'Re-narrating Selectivity' in Margaret M deGuzman and Valerie Oosterveld (eds), *The Elgar Companion to the International Criminal Court* (Edward Elgar Publishing 2021) 307

Klabbers, Jan, *An Introduction to International Organizations Law* (4th edn, CUP 2022)

Klamberg, Mark 'Article 59' in Mark Klamberg (ed.), *Commentary on the Law of the International Criminal Court* (TOAEP 2017) 432

Klamberg, Mark, *Evidence in International Criminal Trials* (Brill 2013)

Kleffner, Jann K, *Complementarity in the Rome Statute and National Criminal Jurisdictions* (OUP 2008)

Klingler, Joseph, Parkhomenko, Yuri and Salonidis, Constantinos (eds), *Between the Lines of the Vienna Conventions? Canons and Principles of Interpretation in Public International Law* (Wolters Kluwer 2019)

Kloss, Bertram, *The Exercise of Prosecutorial Discretion at the International Criminal Court: Towards a More Principled Approach* (Verlag 2017)

Knoops, Geert-Jan Alexander, *Theory and Practice of International and Internationalized Criminal Proceedings* (Kluwer 2005)
Knoops, Geert-Jan Alexander and Zwart, Tom, 'The Flotilla Case before the ICC: The Need to Do Justice While Keeping the Heaven Intact' (2015) 15 ICLR 1069
Kolb, Robert, *Interprétation at création du droit international* (Bruylant 2006)
Kolb, Robert, 'Is There a Subject-Matter Ontology in Interpretation of International Legal Norms?' in Mads Andenas and Eirik Bjørge (eds), *A Farewell to Fragmentation: Reassertion and Convergence in International Law* (CUP 2015) 473
Kolb, Robert, *Théorie du ius cogens international: Essai de relecture du concept* (PUF 2001)
Koskenniemi, Martti, *From Apology to Utopia* (CUP 2005)
Kreß, Claus, 'International Criminal Law', MPEPIL (2009)
Kreß, Claus, 'The Procedural Law of the International Criminal Court in Outline: Anatomy of a Unique Compromise' (2003) 1 JICJ 603
Kreß, Claus and Barriga, Stefan (eds), *The Crime of Aggression: A Commentary, Vols 1 and 2* (CUP 2016)
Kuczyńska, Hanna, *The Accusation Model Before the International Criminal Court: Study of Convergence of Criminal Justice Systems* (Springer 2015)
Kumar, Amit, 'Is Article 21 of the Rome Statute Aiming for Legality or Hierarchy? A Dilemma' (2020-2021) 20 *ISIL Year Book of International Humanitarian and Refugee Law* 56
Labuda, Patryk I, *International Criminal Tribunals and Domestic Accountability: In the Court's Shadow* (OUP 2023)
Lanciotti, Alessandra, *La Corte penale internazionale e la repressione delle gravi violazioni del diritto umanitario* (Giappichelli 2013)
Lang, Winfried, 'Les règles d'interprétation codifiées par la Convention de Vienne sur le Droit des Traités et les divers types de traités' (1973) 24 *Österreichische Zeitschrift für öffentliches Recht* 113
Lanza, Giulia, *Indirect Perpetration and Organisationscherrschaftslehre: An Analysis of Article 25(3) of the Rome Statute in Light of the German Differentiated and Italian Unitarian Models of Participation in a Crime* (D&H 2021)
Lattanzi, Flavia, 'Concurrent Jurisdictions between Primacy and Complementarity' in Roberto Bellelli (ed.), *International Criminal Justice: Law and Practice from the Rome Statute to Its Review* (Ashgate 2010) 181
Lattanzi, Flavia, 'La complementarità' in Giorgio Lattanzi and Vito Monetti (eds), La Corte Penale Internazionale: Organi – competenza – reati – processo (Giuffrè 2006) 179
Lattanzi, Flavia, 'Les techniques interprétatives des tribunaux pénaux internationaux' (2011) 115 RGDIP 435
Lauterpacht, Elihu, 'The Development of the Law of International Organization by the Decisions of International Tribunals' (1976) 152 *RdC* 377
Lavrysen, Laurens and Mavronicola, Natasa (eds), *Coercive Human Rights: Positive Duties to Mobilise the Criminal Law under the ECHR* (Hart 2020)
Le Bouthillier, Yves, 'Article 32 – Conventione de Vienne de 1969' in Olivier Corten and Pierre Klein (eds), *Les Conventions de Vienne sur le droit des traités: Commentaire article par article* (Bruylant 2006) 1339
Lee, Roy S (ed.), *The International Criminal Court: The Making of the Rome Statute* (Kluwer Law 1999)

Leisner, Kate, 'Prioritizing the Taliban at the ICC: Is the Court Able to Curb Political Prosecutions?' (2022) 37 Maryland JIL 93

Lentner, Gabriel M, *The UN Security Council and the International Criminal Court: The Referral Mechanism in Theory and Practice* (Edward Elgar Publishing 2018)

Lenze, F, 'The Linguistics of Seriousness Standards Regarding Internationally Wrongful Acts of the State and Individual Crimes in the Light of the Work of the ILC and the Statute of the International Criminal Court with Special Reference to Massive or Systematic Violations of Human Rights' in Kalliopi Koufa (ed.), *The New International Criminal Law: 2001 International Law Session* (Sakkoulas 2003) 1077

Linderfalk, Ulf, 'Is Treaty Interpretation an Art or a Science? International Law and Rational Decision Making' (2015) 26 EJIL 169

Linderfalk, Ulf, *On the Interpretation of Treaties* (Springer 2007)

Linderfalk, Ulf, 'The Exercise of Discretion in International Law – Why Constraining Criteria Have a Proper Place in the Analysis of Legal Decision-Making' (2019) 62 German YIL 407

Linderfalk, Ulf, 'The Functionality of Conceptual Terms in International Law and International Legal Discourse' (2013) 6 EJL*S* 27

Linderfalk, Ulf, *Understanding Jus Cogens in International Law and International Legal Discourse* (Edward Elgar Publishing 2020)

Liwanga, Roger-Claude, 'The Meaning of "Gross Violation" of Human Rights: A Focus on International Tribunals' Decisions over the DRC Conflicts' (2015) 44 *Denver JILP* 67

Lo, Chang-fa, *Treaty Interpretation under the Vienna Convention on the Law of Treaties* (Springer 2019)

Longobardo, Marco, 'Everything Is Relative, Even Gravity: Remarks on the Assessment of Gravity in ICC Preliminary Examinations, and the *Mavi Marmara* affaire' (2016) 14 JICJ 1011

Longobardo, Marco, 'Factors Relevant for the Assessment of Sufficient Gravity in the ICC. Proceedings and the Elements of International Crimes' (2016) 33 Zoom-In QIL 21

Longobardo, Marco, 'Lotta alla povertà in territorio occupato: potenzialità e limiti del diritto dell'occupazione bellica' in Massimo Starita (ed.), *La povertà nel diritto internazionale e dell'Unione europea* (Editoriale Scientifica 2025) 163

Longobardo, Marco, 'The Italian Legislature and International and EU Obligations of Domestic Criminalisation' (2021) 21 ICLR 623

Lopes Fabris, Alice, 'The Collective Interest at the ICC: International Community as a Victim of International Crimes' in Alberta Fabbricotti (ed.), *Intentional Distruction of Cultural Heritage and the Law: A Research Companion* (Routledge 2025) 355

López, Rachel, 'The Law of Gravity' (2020) 58 CJTL 565

Lostal, Marina, 'De-objectifying Animals: Could they Qualify as Victims before the International Criminal Court?' (2021) 19 JICJ 583

Lostal, Marina, 'The Misplaced Emphasis on the Intangible Dimension of Cultural Heritage in the *Al Mahdi* Case at the ICC' (2017) 1 *Inter Gentes* 45

Lowe, Vaughan, 'The Politics of Law-Making: Are the Method and Character of Norm Creation Changing?' in Michael Byers (ed.), *The Role of Law in International Politics: Essays in International Relations and International Law* (OUP 2000) 207

Loyo Cabezudo, Joana, 'La llave del "interés de la justicia" en el Estatuto de Roma: su controvertido empleo en el caso de Afganistán' (2021) 73 REDI 165

Magnoux, Claire, '*The Sound of Silence*: le pouvoir discrétionnaire du Procureur de la Cour pénale internationale à travers l'utilisation des critères d'intérêts de la justice et de gravité lors de l'ouverture d'une enquête' (décembre 2017 - hors-série) RQDI 9

Maia, Catherine and Poissonnier, Ghislain, 'Cour pénale internationale: de la signification des «intérêts de la justice»' in Catherine Maia and Jean-Baptiste Harelimana (eds), *Réenchanter la justice internationale pénale: perspectives universelles et africaines* (Éditions du Net 2022) 61

Mainetti, Vittorio, 'La Cour pénale internationale face à la destruction du patrimoine culturel: réflexions à propos de l'Affaire *al-Mahdi*' (2017) 39 *Ethnologies* 213

Malby, Steven, *Criminal Theory and International Human Rights Law* (Routledge 2020)

Marchuk, Iryna, *The Fundamental Concept of Crime in International Criminal Law: A Comparative Law Analysis* (Springer 2013)

Mariniello, Triestino, 'Judicial Control over Prosecutorial Discretion at the International Criminal Court' (2019) 19 ICLR 979

Markus, Benzing, 'The Complementarity Regime of the International Criminal Court: International Criminal Justice between State Sovereignty and the Fight against Impunity' (2003) 7 MPYUNL 591

Mbaye, Abdoul Aziz and Shoamanesh, Sam Sasan, 'Article 17' in Julian Fernandez, Xavier Pacreau and Muriel Ubéda-Saillard (eds), *Statut de Rome de la Cour Pénale Internationale: Commentaire Article par Article* (2nd edn, Pedone 2019) 867

McDougal, Myres S, Lasswell, Harold D and Miller, James C, *The Interpretation of International Agreements and World Public Order* (New Haven Press 1994)

McDougall, Carrie, *The Crime of Aggression under the Rome Statute of the International Criminal Court* (2nd edn, CUP 2021)

Mégret, Frédéric, 'Beyond "Gravity": For a Politics of International Criminal Prosecutions' (2013) 107 ASIL Proceedings 428

Mégret, Frédéric, 'La Cour pénale international: a-t-elle fonctionné comme prévu?' in Julian Fernandez and Olivier de Frouville (eds), *Le mutations de la justice pénale internationale?* (Pedone 2018) 81

Mégret, Frédéric, 'The Creation of the International Criminal Court and State Sovereignty: The "Problem of an International Criminal Law" Re-Examined' in John Carey, William W Dunlap and R John Pritchard (eds), *International Humanitarian Law: Prospects* (Brill 2006) 47

Meloni, Chantal, 'The ICC Preliminary Examination of the Flotilla Situation: An Opportunity to Contextualise Gravity' (2016) 33 Zoom-in QIL 3

Merkouris, Panos, *Interpretation of Customary International Law: Of Methods and Limits* (Brill 2024).

Merkouris, Panos, Kammerhofer, Jörg and Arajärvi, Noora (eds), *The Theory, Practice, and Interpretation of Customary International Law* (CUP 2022)

Meron, Theodor, 'International Law in the Age of Human Rights: General Course on Public International Law' (2004) 301 RdC 278

Mettraux, Guénaël (ed.), *Perspectives on the Nuremberg Trial* (OUP 2018)

Milaninia, Nema, 'Conceptualizing Victimization at the International Criminal Court: Understanding the Causal Relationship Between Crime and Harm' (2019) 50 *Columbia Human Rights Law Review* 116

Moreno Ocampo, Luis, *War and Justice in the 21st Century: A Case Study on the International Criminal Court and its Interaction with the War on Terror* (OUP 2022)

Mori, Paola, *L'istituzionalizzazione della giurisdizione penale internazionale* (Giappichelli 2001)

Murgia, Michela, *God Save the Queer: Catechismo femminista* (Einaudi 2022)

Murphy, Ray, 'Gravity Issues and the International Criminal Court' (2006) 17 CLF 281

Neri, Sergio, *Sull'interpretazione dei trattati nel diritto internazionale* (Giuffrè 1958)

Nerlich, Volker, 'Article 85' in Kai Ambos (ed.), *Rome Statute of the International Criminal Court: Article-by-Article Commentary* (4th edn, Beck-Hart-Nomos 2022) 2427

Neroni Slade, Tuiloma and Clark, Roger S, 'Preamble and Final Clauses' in Roy S Lee (ed.), *The International Criminal Court: The Making of the Rome Statute – Issues, Negotiations, Results* (Kluwer Law 1999) 421

Newton, Michael A, 'Absolutist Admissibility at the ICC: Revalidating Authentic Domestic Investigations' (2021) 54 IsLR 143

Nieprzecka, Aleksandra, *Participation in Crime Falling Within the Subject-Matter Jurisdiction of the International Criminal Court* (TMC Asser 2024)

Nouwen, Sarah MH, *Complementarity in the Line of Fire: The Catalysing Effect of the International Criminal Court in Uganda and Sudan* (CUP 2013)

Ntanda Nsereko, Daniel D and Ventura, Manuel J, 'Article 18: Preliminary Rulings Regarding Admissibility' in Kai Ambos (ed.), *Rome Statute of the International Criminal Court: Article-by-Article Commentary* (4th edn, Beck-Hart-Nomos 2022) 1009

Ntanda Nsereko, Daniel D and Ventura, Manuel J, 'Article 19: Challenges to the Jurisdiction of the Court or the Admissibility of a Case' Kai Ambos (ed.), *Rome Statute of the International Criminal Court: Article-by-Article Commentary* (4th edn, Beck-Hart-Nomos 2022) 1033

Nuridzhanian, Gaiane, *The Principle of Ne Bis in Idem in International Criminal Law: Balancing the Interests of Individuals, States, and the International Community* (Routledge 2024)

O'Brien, Melanie, 'Prosecutorial Discretion as an Obstacle to Prosecution of United Nations Peacekeepers by the International Criminal Court: The Big Fish/Small Fish Debate and the Gravity Threshold' (2012) 10 JICJ 525

O'Brien, Melanie, 'The Impact of the Iraq Communication of the Prosecutor of the International Criminal Court on War Crimes Admissibility and the Interests of Victims' (2007) 16 *University College Dublin Law Review* 109

O'Keefe, Roger, *International Criminal Law* (OUP 2015)

Ochi, Megumi, 'Gravity Threshold before the International Criminal Court: An Overview of the Court's Practice' (2016) 19 *International Criminal Database Brief* 1

Okowa, Phoebe, 'Interpreting Constitutive Instruments of International Criminal Tribunals: Reflections on the Special Court for Sierra Leone' in Malgosia Fitzmaurice, Olufemi Elias and Panos Merkouris (eds), *Treaty Interpretation and the Vienna Convention on the Law of Treaties: 30 Years on* (Brill 2010) 333

Olásolo, Héctor, *Corte Penal Internacional: ¿Dónde Investigar? Especial Referencia a la Fiscalía en el Proceso de Activación* (Cruz Roja Española/Tirant lo Blanch 2003)

Olásolo, Héctor, *The Triggering Procedure of the International Criminal Court* (Brill 2005)

Olásolo, Héctor and Carnero-Rojo, Enrique, 'The Application of the Principle of Complementarity to the Decision of Where to Open an Investigation: The

Admissibility of "Situations"' in Carsten Stahn (ed.), *The International Criminal Court and Complementarity: From Theory to Practice* (CUP 2011) 393
Orakhelashvili, Alexander, *Peremptory Norms in International Law* (OUP 2006)
Orakhelashvili, Alexander, *The Interpretation of Acts and Rules in Public International Law* (OUP 2008)
Osiel, Mark, 'When Law "Expresses" More than It Cares to Admit: Comments on Heller' in Carsten Stahn and Larissa Van den Herik (eds), *Future Perspectives in International Criminal Justice* (TMC Asser Press 2010) 254
Oyewole, Oriola O, 'Unveiling the Powers of the ICC Prosecutor: Promoting Access to Justice and Accountability through Sustainable Development Goal 16' (2024) 15 *The Journal of Sustainable Development, Law and Policy* 422
Paige, Tamsin Phillipa, *Petulant and Contrary: Approaches by the Permanent Five Members of the UN Security Council to the Concept of 'Threat to the Peace' under Article 39 of the UN Charter* (Brill 2019)
Palchetti, Paolo, 'Halfway between Fragmentation and Convergence: The Role of the Rules of the Organization in the Interpretation of Constituent Treaties' in Mads Andenas and Eirik Bjørge (eds), *A Farewell to Fragmentation: Reassertion and Convergence in International Law* (CUP 2015) 486
Palombino, Fulvio Maria, *Fair and Equitable Treatment and the Fabric of General Principles* (Springer 2018)
Pan, Kaijun, 'International Organizations' Practice in the Interpretation of Their Constituent Instruments' (2025) 16 JIDS idae021
Papaux, Alain, 'Article 33 – Conventione de Vienne de 1969' in Olivier Corten and Pierre Klein (eds), *Les Conventions de Vienne sur le droit des traités: Commentaire article par article* (Bruylant 2006) 1373
Peat, Daniel and Windsor, Matthew, 'Playing the Game of Interpretation: On Meaning and Metaphor in International Law' in Andrea Bianchi, Daniel Peat and Matthew Windsor (eds), *Interpretation in International Law* (OUP 2015) 3
Pecorella, Giulia, 'The Comoros Situation, the Pre-Trial Chamber and the Prosecutor: The Rome Statute's System of Checks and Balances Is in Good Health', *International Law Blog*, 30 November 2015, https://internationallaw.blog/2015/11/30/the-comoros-situation-the-pre-trial-chamber-and-the-prosecutor-the-rome-statutes-system-of-checks-and-balances-is-in-good-health/
Pellet, Alain, 'Can a State Commit a Crime? Definitely, Yes!' (1999) 10 EJIL 425
Pérez-León-Acevedo, Juan-Pablo, 'Application for Judicial Review of OTP Decision not to Open an Investigation and Authorisation of Investigation at the ICC' in André Klip and Steven Freeland (eds), *Annotated Leading Cases of International Criminal Tribunals, Vol.LXXVI* (Intersentia 2025) 339
Peters, Christopher, 'Subsequent Practice and Established Practice of International Organizations: Two Sides of the Same Coin?' (2011) 3 Goettingen KIL 617
Piccolo Koskimies, Emanuela, 'Sovereignty as Responsibility at the International Criminal Court: The Frontiers of International Judicial Intervention' in Ekaterina Yahyaoui Krivenko (ed.), *Human Rights and Power in Times of Globalisation* (Brill 2018) 69
Picone, Paolo, *Comunità internazionale e obblighi erga omnes* (3rd edn, Jovene 2013)
Picone, Paolo, 'Obblighi *erga omnes* e codificazione della responsabilità degli stati' (2005) 88 RDI 893
Pierini, Jean Paul, 'Le contestazioni della giurisdizione della Corte e dell'ammissibilità del caso' in Giorgio Lattanzi and Vito Monetti (eds), *La Corte Penale Internazionale: Organi – competenza – reati – processo* (Giuffrè 2006) 159

Pino, Giorgio, *L'interpretazione nel diritto* (Giappichelli 2021)
Pinto, Mattia, 'Historical Trends of Human Rights Gone Criminal' (2020) 42 HRQ 729
Pividori, Claudia, *Il principio di complementarità della Corte penale internazionale e il processo di adattamento degli ordinamenti interni* (Editoriale Scientifica 2016)
Poltronieri Rossetti, Luca, 'The Pre-Trial Chamber's Afghanistan Decision: A Step Too Far in the Judicial Review of Prosecutorial Discretion?' (2019) 17 JICJ 585
Poltronieri Rossetti, Luca, *To Investigate or Not to Investigate? Prosecutorial Discretion and Its Judicial Review at the International Criminal Court* (Editoriale Scientifica 2024)
Popalzai, Ghazia and Thobani, Hiba, 'The Complexities of the Gravity Threshold in the International Criminal Court: A Practical Necessity or an Insidious Pitfall?' (2017) 20 MPYUNL 150
Prosperi, Luigi, and Terrosi, Jacopo, 'Embracing the "Human Factor": Is There New Impetus at the ICC for Conceiving and Prioritizing International Environmental Harms as Crimes Against Humanity?' (2017) 15 JICJ 509
Prouvèze, Rémy, 'Cour Pénale Internationale' (2020) 124 RGDIP 699
Pues, Anni, 'Discretion and the Gravity of Situations at the International Criminal Court' (2017) 17 ICLR 960
Pues, Anni, *Prosecutorial Discretion at the International Criminal Court* (Hart 2020)
Rajkovic, Nikolas M, 'What Is a "Grave" International Crime? The Rome Statute, Durkheim and the Sociology of Ruling Outrages' (2020) 16 *Loyola University Chicago International Law Review* 65
Ranganathan, Surabhi, *Strategically Created Treaty Conflicts and the Politics of International Law* (CUP 2014)
Rashid, Farid Mohammed, *Prosecutorial Discretion in the International Criminal Court: Legitimacy and the Politics of Justice* (Routledge 2021)
Rashid, Farid Mohammed, 'The Hidden Discretionary Capacity of the ICC Prosecutor: Revisiting the Analysis of Legal and Relative Gravity' (2020) 24 *The International Journal of Human Rights* 773
Rasi, Aurora, 'Principio di complementarietà e interpretazione dello Statuto di Roma' (2017) 11 DUDI 5
Rastan, Rod, 'What Is a "Case" for the Purposes of the Rome Statute?' (2008) 19 CLF 441
Raz, Joseph, *Between Authority and Interpretation: On the Theory of Law and Practical Reason* (OUP 2009)
Razesberger, Florian, *The International Criminal Court: The Principle of Complementarity* (Peter Lang 2006)
Riccardi, Alice, *Sentencing at the International Criminal Court: From Nuremberg to the Hague* (2016 Eleven International)
Robinson, Darryl, Vasiliev, Sergey, van Sliedregt, Elies and Oosterveld, Valerie, *An Introduction to International Criminal Law and Procedure* (5th edn, CUP 2024)
Roscini, Marco, 'Gravity in the Statute of the International Criminal Court and Cyber Conduct that Constitutes, Instigates or Facilitates International Crimes' (2019) 30 CLF 247
Roscini, Marco, 'Il diritto internazionale umanitario si preoccupa di prevenire o ridurre la povertà?' in Massimo Starita (ed.), *La povertà nel diritto internazionale e dell'Unione europea* (Editoriale Scientifica 2025) 133
Rossi, Pierfrancesco, 'The "Al Mahdi" Trial Before the International Criminal Court: Attacks on Cultural Heritage Between War Crimes and Crimes Against Humanity' (2017) 11 DUDI 87

Ruozzi, Elisa, 'The *Al Mahdi* Case between *Erga Omnes* Obligations and Right to Reparation: The International Community as a Victim or as a Donor?' in Alberta Fabbricotti (ed.), *Intentional Destruction of Cultural Heritage and the Law: A Research Companion* (Routledge 2025) 328

Ryngaert, Cedric, 'Article 59' in Kai Ambos (ed.), *Rome Statute of the International Criminal Court: Article-by-Article Commentary* (4th edn, Beck-Hart-Nomos 2022) 1732

SáCouto, Susana and Cleary, Katherine, 'The Gravity Threshold of the International Criminal Court' (2008) 23 AUILR 807

Sadat, Leila Nadya, *The International Criminal Court and the Transformation of International Law: Justice for the New Millennium* (Transnational Publishers 2002)

Sadat, Leila Nadya and Jolly, Jarrod M, 'Seven Canons of ICC Treaty Interpretation: Making Sense of Article 25's Rorschach Blot' (2014) 27 LJIL 775

Safferling, Christoph, *International Criminal Procedure* (OUP 2012)

Safferling, Christoph and Petrossian, Gurgen, *Victims Before the International Criminal Court: Definition, Participation, Reparation* (Springer 2021)

Salmon, Jean (ed.), *Dictionnaire de droit international public* (Bruylant 2001)

Salmon, Jean (ed.), 'Le fait dans l'application du droit international' (1982) 175 RdC 257

Salmon, Jean (ed.), 'Les métamorphoses de la gravité', in Marcelo G Kohen (ed.), *Promoting Justice, Human Rights and Conflict Resolution through International Law: Liber Amicorum Lucius Caflisch* (Brill 2007) 1175

Sands, Philippe (ed.), *From Nuremberg to The Hague: The Future of International Criminal Justice* (CUP 2003)

Sato, Tetsuo, *Evolving Constitutions of International Organizations: A Critical Analysis of the Interpretative Framework of the Constituent Instruments of International Organizations* (Kluwer Law International 1996)

Scelle, Georges *Précis de droit des gens: principes et systématique, Vol.II* (Librairie du Recueil Sirey 1932-1934)

Schabas, William A, *An Introduction to the International Criminal Court* (6th edn, CUP 2020)

Schabas, William A, 'Complementarity in Practice: Creative Solutions or a Trap for the Court?' in Mauro Politi and Federica Gioia (eds), *The International Criminal Court and National Jurisdictions* (Ashgate 2008) 25

Schabas, William A, '"Complementarity in Practice": Some Uncomplimentary Thoughts' (2008) 19 CLF 5

Schabas, William A, 'Feeding Time at the Office of the Prosecutor', *International Criminal Justice Today*, 23 Nov 2026

Schabas, William A, 'Interpreting the Statutes of the *Ad Hoc* Tribunals' in Lal Chand Vorah, Fausto Pocar, Yvonne Featherstone, Olivier Fourmy, Michael F Graham, John Hocking and Nicholas Robson (eds), *Man's Inhumanity to Man: Essays on International Law in Honour of Antonio Cassese* (Kluwer Law International 2003) 847

Schabas, William A, 'Prosecutorial Discretion v Judicial Activism at the International Criminal Court' (2008) 6 JICJ 731

Schabas, William A, 'Regions, Regionalism and International Criminal Law' (2007) 4 New Zealand YIL 3

Schabas, William A, 'Selecting Situations and Cases' in Carsten Stahn (ed.), *The Law and Practice of the International Criminal Court* (OUP 2015) 365

Schabas, William A, *The International Criminal Court: A Commentary on the Rome Statute* (2nd edn, OUP 2016)
Schabas, William A, *The Trial of the Kaiser* (OUP 2018)
Schabas, William A, *The UN International Criminal Tribunals* (CUP 2006)
Schabas, William A and McDermott, Yvonne, 'Article 66: Presumption of innocence' in Kai Ambos (ed.), *Rome Statute of the International Criminal Court: Article-by-Article Commentary* (4th edn, Beck-Hart-Nomos 2022) 1949
Schabas, William A and Pecorella, Giulia, 'Article 13 – Exercise of Jurisdiction' in Kai Ambos (ed.), *Rome Statute of the International Criminal Court: Article-by-Article Commentary* (4th edn, Beck-Hart-Nomos 2022) 834
Scheffer, David J, 'The United States and the International Criminal Court' (1999) 93 AJIL 12
Schmitt, Bertram, 'Legal Diversity at the International Criminal Court: Reflections of a Judge' (2021) 19 JICJ 485
Schüller, Andreas, '"Gravity" under the Rome Statute: Procedural Filter or Instrument of Shaping Criminal Policy?' (2009) 21 *Humanitäres Völkerrecht Informationsschriften* 73
Schwarzenberger, Georg, 'Myths and Realities of Treaty Interpretation: Articles 27-29 of the Vienna Draft Convention on the Law of Treaties' (1968) 9(1) Virginia JIL 1
Schwarzenberger, Georg 'The Problem of an International Criminal Law' (1950) 3 CLP 263
Scovazzi, Tullio, 'La prima sentenza della Corte penale internazionale in tema di distruzione di beni culturali' (2017) 11 DUDI 77
Shany, Yuval, *Questions of Jurisdiction and Admissibility before International Courts* (CUP 2015)
Siatitsa, Ilia, *Serious Violations of Human Rights: On the Emergence of a New Special Regime* (OUP 2022)
Sicilianos, Linos-Alexandre, 'La dimension humaine du droit international' (2024) 440 RdC 9
Simma, Bruno, 'From Bilateralism to Community Interest in International Law' (1994) 250 RdC 217
Simon, Denys, *L'interprétation judiciaire des traités d'organisations internationals: morphologie des conventions et function jurisdictionnelle* (Pedone 1981)
Sivakumaran, Sandesh, 'The Influence of Teachings of Publicists on the Development of International Law' (2017) 66 ICLQ 1
Sluiter, Göran, 'Human Rights Protection in the ICC Pre-Trial Phase' in Carsten Stahn and Göran Sluiter (eds), *The Emerging Practice of the International Criminal Court* (Martinus Nijhoff 2009) 459
Smith, Stephen Eliot, 'Inventing the Laws of Gravity: The ICC's Initial Lubanga Decision and Its Regressive Consequences' (2008) 8 ICLR 331
Soanes, Catherine (ed.), *The Oxford Compact English Dictionary* (2nd edn, OUP 2003)
Song, Sang-Hyun, 'Preventive Potential of the International Criminal Court' (2013) 3 Asian JIL 203
Sorel, Jean-Marc, 'Article 31 – Conventione de Vienne de 1969' in Olivier Corten and Pierre Klein (eds), *Les Conventions de Vienne sur le droit des traités: Commentaire article par article* (Bruylant 2006) 1289
Spagnolo, Andrea, 'La criminalizzazione degli attacchi ai peacekeepers nella prospettiva della funzione della giustizia penale internazionale al fine del mantenimento della pace' (2017) 11 DUDI 151
Stahn, Carsten, *A Critical Introduction to International Criminal Law* (CUP 2019)

Stahn, Carsten, 'Damned If You Do, Damned If You Don't: Challenges and Critiques of Preliminary Examinations at the ICC' (2017) 15 JICJ 413

Stahn, Carsten, 'Higher Gravity Threshold? A Plea for Caution' in Richard H Steinberg (ed.), *The International Criminal Court: Legal, Policy, and Political Challenges* (Brill 2025) 258

Stahn, Carsten, 'Judicial Review of Prosecutorial Discretion: Five Years On' in Carsten Stahn and Göran Sluiter (eds), *The Emerging Practice of the International Criminal Court* (Brill 2009) 247

Starace, Vincenzo, 'La responsabilité résultant de la violation des obligations à l'égard de la communauté internationale' (1976) 153 RdC 263

Stegmiller, Ignaz, 'Article 15' in Mark Klamberg, Jonas Nilsson and Antonio Angotti (eds), *Commentary on the Law of the International Criminal Court: The Statute Vol.1* (2nd edn, TOAEP 2023) 543

Stegmiller, Ignaz, 'Interpretative Gravity under the Rome Statute: Identifying Common Gravity Criteria' in Carsten Stahn (ed.), *The International Criminal Court and Complementarity: From Theory to Practice* (CUP 2011) 603

Stegmiller, Ignaz, 'The Gravity Threshold under the ICC Statute: Gravity Back and Forth in Lubanga and Ntaganda' (2009) 9 ICLR 547

Stegmiller, Ignaz, *The Pre-Investigation Stage of the ICC: Criteria for Situation Selection* (D&H 2011)

Steinberg, Richard H, 'Politics and Justice at the International Criminal Court' (2024) 57 IsLR 308

Sterio, Milena, 'Individual Criminal Responsibility for the Destruction of Religious and Historic Buildings: The *Al Mahdi* Case' (2017) 49 Case Western Reserve JIL 63

Stigen, Jo, *The Relationship between the International Criminal Court and National Jurisdictions: The Principle of Complementarity* (Brill 2008)

Suhr, Valérie V, *Rainbow Jurisdiction at the International Criminal Court: Protection of Sexual and Gender Minorities Under the Rome Statute* (Springer 2022)

Sur, Serge, *L'interprétation en droit international public* (LGDJ 1974)

Tams, Christian J, 'International Community' in Jean d'Aspremont and Sahib Singh (eds), *Concepts for International Law: Contributions to Disciplinary Thought* (Edward Elgar Publishing 2019) 504

Teitel, Ruti G, *Humanity's Law* (OUP 2011)

Tladi, Dire (ed.), *Peremptory Norms of General International Law (Jus Cogens): Disquisitions and Disputations* (Brill 2021)

Tomuschat, Christian and Thouvenin, Jean-Marc (eds), *The Fundamental Rules of the International Legal Order: Jus Cogens and Obligations Erga Omnes* (Brill 2006)

Trahan, Jennifer, 'Prosecutor De-Prioritizes ICC Investigation of US Torture Program', *Opinio Juris*, 1 Oct 2021, https://opiniojuris.org/2021/10/01/prosecutor-de-prioritizes-icc-investigation-of-us-torture-program/

Trenga, Anna, 'The Gravity Threshold of Article 17(1)(D)' (2015) 11 *Eyes on the ICC* 79

Treves, Tullio, *La giurisdizione nel diritto penale internazionale* (CEDAM 1973)

Triffterer, Otto, 'The Preventive and the Repressive Function of the International Criminal Court' in Mauro Politi and Giuseppe Nesi (eds), *The Rome Statute of the International Criminal Court: A Challenge to Impunity* (Ashgate 2001) 137

Triffterer, Otto, Bergsmo, Morten and Ambos, Kai, 'Preamble' in Kai Ambos (ed.), *Rome Statute of the International Criminal Court: Article-by-Article Commentary* (4th edn, Beck-Hart-Nomos 2022) 1

Trigeaud, Laurent, 'Article 19: Contestation de la Compétence de la Cour ou de la Recevabilité d'une Affaire' in Julian Fernandez, Xavier Pacreau and Muriel Ubéda-Saillard (eds), *Statut de Rome de la Cour Pénale Internationale: Commentaire Article par Article* (2nd edn, Pedone 2019) 919

Turone, Giuliano, 'Powers and Duties of the Prosecutor' in Antonio Cassese, Paola Gaeta and John R W D Jones (eds), *The Rome Statute of the International Criminal Court: A Commentary* (OUP 2002) 1137

Ubéda-Saillard, Muriel, 'Les techniques interprétatives des tribunaux pénaux internationaux' (2011) 115 RGDIP 421

Urs, Priya, *Gravity at the International Criminal Court: Admissibility and Prosecutorial Discretion* (OUP 2024)

Urs, Priya, 'Situation on the Registered Vessels of the Union of the Comoros, the Hellenic Republic and the Kingdom of Cambodia' MPEPIL (February 2020)

Vagias, Michail, 'The Prosecutor's Request Concerning the Rohingya Deportation to Bangladesh: Certain Procedural Questions' (2018) 31 LJIL 981

Vaid, Kaveri, 'Discretion Operationalized Through Law: *Proprio Motu* Decision-making at the International Criminal Court' (2013) 25 Florida JIL 359

van der Wilt, Harmen, 'Selectivity in International Criminal Law: Asymmetrical Enforcement as a Problem for Theories of Punishment' in Florian Jessberger and Julia Geneuss (eds), *Why Punish Perpetrators of Mass Atrocities? Purposes of Punishment in International Criminal Law* (CUP 2020) 305

van Sliedregt, Elies, *Individual Criminal Responsibility in International Law* (OUP 2012)

Varaki, Maria, 'Introducing a Fairness-Based Theory of Prosecutorial Legitimacy before the International Criminal Court' (2016) 27 EJIL 769

Varaki, Maria, 'Revisiting the "Interests of Justice" Policy Paper' (2017) 15 JICJ 455

Venzke, Ingo, *How Interpretation Makes International Law: On Semantic Change and Normative Twists* (OUP 2012)

Verhoeven, J, 'Article 21 of the Rome Statute and the Ambiguities of Applicable Law' (2009) 33 Netherlands YIL 3

Villiger, Mark E, *Commentary on the 1969 Vienna Convention on the Law of Treaties* (Brill 2009)

Waldron, Jeremy, 'How to Do Things with Standards' in Upendra Baxi, Christopher McCrudden and Abdul Palowala (eds), *Law's Ethical, Global and Theoretical Contexts: Essays in Honour of William Twining* (CUP 2015) 335

Waschefort, Gus, 'Gravity as a Requirement in International Criminal Prosecutions: Implications for South African Courts' (2014) 47 CILJ Southern Africa 38

Webb, Philippa, 'The ICC Prosecutor's Discretion Not to Proceed in the Interests of Justice' (2005) 50 *Criminal Law Quarterly* 305

Weerdesteijn, Maartje and Yanev, Lachezar, 'Assessing Gravity: Should the ICC Consider the Impact of Crimes on the International Community?' in Richard H Steinberg (ed.), *The International Criminal Court: Legal, Policy, and Political Challenges* (Brill 2025) 272

Weiler, Joseph HH, Cassese, Antonio and Spinedi, Marina (eds), *International Crimes of State: A Critical Analysis of the ILC'S Draft Article 19 on State Responsibility* (de Gruyter 1989)

Werle, Gerhard and Jessberger, Florian, *Principles of International Criminal Law* (4th edn, 2020 OUP)

Werle, Gerhard and Burghardt, Boris, 'Establishing Degrees of Responsibility: Modes of Participation in Article 25 of the ICC Statute' in Elies van Sliedregt and Sergey Vasiliev (eds), *Pluralism in International Criminal Law* (OUP 2014) 301

Wheeler, Caleb H, *Fairness and the Goals of International Criminal Trials: Finding a Balance* (Routledge 2023)

Wheeler, Caleb H, 'Human Rights Enforcement at the Borders: International Criminal Court Jurisdiction over the Rohingya Situation' (2019) 17 JICJ 609

Wheeler, Caleb H, 'Strange Bedfellows: The Relationship between the International Criminal Court and the United States' (2024) 14 Wake Forest JLP 35

Wierczyńska, Karolina and Jakubowski, Andrzej, 'Individual Responsibility for Deliberate Destruction of Cultural Heritage: Contextualizing the ICC Judgment in the *Al-Mahdi* Case' (2017) 16 Chinese JIL 695

Wolfrum, Rüdiger, 'Solidarity and Community Interests: Driving Forces for the Interpretation and Development of International Law – General Course on Public International Law' (2021) 416 RdC 9

Wong, Meagan S, 'The Activation of the International Criminal Court's Jurisdiction over the Crime of Aggression: International Institutional Law and Disupute Settlement Perspectives' (2020) 22 ICmLR 197

Wood, Michael and Sthoeger, Eran, *The UN Security Council and International Law* (CUP 2022)

Wouters, Jan, Verhoeven, Sten and Demeyere, Bruno, 'The International Criminal Court's Office of the Prosecutor: Navigating between Independence and Accountability?' in José Doria, Hans-Peter Gasser, and M Cherif Bassiouni (eds), *The Legal Regime of the International Criminal Court: Essays in Honour of Professor Igor Blishchenko* (Martinus Nijhoff 2009) 345

Yasseen, Mustafa Kamil, 'L'interprétation des traités d'après la Convention de Vienne sur le droit des traité' (1976) 151 RdC 9

Zagrebelsky, Gustavo, *Il sistema delle fonti nel diritto* (2nd edn, UTET 1991)

Zakerhossein, Mohammad Hadi, *Situation Selection Regime at the International Criminal Court: Law, Policy, Practice* (Intersentia 2017)

Zakerhossein, Mohammad Hadi, 'To Bury a Situation Alive - A Critical Reading of the ICC Prosecutor's Statement on the ISIS Situation' (2016) 16 ICLR 613

Zammit Borda, Aldo, 'The Situation in Afghanistan, US Sanctions and the Historical Narratives Emerging from the ICC', *EJIL:Talk!* 24 Jun 2020, https://www.ejiltalk.org/the-situation-in-afghanistan-us-sanctions-and-the-historical-narratives-emerging-from-the-icc/

Zappalà, Salvatore, 'Il procuratore della Corte penale internazionale: lucie e ombre' (1999) 82 RDI 39

Zarbiyev, Fuad, *Le discours interprétatif en droit international contemporain: un essai critique* (Bruylant 2015)

Zarbiyev, Fuad, 'The "Cash Value" of the Rules of Treaty Interpretation' (2019) 32 LJIL 33

Zimmermann, Andreas, 'Article 5: Crimes within the Jurisdiction of the Court' in Kai Ambos (ed.), *Rome Statute of the International Criminal Court: Article-by-Article Commentary* (4th edn, Beck-Hart-Nomos 2022) 107

Index